"BEYOND THE LAW"

"Beyond the Law"

The Politics of Ending the Death Penalty

for Sodomy in Britain

CHARLES UPCHURCH

TEMPLE UNIVERSITY PRESS

Philadelphia • Rome • Tokyo

TEMPLE UNIVERSITY PRESS
Philadelphia, Pennsylvania 19122
tupress.temple.edu

Library of Congress Cataloging-in-Publication Data

Names: Upchurch, Charles, 1969– author.
Title: "Beyond the law" : the politics of ending the death penalty for
   sodomy in Britain / Charles Upchurch.
Other titles: Sexuality studies.
Description: Philadelphia : Temple University Press, 2021. | Series:
   Sexuality studies | Includes bibliographical references and index. |
   Summary: "Beyond the Law reconstructs the hitherto untold story of the
   political process through which the death penalty for sodomy was almost
   ended in 1841, emphasizing the ethical, religious, and humanitarian
   arguments used by those who supported the reform"— Provided by
   publisher.
Identifiers: LCCN 2021003992 (print) | LCCN 2021003993 (ebook) | ISBN
   9781439920336 (cloth) | ISBN 9781439920343 (paperback) | ISBN
   9781439920350 (pdf)
Subjects: LCSH: Sodomy—Law and legislation—England—History—19th
   century. | Capital punishment—England—History—19th century. |
   Bentham, Jeremy, 1748–1832—Political and social views. | Lushington,
   Stephen, 1782–1873. | Kelly, Fitzroy, Baron, 1796–1880. | Great
   Britain—Politics and government—1837–1901.
Classification: LCC KD7976.S6 U63 2021 (print) | LCC KD7976.S6 (ebook) |
   DDC 345.42/02536—dc23
LC record available at https://lccn.loc.gov/2021003992
LC ebook record available at https://lccn.loc.gov/2021003993

For Aaron and Jake

Contents

Acknowledgments

———

This project has been a long time in the making. Many of the events presented in the narrative have been examined individually, with the extent and significance of their interconnections only pieced together over time. Because of this, I would like to thank the following groups, organizations, and individuals for the parts they played in allowing me to present and discuss portions of this material through the various stages of its development. The organizers of "Other Lives, Other Voices: A Conference in Honor of Bonnie Smith" at Rutgers University. The organizers of the "Queer Youth Histories Workshop" at the Weeks Centre for Social and Policy Research, London South Bank University. The "Outing the Past" academic conference, and Jeff Evans and Sue Sanders, whose tireless efforts, along with all their supporters, make the United Kingdom National Festival of LGBT History such a success every year. Sean Brady and Mark Seymour, organizers of the "Sodomy Laws to Same-Sex Marriage" conference at Birkbeck, University of London, and Matt Cook, for his comments on the portion of this work presented there. Chiara Beccalossi and Justin Bengry, organizers of the History of Sexuality Seminar at the Institute for Historical Research. Brian Lewis and the participants in the "British Queer History" conference, McGill University, Montreal. The Center for Lesbian and Gay Studies at the Graduate Center of the City University of New York, Scholar in Residence Fellowship Program. Randolph Trumbach, and the participants in the New York Gay and Lesbian History Reading Group, which he founded and ran for many years. Chris Waters and Anna Clark, for their comments on early drafts of this project, and Bruce Kinzer, for his careful reading of a later version. Jongwoo Jeremy Kim and Chris Reed, for helping me read a poem like a poem. Max Likin, Lia Paradis, and Jacob Bloomfield for their comments and encouragements. Sara Cohen, at Temple University Press, for seeing value in the early plan for this book, and Regina Kunzel, Shaun Vigil, Sarah Munroe, Ashley Petrucci, and Heather Wilcox for all of their efforts in helping bring it to completion. The Columbia British History Seminar, Columbia University, and especially Seth Koven, Chris Brown, Judith Walkowitz, and Susan Pederson for their comments. Anne Humphries, Joseph Gerhard, and the members of the Victorian Seminar of the City University of New York Graduate School. The editorial staff at the online journal *Notches*. Rictor Norton and Fr. Frank Ryan, OMI, for all the research they have done. The archivists, research assistants, and administrators associated with the Wertheim Study Room in the Stephen A. Schwarzman Building of the New York Public Library, the Morgan Library, the Weston Library at Oxford University, the British Library, the National Archives of the United Kingdom, the Dorset History Centre, and Strozier Library at Florida State University. John Gillis, for all his support and insights over the years. The community of scholars in Florida State University's History Department, and especially Ed Gray, Jonathan Grant, Nathan Stoltzfus, Suzy Sinke, Claudia Liebeskind, Taylor Tobias, Megan Grongier, Matt McLin, and Kim Kent. Maxine Jones and the Women's, Gender, and Sexuality Studies Program at Florida State University, and Josh Kinchen and Gabriel Abraham for all their work organizing the LGBTQIA students, faculty, and staff on campus. Michael de Nie, Lisa Diller, and the community of scholars of the Southern Conference on British Studies. The Committee on LGBT History of the American Historical Association, which has been an unparalleled resource for young queer academics for decades. Larry Kramer, for his support of the arguments of my first book, and his inspiration to write this one.

"BEYOND THE LAW"

Introduction

I n the nineteenth century, sodomy was referred to as the worst of crimes, and it was described as something that no man would wish to be associated with in any way, lest his reputation be damaged for life. And yet as early as 1835, only three years after the passage of the Great Reform Act of 1832, and two years after the legislated abolition of slavery in the British Empire, in the midst of the period known as Britain's "Age of Reform," the elected representatives of the United Kingdom voted to end the death penalty for sodomy. In a way not previously understood, this 1835 vote was intertwined with the fate of the last two men executed for sodomy in Britain. The legislation that would have saved the lives of these men, who had been convicted for committing a private consensual act behind a locked door, had already passed in the House of Commons. It had been in the House of Lords for weeks at the time of the executions, despite Lord John Russell's efforts to advance it. Although the bill would not pass in the Lords, all subsequent death sentences for sodomy were commuted to transportation or imprisonment in a process overseen by both judges and the Home Secretary, beginning with Russell. The use of the royal prerogative to commute sentences after conviction has been described by Roger Chadwick in *Bureaucratic Mercy* as "a mechanism for accommodating moral change" and "a flexible link between an evolving social perception of justice and the less elastic progress" of the law.[1] Executions for sodomy ended almost immediately after the House of Commons voted that they should, in 1835, even if the process by which that was achieved was precarious.

Several years later, after Russell had pushed through a bill that reduced the number of capital crimes in Britain to fourteen (down from more than two hundred at the start of the nineteenth century), another effort was begun that would have removed the death penalty for sodomy from statute law.[2] The sodomy law had been left out of Russell's sweeping legislation passed in 1837; it was instead a private member's bill, rather than government-sponsored legislation, that was proposed in 1840 to end the death penalty for sodomy, rape, and a few of the other crimes for which it still applied.[3] Russell did not support all the clauses of the private member's bill, but it became clear, through the course of the debates, that he supported its provision ending the death penalty for sodomy.

A judge who had presided over sodomy trials told Russell in 1835 that he was "convinced that the only reason why the punishment of death has been retained in this case is the difficulty of finding any one hardy enough to undertake what might be represented as the defense of such a crime."[4] One of the men who did this, cosponsoring the legislation in 1840 and 1841 that would pass all three of its readings in the Commons—this time with sustained debate—was Fitzroy Kelly. Kelly, who had recently entered Parliament, came from a family saved from financial ruin after the early death of his profligate father by the success of his mother, Isabella Kelly, as a novelist. Isabella was a close friend of the gothic novelist Matthew Gregory Lewis, who was for a time officially the patron of William Kelly, Isabella's son and Fitzroy's brother.[5] Speculation over Lewis's sexual interest in men as well as women was recorded in the early nineteenth century, and scholars in the twentieth century have identified William Kelly as perhaps the most important emotional attachment of Lewis's life.[6] The nature of Lewis's sexual tastes and the nature of his relationship to William remain points of controversy, but there is no doubt that their relationship intertwined the Lewis and Kelly families and also created a familial link to the other cosponsor of the 1840 and 1841 legislation.

That other cosponsor was Stephen Lushington, one of the most prominent abolitionists of the nineteenth century. He voted against the slave trade in 1807 and worked closely with other leading abolitionists of the 1820s and 1830s. His name is one of eight carved on the Buxton Memorial to the abolition of slavery, on grounds adjacent to the Palace of Westminster.[7] His brother was married to Matthew Lewis's sister. Lushington had also, as a younger man, acted as a lawyer for Anne Isabella "Annabella" Noel Byron during her separation from Lord Byron. Lushington is the individual believed to have threatened to use sodomy allegations to force Byron to give

Annabella custody of their infant child, at a time when paternal custody rights were nearly absolute.[8] These actions were remembered and referenced more than a decade later, and Lushington would face criticism in print for intruding into the private decisions made between a husband and a wife in their bedroom.[9]

The relationships between Kelly's and Lushington's personal experiences and their involvement in the 1840 and 1841 legislation remain ambiguous, but their actions in Parliament are less so. As in 1835, the bills put forward in 1840 and 1841 would pass in the Commons, but only in 1840 and 1841 were vote tallies and the transcripts of the parliamentary debates preserved. This record allows us to know, among other things, that Daniel O'Connell voted for the reform, William Gladstone voted against it, Benjamin Disraeli was absent, and Russell delivered a speech that most likely included an argument as to why it was appropriate to lessen the penalty for sodomy, regardless of how one felt about the morality of the act.[10] In the House of Lords, the explicit argument against lessening the penalty for sodomy, delivered by one of the most outspoken defenders of the radical Protestantism in that chamber, was also recorded.[11] It was not, therefore, a typical member of the Lords who stopped this effort, as most men in both houses seem to have been willing to let this change pass into law without comment.

These events, and the meanings ascribed to them by individuals in the early nineteenth century, are the subject of this book. What is presented here is based on records that are fragmentary, incomplete, and at times impervious to satisfying interpretation, but enough details survive to suggest something very different from most historians' current understanding of the potential to end the death penalty for sodomy in the early nineteenth century. What this book demonstrates is that an amalgam of reformist momentum, familial affection, elitist politics, class privilege, Enlightenment philosophy, and personal desires, experienced by different people, and in different ways, almost brought about a reform that would have changed the legal landscape at a time when many believed that such a reform would not have been possible. It was not part of an accelerating "Whiggish" advance toward greater toleration but closer to the opposite, drawing on the last remnants of the greater sexual openness of the Georgian period, just overlapping with the waning momentum of the Age of Reform.[12] An opportunity to end the death penalty for sodomy based on ethical arguments was lost in 1841, and it did not return. When the issue resurfaced, twenty years later, the results of the new law were far more draconian, even if that outcome was masked by the formal end of the death penalty for sodomy in 1861. The pages that follow explain the reasons and provide a broader source base than has been used to date, from within British politics and society, to understand the meaning of the sodomy law at this particular time and place and those who wished to see it changed.[13]

Since the first works of academic gay history were published, the key date associated with the end of the death penalty for sodomy was (reasonably) taken to be 1861. In 1861, twenty years after the events recounted in this book, the death penalty for sodomy was finally removed from statute law, as part of a years-long process of criminal law reform that contained almost no direct discussion of the sodomy law. The dynamic that had made the 1835 and 1840–1841 efforts so intense, stemming from the general reformist tenor of the age and the willingness of various actors to consider a range of moral and ethical arguments in relation to the sodomy law, is absent from the records associated with the 1861 legislation. Anyone looking for a debate related to the sodomy law in these 1861 records will not find one. It is perhaps part of the reason why the end of the death penalty for sodomy in 1861 is regularly mentioned in the secondary literature, but without sustained analysis.

Jeffrey Weeks was the first to set out the legal framework for understanding how sex between men was prosecuted in nineteenth-century Britain. He identified changes in the law related to sodomy in 1828, when the rules of evidence were changed, making convictions easier to obtain, and 1861, and he also identified 1835 as the date of the last sodomy executions. Focused on how changes in the law affected the policing of sex between men in British society, Weeks did not conduct extensive investigations into why those laws were passed. The laws Weeks first identified have been subsequently mentioned in a summary way in most histories of sex between men in Britain.[14] The most extensive and successful subsequent use of the parliamentary papers to analyze prosecutions related to sex between men in Britain was that of Harry Cocks. Cocks first used the statistics gathered by Parliament to demonstrate the importance of attempted sodomy prosecutions in the eighteenth and nineteenth centuries, although his questions and methodology also meant that the parliamentary debates surrounding the passage of statute law in the early nineteenth century did not fall within his study.[15] A further reason for the absence of analysis of the parliamentary debates was that there seemed to be very little material preserved that related to them, as members of Parliament went to great lengths to avoid directly discussing sex between men, even on those occasions when it was a part of the legislation under review. Additionally, for scholars focused on homosexual identity and homosexual politics, details pertaining to specific bills in the early to mid-nineteenth century might seem inconsequential, given that such identities, let alone such politics, were unknown in that period.

But the details matter, because by examining them, we can uncover some of the unexpected reasons why the majority of the elected members of Parliament were willing to lessen the penalty for sodomy, and understand how a diverse range of individuals within British society felt about this. The best account to date of what occurred in 1841 is covered in a few pages of legal historian Leon Radzinowicz's multivolume *A History of English Criminal Law*, but it contains distortions that have obscured the story.[16] Radzinowicz mentions the 1841 attempt to end the death penalty for sodomy briefly, arguing that by 1840, "Russell had decided that public opinion would support abolition of the death penalty at least for rape and carnal knowledge," and that he "attempted at the same time to get it removed for unnatural offences, but this provoked such high feelings in the Lords that it had to be withdrawn lest the whole Bill would be lost."[17] The debates cited in the accompanying note, however, were for the Lords debates on the bill presented by Kelly and Lushington. Kelly is mentioned by name, six pages later, as sponsoring the same bill, with Russell now presented as opposing it.[18] Following the actions of Kelly and Lushington, rather than Russell, links these debates to individuals who argued far more forcefully against the sodomy law and who also argued for the naturalness of same-sex desire and opposite-sex desire within the same individual.

Recovering the details that allow us to understand what these debates meant to the individuals participating in them is extremely difficult, not only because of the lack of sources but also because of the intellectual pitfalls of which such a project has often been assumed to run afoul. On those few occasions when this topic has been addressed at all, the early-nineteenth-century efforts to end the death penalty for sodomy are treated as one aspect of the larger effort to restrict or end the use of the death penalty in Britain.[19] Yet, time and again, the sodomy law is separated out from this general reform process, treated as an exception to the rule, for reasons often not specified, at least not in the moment. Two generations of gender historians and historians whose work is informed by critical race theory have demonstrated that such exceptions to the rule, when made in relation to gender or race, are anything but natural or self-evident and instead are points at which to investigate the workings and logics of power through the ways in which such exclusions were created, justified, and maintained.[20]

Attempts to focus on the specific treatment of sodomy laws in the context of general law reform are sometimes dismissed as an attempt to find modern homosexual identity in a period before the late nineteenth century or to read the evidence of the past through the categories of the present.[21] What must be done to avoid projecting modern understandings into the past is to fully historicize what sodomy law reform meant to all the relevant early-nineteenth-century individuals and in all the relevant early-nineteenth-century contexts. Only by devoting meticulous (and time-consuming) attention to understanding the different meanings that this concept had in that particular time and place is it possible to begin to speculate on an individual's motivation for a particular action, let alone on a self-understanding. Even after doing this work, in many cases meaningful understandings still cannot be known for lack of evidence.[22] Scholars must be prepared for and acknowledge these limitations in their texts, even as they recount as much as can be credibly established. This is the approach that Laura Doan calls for in *Disturbing Practices: History, Sexuality, and Women's Experience of Modern War*, referring to it as "critical queer history" while acknowledging it as the method of critical history in general, first spelled out in Michel Foucault's *Archaeology of Knowledge*.[23]

A version of this methodology is employed in the pages that follow—not to speak primarily to issues of identity, because these only surface briefly in Chapters 5 and 6 and then more extensively in the Conclusion, but rather to establish the contexts within which the ideas of sodomy, law, and reform gained meaning in the early nineteenth century. Each of these concepts had multiple distinct meanings, depending on where, when, or by whom they were being considered. Meanings multiplied, became more complex, and moved differently through the political system, depending on which groups or which contexts were defining the term and when and whether the above three terms were linked, either all together or in pairs.

Sodomy, for instance, was most widely understood through a range of religious contexts that condemned or disparaged it, but this understanding did not go unchallenged. In his published work, Jeremy Bentham creates a rationalist philosophical context that places sodomy outside the scope of behaviors that could be regulated by the state, and in his private writing, he goes so far as to assert that sodomy is a benign or even positive force.[24] These ideas, along with those stemming from religion, can be seen to influence the political debates of the 1830s and 1840s. It was possible to vote for lessening the penalty for sodomy as Bentham defines it but almost impossible to do so based on how a Protestant evangelical like the Earl of Winchilsea did in the House of Lords in 1841. Sensitivity to the range of ways in which the term was understood at the time also brings in the context of marriage. Sodomy between men is described in a handful of written sources as a natural taste of some men, but those men are also described as naturally desiring sexual relations, including sodomy, with women as well. This interpretation had the potential to place sodomy within marriage and thus place religion, which was the guardian of the sacramental space of marriage, in tension with the authority of the state. This issue was never argued in Parliament, but it was raised in a publication associated with the parliamentary debates.[25]

Meanings of reform likewise varied if it was deployed in the context of Tory political discourse, Whig political discourse, or radical political discourse.[26] The process of Tory law reform was different from that of Whig law reform, and each addressed the issue of the sodomy law in the 1820s, 1830s, or early 1840s. Most prominent Whig and Tory politicians wrote nothing on the concept of sodomy, but it is possible to observe how individuals did or did not remain consistent in their avowed principles of law reform when the sodomy law was in question. This tells us something important about how they understood what the sodomy law meant. The fine distinctions made in the framing of the laws, and in the development of the arguments in 1835, 1840, 1841, and 1861, provide multiple points through which to gain such insights.

The radical perspective is not so clear from the parliamentary debates, but other sources show that for radicals, the sodomy law was often seen as a hated tool of class privilege and religious hypocrisy that was applied only to the poor, while the rich escaped prosecution. In some radical writing, men convicted of sodomy or its attempt are described as "poor buggers," while far worse invective is directed at the system that protected upper-class men who had committed the same acts.[27]

Additionally, the "sodomy law" was something far more expansive than the concept of sodomy itself. As Cocks has shown, the law against *attempted* sodomy, from the early eighteenth century forward, provided the vast majority of prosecutions for sex between men recorded in the criminal returns. The vagueness of what constituted an attempt at sodomy under the law meant that a wide and subjective range of behaviors might lead to a conviction.[28] In addition, nineteenth-century newspaper reporting of cases involving "indecent assault" between men, which were not recorded separately in the parliamentary papers, suggests that these prosecutions were far more numerous than those for attempted sodomy and that no more than a suggestive touch was necessary to bring about a prosecution.[29] What constituted a criminal sexual advance between men, therefore, was based on the understandings of the accuser, the presiding magistrate, and the jury. The death penalty for sodomy, although comparatively rarely used, helped anchor the system of men's policing of the masculinity of other men, and we know that its abolition mattered to some men at the time as a step toward delegitimizing this policing, based on the writings they left behind.

Placing the focus on understanding the social and cultural contexts of sodomy law reform significantly increases the body of relevant source material. Because this is a story concerned in part with parliamentary politics, many of the individuals involved are well documented, and the highly structured nature of parliamentary debate allows for small fragments of information to reveal far more than they would in another context. Russell, for example, never spoke the word "sodomy" in his speech arguing that moral objections to sodomy were not enough of a reason to continue to make it a capital crime, nor did he use any of the euphemisms for sodomy associated with the period. However, in the speech where he argued that an unnamed "offence was beyond the law and above the law," Russell was giving his views on each of the clauses of the bill that Kelly and Lushington had put forward, and he was doing so in the order in which those clauses appeared in the text of the bill.[30] In this and many other ways, the systematic nature of parliamentary records allows us to discern what would otherwise be unknown.

Parliament provides one context in which seemingly small amounts of evidence reveal a great deal; family, as shown in the pioneering work of John Gillis, provides another. From Matt Cook's work on queer domesticity in the late nineteenth and twentieth centuries to Emma Rothschild's demonstration in *The Inner Life of Empires* of the importance of family life and family networks for members of Parliament and the commercial class, a range of recent work has shown that examining family is a key to understanding the self in relation to sexuality, in the case of Cook, or the meaning of the Enlightenment as a lived experience, in the case of Rothschild.[31]

The examination of family also begins the process of expanding the range of political actors beyond those who sat in Parliament or voted in elections, as historians from E. P. Thompson to James Vernon have long called for.[32] More popular forms of politics, carried out in the public sphere, preserve the perspective and the writing of political radicals, working men and women, and women writers of the middle and upper classes. The chapters that follow look at a diverse range of political actors, accessible as never before thanks to the digitization of sources.[33] The political networks of poor radicals can be traced, as can obscure literary references meant to be opaque to most readers. It is now also possible to quickly reconstruct the career of a backbench Member of Parliament (MP), to learn something of his family, and to explore the failed initiatives that provide insights into otherwise unre-coverable aspects of British culture. Approaching these sources with a com-mitment to foregrounding issues of class, gender, race, and sexuality leads to a political history focused on those who challenged the hegemonic values of Georgian and Victorian Britain and provides a new source base for the his-tory of sexuality before the late nineteenth century.

The material that is presented in the pages that follow is organized chron-ologically and thematically. The chronological organization is necessary to make the relationships between these events comprehensible. Some of the in-cidents described in this book have been addressed in other scholarly works. Such incidents as the Bishop of Clogher affair or the evidence of Lord Byron's sexual interest in men and women have long been referenced within queer histories of Britain, but they take on new significance when seen as part of a sequence of events.[34] The material is also arranged thematically, with each of the first six chapters addressing an aspect of the cultural context of the late Georgian, Regency, and early Victorian periods relevant to the analysis of the parliamentary debates that are explored in the final chapters.

To this end, the first chapter addresses Bentham's public and private at-tempts to establish a new context in which the state regulation of sodomy could be understood and reformed. This chapter asserts that one of Ben-tham's most widely read and influential works on legal reform, *An Introduc-tion to the Principles of Morals and Legislation*, published in 1789, contains arguments against the criminalization of sex between men.[35] Bentham's ar-gument is presented obliquely, but consideration of Bentham's text as a whole makes clear that several passages directly argue against the criminalization of sex between men, and at least some of those who desired this reform knew that they had the support of the most prominent philosopher and legal theo-rist of the day.[36] The chapter then analyzes the public debate that occurred in the newspapers in 1772 over whether the death penalty should apply to men who had sex with men, demonstrating that Bentham was not alone in the Georgian period in being willing to publicly express skepticism over the practice of executing men for this reason.[37] The final section of the chapter examines how the dramatic increase in the number of executions for sod-omy in the first two decades of the nineteenth century inspired Bentham to go further than he had before. In the 1810s, he plotted out a new work, as systematic as his earlier *Principles of Morals and Legislation*, but this time fo-cused primarily on undermining the state's arguments for regulating forms of sexuality. Whole chapters of this book would be dedicated to contesting the state's rationales for prosecuting men who had sex with men. Knowing how controversial these ideas would be, he attempted to recruit William Beckford, the novelist and sitting MP (who had been ostracized for more than thirty years after being caught having sex with a young man of his own social class), to help him promote his proposed work.

It was not Beckford in the 1810s who brought this issue to the floor of the House of Commons, though, but Kelly and Lushington in the 1840s. Chapter 2 explores the ways in which family experiences shaped Kelly. His brother, William, spent much of his adult life as an unsuccessful actor, and Lushington's relation Matthew Lewis was a famous novelist and playwright. Matthew was publicly the patron of William, and the chapter explores the affective and ethical connections that Matthew and William's relationship created between their families. Central to these connections was Fitzroy's and William's mother, Isabella, who, like Lewis, was a successful novelist. Elements of the relationships between the Lewises, the Kellys, and the Lushingtons are reconstructed in the chapter, as they relate to the relationship between Matthew and William and as they concern Matthew's response to the ethical crisis that he faced after inheriting more than three hundred enslaved individuals from his father.[38] Matthew did not repudiate his ownership of enslaved people, but he did visit his estates in Jamaica twice in the few years that he lived after inheriting them; there, he abolished the use of corporal punishment, considered a far-reaching reform at the time.[39] This chapter argues that at least part of the reason why Kelly was willing to propose the legislation that he did in 1840–1841 can be found in the web of affective and ethical ties that connected and constituted his family.

Chapter 3 shifts the focus to popular politics in the 1810s and 1820s and examines the attempts of radical and ultra-Tory newspapers to tie the idea of "sodomy" and the "sodomite" to political opponents.[40] The chapter establishes the degree to which such radicals as William Cobbett and William Benbow used incidents involving sex between men as part of their broader critique of the unreformed political system. The chapter highlights the contrasting political uses of the Duke of Cumberland scandal of June 1810 and the Vere Street molly-house raid in early July 1810. In the Cumberland scandal, allegations appeared in the radical press that sex between men was a critical factor in a suspicious death in St. James's Palace and that the government was trying to hide this information. By contrast, just a few weeks later, the ultra-Tory press, and the respectable press in general, emphasized the public's uniting behind the state's punishment of lower-class "sodomites" during the widely publicized Vere Street molly-house raid. The partisan practice of linking the accusation of sodomy to political opponents was most starkly demonstrated in relation to the 1822 Bishop of Clogher affair. Clogher, a bishop in the Church of Ireland, was caught having sex with a soldier in a London public house and was subsequently discovered to have destroyed the lives of lower-ranking men who had accused him of sexual assault.[41] Previous scholarship has underestimated the degree to which sex between men was politicized before 1832 and has consequently missed the significance of changes in the criminal law that focused on sex between men, facilitated by Robert Peel, that stemmed directly from the Bishop of Clogher affair.

In the space of just a few years, between 1822 and 1825, Peel dealt with allegations related to sex between men leveled at two close parliamentary colleagues, and he twice changed the law in relation to extortion based on accusations of sex between men. One of the men facing these allegations was Viscount Castlereagh, who, in the days after the Bishop of Clogher scandal broke, confessed to George IV, the Duke of Wellington, his friend Harriet Arbuthnot, and others that he was being blackmailed for expressing sexual interest in other men. He then took his own life.[42] The sole book-length investigation of whether a blackmail played a part in Castlereagh's suicide was written in 1959, by a close friend and one-time employee of Castlereagh's descendants. Chapter 4, for the first time, analyzes the findings of H. Montgomery Hyde in *The Strange Death of Lord Castlereagh* in relation to Peel's subsequent changing of the law on extortion related to sex between men. Hyde's work is scrupulously researched and accurate on almost all its points, except for the one that is most often quoted in subsequent work. Peel's 1823 Threatening Letters Act, as amended in early 1825, would have afforded Castlereagh legal tools to face his accusers, and its passage was followed by a wave of widely reported court cases in the summer of 1825, many of which were based on such extortions. During that summer, two men were forced out of Parliament due to accusations that they had had sex with men. Letters survive in which one of these men, Richard Heber, negotiates his exile and resignation with Peel. Chapter 4 pieces together the public and private efforts of the government to alter the ways in which sex between men was punished (and not punished) up to the summer of 1825 and examines the logic of Tory law reform that underpinned the legal changes.

These legislative changes and arrests in the summer of 1825 did not go unnoticed, and shortly thereafter, an individual penned an outraged protest of what Peel had done, calling out individual members of the Commons known for their humanitarian sympathies and chastising them for not resisting Peel on this issue. This protest is a portion of the multiauthored text published under the title *Don Leon*. Chapter 5 establishes for the first time the connection between *Don Leon* and Beckford, linking it to Bentham's earlier invitation to Beckford to support his efforts to end the sodomy law.[43] The chapter traces the ways in which *Don Leon* was altered by several individuals, from a wealthy landowner to a radical pressman, in a period that spanned the late 1810s through the late 1850s. The initial portion of the work is identified as the first six hundred lines of *Don Leon* (which argues that the sodomy law is an offense to companionate same-sex couples) and the appended poem "Leon to Annabella" (arguing that the sodomy law is a threat to married couples). The chapter examines the details of the multiauthored *Don Leon* to argue that its primary purpose was to argue from and for the perspective of an individual who naturally feels sexual desires for men and women and who therefore, if otherwise acting morally and ethically, is undeserving of punishment.

Within a few years of the writing of *Don Leon*, larger political events provided an opportunity to bring about the end of the death penalty for sodomy. The Tory control of government that had persisted for more than two generations was finally ended, and a host of reforms, many first considered before the French Revolution, began to be enacted. Whig governments, from 1830 on, proceeded with franchise reform, the abolition of slavery, factory reform, poor-law reform, municipal-government reform, and a host of other reforms, including the dramatic reduction in the use of the death penalty within the criminal law.[44] Chapter 6 examines the philosophy that underlay Whig reform of the criminal law and the degree to which protégés of Bentham controlled the process. At least one of these protégés, John Austin, can be shown to have directly engaged with Bentham's arguments against the criminalization of sex between men. The chapter then provides the first scholarly examination of the parliamentary attempt to end the death penalty for sodomy in 1835, which saw the first House of Commons majority ever secured for such a reform. The relationship of this effort to the plight of James Pratt and John Smith, who were executed within weeks of the stalling of the 1835 effort in the House of Lords, is also explored.[45] Pratt and Smith were two adult men who were observed having consensual sex with each other behind a locked door. Charles Dickens was among those who took notice of their plight.[46] They became the last men in Britain to be executed for sodomy, and the impact of their widely reported story on Russell and on the parliamentary effort to end the death penalty for sodomy in general is told in this chapter.

Compared to the 1835 effort, the parliamentary maneuverings of 1840 and 1841 are far better documented. This effort brought Kelly and Lushington together, and during this effort, Kelly tirelessly shepherded his bill past multiple setbacks. Chapter 7 reconstructs for the first time the details of that legislative process and shows how it was possible to have a majority of men in the Commons vote to end the death penalty for sodomy, not in the context of an omnibus bill but in a vote just on a clause ending the death penalty for sodomy and rape. The logic by which Parliament linked sexual violence against women with a category that conflated forced and consensual sex between men is analyzed, as are the parliamentary records of the men who sided with Lushington and Kelly and the nature of the support offered by Russell.[47] The bill would pass all three readings in the Commons, where the word "sodomy" never appears in the transcripts of debates, but it faltered in the Lords, where one outspoken member repeatedly used that word in a way that cast aspersions on the bill and those who supported it.

The concluding chapter demonstrates how different the political situation of 1861, when the death penalty for sodomy was finally eliminated, was from that of 1835, 1840, and 1841. Events in these years were not the start of a steady march toward reform in relation to sex between men but instead the result of a unique configuration of ideas, individuals, and circumstances that did not extend past the early 1840s. In the later 1850s, in a brief window when Kelly served as Attorney General, he inserted clauses ending the death penalty for several crimes, including sodomy, into a broader law reform bill that had been under development for years. After the ministry that Kelly was a part of fell, though, the sodomy provisions of the bill suffered punitive amendments, so that by the time of its final passage in 1861, the death penalty for sodomy no longer existed, but the maximum punishment for "attempted sodomy" and "indecent assault" was raised from two to ten years of imprisonment. A later government in 1880, building off the work of an 1879 Royal Commission, would attempt to undo this punitive amendment, not by lessening the penalty for attempted sodomy and indecent assault but by establishing the category of "indecent acts," with a two-year maximum sentence, for the punishment of sex between men.[48] This chapter argues that the passage of the Labouchere Amendment to the Criminal Law Amendment Act of 1885, and with it the establishment of the charge of "gross indecency," should be seen as the culmination of these earlier efforts.

This new interpretation of the Labouchere Amendment, derived in part from the questions asked and the methodologies employed over the preceding chapters, is then used to bolster the call for a renewed emphasis on queer history that examines the period before the late nineteenth century. As the identity categories created in the late nineteenth century are increasingly called into question in the present day, the absence of such identities in earlier periods need not be the barrier to research that it once was. Investigating how marginalized individuals created political arguments and political alliances to bring about ethical reforms in a hostile political climate seems to be a topic of vital interest to contemporary queer studies. It emphasizes the importance of seizing the opportunities that are present in the moment rather than waiting for more ideal conditions that might never arrive. It is an approach that will help us better understand our own past and provide insights that might inform efforts to shape a better future.

1

Bentham's Public and Private Arguments

Executions for sodomy in London occurred at a rate approaching one per year between 1804 and 1816. This was a new phenomenon. A man born in the same year as Jeremy Bentham, 1748, would have seen only four executions for sodomy in the capital in his first fifty-five years. He might even have known that executions for sodomy were as rare in the preceding fifty years, and largely nonexistent before that. But starting at age fifty-five, he would have lived through executions for sodomy in London in 1804, 1806, 1808, 1809, 1810 (two), another in 1814, another in 1815, and 1816 (two). Given that between 1812 and 1818 only about twenty individuals were executed in London each year, this was a significant number.[1] There is more to England than London, of course, but a substantial proportion of all sodomy executions occurred in the capital city, and only for London is it possible to know the circumstances of each case, starting in the late seventeenth century and continuing until details stopped appearing in the court records, after being deemed "so indecent . . . [that they were] unfit for Publication" in the mid-1790s.

Bentham considered the execution of a man for having consensual sex with another man to be profoundly unjust. No later than in his early twenties, he had reasoned that criminal punishments for consensual sexual acts were an abuse of state power, but he was also aware of the extreme prejudice common in British society toward men who had sex with men. He includes arguments against punishing such acts in one of his most influential works of legal and moral theory, published in 1789, although he presents them in a way that only legal scholars would likely follow. Years later, as the number of sodomy executions increased during and just after the Napoleonic Wars, Bentham wrote another work, this one focused primarily on sexuality and the logic that should govern the state's regulation of it. In that work, Bentham argues that the state should not punish consensual sexual acts, with multiple chapters making this argument in relation to sex between men. Following the logic of utilitarian philosophy, he argues that allowing the men who desired one another to pursue such passions had beneficial effects for society as a whole. Fully aware of the resistance that these ideas might face, he wrote an appeal in the mid-1810s to William Beckford, a Member of Parliament (MP) well placed to help him circulate these ideas to a wider public.[2]

While Bentham wrote the eighteen-page prospectus that he hoped would draw Beckford into his reform project, Beckford was rapidly exhausting what had been for a time the largest fortune in the country. He was a widower after the untimely death of his wife, Lady Margaret Gordon, and the father of two adult daughters, Maria Margaret Elizabeth and Susan Euphemia. He was best known as the author of the gothic novel *The History of the Caliph Vathek*, for the construction of the Gothic mansion Fonthill Abbey, and for the affair he had had decades earlier with William Courtenay, eight years his junior and the son of a viscount. Beckford had become a social outcast since the brief relationship with Courtenay had been made public in 1784, but this ostracism did not preclude his publishing multiple works to good reviews in the press; his continuing to reside at Fonthill Abbey; his maintaining a good relationship with his son-in-law, Alexander Douglas, from 1819 the tenth Duke of Hamilton; and his holding a parliamentary seat, albeit for the rotten borough of Hindon, from 1790 to 1794 and again from 1806 to 1820.[3] Bentham feared the destruction of his reputation that might come from being too closely associated with sex between men, but Beckford had already suffered that fate thirty years before and might be convinced to use his wealth, his literary skill, and his membership in Parliament to challenge the prejudice that had so shaped his own life.

To effect this change, Bentham had to contest the pervasive and powerful understanding of sex between men as "sodomy," grounded in the ascetic tradition within Christianity and reinforced by the more recent legal interpretations of William Blackstone. This understanding left little room for reform and little space for sympathy for men who had sex with men.[4] In his work of the 1810s, Bentham not only sets out a philosophical argument against such animosity but also takes aim at that Christian understanding of "sodomy," not to question the religion of Jesus but to undermine the legitimacy of the tradition that had been developed by interpreters starting with Saint Paul.

The religious argument would be key to the overall success of Bentham's effort to end sodomy executions, but Bentham also believed that his ideas would reach a wider audience if they were coupled with evidence from the ancient world and presented in a lively manner. Bentham explained in his letter to Beckford that "from the aspect shown by classical antiquity toward pleasure in the shapes in question, much curious matter might be collected, and no small addition made to the amusingness of the work, and the consequent extent of its circulation."[5] Thus, Bentham envisioned grafting Beckford's literary and poetic genius to his own philosophical and theological expertise to counter the hegemony of the legal views of Blackstone and the moral definitions of the ascetic tradition within Christianity. This chapter tells the story of the ideas and events that led up to Bentham's proposal to Beckford of this remarkable alliance.

Bentham's Published 1789 Argument

When Bentham was eighty years old and at the height of his reputation, Lord Brougham, soon to be Lord Chancellor, during an important speech to Parliament on law reform, observed that "[the] age of Law Reform and the age of Jeremy Bentham are one and the same." When Brougham made this observation, Bentham was, according to Leon Radzinowicz, the "founder and acknowledged leader of a new school of thought[;] surrounded by a team of eminent and devoted pupils, he had the good fortune to witness the gradual adoption of his ideas."[6] The principles that underpinned that new school of thought had been first published by Bentham decades before, in *An Introduction to the Principles of Morals and Legislation*. This highly influential work lays out ideas that would inform Tory criminal law reforms in the 1820s and Whig criminal law reforms in the 1830s. Also, contrary to most current understandings, the book sets out arguments against the criminalization of sex between men.

Bentham first started drafting arguments against the criminalization of sex between men in the early 1770s, when he was in his mid-twenties. He printed some of those arguments in 1780, and in 1789, they were published in *An Introduction to the Principles of Morals and Legislation*, one of his most important and influential books.[7] Among its many avid readers was Napoleon Bonaparte, who hailed it as "a work of genius," and its ideas were drawn on in the process of drafting the Napoleonic Code.[8] *Principles of Morals and Legislation* was also influential during the efforts to draft new legal codes in Spain, Portugal, Greece, and several of the new republics in Central and South America. Bentham's writings on the law had international appeal,

Figure 1.1 *Jeremy Bentham* by Aimée Pages, lithograph, 1829. (© National Portrait Gallery, London.)

"partly because he sought to create a philosophical system which he could bring to bear on hitherto largely emotive issues of crime and punishment."[9] In this work, Bentham identifies what he takes to be the first principles of human motivation and social interaction and then rigorously applies those principles to develop an understanding of what should and should not be regulated by law. Only a few pages of *Principles of Morals and Legislation* directly address sex between men, although the logic by which Bentham rejects its criminalization is established throughout the work.

This published refutation of the criminalization of sex between men by Bentham has been overshadowed by the discovery of Bentham's far more copious unpublished writing on the topic. At the midpoint between printing and publishing *Principles of Morals and Legislation*, circa 1785, Bentham produced almost sixty manuscript pages elaborating his arguments for reforming the laws related to sex between men. That work was first discovered by Louis Crompton and published in its entirety in 1978 in the *Journal of Homosexuality*.[10] Crompton's extraordinary historical find was identified at the time as "the earliest scholarly essay on homosexuality presently known to exist in the English language."[11] Along with the essay, Crompton also published accompanying notes by Bentham that "revealed his personal anxieties" about making these views public. Bentham writes that "on this subject a man may indulge his spleen without controul" and that "if you let it be seen that you have not sat down in rage you have *given judgment against* yourself at once."[12] Bentham also writes, "I am ashamed to own that I have often hesitated whether for the sake of the interests of humanity I should expose my personal interest so much to hazard as it must be exposed to by the free discussion of a subject of this nature." Because of these statements, it has been asserted that Bentham kept these views on sex between men secret for fear of discrediting the whole of his philosophy.[13]

The arguments against the criminalization of sex between men presented in *Principles of Morals and Legislation* are not nearly as extensive as what Bentham wrote privately in 1785, but neither are they equivocal. Both address key points in the same order, and both examine sex between men under the same general title: "Offences Against One's Self." The title is taken from one of the subheadings in *Principles of Morals and Legislation* and has greater meaning when understood in relation to all the categories of offenses described in that work. But, lacking the context to make the meaning of the title clear, Bentham adds "Paederasty" to the title in the unpublished manuscript pages. The similarities between the two works point to the ways in which the manuscript pages are elaborating and working through ideas presented concisely in the published work.

The first of Bentham's two arguments to directly undermine the justification for the punishment of sex between men is in the second chapter of *Principles of Morals and Legislation*. The first chapter sets out to establish that mankind is governed by considerations of pain and pleasure, while the second chapter examines other principles on which moral systems have been based—improperly, in Bentham's view. The ascetic, or self-denial principle, is disposed of first, while the rest of the chapter takes on "that principle which approves or disapproves of certain actions . . . merely because a man finds himself disposed to approve or disapprove of them: holding up that approbation or disapprobation as a sufficient reason."[14] Bentham then describes ten systems based on this principle, beginning with "Moral Sense" and "Common Sense" and ending with the category of "Repugnance to Nature." Unsparing in his dismissal of the idea of the "unnatural," he writes:

> Unnatural, when it means any thing, means unfrequent. . . . But here it means no such thing: for the frequency of such acts is perhaps the great complaint. It therefore means nothing; nothing, I mean, which there is in the act itself. All it can serve to express is, the disposition of the person who is talking of it: the disposition he is in to be angry at the thoughts of it.[15]

Bentham then writes that only the principle of utility could determine whether such distaste for the act is warranted, implying that the question would be addressed later in the book. He ends the section with the observation that a person invoking "repugnant to nature" means only that "I do not like to practise it; and, consequently, do not practise it. It is therefore repugnant to what ought to be the nature of every body else."[16]

That hinted-at argument is ultimately spelled out, but not until the penultimate chapter. Given that Bentham's text is an all-encompassing guide to what the law should and should not do, it seems logical that sex between men would be a minor theme. After identifying the primary motivators of individuals, based on pleasure and pain, Bentham then postulates four main sanctions that can be inflicted on an individual (Chapter 3), how to determine a just measure of pain (Chapter 4), the main varieties of pleasures and pains (Chapter 5), and how individuals experience pleasures and pains differently (Chapter 6). The range of individual acts (Chapter 7), the consciousness and motivations of individuals who perform these acts (Chapters 8, 9, and 10), and the range of individual dispositions (Chapter 11) are also systematically laid out. By Chapter 12, almost 150 pages into the book, Bentham begins his discussion of the consequences of "mischievous acts." Discussion of circumstances under which punishment should not be applied (Chapter 13), the proper relationship between punishment and offenses (Chapter 14), and what a punishment should be (Chapter 15) follow; it is not until Chapter 16 that Bentham offers what he believes is a complete list of behaviors that the law may fairly regulate. This chapter extends for more than 100 pages, in a book that runs just over 330 pages.

The offenses related to sex between men are covered in fewer than five pages, under the heading of "self-regarding offences: offences against one's self." They comprise "class three" of the five classes of offenses, which also include private offenses, semipublic offenses, public offenses, and multiform offenses. "Class three" is the least developed of the five, in part because Bentham follows the convention of his age to discuss sex between men only briefly, and with language that is not explicit. Yet it is also in part because Bentham disagrees with the criminalization of the acts grouped in this category, which he directly states in his text.[17] In a footnote, Bentham writes of the offenses in this category, "most of them are apt to be ranked among offences against the law of nature."[18] The inclusion of this note makes Bentham's stance against the criminalization of sex between men evident to careful readers of his earliest influential work on legal reform.

While circumscribed by reticence, the arguments in this short passage are clear. Bentham writes that "in individual instances it will often be questionable, whether they are productive of any primary mischief at all: secondary, they produce none." The lack of primary mischief is due to the fact that the person committing the act "shews by his conduct that he is not sensible of it" causing negative consequences. Bentham then argues that those engaging in such acts "affect not any other individuals . . . unless by possibility in particular cases; and in a very slight and distant manner the whole state."[19] Because no one else is affected, no other individual can claim compensation from or retaliation against men committing such acts. "No person has naturally any peculiar interest to prosecute them," he writes, although "in certain countries it is not uncommon for persons to be disposed to prosecute without any artificial inducement, and merely on account of an antipathy, which such acts are apt to excite."[20]

Bentham continues by arguing that the mischief these acts "produce is apt to be unobvious, and in general more questionable than that of any of the other classes." It was "the two false principles; the principle of asceticism, and the principle of antipathy" that caused individuals committing the offenses classed in this category to be singled out for unusually harsh punishment, Bentham argues.[21] He ends the section by noting that the "best plea for punishing them is founded on a faint probability there may be of their being productive of a mischief, which, if real, will place them in the class of public ones: chiefly in those divisions of it which are composed of offences against population, and offences against the national wealth."[22]

This final passage might suggest a potential justification for the punishment of sex between men, outside the category of "offences against one's self," but this proves to be a very limited punishment within the logic and categories of *Principles of Morals and Legislation*. Bentham borrows the concept of "offences against one's self" from Montesquieu to overcome his difficulty in finding any suitable legal category by which to justify the punishment of sex between men.[23] Having undermined "offences against one's self" as the basis for punishment, though, Bentham replaces it only with the "*faint* probability that there *may*" be cause to punish such acts as an offense against population or national wealth.[24] Yet both of these are minor points in *Principles of Morals and Legislation*, and both are only discussed within the broader category of "offences against the national interest in general." Within Bentham's framework, "such acts . . . collected together under a miscellaneous division by themselves, and stiled offences against the national interest in general," are grouped as the eleventh and last division of the class of offenses against the state.[25] In the one place in *Principles of Morals and Legislation* where Bentham enumerates acts in the category of "offences against the national interest in general," he lists "immoral publications" and excessive gambling or taking presents from rival powers without leave by "persons who are about the person of the sovereign, though without being invested with any specific trust."[26] Such offenses might be punished with a fine or dismissal, but nothing more severe than that.[27]

Thus, the reader who invested time in *Principles of Morals and Legislation* would find only the "*faint* probability that there *may*" be cause to punish such acts with a mild sanction. While this argument might have been lost on many who read Bentham, it was almost certainly understood by John Austin, one of the six men most responsible for advising the British government on reducing the use of the death penalty. We can suspect this not only because Austin was one of the most well-read legal scholars of his generation, or because he was a close friend of Bentham's, but because Austin's personal copy of *An Introduction to the Principles of Morals and Legislation* survives in the Inner Temple Library in London, and the passages discussed in the preceding pages are among the more heavily underlined in the book.

What Could Be Said in Public: The 1772 Debate

Bentham was the most influential British philosopher of the first third of the nineteenth century, and certainly the one who had the greatest impact on the legal reforms implemented during Britain's "Age of Reform." Because his published arguments against the criminalization of "unnatural acts" were mixed into the logic of his larger philosophical work, Bentham did not face the public censure that had occurred when *Ancient and Modern Pederasty Investigated and Exemplify'd* was published in 1749. That work, which includes defenses of same-sex desire, was almost immediately suppressed, with the author, Thomas Cannon, and publisher prosecuted and convicted.[28]

The death penalty for sodomy was being publicly debated while Bentham was writing on the topic, though. Up to that point, only one man had been executed in London under the sodomy law in Bentham's lifetime, for bestiality, and before that, there had been no execution for sodomy in London since 1730, before Bentham was born.[29] Five other men had been convicted and sentenced to death under the sodomy law in London in this same period. One of those three men was convicted of raping a minor, another of bestiality, the third of making an unwanted sexual advance on another married man (his neighbor), and the final two were a couple of adult men who had consensual sex with one another, but all five had been reprieved. Executions for sodomy in London were not common, then, when Robert Jones was sentenced to death in 1772.

Jones was eventually pardoned, but the circumstances around his case sparked perhaps the most extensive newspaper debate related to sex between men between 1740 and 1870. Surveying the contents of British newspapers for references to sex between men over these years reveals that 1772, 1806, 1810, 1822, 1825, 1833, 1841–1842, and 1870 had the highest number of such reports.[30] However, 1772 is unique in that the survey turned up more than 120 newspaper articles or letters, twice as many as were found in any other year, of which more than 90 were related to Jones and his pardon.[31] Of those, forty-eight were letters to the editor. Rictor Norton has called 1772 the year of "the first modern debate on homosexuality," and, terminology aside, his description seems warranted.[32]

The central event of the case was the rape of a minor by Jones. The jury believed the victim, who was a few weeks away from turning fourteen at the time of the assault, and found Jones guilty of sodomy, after which he was sentenced to death. Jones, though, was an officer in the army, often referred to as "Captain Jones," and a well-connected man of fashion, and he received a royal pardon. It was after the pardon that the debate broke out in the press over the proper handling of offenders like Jones. The debate spread from the specifics of the case to broader issues, including the justice of executing men for sodomy, the justice of the criminalization of sex between men generally, and the proper exercise of royal prerogative. The majority of voices in the debate condemned the act of sodomy, and some went so far as to argue that failure to punish the crime would lead to divine retribution on the whole of Britain. But others publicly argued that it was not the place of the law to punish such acts and that public disapproval of them was enough to keep the behavior in check. It was also argued that the rich and the poor faced different standards of justice when these cases were prosecuted.

Most voices raised in the 1772 newspaper debate were in favor of the state's retaining the death penalty for sodomy, but they also were challenged to provide their reasons for believing this.[33] Newspapers took a variety of stances when discussion of the case of Captain Jones broadened to address the question of consensual sex between adult men. A theme of the editorials of the *Public Ledger* was that men who had sex with men should not be executed, but they should be shamed into less public behavior. A correspondent to the paper, in response, offered observations regarding "military maccaronis" and the effect that they could have on the strength of the nation. He wrote:

You will wonder, my Dears, why I thus rudely address you; you will deem it a mark of prodigious impoliteness thus to accost a Race, who, however addicted to the crime for which Jones—suffers, have, as yet, escaped detection, and therefore cannot fairly be charged with the criminality; but Suspicion, that jealous, troublesome passion; Suspicion is got abroad—the carriage—the deportment—the dress—the effeminate squeak of the voice—the familiar loll upon each others shoulders—the gripe of the hand—the grinning in each others faces, to shew the whiteness of the teeth—in short, the manner altogether, and the figure so different from that of Manhood; these things conspire to create Suspicions; Suspicion gives birth to watchful observations; and from a strict observance of the Maccaroni Tribe, we very naturally conclude that to them we are indebted for the frequency of a crime which Modesty forbids me name.[34]

The editorials in the *London Evening Post*, by contrast, centered mostly on the politics of the pardon, harshly criticizing the government and the monarch for issuing it and arguing that the government was losing the support of its people by such actions.[35]

The paper publishing the greatest number of arguments against the death penalty for sodomy, and the most extensive arguments questioning the criminalization of sex between men generally, was the *Morning Chronicle*. One letter writer asked whether "judgment of death is not too penal for a fact not so very material in its consequences, which the philosophy and legislators of Greece and Rome esteemed as an indifferent thing? [A]nd although it is become sinful under the Christian dispensation, whether the punishment should not be somewhat of an ecclesiastical nature, as excommunication or outlawry."[36] Another letter in the *Morning Chronicle*, published a few days later, argued that a "man may doubtless be addicted to this black crime, without being a ruffian, a murderer, and a cheat; and he may be a good engineer, *bomb*-barder, scaramouch and punch."[37] Another letter, published a week later, questioned the validity of the sodomy law, calling it "a political stink-trap, invented by Henry VIII, demolished by his daughter Mary, and restored by Elizabeth, during the contentions betwixt the clergy and laity for dominion." The author of this letter agreed that the act deserved punishment, but punishment short of execution.[38]

Other correspondents disagreed. One declared, "For God's sake, Mr. Printer, what are you about? [S]urely you carry your ideas of *impartiality* too far!"[39] Another correspondent, reacting to the idea that excommunication would be enough of a punishment for sodomy, wrote, "O pious [George]! What abominations has thy ill-timed lenity encouraged, when such advocates dare publish their infamous tenets in open day?"[40] One of these men

Figure 1.2 Note the placement of the shaft of the soldier's sword and the hilt of the gentleman's. Original from the time of the Captain Jones affair. "Eternal Infamy, that Wretch Confound, Who Planted first this Vice on English Ground A Crime; that spite of Sense and Nature reigns. And Poisons Genial Love & Manhood stains." *Refin'd taste*, by Matthew Darly, published by Robert Sayer, London, 1770–1775. (© The Trustees of the British Museum.)

argued of sodomy, "Is it not a crime against the law of reason, conscience, nature, and God?" A theme of their arguments was that "in this luxurious and abandoned age, the natural horror and detestation of unnatural crimes is worn off by excess of profligacy." It was argued that the death penalty was needed for "checking the diabolical depravity, and annexing the ideas of horror, death and infamy, to such shocking eccentrical sallies of intemperance. When sod-my stalks abroad at mid-day, and every day brings forth a fresh culprit, [it] is no season to talk of relaxing the penalty."[41] A regular theme of these letters, also, was that God would collectively punish Britain if it allowed such men to openly flout divine law.

Individuals supporting a more lenient attitude toward sex between men addressed their critics directly. One man recommended that such "noisy correspondents" to the *Morning Chronicle* read "the late learned remarks of Dr. Kenrick on this subject; who, like Aristophanes of old, seems to consider it as a mere matter of ridicule or satire."[42] Another writer took on a critic's conflating the crimes of sodomy and rape, arguing that violence was inherent in the latter, but not the former. The letter writer argued that sodomy was not naturally a capital crime but only made one by act of Parliament, and he reminded readers that "witchcraft, heresy, and many more such damnable sins" had also been made capital crimes by Parliament, but those punishments "ha[d] been since repealed."[43] He went on to say that "if every sinner was to be put to death without mercy for such sins, crimes, or impunities, I doubt your friend to nature, who can be no better than an infidel, would stand but a poor chance for his life."[44]

Another man argued for the continuation of the debate within the press, as the "matter is the subject of universal conversation; the public are interested in it, and ought to have every information upon it." This author focused primarily on the issue of the death penalty and framed his comments as based solely on dispassionate reason. He argued that the death penalty should only be used for those who would otherwise be a danger to society. The author then wrote that Jones's crime did not meet this standard. He challenged the idea that passionate denunciations of sodomy could really count as the basis of a reasoned argument, writing that "[t]he only *argument* I ever heard used (for the *words unnatural, shocking, detestable, abominable*, &c. &c. though they shew an honest and generous indignation against the offence, yet they carry no degree of conviction to a cool, deliberate mind) to prove the enormity of this crime, is, that if it was practised in its full extent, it would stop the propagation of mankind." The author then went on to say that such arguments could not be taken seriously and asked whether "so phantastical a fear ever have had possession of the brain of any mortal?" He then went on to quote the ancient authors Solon and Cornelius Nepos, who "did not look upon this vice as threatening the destruction of society," before recounting how contemporary "Turks seldom to make enquiries after *secret* criminals, being unwilling to seek occasion for scandal; the severity of their laws is directed against open breaches of the peace of society." The author continued that sodomy would always invoke "unavoidable and general detestation of mankind" and that this threat would be enough to keep it in check, but at the same time, he argued that people should question the wisdom of publicly prosecuting such acts.[45]

The quoted letters represent only a small portion of the public debate sparked by the Jones case, but they highlight the openness with which arguments against the death penalty for sodomy (and even against the sodomy law itself) could be made publicly as early as the 1770s. Bentham was in London, with chambers in Lincoln's Inn after having been admitted to the bar in 1769, when this case became "the subject of universal conversation," and we know that he spent years thinking about whether to include a discussion of the sodomy law as a part of his larger treatise on morals and legislation. Bentham left many private writings on this topic, not only on the relationship of the law to sex between men but also on the ways in which social norms and public debates, such as that sparked by the Jones case, shaped individual desires.

Bentham and the Nature of Same-Sex Desire

Bentham thought that the greater animosity directed at acts of same-sex desire in his own age, as compared to the ancient world, was altering how the contemporary individual who felt that desire understood it. In his unpublished 1785 "Essay on Paederasty," Bentham argues that while same-sex desires were natural, having such desires exclusively was not. He observes that "in all antiquity there is not a single instance of an author nor scarce an explicit account of any other man who was addicted exclusively to this taste."[46] To desire men but not women is also referred to by Bentham as a corruption. He writes in negative terms of the state wherein "a man's taste [might be] even so far corrupted as to make him prefer the embraces of a person of his own sex to those of a female."[47]

But then Bentham begins to argue that individuals who are exclusively drawn to their own sex might be more prevalent in his own day than in the ancient world because of society's condemnation. Bentham argues:

> The persecution they meet with from all quarters, whether they deserve it or not, has the effect in this instance which persecution has and must have more or less in all instances, the effect of rendering those persons who are the objects of it more attached than they would otherwise be to the practice it proscribes. It renders them the more attached to one another, sympathy of itself having a powerful tendency, independent of all other motives, to attach a man to his own companions in misfortune.[48]

This is not a view that Bentham develops extensively in his work, but it does seem worth noting that an individual in the 1780s saw a relationship between prohibitions and desires in relation to sex between men.[49]

If in Bentham's view exclusive feelings of same-sex desire in men were an unfortunate corruption of taste, the lack of any such desire in a man was also problematic and might lead to a failure to empathize. At several points, Bentham admonishes men who had never desired another man for criminalizing the actions of those who did. He writes:

Those who choose to the most extravagant expressions to vent their antipathy against it, and who think that there are other methods of displaying their virtue pouring forth their fury at free cost against a Vice of which they are secure from the temptation, scruple not to avow their sentiments that a bad taste is a very bad reason for a man's being thrust into perdition with the vilest, and that to thirst after a man's blood who is innocent, if innocence consists in the doing of no harm to anyone, is a much worse taste.[50]

Bentham here declares it "a much worse taste" for men "to thirst after a man's blood" for doing something that "consists in the doing of no harm." If such a thirst constituted a deep conviction of most men, there would be little chance of ending the death penalty for sodomy through parliamentary action, but there is evidence that it was not. Within the upper class, exile or social ostracism was often considered sufficient punishment for one caught having sex with another man, and it was the only punishment to which William Beckford, William Courtenay, the Bishop of Clogher, Richard Heber, James Stanhope, and William Bankes were subjected.[51]

Examples such as these help illustrate how men like Beckford might have continued to function, albeit in a limited way, in upper-class society even after being identified as having sexual interest in other men.[52] Many seemed unwilling to treat acts of sex between men either as unproblematic or as harshly as the dominant legal and religious rhetoric built around the concept of "sodomy" required. What was needed for those who disagreed with the dominant discourse on "sodomy" was an alternate construct also grounded in moral and legal principles. Thus, amid the most sustained wave of executions for sodomy that England had ever seen, Bentham, one of its most important philosophers, worked out just such a comprehensive understanding and drafted an invitation to Beckford, an MP, asking for his help in inserting these ideas into the public and political debates.

The Problem of Criminal Law Reform

In the later 1810s, when Bentham wrote to Beckford, any challenge to the use of the death penalty was met with fierce resistance in Parliament. Throughout the eighteenth century, supporters of the existing system argued that extreme intimidation through the use of the death penalty was the only effective deterrent to crime.[53] Without a robust system of policing to detect and prevent crime, without a developed system of secondary punishments that could substitute for execution, and with a haphazard set of criminal procedures that led to the failure of many prosecutions, making examples of the convicted through public execution was considered by many essential to maintain compliance with the law.[54]

Advocating for these views, and arguing that the numerous capital statutes then active should be more rigorously put into effect, were such men as Henry Fielding. Fielding had risen to prominence as the magistrate who reformed London's Bow Street police office in the mid-eighteenth century, making it into the most important model for judicial reform of the time. Fielding did not argue that any man "of common humanity nor common sense can think the life of a man and a few shillings to be of an equal consideration"; instead, he argued that the terror of the example of a man being executed for petty theft was meant to deter thousands from considering the same crime.[55] Fielding also emphasized "the extreme social danger" that the vices of the poor, such as "expensive amusements, drunkenness, and gaming," represented, although he did not view these same vices as socially dangerous when exhibited by the upper classes.[56] This attitude was shared by many contemporary moralists and reformers who were "instrumental in initiating the movement for the improvement of manners," which advocated for extending the scope of the criminal law to better regulate individual behavior. William Paley's 1785 *The Principles of Moral and Political Philosophy* sums up many of these ideas, adding that the most severe punishments should be applied to the crimes that were hardest to detect and emphasizing that the extensive use of capital punishment was mitigated by allowing judges to weigh the circumstances of each case and follow through with only a limited number of executions.[57]

In the second half of the eighteenth century, reformers in England, drawing on criminal law reforms on the continent, first started to raise challenges to these ideas. Two Committees of Inquiry were formed by Parliament in this period to investigate the reform of the criminal law, although almost nothing came from these earliest efforts. Building from the work of the 1750 Committee, a bill passed the House of Commons in 1752 to allow felons to be confined to the Royal Dockyards with hard labor as an alternative to execution, but this effort failed when the House of Lords opposed it as a relaxation of the criminal law.[58] Building from the work of the 1770 Committee, a bill passing in the Commons in 1772 would have eliminated the death penalty for six capital crimes that had largely fallen into disuse, but this bill, too, was rejected by the Lords as a "dangerous innovation, tending to subvert the established legal system," even as supporters of the measure countered that the rapid increase in capital statutes over the previous decades was the actual innovation.[59]

In 1787, two years before Bentham would publish *Principles of Morals and Legislation*, a Commission of Inquiry was proposed in the Commons to consider a more systematic reform of the penal laws. This commission would have considered whether the law should make greater differentiations in the punishments assigned to different types of crime, ranging from murder to petty larceny. Rather than punishing all these crimes with the death penalty, the proposal was for a revision of criminal law based on "a new classification of offences according to their gravity."[60] The rapid increase in capital statutes in the previous decades was cited as a justification for the commission, which was to be made up of judges and other "professional men" familiar with the workings of the legal system.

William Pitt rejected the idea, though, making arguments that "were taken up and consistently repeated by all future opponents to reform." Pitt argued that "it would be extremely dangerous to take any step which might have the smallest tendency to discrediting the present existing system, before proper data and principles should be established whereon to found another." Pitt also cited the enormity of the task, the need to consider fully the ramifications of any changes before they were made, and the need to employ men of "the highest stations in the Law department" to carry out this work.[61] Based on this criticism, the motion for the bill was withdrawn by the individual who had proposed it, declaring that "he had not brought the subject forward as a Party matter." Bentham's *Principles of Morals and Legislation* would provide the basis for part of such a systemic reform, but it would take years for its influence to grow to the point where it would inform such broad changes.

The British criminal-justice system thus entered the nineteenth century unreformed, with its traditional procedures firmly entrenched, having amassed more than two hundred capital statutes and remaining reliant on the terror of the gallows as a primary deterrent to crime. The domestic tensions and repressions brought about by the British government's response to the French Revolutionary and Napoleonic Wars put severe strains on the system and exacerbated its many defects. The reform of criminal laws, criminal procedures, secondary punishments, and policing were interconnected, making any change difficult, and all the more so at a time when any questioning of traditional institutions might be considered seditious. It would not be until 1808, with the start of the decade-long and largely unsuccessful campaign of Sir Samuel Romilly, that there would be a prominent and persistent advocate in Parliament for reducing the use of the death penalty.[62]

Sodomy Executions in the Early Nineteenth Century and Bentham's Response

It was in this context that executions for sodomy in Britain reached their highest levels. Since the 1970s, scholars have been aware of the spike in prosecutions for sex between men in England during the wars against Revolutionary and Napoleonic France. Arthur Gilbert, Louis Crompton, and Seth LeJacq have made connections between the repressive nature of the British state in wartime and the increase in the number of executions for sodomy in these same years.[63] Crompton, among other scholars, has observed that "at least a dozen executions [for sodomy] took place in England [in the eighteenth] century . . . and more than 60 in the period 1806–1835."[64] As the executions become more frequent in the early nineteenth century, though, evidence of the circumstances leading to them becomes more difficult to recover.

The circumstances of almost all the sodomy cases leading to executions in eighteenth-century London are known. The three between 1700 and 1730 were a result of a molly-house raid in 1726.[65] Of the remaining three men executed for sodomy in the eighteenth century in London not yet mentioned in this chapter, one had committed bestiality, while another had had consensual sex with another man in a room with a dozen others present and had been identified as someone who "washes and irons and cooks . . . for these sodomites; and picks up young fellows for them."[66] The circumstances of the last case, in 1797, remain unknown, since by this point the Old Bailey and the newspapers were declaring the contents of this and similar cases unfit for publication.[67]

Beyond 1797, newspapers reported on the executions, but those reports often included only moralizing descriptions of a man's final moments on the gallows and did not describe the case details. This approach seems significant, since in the *Report of the Select Committee on Criminal Laws* and in other documents produced in relation to criminal law reform in Britain in the early nineteenth century, it is stated that the public and open nature of criminal-law proceedings was one of the primary guarantors of British liberties.[68] The ability of Britons to scrutinize the actions of the courts in relation to the sodomy law was largely eliminated only a few years before the substantial increase in the number of executions for sodomy.

In 1817, at a point when ten men had been put to death for sodomy in London in the space of a dozen years—an execution rate unlike anything that had taken place in England and Wales in the eighteenth century—Bentham wrote to Beckford, explaining his plan to combat this injustice and so-

Figure 1.3 *William (Thomas) Beckford*, by Frederick Bromley, published by Henry Graves & Co., after Sir Joshua Reynolds, mezzotint, 1862 (1782). (© National Portrait Gallery, London.)

liciting Beckford's help.[69] Bentham hoped to write a philosophical treatise, as systematic and logical as his earlier *Principles of Morals and Legislation*, that would foreground his refutation of the moral and philosophical foundations of the laws that allowed men to be put to death for having consensual sex with one another. Given that Bentham's published work from the 1780s had helped inspire the revision of law codes, altering and improving the conditions of life for millions, Bentham had good reason, based on past experience, to believe that his efforts with this new work might also lead to similar improvements in the law. In his letter to Beckford, Bentham never referred to those acts as "sodomy," most likely sensing the rhetorical advantage the term gave to his opponents, and instead employed a more neutral term, the "Attic taste."[70] Bentham's understanding of the "Attic taste" was a product of the cultural context of the early nineteenth century, and to understand the concept, it is necessary to look in detail at how Bentham presented it to Beckford.

In the eighteen pages Bentham wrote to Beckford, consisting of a four-page letter and a fourteen-page prospectus, Bentham described his project not as a defense of a persecuted minority but as a work that "has for its general object the good of mankind: the greatest happiness for the greatest number." Following the principles of utility, Bentham looked to defend "the liberty of Taste against the . . . hostility of the principle of *asceticism* and the principle of *antipathy*."[71] His title for the work, specifically chosen to generate popular interest, was *Not Paul, but Jesus*. He described the title as an "advantageous expedient, for giving extent to the circulation of the work," since it "should promise to attract attention, and excite circulation, in the breasts of religionists in general."[72]

Bentham hoped to jar individuals out of a fundamental error of religious interpretation. One of his principal objects was "reclaiming the public mind, from the errors into which it has been led by the principle of asceticism," from the "gloomy and antisocial, pernicious notions, involved in the Calvinistic and various other modes of the religion of Jesus, and the antipathies that have sprung out of them."[73] Bentham argued that it was from "religious terrors . . . that the principle of asceticism derives, it is believed, the greater part of its influence: and it is from these writings of St. Paul, as contradistinguished from the acts and sayings ascribed to Jesus, that . . . these terrors have exclusively been derived." Bentham believed that so long as "what is peculiar to Jesus remains unimpeached" in his work, his defense of the "Attic taste" might be fairly considered by the public.[74]

Bentham planned to publish *Not Paul, but Jesus* in two parts. The first was meant to be primarily theological. He explained to Beckford that "upon examination, nothing, it has been found, can be slighter, or more easily cut, than the thread by which the religion of Paul has been attached to the religion of Jesus." Of Paul's writings, Bentham described their "repugnancy to the acts and sayings ascribed to Jesus, and the pernicious nature of the doctrine of asceticism on which they were based." Paul, Bentham claimed, had erected "an empire to himself" on the foundation of Jesus that had brought on the "destruction of human happiness."[75] Bentham's plan was to publish these theological arguments first, believing that they would be less controversial than those on sexuality that would follow, and after publication, "some judgment may be formed, concerning the reception likely to be given to Part II, and what course it may be most advisable to take in consequence." Assuming that Beckford's primary interest would be in those more controversial arguments related to sexuality, Bentham described that part of his work in far more detail.[76]

Not Paul, but Jesus, Part II, as Described by Bentham to Beckford

The fourteen-page prospectus that Bentham wrote for Beckford described the subject of Part II as the pleasures of sense, establishing that the only grounds for condemning any such pleasure would be if it resulted in a greater amount of pain. Any pleasure that increased the aggregate happiness of humanity should be accepted.[77] To support this premise, Bentham referenced his more extended arguments in his *Principles of Morals and Legislation*. Bentham then asked why certain pleasures of the senses, primarily those related to sexuality, had been the subject of harsh penalties and regulations, while others, such as those derived from hearing, sight, or taste, were not regulated at all or subject only to mild sanctions. Bentham then quantified the various types of pleasure and pain that might stem from the senses according to their frequency, duration, intensity, and other categories, much as he had systematically quantified the various kinds of crimes and punishments in his *Principles of Morals and Legislation*.

Before laying out the contents of the chapter he called "Physical Divisions of the Subject," Bentham stated that the object of the chapter was to show "the absence of distinction in respect of noxiousness, between those modes of sensual gratification, on which condemnation is generally passed by the laws and public opinion, and those on which no such condemnation at all is passed, or none but what is much less severe."[78] Bentham clearly believed that this point would be most salient for Beckford, and he ensured that it was not lost in the details that followed. Bentham then discussed the relationship between those instances when the pleasure derived from an act was immediate and those when the benefits were more long-term. The pleasures of eating in the present might be assessed in relation to the value of nutrition over the longer term, or the pleasures of sex in the moment could be assessed in relation to the value of births in the future. If individuals were not condemned when they ate for reasons other than nutrition, Bentham argued, why should they be when they had sex for reasons other than procreation?[79]

Once the divisions of his subject had been clarified in this way, Bentham ranked types of sexual acts and social circumstances that might lead to procreation, ordered according to the praise or condemnation that they received within the culture. Sex within marriage was ranked highest, followed by fornication, single and then double adultery, bigamy, seduction, and finally sexual acts accompanied by violence. Forms of sex within marriage by which conception was not possible were discussed next, with Bentham reminding his readers that Leviticus 20:18 prescribes death for a man who has sex with his wife while she is menstruating.[80] Public opinion regarding the pleasures of sense, he argued, was filled with great errors and inconsistencies in how it determined which acts were noxious and which were not, and for each of these cases, Bentham planned to reassess the act in question according to the principles of utility.

Next, Bentham ranked eighteen different categories of sexual contact outside marriage by which conception was not possible, starting with "the act, solitary"; then moving through a variety of couplings involving a man and a woman, two women, and two men; and ending with "Parties: three or more."[81] After analyzing all these different permutations, Bentham wrote that "in no instance, other than this of the act of *sexuality*, has any act of sensuality been considered as being subjected—subjected by *nature*, as the phrase is—to any *restrictive rule*, other than the rule of *probity*."[82] In the next two chapters, Bentham planned to explain that it was only "blind antipathy" and asceticism that sustained the current prohibitions and laws related to sexuality.

In the next chapter, the ninth, Bentham would focus exclusively on the "gratifications deemed *irregular* of the sexual appetite," identifying this as the mode of "sexuality termed by Beccara *the Attic*."[83] Bentham planned to show the "absurdity of the epithet *unnatural* as applied in this case," and here he referenced his debunking of that term in *Principles of Morals and Legislation*. The tenth chapter would then systematically refute the objections to lifting the legal and social sanctions then applied to the "Attic taste." To the objection of "*enervation*," Bentham argued that the history of Greece and Rome showed that a society could remain vibrant and vital where this taste was accepted. To the idea that this acceptance would cause a "*diminution of sympathy*" between men and women, Bentham wrote that in no country where the "Attic taste" was unpunished had this come to pass. They included "the nations on the Continent, in which, though proscribed by the laws, it is regarded with so little acrimony by public opinion, that the laws remain universally unexecuted."[84] Bentham likewise refuted the claim that acceptance of the Attic taste would constitute a threat to the population of the nation, again citing the example of ancient Greece.

Many passages about Chapter 10 remind the reader of the conceptual divides that separate Bentham's understanding from our own. Prostitution between men and boys in Japan was cited unproblematically here as evidence that acceptance of the Attic taste would not diminish the desire in men for women. When addressing cases of "infidelity committed with a paramour of the same sex," Bentham framed it as a "danger of a wound more severe to the feelings of the wife, than if with a person of the opposite sex."[85] Bentham's response was that the physical attractions of a youth fade by age twenty, and therefore such affairs would not be long lasting for married men. When addressing the danger that preceptors and pupils might have sex, Bentham argued that while such an affair would be preferable to masturbation, "to a youth of the pupil age, a youth of the like age, will naturally be a more inviting paramour, than a man of the preceptorial age." Nevertheless, Bentham went on to write, "In respect of injury to health by excess, in this mode the danger will, on various accounts, be less from one preceptor than from a multitude of fellow pupils."[86] Bentham began with the premise that the relations under discussion in this section were consensual, but such issues as the unequal power relationship between a man and a boy, or between a preceptor and a pupil, were entirely unaddressed, as was the fact that only the sexual agency of the man and not that of "the wife" was considered in other examples.

In the following chapter, Bentham would move through the reasons behind society's "improperly grounded causes of condemnation" of the Attic taste, beginning with the ascetic religious condemnation and followed by antipathy "towards individuals considered as addicted" to this taste. Also included here was the "desire of praise on the score of virtue." But the list went on to include "Envy" on the part of those who did not feel such desires and, finally, "precautionary self-defence against the imputation" for those who had the Attic taste but wished to keep it secret, with Bentham citing James I as an example, due to his placing it "on the short list of unpardonable crimes."[87]

Bentham then listed the social harms that came from punishing the Attic taste. First among them was "loss of the whole mass of pleasure derivable from this source."[88] "Unsatisfied desire" was listed as another social harm, and it was also in this section where Bentham argued against the death penalty specifically. Briefly dropping his scholarly restraint, he wrote, "What a point, for life and death to turn upon!"[89] After this aside, most of the remaining chapter was to be devoted to the harm that the law caused to men who were or were not subject to the Attic taste, due to the ease with which either could be blackmailed on charges of sexual interest in other men.

The final chapter that Bentham sketched out for Beckford was to be titled "Beneficial Effects of Certain of These Modes," and its description took up more than a fifth of the total proposal.[90] It emphasized his earlier point that society benefitted from the happiness obtained by individuals who had sex with their preferred partners rather than having less satisfying sex with more socially appropriate partners or sexually gratifying themselves alone. He then analyzed a broad range of couples, relationships, and consequences to make his final assessments. A few new facts were added here, such as one instance where he specified that the individuals in a series of case studies were "not immature," although the age at which Bentham believed consent to be possible was not given.[91] The chapter description and the prospectus as a whole ended rather abruptly, with more tightly packed words written at the bottom of the final page and a note that there was "no room here for the specification" of further points.

Bentham's final point, which was somewhat inconsistent with his previous arguments, was that given the state of public opinion, banishment could be used as a punishment, but only in cases that had two uninvolved witnesses.[92] It seems likely that Bentham meant this suggestion to be a replacement for the death penalty for sodomy, but, as was the case throughout this document, Bentham never used that word, and his meaning here must remain somewhat ambiguous.

The Invitation to Collaborate

Bentham shared his progress toward publication and his plans for financing the project with Beckford. He considered Part I to be largely finished, as he had already worked through the necessary material on the Epistles and the Acts of the Apostles. He also believed that it would be relatively easy to find a publisher for this first part, although he did not expect there to be anything in the way of profits derived from sales. While much of the material for Part II had been "in like manner traveled over and written upon," Bentham believed that "to render it satisfactory to the author, no inconsiderable part of it would require to be written anew."[93]

Bentham's letter to Beckford became more pointed when he began to discuss the animosity that he believed might be generated by Part II. Bentham put it bluntly: "In case of his being known to be the author of such a work, there is no saying to what degree every prospect of future usefulness might, in this instance, be destroyed."[94] He cited the recent example of Sir William Meredith, "an excellent statesman . . . well qualified to render in various ways important service to his country and mankind," who had been driven into exile "for no other cause than his having partaken of gratifications, the innoxiousness of which it is one main business of this work in question to demonstrate."[95] It would not have been lost on either man that Beckford had already been ruined in this way by his association with Courtenay and therefore might have little left to lose. Furthermore, Beckford's private fortune, his seat in Parliament, and his literary skill and reputation might all enhance and complement Bentham's efforts. Bentham made the case explicitly as he closed his letter:

> In this state of things, it will hardly be matter of wonder, that the author is desirous of finding, in an appropriate social intercourse,

and external support for his faculties under a burden of such a magnitude:—a sort of patron, in whose honour, in point of secrecy and all other points, he could confide, and by whose sympathy he might be cheered and supported: a co-operator, in whose literary talents what every deficiency there may be in his own might find a supply; who, in his own person, might find an amusement in giving form and order, and superior expression, and perhaps additional quantity, to the materials which are in readiness to be supplied. . . . For all this the author's eye has turned itself to the author of the *History of the Caliph Vathec*.[96]

Bentham also invited Beckford to go beyond patronage of the project by joining him to help produce an additional argument. Bentham believed that a compendium of citations from classical antiquity defending the "pleasures in the shapes in question" would add to the popularity of his arguments and increase their circulation. Bentham stated that he had seen many such references but did not have the time to compile a comprehensive collection of them. Bentham added that if Beckford were "not disposed to engage in it himself, [he] might perhaps be disposed, and able, to find some other hand that would."[97] Beckford was thus asked by Bentham to produce a work that was to be built on classical references defending sexual acts between men and that was meant to be lively and draw in a large readership for the purposes of popularizing reform. Based on the newspaper clippings collected by Beckford and now held in the Weston Library at Oxford University, evidence suggests that Beckford at least partially accepted this invitation from Bentham, resulting in the portion of the work that has come down to us today as the poem *Don Leon*.

Conclusion

What became of this proposed alliance between Bentham and Beckford cannot be said with certainty. Bentham would publish Part I of *Not Paul, but Jesus* in 1823, but pseudonymously, with no help from a powerful patron. Part II of *Not Paul, but Jesus* was written by Bentham but not published in the nineteenth or twentieth century. As described in Chapter 5, material in the Beckford papers links Beckford and the poem *Don Leon*, a fifty-page defense of transgressive sexual desires, but that work, too, was circulated and published anonymously. If Beckford did lend his literary talents and political connections to Bentham's efforts, he did not do so publicly.

But another man did. Beckford's collection of newspaper clippings includes one story about Fitzroy Kelly and his effort in 1840 to pass the Punishment of Death Bill that would have ended the death penalty for sodomy. More than any other man, Kelly had made himself the public face of the effort that would have ended the death penalty for sex between men, an effort that a majority in the Commons supported on multiple separate votes, even though it would be denounced in the Lords loudly and publicly as supporting "sodomy." Bentham tried to use logic and reason to fight the brutal prejudices that coalesced around the concept of "sodomy," and those reasoned arguments likely influenced some who voted with the majority in the Commons. But those reasoned arguments seemed less effective in motivating specific individuals beyond Kelly to make a public stand, to make public statements, and to thereby risk their reputations for a principle, no matter how just.

When examining Kelly's possible motivations for doing what he did, an additional causal factor, aside from the power of reasoned arguments, is suggested by his personal biography: that of love within a family. Fitzroy Kelly may have acted for his brother, William Kelly, who years before had been in a relationship with Matthew Gregory Lewis, the gothic novelist and playwright. The relationship was emotional, financial, and possibly romantic, and it entwined the Lewis and Kelly families more tightly than they had been before. The next chapter tells the story of William and Matthew's relationship and the web of family connections that linked some of the men who were willing to brave the wrath of those who wielded the rhetorical bludgeon of "sodomy."

2

Family, Compassion, Empathy,
and Reform

Fitzroy Kelly, the man who did the most to advance the 1840 and 1841 bills that would have eliminated the death penalty for sodomy, was as much of an outsider in the world of patriarchal politics as could be found in the House of Commons. Although his parents were from prominent families, his father was improvident, and possibly illegitimate, and left his family in financial straits before and after his early death.[1] It was Isabella Kelly, Fitzroy's mother, who overcame repeated setbacks to ensure that her two sons and daughter received educations. She had displayed literary talent from an early age and in her thirties became a successful novelist. She secured a law education for Fitzroy and a patron from the literary world for her other son, William, and tutored her daughter, Rosa, so that she, too, might pursue a career in letters.

Lack of economic resources made the Kelly family's association with the upper ranks precarious. Isabella's efforts produced access, but time and again, individual family members faced setbacks that brought them to the edge of destitution. The primary benefactor of the Kelly family was Matthew Gregory Lewis, author of *The Monk* and other popular works of gothic fiction. The nature of the relationship between Matthew Lewis and William Kelly, Isabella's son and Fitzroy's brother, has been debated by scholars since at least the 1930s; whatever its particulars, it intertwined the Kelly and Lewis families for more than a decade.[2] Fitzroy Kelly grew up seeing Matthew Lewis assist his mother in her career, provide for his brother William's education, and help place William in a position in the War Office. He saw Matthew's assistance to William continue even as William's habits became profligate.

In at least one letter, Matthew referred to the connections between the Kellys and the Lewises as familial, and if so, then the web of kinship would have extended from the Kellys to the Lushingtons.[3] This is because Maria, Matthew's sister, married Henry Lushington, the brother of Stephen Lushington. Stephen was the first cosponsor of Kelly's Punishment of Death Bill, denounced in the House of Lords as supporting sodomy because it would have ended the death penalty for those convicted of that crime.[4] On Matthew's death, Maria inherited one of Matthew's Jamaican estates, while her husband, Stephen Lushington's brother, inherited all of Matthew's personal papers.[5] Those papers included the journal that Matthew had kept on his visits to Jamaica, during which he had attempted to abolish corporal punishment on the estates he had inherited only a few years before. The abolition of slavery was the consuming passion of Stephen Lushington's life.[6]

Fitzroy Kelly did not leave a collection of personal papers, making it difficult to ascertain his reasons for framing the 1840 and 1841 bills in the way that he did. What Fitzroy Kelly might have known of Matthew Lewis's sexual tastes is not recorded, but Matthew was thought by some who knew him to be attracted to other men. Veiled allusions to this belief were made, for example, by parodist James Smith, who quoted Lord Byron as saying that he would not accept a dinner invitation again from Lewis, as "I never will dine with a middle-aged man who fills up his table with young ensigns."[7]

The pages that follow trace some of the familial and ethical influences on Fitzroy Kelly and Stephen Lushington, the two men who were most willing to risk publicly associating themselves with reform of the sodomy law. The degree to which Fitzroy Kelly was raised by, protected by, and shared his life with a family who was far removed from the practices of patriarchal masculinity receives the primary focus.[8] While it is difficult to say what motivates an individual to take a particular action, experiences of a lifetime play a role in shaping moral decisions, just as more literal cultural texts do. We know that Kelly read the published work of Jeremy Bentham, and if he did so closely and thoroughly, he would have known Bentham's views on the criminalization of sex between men. Likewise, if he had reason to believe what others whispered about his mother's colleague and brother's benefactor, he might have had a deeply personal reason for dismissing the harshest condemnations of the Attic taste.[9] We cannot know whether such personal experiences motivated Kelly in 1840 and 1841, and, to be sure, the bill he and Lushington proposed together would have eliminated the death penalty for several other crimes as well. Even so, their actions would have weakened the link between patriarchal masculinity and the denunciation of sodomy, challenging the masculine standards that defined the public image of many of their parliamentary colleagues.[10] There is a significant literature on the effort to end the death penalty in 1830s Britain, and Fitzroy Kelly did not take the lead in any of those earlier initiatives.[11] It is worth trying to understand some of the reasons why, in this case, he did.

Isabella Kelly and Her Children

The strongest influence in Fitzroy's formative years was his mother, Isabella Kelly. Both of Isabella's parents were from wealthy Scottish families, but both were disinherited after they clandestinely wed in the 1750s. Despite the lack of family support, her parents persevered, with her father rising to the rank of captain in the Royal Marines and serving for a time as a groom of the bedchamber to George III. Just as she was turning thirty, in 1789, Isabella married Robert Hawke Kelly, the eldest son of Col. Robert Kelly, a prominent figure in the affairs of the East India Company in the second half of the eighteenth century.[12] But in 1790, less than a year into the marriage, Colonel Kelly died during the siege of Sathyamangalam in the Third Anglo-Mysore War. Isabella later wrote that the death of her father-in-law "gave the first blow to our independence," as her husband, who was then in the cavalry of the East India Company Army, had been dependent on his father for income and was forced "for financial reasons into the English service."[13] Other family members also blocked Isabella and her husband from inheriting, with accusations that Robert was born out of wedlock, only the natural son of his father, and therefore not a legitimate heir.[14]

The family still had some resources after Colonel Kelly's death. Isabella wrote that "the first Lord Hawke had loved [her husband] as a son," and he and his heir provided the couple an annuity.[15] Even so, Robert did not adjust his spending to meet their reduced circumstances, and "instead of . . . accommodating his mode of life to his fallen fortunes, continued to pursue an idle and even dissipated course, and to mix in the highest society; leaving his highly-gifted, but ill-fated, partner, to struggle with the buffets of the world as best she might."[16] This was the reason why, five years into their marriage, Isabella began publishing her writing. Isabella "had in idle or leisure hours put together some passages of [her] own early life," and she later wrote, "It struck me in my desolateness that [if] I embellish[ed] them with some fiction it might produce a novel."[17] Her first book, *A Collection of Poems and Fables*, was published in 1794 and includes poems that reference an unhappy marriage, a possible desertion by her husband, and the death of a child.[18] Isabella later indicated that a number of her works were to some degree autobiographical.

Over those years, Isabella, already in her thirties, and Robert had three children: William in 1795, Fitzroy in 1796, and Rosa in 1800.[19] Despite having to raise the children with little help from her husband, she embarked on a prodigious period of writing, publishing six novels between 1795 and 1799. For a time, Isabella became one of the leading authors of the Minerva Press, which specialized in sentimental gothic fiction and supported many female authors.[20] The press had been founded by William Lane and was attached to a circulating library that he ran in London starting in the early 1790s. Her novels went into multiple editions, were financially successful, and received positive reviews from literary critics. Isabella later wrote, "I was delighted with my success and thanked God for such a refuge from want as my pen promised."[21]

In 1802, when Isabella was at the height of her professional success, her publisher introduced her to Matthew Gregory Lewis, then twenty-seven years old and one of the most prominent gothic novelists and playwrights of the day.[22] Matthew's first novel, *The Monk*, published in 1796, had quickly become a sensation, bringing him into the first circles of Regency society, even though (or because) it was attacked as pornographic and blasphemous.[23] Matthew had recently been elected to Parliament, also in 1796, holding the rotten borough seat for Wells that had been William Beckford's until 1790.[24] Matthew followed his first novel with a play, *Castle Spectre*, that was performed to extremely positive reviews at Drury Lane in December 1797.

Mrs. Cornwell Baron-Wilson, Matthew's first major biographer, argues that Matthew saw something of himself in Isabella. Isabella's efforts to establish herself as an author while struggling with financial and family constraints resonated with Matthew's own story. Matthew had originally been educated and groomed by his father for a career in the diplomatic service, but after moving to Saxe-Weimar-Eisenach to learn German in preparation for that career, Matthew continued to pursue the literary and dramatic interests for which he had shown an aptitude since childhood. His time in Weimar also exposed him to the German Schauerroman ("spine-chiller") that would shape his most popular work in Britain.[25] Matthew's writing gave him a degree of economic independence from his father, allowing him to leave behind the career that his father had chosen for him. With Isabella and Matthew sharing talent, desire, and the spur of necessity, a strong bond of friendship soon formed.[26] Defending his close association with someone significantly beneath him socially, Matthew stated, "I care nothing about rank in life,

Figure 2.1 *Monk Lewis,* by J. Hollis, published by John Samuel Murray, after George Henry Harlow, stipple engraving, published 1834. (© National Portrait Gallery, London.)

nothing about what other people may think or say; and have always, in both my public writing and private life, shown . . . a pleasure in spitting in the face of public opinion."[27]

The connections between the Kelly and the Lewis families intensified. Isabella and Matthew engaged in a degree of literary collaboration, at least until press speculation over Matthew's involvement in Isabella's writing led Matthew to stop reading her work prior to publication in 1804.[28] Matthew's mother, Frances, also formed a friendship with Isabella. Frances shared Matthew's and Isabella's desire for success as a novelist. Matthew, however, strongly discouraged his mother from this pursuit, his stated reason being fear of gossip in the press over the degree to which he was involved in her work.[29] It was not just for himself, Matthew wrote his mother, but also for his sister, Maria, that he was concerned. Matthew explained to his mother, "Maria's interest [was] certainly . . . that she should be loved and respected by her husband's relations; and from what I know of them, I am persuaded she would not be thought better of by them for having an authoress for a mother."[30] Matthew believed that Lady Lushington, Maria's mother-in-law, did not disapprove of Frances currently, despite the scandals that were associated with her (described in the following paragraph), but that if Frances became a public figure through her writing, Lady Lushington "would be displeased" and "Maria would most probably feel the effects of displeasure."[31] In a lost letter, Frances seems to have told Matthew that she felt "stabbed in the heart" by his resistance to her embarking on her own literary career.[32]

Lacking the financial imperative that compelled Isabella to take on a public role, Frances deferred to her son, and this dispute did not long interrupt the affectionate tone that is a hallmark of the extensive correspondence between mother and son. It helped that Matthew provided Frances with a generous allowance, allowing her independence from her husband, from whom she had separated in 1781. Only six years old at the time of the separation, Matthew was Frances's eldest child, referred to as "his mother's pet companion." He remained loyal to her over the years, even though it was Frances who had broken her marriage by having an affair with a music instructor and then bearing his child. Yet Matthew's attachment to Frances remained strong. He assured her in the process of dissuading her from embarking on her own writing career that she "w[ould] be always loved and respected by those who live with you and are sufficiently intimate to know the good qualities of your heart; but those who know you by report, can only know that you formerly took a step in defiance of the declared principles of society."[33]

Matthew may not have approved of his mother's literary ambitions, but he did approve of the plan for Isabella and Frances to share a household in Chelsea, which was well developed but ultimately not realized.[34] Frances and Matthew also took an interest in Isabella's eldest son, William, and many letters about him passed among the three of them. Matthew offered to sponsor William's education, "so as to enable him to become a useful and honourable member of society." He also added that once William's education was complete, he "may have interest enough to place him in the War Office," where Matthew's father continued to hold a high post.[35]

Even as Isabella's talents and friendships were advancing her career, other forces worked to pull her down. In 1805, the Second Baron Hawke died, and the allowance that Isabella and Robert had received up to that point stopped. This event, combined with Robert's continued "expensive habits," led him to accept "an offer to go to the West Indies with a civil appointment; he lived only ten days after his arrival," dying in Trinidad in 1807.[36]

In a later letter, Isabella indicated that wealthy friends at this point helped her establish a school for the care and instruction of youths. Through this school, Isabella met Joseph Hedgeland, a merchant whose daughters were pupils there. Isabella wrote that he "offered me his hand and promised to be the guide and father of my sons. I married him and he was the best of human beings, his pride and pleasure it was to render me independent and happy." But again, misfortune struck. Betrayed by a friend, Hedgeland lost all his money in a commercial speculation. Isabella related that he "died of a broken heart and left me to struggle with penury."[37] Despite this hardship, Isabella was able to keep Fitzroy in the Chelsea day school of the Rev. Mr. Farrer.

After paying for William's education, Matthew did get William a position in the War Office. William's behavior in the post became an issue, though, with reports soon getting back to Matthew of his "profligacy and ill-courses, gossip which [Matthew] refused to believe as often as his favourite [William] vowed the tales were false."[38] Isabella was unhappy with William's behavior and "wept and pleaded with her wayward son in vain."[39] For a time, William seems to have retained the support of Matthew. In one letter to his mother, Matthew told her to tell Isabella that he was, "if not entirely content—at least not seriously displeased with William."[40] In another letter, Matthew told his mother to tell Isabella that he had seen William and had "parted with him kindly enough" and that "the late complaints against him have made no alteration in me towards him."[41] Yet in her two-volume biography of Matthew, Baron-Wilson presents only a few letters "selected out of the many on the same subject [that] show the anguish . . . [that] Lewis felt at the overthrow of the hopes he had formed for his youthful favourite."[42]

There has been a great deal of speculation, at the time and subsequently, over Matthew's sexual tastes and the nature of his relationship with William. Baron-Wilson claims that in the 1830s, Matthew was enamored with Lady Charlotte Campbell, daughter of the fifth Duke of Argyll, while Montague Summers, writing in the 1930s, argues that "Lewis, who was homosexual, had many affairs and intrigues, but there can be no question that William Martin Kelly was the absorbing passion of his life."[43] Louis Peck, who wrote a biography of Lewis in 1961, argues that "the statement that Lewis was homosexual . . . would require for confirmation more convincing evidence than has been presented" and that it is "impossible to confirm or disprove."[44] George Haggerty claims that Matthew's tastes were "deeply rooted in aberrant desire and guilt-ridden fear."[45] Matthew Lewis never married, and he left no record of sexual relationships.

The most recent scholarly work to address the question comprehensively is David Lorne Macdonald's *Monk Lewis: A Critical Biography* (2000). It quotes Byron as stating that Lewis "was [more] fond of the society of younger men than himself. . . . I remember Mrs. Hope once asking who was Lewis's male-love this season!"[46] Macdonald argues that "the evidence is abundant enough to be cumulatively suggestive, even if it would not be quite conclusive in a court of law."[47]

Whatever the nature of Matthew and William's relationship, it deepened the connection between their families, it was more personal and emotional than most patron-client relationships, and it involved a significant financial component. Once Matthew came into his inheritance in 1812, he added William to his will. William was to receive five shares in Drury Lane, worth £100 each; £500 to be invested by the will's executors; and £500 as a cash payment.[48] The gift of theater shares would have been fitting. One of the few things known about William after 1818, the year of Matthew's death, is that he pursued an acting career under an assumed name.

During the time when he worked at the War Office, William took liberties that tested Matthew's patience. William ran up debts by telling tradesmen that Matthew, his patron, would pay them. William also cashed a draft on Matthew, which Matthew called a "most monstrous piece of ingratitude, for which I think drunkenness and debauchery no excuse."[49] William's debts and dissolute behavior would lead to his arrest, with Matthew posting the bail in 1815 (and not for the first time) to secure his release. Matthew was so furious at William for these escalating transgressions that he told William not to contact him directly but to send all communication to him through Frances.[50] Even so, Matthew told William, "I shall not forget you, and my mother can make known to me what you want to say, and through her I shall return my answer."[51]

In 1815, after being reprimanded by his superior at the War Office, William quit his job. When Frances asked whether Matthew could get William reinstated in his position, he replied, "So help me God! Re-establish him in the office! I could as soon get him into the moon."[52] In 1815, Matthew wrote to William:

> I need not tell you that I have been equally surprised and grieved at the accounts which I have lately heard of your conduct. . . . I can now only say, that penitence and good conduct may yet induce me to notice you. But I must have proofs before I can interfere further in your concerns.[53]

When he broke with William in 1815, Matthew was thirty-nine years old and three years into the inherited responsibilities of managing estates on both sides of the Atlantic. While William, then twenty, would continue to struggle in the following years, Matthew would rise to the challenge of new responsibilities, testing the courage and meaning of an antislavery position that he had publicly expressed years before. His first play to be produced, in 1797, had included African characters, one of whom, Hassan, denounces slavery, contributing to controversies surrounding the play.[54] But at that point, his father, with whom he already had strained relations, was the slave owner. Now his own fortunes were sustained in part by the enslavement of others. After spending his life inventing stories of gothic horror, Matthew was now directly responsible for the real horrors that contributed to his social position. Confronted with this moral dilemma, he did more than most and determined to see for himself the lives of those whose enslaved labor supported his privilege.

In the remaining three years of his life, he made two trips to inspect the living conditions of the more than three hundred enslaved people on his estates and to look into the possibility of improving them. He first left England in November 1815 and returned in March 1816, keeping an extensive journal of his experiences. On returning to England, Matthew met with William Wilberforce to discuss what he had seen, and he wrote a codicil to his will insisting that future owners of his Jamaican estates go once every three years to evaluate the conditions under which the enslaved people lived.[55] He then traveled in Europe for a year and a half, visiting Lord Byron, Percy Bysshe Shelley and Mary Shelley, and others at the Villa Diodati in Geneva in August 1816. He again left for Jamaica in November 1817 to evaluate the impact of the reforms that he had implemented during his first visit. On his second trip home from Jamaica, in 1818, Matthew died from yellow fever.

Matthew may have broken off relations with William in 1815, but he ensured that William would be provided for. Matthew had been giving his mother, Frances, an allowance of £1,000 a year. Matthew did not give William an allowance directly, but Frances did, with Matthew's knowledge and consent, and Matthew increased the amount he gave his mother by the amount that she gave William.[56] His will provided that William would continue to receive £2 a week after his death, with Matthew observing, "I have no other means of securing him from starving, through his own imprudence and misconduct of every kind."[57]

What is known of William after Matthew's death is tinged with sadness. He attempted to establish himself as an actor under the assumed name of William Horace Keppell, making his theatrical debut in London at the Queen's Theatre, near Tottenham Court Road. Before the performance, William wrote to an influential acquaintance, William Jerdan, who had resided in a cottage next to Isabella's during the time she was married to Joseph Hedgeland.[58] Jerdan was a longtime editor of the *Literary Gazette*, and William asked whether Jerdan could help encourage a large audience for the performance. He went so far as to offer to send Jerdan "any number of tickets you think you can disperse," especially for those willing to fill the pit of the house. William's performance "failed to make a sufficient impression upon the public," though, and his appearance as Hamlet in New York in 1831 was no different. Jerdan wrote that William "was hardly ever known beyond a very limited circle, and is now forgotten."[59] William's failure as an actor, Jerdan added, was not because of lack of talent, "nor were his endowments of a mediocre order," but because "fortune did not smile on him." Jerdan's final comment on William was that, "after suffering great mortifications, he died prematurely with an almost broken heart."[60]

Fitzroy Kelly and His Mother

As his brother's life lurched from one disappointment to the next, Fitzroy Kelly was beginning to achieve recognition. Isabella struggled to keep him in a day school in Chelsea, and he never went either to public school or university, a fact that would be referenced at various times throughout his career by adversaries.[61] His education in the law began at Lincoln's Inn in 1818, where he read with Abrahams and Wilkinson, well-known pleaders, and until 1824 Kelly worked only as a pleader, drafting statements without appearing in court. It was because of the unusual circumstances of a particular assize case on the Norfolk Circuit that Kelly got his chance to prove himself. In that matter, one side "had engaged all the leading counsel on the circuit, and the attorney [for the opposing side], wandering in the town at his wit's end," was persuaded to give Kelly a try. Fitzroy, then twenty-eight, took and won the case, and from this point on, he "was in all the important cases" on the Norfolk Circuit.[62] Fitzroy was also married in 1821, to Agnes Scarth, and the couple soon had a daughter.

Although Fitzroy was now on a professional track, Isabella's finances remained unsettled. She worked for a time as a governess, and in 1828, she made her first appeal to the Literary Fund for assistance.[63] Like most asking for financial help, Isabella gave up a degree of privacy; she was forced to spell out the hardships of her life, many of which have been recounted previously in this chapter. She confessed that to ask for help in this way was "painful" and "humiliating," but she also preserved her dignity, basing her request for assistance on the artistic and moral merit of her professional work. After listing all the (more than a dozen) books she had written, she added that at the age of sixty-seven, "declining health, defective sight, [and] pecuniary embarrassments which duty and affection to some and a wrong placed confidence in others altogether combine and overwhelm me, and I am rendered as unable to pursue my literary avocations." Isabella did mention Fitzroy, who was "now on the circuit" and currently difficult to reach. She described him as "a rising young man, at The Bar . . . [but] who is married and has a family to support." She did not mention William, but she did discuss her daughter;

the 1828 letters are, in fact, one of the best sources of information on the life of Isabella's daughter and Fitzroy's sister, Rosa.[64]

Rosa's life had many parallels to that of her mother. Isabella had tutored Rosa so that she might also have the option of supporting herself through writing, and several times the letters in Isabella's Literary Fund case file show her trying to interest individuals at the fund and elsewhere in the writing talents of her daughter. Rosa did not have the writing success of her mother, though, and as a young woman without a dowry, she had only a slim chance of marrying into the social circles of her mother's youth. Indeed, parish records indicate that in January 1824, Rosa married a clerk, George Crookshank, with Isabella and Fitzroy as witnesses. Rosa and George had two children, Alexander, born in November 1824, and Sara, born in 1826.[65] In her 1828 application to the Literary Fund, Isabella indicated that Rosa and her children were living with her, but she did not explain why or mention the whereabouts of Rosa's husband.

The Literary Fund awarded Isabella £30 in 1828, and while the money may have helped in the short term, Isabella was in an even more desperate situation when she wrote another series of letters four years later. Rosa's husband's death in 1831 seems to have worsened the family's financial plight. Isabella wrote to the Literary Fund that "now in my declining years with all my energies weakened, my constitution impaired and my heart nearly broken I have and do resort to my pen for help to support my dear child and her children." She mentioned William in these later letters, but only to say that he was living abroad and unable to help her, with the dates corresponding to his known theatrical performances in New York.

More than seventy years old and with renewed family burdens thrust upon her, Isabella still grounded her appeal as much in her professional status as in her distress. She wrote of the literary and educational works that she and her daughter had produced in recent years, but she also noted the difficulty of getting Londoners to pay attention to the works of provincial presses. She had another novel prepared and almost ready for publication but was concerned that her writing style might no longer be in fashion, and she hoped to get the opinion and support of individuals connected with the Literary Fund to review and perhaps endorse the work. Isabella listed the prominent friends and relations who had patronized her work, including "the late Duchesses of Gloucester and York, Warren Hastings . . . [and] Mr. Lewis," but then remarked, "Alas! where are they? All gone to their reward."[66] She continued, "My friends who would have powerfully aided me are gone. My great relations are now the second generation from those who loved me in my youth."

Isabella received £20 from the Literary Fund in 1832, and it was the last time that she needed to ask. After years of struggle, the Kelly family's fortunes finally began to turn on the strength of Fitzroy's legal career. In the 1830s, he became known as a specialist in commercial law and became a standing counsel for the East India Company and the Bank of England. As an advocate, it was said, "he was almost unrivalled in his ability to make an intricate case intelligible to a jury."[67] His mastery of commercial law would eventually make his London legal practice, for a time, the second most lucrative in the country. Years later, after he became a judge, he was known for being "precise and painstaking" in his decisions. It was remarked of him that "whatever his decision, you went away satisfied that you had been fairly dealt with. . . . [Y]ou never smarted under a sneer, or had to put up with a mediocre jest."[68]

His political skills were less sure. He failed in his first three election campaigns, and he was only brought into Parliament for Ipswich by petition in 1838, a year after he lost the race for the seat. He would lose the seat again in the 1841 election and only gain more stability after running for one of the relatively safe seats for Cambridge two years later. Once in Parliament, his legal talents brought him into leadership roles within the government, including the office of Solicitor General under Robert Peel and Attorney General under Lord Derby. Although he supported conservative interests, Kelly often "ignored the traditional boundaries of party politics" and gave generous support to reforms promoted by his political opponents, such as those by Sir Richard Bethell, a Whig best known for his work in passing the Matrimonial Clauses Act of 1857. On Kelly's death, the *Times* remarked that his many achievements came not through introductions or influence but solely by "his own fearless energy, sound learning, and unwearied combativeness."[69]

Fitzroy's success was also extended to his mother. After hardships lasting into the eighth decade of her life, Isabella seems to have finally secured some comfort in her final years. A newspaper story from 1848, three years after Fitzroy became Solicitor General, was saved in her Literary Fund case file. In the article, titled "The Mother of Sir Fitzroy Kelly," Isabella was described as "a celebrated novelist in her day, fifty years ago." She was living in a nice neighborhood in London, and, at ninety years of age, she "retain[ed] her faculties and read[] the smallest print without spectacles." The article included laudatory words about the family from which she had descended, while of her own children, all that was said was that "Sir Fitzroy Kelly is her only son."[70]

Stephen Lushington and
Matthew Lewis's Jamaica Journal

Stephen Lushington was far less involved in the 1840 and 1841 bills than was Fitzroy Kelly. Kelly had originally approached William Ewart to cosponsor or even take the lead on the legislation, as Ewart was the individual most identified at the time with the campaign against capital punishment. But when Ewart declined, Lushington agreed.[71] Kelly and Lushington were of different political parties, although both had reputations for working across party lines for causes they believed in. The recorded debates regarding the Punishment of Death Bills in 1840 and 1841 include only one speech by Lushington; its subject is the protection of women from rape. This cause was consistent with Lushington's insistence, as a counsel and later a judge in matrimonial cases, that strenuous advocacy for women was warranted, given their disadvantages under the law.[72]

From 1808, Lushington was a member of the Doctors' Commons, which oversaw ecclesiastical law, and as such, he represented individuals in marital disputes. Among those clients were Lady Byron, in her separation from Lord Byron, and Caroline, in her efforts to prevent George IV from dissolving their marriage. Lushington's efforts were central to Lady Byron's securing her separation, and she remained grateful to him for the rest of her life.[73] Lushington also remained close to Caroline after arguing her case in the House of Lords. He was present at her death, accompanied her body back to Brunswick, and served as the executor of her will. Starting in 1828, he was a judge for the Consistory Court of London, the most important diocesan court in the country, with jurisdiction over matrimonial cases. He was known for handing down many decisions favoring women, and "he went out of his way to make provision for the wife by extraordinary means."[74]

Lushington's legal advocacy for women had led him to be associated with an allegation of sodomy early in his career. As discussed in Chapters 5 and 7, Lushington likely used the threat of a sodomy allegation to help Lady Byron keep custody of her infant child when she separated from Lord Byron, which would otherwise have been difficult to secure, given the near-absolute rights of fathers at the time. Criticism of this action, disparaging Lushington for extending the sodomy law into the marital bed, was published decades later as a part of the main work advocating for the end to the death penalty for sodomy in the early nineteenth century.

Lushington was best known, though, for his opposition to slavery. He was a Member of Parliament starting in 1806, and in 1807, when he was only twenty-five, he delivered an important speech against the slave trade before voting for its abolition. Lushington's independence in Parliament irritated his patron, and in 1808, he lost the seat he had won with the patron's support. He would not return to Parliament for another dozen years, with the first of what would become an almost unbroken string of electoral successes. Lushington was primarily responsible for the 1824 legislation that abolished the transfer of slaves between British colonies. He was also one of the architects of the 1833 emancipation legislation, on which he worked closely with T. F. Buxton, Wilberforce's successor as leader of the abolitionist movement. Buxton's son later wrote that "every idea, and every plan, was originated and arranged between them."[75]

Religion was a key to Lushington's moral and ethical choices. A loyal churchgoer, he occupied the principal pew at his local parish church at Ockham. His liberal principles often clashed with his duties as an ecclesiastical judge on such issues as the church rates and the obligations of dissenters to pay them. He did not support the revival of Gothic or High Church forms, which he saw as reintroducing Catholic elements into the Church of England, but he was not an evangelical, either, and "his friends in the anti-slavery movement regretted that he was not 'truly religious.'"[76]

Given the place that religion, morality, and ethics played in Lushington's life, he might have looked askance at Matthew Lewis, who at the time they became related, through the marriage of their siblings, was most known for a book that Samuel Taylor Coleridge, among others, had denounced as immoral and blasphemous.[77] But Lushington also knew of the literal and ethical journey that Matthew had taken in the 1810s, as the result of the choices he had confronted when he had inherited enslaved individuals. Matthew had considered having his Jamaica journal published as early as March 1815, although nothing had come of it before the start of his second, fatal voyage to Jamaica. An 1819 letter documented efforts by Matthew's sister Sophia to enlist Walter Scott to approach publishers, although it was not until 1833 that John Murray agreed to publish the journal, promising to get the book out quickly, since "it is the right moment for publishing . . . now that people are full of interest about the (West) India question."[78]

Matthew's *Journal of a West India Proprietor* was praised in the *Edinburgh Review*, the *Quarterly Review*, and other publications.[79] One critic thought the journal worthwhile, even though he did not think much of Matthew as a poet, playwright, or novelist, saying that Matthew had previously built his reputation "upon the excitement of no nobler passion of the mind than fear."[80] Others, including Coleridge, considered the journal to be "by far

[Lewis's] best work, [which] will live and be popular."[81] This was, in part, because *Journal of a West India Proprietor* carries a message of empathy, reason, and atonement that resonated with the times.

It was common for the religious literature of the early nineteenth century to describe the lives of flawed individuals struggling to confront their shortcomings and engaging in the hard personal work of self-examination to achieve renewal.[82] Matthew does not write in his journal of religion's being the catalyst for his ethical awakening in relation to slavery, instead crediting his personal interactions with those who were enslaved in Jamaica.[83] Matthew's transformation was more one of empathy and experience than of revelation, but when his story became public with the publication of his journal in 1834, much of Britain was embarking on a similar journey, as the nation took the most meaningful step to date to address the inhuman system of mass enslavement that it, too, had inherited from past generations and from which it had profited so greatly.

Matthew knew that slavery was immoral and that he had benefited personally from that immorality. He knew that he would not be harmed if he allowed it to continue, while he might be if he strenuously opposed it. Yet his interaction with individuals who personally suffered the hardship of enslavement convinced him to take risks to improve their circumstances. Because of the significance of that transformation for Matthew, because of his relationship to the two men who cosponsored the 1840 and 1841 Punishment of Death Bills, and because of the need not to ignore the systems of foreign and domestic coerced labor that sustained the privileged spaces within which parliamentary debate and upper-class social life occurred, it is worth examining the contents of Matthew's *Journal of a West Indian Proprietor* in detail.[84]

Matthew's Jamaica Journal

Matthew first describes the sights and sounds of Gravesend, a seat of "melancholy" where "nowhere else did I ever see the sky look so dingy, and the river so dirty."[85] These rich descriptions of the port of embarkation foreshadow the later discussion of the vibrant and invigorating climate of Jamaica and, along with the dozens of literary allusions, witty observations, and anecdotes about his experience of voyage, remind the reader that the journal was written by one of the foremost playwrights and novelists of the day. Also in this first section are reflections on the theme of the pains, discontents, and pleasures of romantic relationships as well as a long poem focused on the theme of lost romantic love, inspired by the sight of a twenty-year-old sailor on the ship:

That sailor I've noted—his cheek, fresh and blooming
With health, scarcely yet twenty springs can have seen;
His looks they are lofty, but never presuming,
His limbs strong, but light, and undaunted his mien.
Frank and clear is his brow, yet a thoughtful expression,
Half tender, half mournful, oft shadows his eye;
And murmurs escape him, which make the confession,
If not check'd by a hem, they had swell'd to a sigh. . . .
So mournful, and yet they're prolong'd with such pleasure
Oh, nothing but love could have prompted the strain.
Yet, whate'er be the cause of thy sadness, young man,
That the weight be soon lighten'd, I send up my vow;
From the stings of remorse, I'll be sworn, thou 'rt a freeman,
No guilt ever ruffled the smooth of that brow!
That sigh which you breath'd sprang from pensive affection;
That song, though so plaintive, sheds balm on the heart;
And the pain which you feel at each fond recollection,
Is worth all the pleasures that vice could impart.[86]

These themes of love and loss fade as Matthew's ship reaches the Caribbean and his work begins. There are few references to love or longing in the rest of the journal, let alone any indications of new romantic interests. This shift is in large part because Matthew's narrative presents him as focused exclusively on his mission, but also because, as Matthew writes, one of the greatest drawbacks of being in Jamaica is "being obliged to live perpetually in public . . . [with] every thing done by him being seen and known."[87]

Vivid descriptions of the shimmering colors, flying fish, and tropical birds fill the pages as the ship moves from Antigua, past Puerto Rico, and then on to Jamaica, but the threat of violent resistance to the plantation system is ever present.[88] After reaching the Caribbean, the crew has to take precautions as they enter waters with pirate ships populated by "negros and outlaws of all nations, their numbers generally running from one hundred to one hundred and fifty men."[89] Matthew's ship is not attacked by these free Africans and their allies, but he learns that another vessel was, the *Saint Elizabeth*, which had embarked from England around the same time. Almost all the ocean voyages described in the book are marked by such fears of piracy.[90]

Matthew next describes arriving at his Jamaican estate, Cornwall. By his account, he allows himself to be confronted by those he holds in slavery. As he describes a scene where he is greeted with cheers by enslaved individuals, he pauses over "several old women, wrapped up in large cloaks, their heads bound round with different-coloured handkerchiefs, leaning on a staff, and standing motionless in the middle of the hubbub, with their eyes fixed upon the portico which I occupied, form[ing] an exact counterpart of the festivity of the witches of Macbeth."[91] These women are the first of several individuals whom Matthew allows to stand in judgment of him, and the description of the women's gaze is almost immediately followed by his statement that "I could not help being affected; perhaps it was the consciousness that all these *human beings* were my *slaves*."[92]

This scene is framed by text describing the enslaved as being grateful to Matthew, and yet Matthew states, and not for the only time in the narrative, that "whether the pleasure of the negroes was sincere may be doubted."[93] In such moments, he acknowledges, his interactions with individuals on his estate are determined by his power over them. This view can be seen again in the narrative when, after hearing another man identify himself as his slave, he writes:

> The word "slave" seemed to imply, that, although he did feel pleasure then in serving me, if he had detested he must have served me still. I really felt quite humiliated at the moment, and was tempted to tell him,—"Do not say that again; say that you are my negro, but do not call yourself my slave."[94]

Throughout the journal, Matthew casts himself in the part of the paternalistic landowner, listening to and responding to those who work on his estate. He visits the "negro village" and describes it in detail, noting that "there are many very old people" there and taking their presence as "strong proof of the good treatment [to] which the negroes on Cornwall have been accustomed."[95] Matthew also raises other topics, such as the property rights of the enslaved, and the ways in which the conditions of the enslaved are superior to those of the factory workers of England.[96] Typical of this material is a six-page description of a dispute between two men who are enslaved on the estate. The case had first appeared before Matthew in his role as magistrate, and he describes himself as visiting the men in their homes, meeting their families, and learning about their religious practices. At the end of the section, Matthew declines an invitation to go to a dinner and ball at Montego Bay, "being determined to give up my whole time to my negroes during my stay in Jamaica."[97]

Matthew is invested in showing the positive effects of the abolition of the slave trade, which had occurred less than a decade before his visit. Of the trauma caused by pre-1807 practices, Matthew writes, "Poor creatures! what with the terrors and sufferings of the voyage, and the unavoidable hardships of the seasoning, those advantages were purchased more dearly than any in this life can possibly be worth. God be thanked, all that is now at an end."[98] Matthew describes some estates that have been abandoned due to lack of workers and his belief that "with the difficulty of procuring more negroes— (which can now only be done by purchasing them from other estates) . . . I am fully persuaded that instances of tyranny to negroes are now very rare, at least in this island."[99]

And yet, finally, more than one hundred pages into the book, the silences that have sustained the placid surface of Matthew's narrative are broken by the first indication of the violence necessary to maintain a slave society.[100] He writes that the enslaved individuals on his estate had been brutally mistreated by unsupervised overseers before his arrival and that "the public magistrature was obliged to interfere to protect them from his cruelty. . . . [I]f I had not come myself to Jamaica, in all probability should I ever have had the most distant idea [of] how abominably the poor creatures had been misused."[101]

In a work purporting to be a chronological account of Matthew's journey, these revelations of extreme cruelty (the details of which are never fully described) are a reminder of the artificial nature of the narrative. The passage indicates that he has been gaining first-hand knowledge of the violence inherent in the system over the previous weeks, but this information is revealed to the reader only at the moment when Matthew acts to correct it.[102]

Immediately following this passage, Matthew writes that the whip will no longer be used on his estate, and as the book unfolds over the remaining three hundred pages, it becomes clear that instituting this reform is central to what Matthew seeks to accomplish with his visit. Matthew writes that he is "indeed assured by every one about me, that to manage a West-Indian estate without the occasional use of the cart-whip, however rarely, is impossible" and that British soldiers and sailors receive similar punishments.[103] But then he argues, "All this may be very true; but there is something to me so shocking in the idea of this execrable cart-whip." He states that he has "positively forbidden the use of it on Cornwall; and if the estate must go to rack and ruin without its use, to rack and ruin the estate must go."[104]

Matthew then reiterates that it is specifically his visit to Jamaica and his personal interactions with individuals who had been brutalized in this way that have led him to this decision. He writes:

> Probably, I should care less about this punishment, if I had not been living among those on whom it may be inflicted; but now, when I am accustomed to see every face that looks upon me . . . one must

be an absolute brute not to feel unwilling to leave them subject to the lash.[105]

Ending most corporal punishment is the cornerstone of a series of reforms that Matthew implements in his three months at his main Jamaican estate. Other reforms include additional time off to cultivate individual plots, which provide all of an enslaved person's food; the construction of a new hospital on the estate; and the requirement that punishments be delayed for at least twenty-four hours, to avoid acting in the heat of the moment. One form of sexual violence against enslaved women is also addressed.[106]

Rebellions, Resistance, and Benevolence

Throughout the journal, Matthew frames his discussion of these reforms in terms of benevolence, but he also reveals that individual and group acts of rebellion in the Caribbean might have shaped his views. The fear of being poisoned by those who prepare his food, for example, is a recurring theme in the journal. Obeah men, with their knowledge of poisons and ability to distribute them to almost anyone, are depicted as a regular presence in the region, despite the efforts of Matthew and others to suppress them.[107] Concerning the trial of a young woman who poisoned her master, Matthew expresses shock that "she stood by the bed to see her master drink the poison; witnessed his agonies without one expression of surprise or pity. . . . Even since her imprisonment, she could never be prevailed upon to say that she was sorry for her master's having been poisoned." The young woman would be executed for her actions, but "she heard the sentence pronounced without the least emotion; and I am told, that when she went down the steps of the courthouse, she was seen to laugh."[108]

Matthew also discusses several large-scale rebellions that have occurred or been threatened. White fears are often stoked by rumors among those enslaved "that *The Regent and Wilberforce* had actually determined upon setting them all at liberty at once . . . but that the interference of the island had defeated the plan."[109] Furthermore, Matthew writes, "discontent was most carefully and artfully fomented by some brown Methodists, who held secret and nightly meetings on the different estates," or by mysterious individuals, such as "a *black* ascertained to have stolen over into the island from St. Domingo, and a *brown* Anabaptist missionary."[110] That such uprisings might lead to, "in all probability, a general massacre of the whites, and a second part of the horrors of St. Domingo," is also a common refrain.[111] One man, taking on the title of "the King of the Eboes" in preparation for such an uprising, declares after his capture that he has "left enough of his countrymen to prosecute the design in hand, and revenge his death upon the whites."[112]

As many scholars have noted, the reality of plots and rebellions often had little in common with what whites knew or said of them, which could be exaggerated to justify brutal reprisals on the enslaved populations.[113] Nevertheless, the danger was real and ever-present, and perhaps felt by Matthew every time he doubted the sincerity of the responses he received from those he kept enslaved.

Meeting as Fellow Humans, and Its Limits

One of the more poignant moments in the journal occurs during an extended conversation between Matthew and the man who takes him around Port Royal by canoe. They speak of Christianity and of the treatment of enslaved individuals, which this man is. The man tells Matthew "that kindness was the only way . . . and that, if that failed, flogging would never succeed." Matthew then quotes the man as saying, "'Blacks must not be treated now . . . as they used to be; they can think, and hear, and see, as well as white people: blacks are wiser . . . than they were, and will be wiser still.'"[114] Matthew's empathetic presentation of statements like this, though, is followed by passages showing that he clearly believes himself to be superior to black people, who he complains have great difficulty executing tasks properly.[115]

Matthew's text only once addresses the abolition of slavery directly. He states that "every man of humanity must wish that slavery, even in its best and most mitigated form, had never found a legal sanction, and must regret that its system is now so incorporated with the welfare of Great Britain as well as of Jamaica, as to make its extirpation an absolute impossibility, without the certainty of producing worse mischiefs than the one which we annihilate."[116] In these statements, Matthew falls far short of those in Britain in the 1810s who argued that abolition must be achieved, regardless of the "mischiefs" that might ensue. Yet he is well advanced over many of his fellow planters, some of whom, including a magistrate, publicly rebuke Matthew. Matthew's reforms and his willingness to listen to charges that enslaved individuals made against whites are the cause of the magistrate's concern, but Matthew represents himself as not only unfazed by the criticism but flattered by it.[117]

Matthew never gave up his ownership of other individuals or his ability to coerce them to increase his personal wealth. And yet he was at least willing to see for himself the system that sustained his life in England. He was willing to meet individuals whom he kept in slavery, and he was affected by the experience. Even as he strained to see these individuals as a content peasantry, better off than English factory workers, he also recognized some of the injustices of slavery and made changes in the operation of his estates that could potentially lessen their value. These steps were made fewer than three years after he inherited the estates. Whether he would have gone further in later years cannot be known, as his life was cut short by yellow fever on his second voyage home from Jamaica, only a few weeks after he wrote the last entry in his journal.

Final Reflection

One of the greatest benefactors of Fitzroy Kelly's family became an example to the nation, posthumously, of the capacity of individuals to empathize with the suffering of others and to take at least some personal risk, however modest, given the scale of the injustice, to make the communities they influenced more ethical. Matthew never distanced himself from either his earlier writing or the behavior that caused some to suspect that he was sexually interested in men. These were all parts of the same ethical subject.[118] They were all parts of the Matthew Lewis whom Fitzroy Kelly knew and whom Stephen Lushington also knew, albeit to a lesser degree. Matthew Lewis stated that it was specifically because he had met enslaved individuals that he altered his opinion over how they should be treated. Might Fitzroy's and Stephen's personal interactions with Matthew have increased their ability to empathize with him?

Matthew's influence on the two men who in 1840 and 1841 would unite to make ending the death penalty for sodomy one of the key features in their Punishment of Death Bills cannot be known. It can be conclusively established, though, that Jeremy Bentham, as shown in Chapter 1, and Lord John Russell, as shown in Chapter 7, supported the reform, even while taking steps to publicly distance themselves from it. But Fitzroy Kelly and Stephen Lushington together publicly proposed and defended the bill that would be explicitly denounced in the Lords as seeming to condone sodomy. A complex, admirable, and ethical figure, Matthew Gregory Lewis was the primary link between Kelly and Lushington, a link that was embedded not in the caprice and brinksmanship of parliamentary politics but in the emotional and affective bonds of family.

3

"Sodomy" in Popular Politics

The politicization of sexual immorality intensified in the first decades of the nineteenth century due to the wartime and immediate postwar crises. This period saw the founding of the Society for the Suppression of Vice in 1802; by 1804, it had become a mass subscription society and inspired similar groups across Britain. These groups drew a direct connection between moral disorder and social disorder, arguing that "England was indeed infected with the spirit of licentiousness and of rebellion against authority" that had brought about the French Revolution.[1] They highlighted what they saw as the "consequences of rebellion against traditional values and institutions, and [warned] the English of the intentions of the Almighty should they fail to turn from their wickedness."[2] These groups were powerful allies to the government, but their support came with a price, such as the pressure they exerted to end the slave trade. While the government was reluctant to undercut the profitability of Britain's slave-based Caribbean sugar production in a time of war, for some of those pressing for the reform, it was an act of atonement for the national sin of slavery.[3] The Vice Societies saw the domestic campaigns against Sabbath-breaking, profanity, and lewd and disorderly behavior in a similar light.

Radical politicians, such as William Cobbett and William Benbow, disagreed and argued that such groups only prosecuted the crimes of poor men while those of the wealthy were left unchallenged and that the members of such groups were often ruthless in their economic exploitation of the lower classes in Britain. Cobbett was one of the best-known and more financially secure radical leaders of the day, while Benbow, from the lowest social levels, was connected to the 1816 Spa Fields conspiracy and the planned revolutionary government to follow.[4] He was an especially effective communicator to the lower classes, and, as Iain McCalman has observed, he was able "to tap the ardent popular passions generated by unlearned enthusiastic preachers" and made use of his "plebeian and vernacular credentials" to appeal to a wide audience.[5] The threat posed to the government by such radicals was never greater than it was in the 1810s and 1820s, and Cobbett and Benbow used examples of unpunished sodomy and sex between men within the upper class as part of their argument against a corrupt upper class that put itself above the law.[6]

The degree to which sodomy and sex between men were used as tools in partisan politics in this period has been underestimated. This topic became an unavoidable issue for the government in June 1810, when the Duke of Cumberland, at that point sixth in line to the British throne, was discovered in St. James's Palace, covered in blood, with the body of his dead valet down the hall. Accusations would appear in the radical press immediately thereafter, and resurface periodically in the years following, that the duke had murdered his valet to avoid being accused publicly of having had sex with a man. A few weeks later, the Vere Street molly house would be raided, leading to unprecedented displays of loyal subjects joining in the public condemnation of lower-ranking "sodomites."

The two narratives associated with 1810—one related to the Duke of Cumberland and the other to the Vere Street molly-house raid—allow for the examination of how sex between men factored into political contests before the Reform Act of 1832.[7] For the Tory government in the 1810s and 1820s, the punishment of "sodomites" could be used to reinforce its moral credentials; for radicals, the failure of the upper classes at all levels to observe the moral standards that they enforced among the poor was a powerful illustration of hypocrisy and the need to sweep away the abuses of "Old Corruption."

These same issues were drawn in stark relief in a way that drew the attention of the nation and would be remembered decades later when a bishop in the Church of Ireland was caught having sex with a soldier in a London public house in 1822. It was not just that the bishop was allowed to escape on bail while the solider faced prosecution that made this issue so explosively partisan; it was the further revelations that this same bishop had destroyed the lives of other lower-class men who had accused him of making sexual advances, with local elites closing ranks to support the bishop. Radicals led by Cobbett and Benbow used the Bishop of Clogher scandal and other examples of unpunished acts of sex between men involving the upper classes as components of their broader assault on the injustices of the political system. The Bishop of Clogher scandal led to the first significant change in the state's regulation of sex between men in the nineteenth century, carried out by the Tory government in 1823 and 1825, amplifying the class bias in the implementation of the law as it related to sex between men.

The significance of these events in 1810, 1822, and 1825 and their relationship to one another were noticed at the time. In the summer of 1825, during a wave of prosecutions carried out under the new law passed by Robert Peel, the *Morning Chronicle* observed that "it is always with the greatest reluctance that we break silence with regard to those unnatural offences and disgusting practices which now, unfortunately, engross so much of the public attention."[8] The reporter lamented that there was no longer "the same understanding on the part of the Press not to allude to unnatural crimes, which there is in decent society." There had been, it was observed, "something like an understanding of this sort, in consequence of the disgusting scenes of 1810, which was tolerably well observed, till the case of a certain Bishop broke down every restraint of the kind."[9] This chapter recovers the political history of sex between men that this reporter knew, demonstrating the degree to which sex between men was an issue in partisan politics and the consequences of that issue for the Tory government in the 1820s.

Radicals, Rumors, and the Duke of Cumberland

In 1810, Ernest Augustus, the Duke of Cumberland, then sixth in line to the British throne (and later second, behind only Victoria), was found wounded and covered in blood in St. James's Palace, while one of his valets, Joseph Sellis, lay dead down the hall with his throat slit. Reporting of this incident in the press was immediate and intense, with factions ranging from the ultra-radicals to the High Tories offering incompatible accounts.[10] Some perspective on the political stakes in this contest was provided years later in the *Morning Chronicle*, in a report on one of the libel trials sparked by the valet's death.[11] The *Morning Chronicle* recounted a radical view of the events when it reported that "on the morning of the 1st of June an astounding communication was made by the daily Papers, that his Royal Highness had been surprised in the night, and that his life had been attempted by one of his valets, named Sellis. *Many reports were circulated, and the general opinion was, that the Duke was the murderer.* Of course the High Tory party took no small pains to propagate the opposite sentiment, but the former was most generally believed, from the analogy of attending circumstances."[12] The *Annual Register* was strong in its royalist support, but it also reported that "there were persons sufficiently evil-

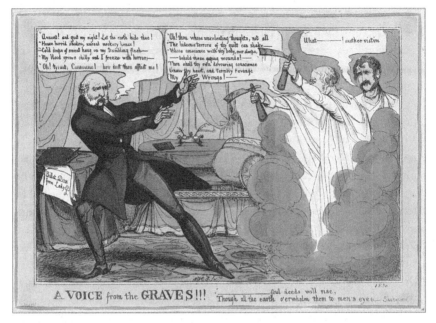

Figure 3.1 The Duke of Cumberland recoils in horror from two ghosts, one of whom is Sellis, who declares, "What _____! Another Victim." *A Voice from the Graves!!!, _____foul deeds will rise, Though all the earth o'erwhelm them to men's eyes—Shakspeare,* Thomas Howell Jones, Publisher not named, etching hand-colored, England, 1830. (Library of Congress.)

minded to insinuate that the Duke of Cumberland himself had murdered Sellis. From that time until . . . the present . . . his Royal Highness had been incessantly made the victim of the scandalous calumnies of some obscure slanderer or slanderers."[13]

According to the palace, Sellis, in a fit of madness, had attempted to assassinate the duke. The coroner's inquest was held on June 1 at St. James's Palace, with Francis Place acting as foreman of the jury.[14] It was reported in the *Annual Register* that "when the jury inspected Sellis's room, they examined minutely the body" in an inquest that lasted from 3:00 P.M. until 11:00 P.M., with seventeen witnesses called. The jury took two hours to conclude that Sellis had made an unsuccessful attempt to kill the Duke of Cumberland and then committed suicide. The government left the blood on the walls of St. James's Palace, allowing, it was said, the public to come in and inspect for itself.

Testimony of the witnesses at the inquest, published in newspapers in the following days, demonstrated the closeness that had existed between Sellis and the duke. Cumberland was the godfather of Sellis's most recent child and had prevailed on his sister, Augusta, to be godmother.[15] As a consequence, "Sellis became in some sort an object of particular attention to all the branches of the royal family, from whom he and his children received many little presents and marks of notice."[16] Multiple servants in St. James's Palace echoed the statements of one man that "the Duke was particularly partial to Sellis, and behaved better to him, he thought, than to any other servant."[17] At St. James's Palace, Sellis and "his family were accommodated with lodgings over the gate-way, leading into the Kitchen-court from Cleveland Row; from which there was a communication with the Duke's suite of apartments." Another servant confirmed that a "special privilege was allowed to Sellis, of a bell being permitted to be put up, to bring him to the Duke from his family's apartments."[18] Other familiarities were described, such as the fact that "Sellis used, some years since, to ride in the carriage with the Duke."[19] It was also sworn under oath that Sellis "and his family were in so much favour that every Court day, when the Queen came to dress at the Duke's apartments, for the drawing-room, Sellis's wife and children were had down."

The greatest household tensions described in the testimony were between Sellis and Cornelius Neale, another servant who seemed to be attracting the duke's favor and who was increasingly called on to attend to the duke privately, in place of Sellis. At one point, Sellis accused Neale of stealing from the duke, and "Sellis made a charge against him at the Bow street Office, 8 or 9 months since," but nothing came of it. One servant in the depositions, a valet named James Pauler, said that "Sellis often talked about leaving the Duke's service, saying, *he could not remain in the family* if Neale did."[20]

Some time later, the radical *Independent Whig* published a series of questions directed at the "Duke of C." It asked "whether it be not true, that several attempts were made, before a Coroner's Jury could be found" willing to declare the death a suicide.[21] It also questioned why the duke insisted that Sellis be given a Christian burial by the duke's chaplain, despite the fact that this treatment was not allowed for suicides but would prevent the body from being seen by others.[22] "The other queries go to the other facts of the case, as *long since laid before the public,* in relation to the razor [which had slit Sellis's throat and was found far from the body], to the basin, in which it appeared that hands stained with blood had been washed, to the bloody coat, &c. all of them going to insinuate that Sellis could not have fallen by his own hand."[23]

The most persistent alternative explanation for these events, the one that was central to one of the most prominent libel trials, was that, according to the *Annual Register,* "a short time before this dreadful catastrophe, the Duke had been surprised in an improper and unnatural situation with this Neale by the other servant, Sellis, and exposure was expected."[24] It was argued that the duke had killed Sellis to prevent his going public with his accusations and then had wounded himself superficially to make his story more plausible. Another version of the rumor was that it was the Duke of Cumberland and Sellis who had been most intimately involved and that tensions had developed when the duke's affections seemed to turn toward Neale.[25] Working against Cumberland's credibility, at least for some, was the "considerable disgust in many persons who were acquainted with the more private life and habits of the Duke."[26]

Accusations made in radical publications against members of the royal family in this period cannot be taken at face value, but they had political power. Only a year before, the revelation that the Duke of York had allowed his mistress to sell government offices was used to deny him the command of the British Army in the Peninsular War, a command instead given to the Duke of Wellington. Most in the British government believed Wellington to be a far superior general, but to oppose the Duke of York's appointment might have been seen as politically seditious without the pretext of the sex scandal to provide political cover.[27] A decade later, liberal and radical politicians, through their support of Caroline's efforts to prevent George IV from divorcing her, were able to oppose the government in a way not possible in the years since the outbreak of the French Revolution. Criticizing the morals and the ethics of the king and his government was allowable in a way that direct public criticism of policies was not, and this option was a powerful tool for undermining the legitimacy of opponents.[28]

The Duke of Cumberland scandal did not fade in the weeks that followed. Dissatisfaction with the official story of what had occurred in St. James's Palace persisted, and on July 5, more than a month after the death of Sellis, the *Times* reported that "some of our contemporaries are publishing the whole of the depositions taken before Mr. Read, the magistrate in relation to the worried attempt upon the Duke of Cumberland's person," but the *Times* refrained from doing so.[29] The *Morning Chronicle* published some of the depositions, while *Cobbett's Weekly Political Register* took up most of its thirty-page July 7, 1810, issue with more than two dozen depositions, opening the issue with Cobbett's letter to his readers in which he explained that "now, for the first time in my life on any account whatever, I am a prisoner, after having been a public Writer for ten years in England."[30]

William Cobbett's Story

By that point, Cobbett was a persistent and vocal critic of the government. An informally educated son of a farmer and publican, he had held positions of increasing rank and responsibility in the army. After being discharged in 1791, he published *The Soldier's Friend*, a scathing and impassioned look at how poorly common soldiers were paid and treated. To escape prosecution for this work, he fled to the United States in 1792. The events of the French Revolution inspired him to begin publishing newspaper articles and pamphlets in the United States under the pen name "Peter Porcupine."[31] Cobbett attacked Thomas Paine for his politics and his religious views, and he most identified with the Federalist faction in American politics led by Alexander Hamilton. In 1800, when the threat of a libel case in America convinced Cobbett to return to England, he was offered control of a government-run newspaper, so aligned with the state interests were his views thought to be.

It did not take long after his return to England, though, for distance to open between his views and those of the government. In *Cobbett's Weekly Political Register*, which he founded in 1802 after declining to take control of the government-owned newspaper, he grew increasingly vocal in his attacks on the policies of taxation, debt, and the use of paper money.[32] These practices, according to Cobbett, not only exacerbated the ruinous costs of the war but also, along with the seemingly unabated system of unmerited sinecures that the government continued to dole out to the upper classes, made a mockery of any concept of shared burden when juxtaposed with the desperate plight of the poor in the countryside, with whom Cobbett was particularly concerned. By 1807, Cobbett had sided strongly with Maj. John Cartwright and others who saw radical parliamentary reform as the only viable solution to the problems of the nation.[33]

The detailed depositions published in *Cobbett's Weekly Political Register* seemed to undermine the official story of Sellis's death. They showed a man who exhibited neither signs of madness nor thoughts of contemplating an assassination. Mary Ann Sellis, Joseph Sellis's widow, reported that her husband "had been with her nearly the whole of yesterday; that he went to market, and afterwards walked with her and the children in the Park, and did not leave her till ten o'clock that night."[34] Mary Ann's deposition showed a seemingly untroubled man enjoying a day with his family. Other depositions called into question the interpretation of key pieces of physical evidence, such as slippers said to belong to Sellis that had been found in the Duke of Cumberland's room.[35] The dueling accounts of what may have led to the death of Sellis did not continue in the press, though, as the day after the extended depositions were published in *Cobbett's*, the Vere Street molly house was raided, beginning an unprecedented wave of newspaper reporting on sex between men, in which the nation, it was shown, rallied behind the state in its action against "sodomites."

For a government facing the persistent allegation that it was defending a man who was willing to murder to conceal his attraction to other men, the timing of the Vere Street matter could not have been more fortuitous. It generated more newspaper coverage than any other event involving sex between men in more than eighty years. And, unlike in the case of Capt. Robert Jones forty years before, no part of the press offered sympathy for those arrested or seemed to regret the brutal punishments that they faced. Instead, the newspaper reports made clear just how different "sodomites" were from ordinary men of any class, amplifying the state's and the public's excoriation of such deviants.

Addressing Vere Street

The Vere Street molly-house raid has consistently been cited as evidence of English attitudes toward sex between men in the early nineteenth century.[36] The arrest of twenty-seven men at the White Swan, in Vere Street, was first reported on July 9, 1810, and from the earliest reporting, it was noted that the men were met by the "mob . . . expressing their detestation of the offence of which the prisoners were charged."[37] The men were described as being of the lower classes, as habitually engaging in the act of sodomy, as creating a separate and secret space in which they carried out that act, and even as sometimes carrying out mock childbirths.[38] Also frequently cited in contemporary accounts was the pillorying of six of the men who were convicted of attempted sodomy. Among the daily papers, the *Times*, the *Morning Chronicle*, the *Morning Post*, the *Evening Mail*, and others published reports with passages that contained almost exactly the same wording, with similar accounts published a few days later in the *Saunders's News-Letter*, the *Hampshire Chronicle*, *Bell's Weekly Messenger*, *Kentish Weekly Post*, and other provincial and weekly newspapers, and then still later in the *Annual Register*.[39] Typical was this account from the *Star*:

> The disgust felt by all ranks in society at the detestable conduct of these wretches occasioned many thousands to become spectators of their punishment. At an early hour the Old Bailey was completely blockaded. . . . The shops from Ludgate Hill to the Haymarket were shut up, and the streets lined with people, waiting to see the offenders pass. . . . The miscreants were then brought out and placed in the caravan . . . having cast their eyes upwards, the sight of the spectators on the tops of the houses operated strongly on their fears, and they soon appeared to feel terror and dismay.—at the instant the church

clock went half past twelve, the gates were thrown open. . . . The caravan went next, followed by about 40 officers and the Sheriffs. The first salute received by the offenders was a volley of mud, and a serenade of hisses, hooting, and execration, which compelled them to fall flat on their faces in the caravan. The mob, and particularly the women, had piled up balls of mud to afford the objects of their indignation a warm reception. . . . At one o'clock four of them were exalted *on a new pillory, made purposely for their accommodation.*— The remaining two, Cook and Amos, were honoured by being allowed to enjoy a triumph in the pillory alone. . . . Upwards of fifty women were permitted to stand within the ring, who assailed them incessantly with mud, dead cats, rotten eggs, potatoes, and buckets full of blood, offal, and dung, which were brought by a number of butchers' men, from St James's Market. . . . [T]he remaining two, Cook (who had been the landlord) and Amos, alias Fox, were desired to mount . . . and in one minute they appeared a complete heap of mud and their faces were much more battered than those of the former four. . . . Cook appeared almost insensible, and it was necessary to help them both down and into the cart, whence they were conveyed to Newgate by the same road they had come, and in their passage they continued to receive the same salutations the spectators had given them going out. Cook continued to lie upon the seat in the cart, but Amos lay down among the filth, till their entrance into Newgate sheltered the wretches from the further indignation of the most enraged populace we ever saw.[40]

Men had been placed in the pillory for having sex with men many times before. But no other account of pillorying men for attempted sodomy in the eighteenth or early nineteenth century comes close to matching these descriptions of thousands of spectators lining the streets for hours, some having collected putrid items for days, and covering the accused in heaps of garbage until they were hardly recognizable as humans. The images described are so graphic that it is difficult to get them out of mind. Perhaps that is why Vere Street is mentioned in almost every work that discusses sex between men in nineteenth-century Britain, even when almost none of these same works mention the Duke of Cumberland affair of only a few weeks earlier.[41]

The state did not compel people to line the streets to taunt and torture the men arrested at Vere Street. But someone, at some level, did decide to build new pillories "made purposely for their accommodation," so that the men arrested at Vere Street could be best displayed to the crowd.[42] If this as-

Figure 3.2 The Duke of Wellington and the Duke of Cumberland, with contrasting postures of skepticism and ingratiation. *Another Ominous Conjunction*, by John ("HB") Doyle, printed by Charles Etienne Pierre Motte, published by Thomas McLean, lithograph, 1831. (© National Portrait Gallery, London.)

pect of the event was stage-managed, other aspects of the event might have been as well, in ways that might have influenced the reporting of the event. At least one newspaper, in the context of a later scandal, directly stated that the goal of the press at such moments should be "to preserve *and strengthen* that detestation" that the public had for acts of sex between men and that doing so was "a public duty."[43] When stating his reasons for publishing specific details and invective rhetoric related to sex between men, the editor of *Bell's Life in London and Sporting Chronicle* argued that the press played a key role in ensuring that sodomy would never be as common in Britain as it was in Italy or France. He argued:

> If those who ought to be the guardians of the public morals—those who really are so when they properly discharge their duty—we mean,

the writers in the public papers . . . do their duty, Britain will still be undefiled, and the abhorrence of the foul crime will descend to future generations; but we will maintain, that to effect this, *the INFAMOUS must be pointed out* when detected, *and the indignant execration of the populace must be encouraged* rather than stifled.[44]

This editor believed that it was his duty not just to report the anger that might be expressed at "sodomites" but to encourage it.[45] It was an idea that informed radical and ultra-Tory press coverage of sex between men, with the difference being which scandals were selected by each side for emphasis and which for silence.

Only a few other molly-house raids were documented in the first fifty years of the nineteenth century, and none received anything close to the same level of press coverage. The possibility of more than a temporal relationship between the Duke of Cumberland affair and the Vere Street molly-house raid is suggested by the many newspapers that mentioned that the Duke of Cumberland was spotted in the crowd at the execution of two of the Vere Street convicts.[46] One paper, the *Carlisle Journal*, even added three exclamation points: "The Duke of Cumberland, Lord Sefton, Lord Yarmouth, and several other Noblemen, were in the Press Yard ! ! !"[47]

"Unrespectable" Pressmen: Stoddart and the "Man-Mistress"

Radical and ultra-Tory pressmen took advantage of high-profile incidents involving sex between men to further their own political agendas; some even went so far as to fabricate sodomy charges. Many argued that the allegations against the Duke of Cumberland were just such fabrications by radicals. The case for fabrication seems to be much more compelling, though, regarding allegations centering on sex between men derived from a single ultra-Tory pressman in 1818, designed to discredit some of the leading radical politicians of the day in the run-up to a parliamentary election.

Cobbett was one of those involved in this 1818 incident, although this time from abroad. After his 1810 conviction and two years' imprisonment in Newgate for publicly criticizing the government for an incident that had occurred years before, Cobbett returned to his Hampshire farm where he lived with his family, continuing to publish the *Political Register* as he had done throughout his incarceration. The severe economic downturn following the end of the Napoleonic Wars, along with the 1816 harvest failure, was the catalyst for Cobbett's move in an even more radical direction, sparking him to create a mass-circulation version of the *Political Resister*. He sold forty-four thousand copies of the first issue, in which he urged the election of radical reformers to Parliament. Fearing arrest due to the increasing stridency of his writing, Cobbett returned to the United States in 1817, but he continued to publish the *Political Register* from abroad.[48]

The man who sparked the 1818 incident had also received an offer from the government, similar to the one extended to Cobbett years before, to help him establish a newspaper. Unlike Cobbett, John Stoddart accepted. Stoddart was from a more privileged background than Cobbett's, with the Bishop of Durham acting as his first patron at Oxford. But as a student, Stoddart embraced the writings of William Godwin and the republicanism of revolutionary France, leading to a break between him and the bishop. While traveling in radical circles and adopting the close-cropped hairstyle of the sansculottes, Stoddart also continued to study for the bar at Grays's Inn, earning his Doctorate of Civil Law in 1801.[49] His revolutionary fervor waned over time and then fully retreated, so that when he became the editor of the *Times* in 1812, he was known for his pro-Tory editorials and support of the French ultraroyalists. Many of his former radical associates felt betrayed by this transformation, and he and his former friends traded public attacks in the pages of the *Times* and other newspapers. Stoddart was eventually dismissed by the owner of the *Times* over these extreme views. The following year, he founded the *New Times* with money from the government and French ultraroyalists; for the next decade, he used it as a platform from which to attack radicals.[50]

The focus of Stoddart's 1818 libelous accusation was Thomas Cleary, an electoral agent of the radical Major Cartwright, who was then running for a seat in Parliament to represent Westminster. Cleary had read a letter on the hustings in support of Cartwright, sent over from America by Cobbett. The letter was somewhat disparaging of Henry Hunt, another prominent radical leader, and Hunt questioned whether the letter had actually been written by Cobbett. Shortly thereafter, a letter appeared in the *New Times*—signed "H. Hunt" but most likely penned by Stoddart—that charged Cleary with forging the letter he had read at the hustings and described him as "a kept man-mistress, who had not a shilling but what he obtained by his own prostitution."[51]

The libel trial that followed opened with an emphasis on the enormity of the accusation that had been made against Cleary. The counsel of the plaintiff framed the case by telling the jury that if "they were for a moment to estimate the nature of the libel from any they had previously heard discussed, they would form a very inadequate idea of its magnitude." He added that "it exceeded, in the bitterness of its sting, any thing which he had ever experienced."[52]

Figure 3.3 From the time of the "man-mistress" trial. Note the gazes of the couple in the center of the image and the soldier on the far right. *Monstrosities of 1818*, by George Cruikshank, published by G. Humphrey, London, etching, hand-colored, 1818. (Courtesy of the Lewis Walpole Library, Yale University.)

Stoddart's defense took several tacks. Stoddart denied responsibility for the letter, arguing that it represented the view of a reader. He also argued that the letter implied that Cleary had been kept by a woman, as Tom Jones had been by Lady Bellaston in Henry Fielding's novel. Stoddart's defense admitted that it had been a lapse to suggest that Cleary had prostituted himself to a woman but that this accusation was not as serious as charging him with having done the same with a man.[53] Stoddart's explanations were implausible, and he was fined £100 for libeling Cleary, a slap on the wrist that did not seem to alter his editorial policies.

This sort of lawsuit was a regular occurrence in these years, sparked by accusations and innuendos in the radical and the ultra-Tory press. In addition to lawsuits instigated by individuals, the radical pressmen also had to face well-funded prosecutions by the government for sedition or by the Society for the Suppression of Vice for blasphemy. Consequently, it was common for more prominent and wealthier radicals to fund the publishing efforts of lower-class men, with those men becoming the public face of the inflammatory material.[54] Those lower-class men then faced liability and sometimes imprisonment, but it was also a bargain that gave some radicals an unprecedented opportunity to participate in the public debate. Such an alliance would be formed between a wealthy patron, George Cannon, and William Benbow in the years immediately preceding the Bishop of Clogher affair.[55]

Percy Jocelyn's Unethical Choices

Before having consensual sex with a soldier in private space in 1822 put him at the center of a national scandal, Percy Jocelyn, the Bishop of Clogher, made several deeply unethical and reprehensible choices. He was born the third son of the Earl of Roden, and at age twenty-one, he graduated from Trinity College, Dublin. In college, Jocelyn was described as "a tall thin young man with a pale, meagre and melancholy countenance, and so reserved in his manners and recluse in his habits, that he was considered by everybody to be both proud and unsociable." Jocelyn was said to have largely confined himself to his chambers, and although he studied a great deal, he did not gain academic honors.[56] He was promoted within the Church of Ireland, moving from being a rector in the diocese of Armagh in 1787 to the Bishop of Ferns and Leighlin by 1809, when he was forty-five years old.[57]

On more than one occasion, Jocelyn used his social and familial privileges to protect himself after sexually assaulting other men. When visiting his oldest brother, then the second Earl of Roden, Jocelyn allegedly made an unwanted sexual advance toward John Beddy, a servant in the house. It was said that Jocelyn used promises of favors and physical force on Beddy. Beddy in turn beat Jocelyn so severely that he remained in his room for two weeks until the marks of his injuries abated, with the rest of the household told that he had been injured in a fall.[58]

Jocelyn's greatest moral failings seem to have arisen from the desire to cover up his attack on James Byrne. In 1811, Jocelyn had forced himself sexually on Byrne, a coachman who, like Beddy, also worked for Jocelyn's brother.[59] Byrne wanted to complain, and he had two letters containing evidence of Jocelyn's advances, but these "were taken from him by a stratagem, and he, being thus deprived of the only documents by which he could support his charge against the Bishop, was brought to trial for defamation and found guilty."[60] Byrne was sentenced to two years' imprisonment and two or three floggings. It was reported that after the first flogging, where "he was bled and tortured until the last spark of life and feeling had nearly become extinct," he was advised to recant his accusation on the promise that the other floggings would not follow. Even then, "he did not yield until after repeated menaces of utter destruction, and until his wife and four children were brought to his dungeon, and had thrown themselves on their knees, and actually *wept him* into acquiescence." It was reported that Byrne, on signing the confession, told the sheriff, "But mind, *I am about to put my name to a falsehood*!!!"[61]

After the flogging, Byrne went on to face two years' imprisonment, financial ruin, and a physical decline. In Dublin, by contrast, Jocelyn lived well with a servant, a man described as "like himself, his man-mistress."[62] By the time he held the Bishopric of Clogher, in 1820, he was making at least £13,000 a year.

What Everyone Knew by Saturday

On the night of Friday, July 19, 1822, Jocelyn, the Bishop of Clogher, was caught in the White Lion public house having sex with John Moverley, a twenty-two-year-old Grenadier Guard. The two had planned to meet there at 9:00 P.M., each going separately to a back parlor. Moverley was in his military uniform, while Jocelyn, who had spent the day in the House of Lords, was wearing clothes that gave him "the appearance of a gentleman."[63] The first person to witness them having sex with each other, by peering through a

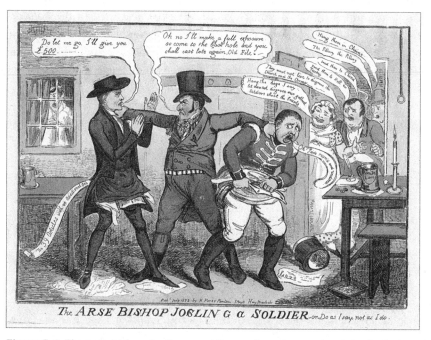

Figure 3.4 *The arse bishop Joslin g a soldier-or-do as I say not as I do.*, by Isaac Robert Cruikshank, published by H. Fores, London, 1822. (© The Trustees of the British Museum.)

window on the back of the public house and through a small gap in the drawn curtain, called the landlord, who in turn called a watchman and several other regular patrons of the public house. They watched Jocelyn and Moverley for some time before breaking in and making the arrest. The pair was roughly escorted to the St. James's watch house in a state of partial dress, with a mob following. A letter in Jocelyn's possession revealed his identity. When the two men were brought before the Marlborough Street magistrate the next day, Saturday, July 20, Jocelyn's bail was set at only £1,000, an amount so low for a man of his fortune that it all but assured that he would flee the country, as he almost immediately did. Moverley, unable to make bail, remained in jail.[64]

William Cobbett's Attack on
the "Respectable Press"

All this information was known early enough on Saturday, July 20 to be included in the Sunday papers as well as in the daily and triweekly papers that would be published starting on Monday. But the fact that so many of the newspapers avoided the story, or referred to it only obliquely, infuriated Cobbett and led him to devote the entirety of the next issue of the *Political Register*, dated Saturday, July 26, to a review of the conduct of all the London papers over the previous week. He classified papers as "respectable" or not based on how they had handled the accusations against the bishop and the soldier.

The subject of Cobbett's coverage was not sex between men but the differing standards applied to the crimes of the rich and the poor. On the first page of the thirty-two-page issue, Cobbett declared:

> If the laws of any country, hanged men, in one situation of life, for murder, and punished men, in another situation of life, with transportation, or something short of death, those laws would be *unjust*, and would, in fact, be acts of *tyranny so outrageous as to justify, and fully justify, the use of effectual means to overthrow the Government that had made such laws.*[65]

Cobbett went on to say that this "*respectable* part of the press, which was so loud, so vehement, in the case of the *poor* miscreants of *Vere-street*, has now been either silent (as the *Old Times,*) or, has been hatching apologies, as the case of the *New Times*."[66] Had the other arrested man "been a tradesman, artisan, or labourer" instead of a bishop, Cobbett went on, the "respectable" press "would have blazoned forth the name and the act, day after day, as it has done on so many occasions."[67] To clearly demonstrate the cause of his anger, Cobbett then stated that "we shall lay before our readers an account of the conduct of the 'respectable' and the infamous part of the press, upon this occasion; naming the several papers; and making them as notorious as it is in our power to make them."[68]

Cobbett gave credit to the *Observer* for describing the incident in its Sunday, July 21, issue and then noted that Sir William de Crespigny, a Member of Parliament, had spoken on the matter in the House of Commons on Monday, July 22. The *Statesman Newspaper* had also published some of the details in time to be mentioned in Crespigny's speech. But the *Morning Post*, Cobbett wrote, published only one-fifth of the *Observer*'s story, and "at the bottom of a column, in a part of the paper likely to escape observation."[69] The *Morning Advertiser* stated only that "a person of consideration and a soldier were taken to the office and charged with a gross misdemeanor." Cobbett chided the *Morning Chronicle*, "which can spare just seven lines put in the very obscurest part of all the paper," saying only that "two persons" had been caught and neglecting to mention that one was a bishop.[70] Cobbett then contrasted the silence of the *Times*, the *John Bull*, and the *New Times* on this issue to the avalanche of coverage "they showed in the case of the Vere-street Gang," ascribing the difference in coverage to "the rank and riches of the party now offending, and the obscurity and poverty of the parties then offending."[71]

Bell's Life in London and Sporting Chronicle also claimed to have been among the first to mention the bishop, reporting that in its July 21 issue, it had noted that one of the arrested men was "P**** J******, bishop of C*****, in Ireland!"[72] In its next issue a week later, *Bell's* chided the rest of the press, stating that the daily papers had "acted most unwisely by their apparent endeavors to *hush up* this brutal transaction."[73] The editor went on to note that some in Parliament and elsewhere distinguished between the "respectable" and the "unrespectable" press, and he could understand the motives of the respectable portion in not wanting to draw attention to sex between men, even if he disagreed with the decision. He was less charitable with the "unrespectable" publications, such as the ultra-Tory *New Times*, whose reticence on this issue seemed to derive purely from partisan motives. Concerning the case, the usually outspoken *New Times* obliquely noted that "an ecclesiastic of considerable eminence in a neighboring kingdom, has been detected in practices not to be counted for, but on the supposition of his having fallen under the influence of insanity."[74]

Many representatives of the "respectable" press eventually felt the need to explain their reasons for delaying coverage. In its first report on the incident, on Thursday, July 25, almost a week after the arrest, the *Times* related that "an exposure of monstrous depravity has taken place within these few days, all allusion to which we have hitherto suppressed."[75] This admission was printed on the same day that the *Times* first reported on what had happened to James Byrne at the hands of Jocelyn, and most of the subsequent coverage in the *Times*, and many other respectable newspapers, focused on Byrne and not the soldier. The next day's *Times* reported that Byrne had been "the poor victim of this audacious hypocrite" and had been "unrelentingly flogged" after the bishop had him prosecuted, faulting *"the state itself, through whose erring tribunals the innocent man was tortured,* and the guilty enabled to triumph over him."[76]

The revelations concerning Byrne seem to have focused the attention of the respectable press on the Bishop of Clogher story.[77] Newspapers that had not reported the arrest of Jocelyn and Moverley when it seemed to concern only consensual sex between an upper-class man and a soldier now described in detail how the character of Byrne had been denigrated in 1811. Some 1822 reports were in large part devoted to statements from the 1811 trial documents, wherein "the attention of the jury [was called] to every act of [Percy Jocelyn's] life, and they would find them marked by the display of *virtue, piety, and benevolence*." Jocelyn had been praised, as had his family and "the other noble branches of this stock," and all this had been used as "the most undeniable evidence to prove, that every tittle which this most atrocious wretch [Byrne] ha[d] alleged [wa]s utterly false."[78] And yet exactly the opposite was true. Someone of the highest birth, with one of the highest positions in the church, was shown to have lied remorselessly, sending an innocent man to be flogged nearly to death and destroying his family, simply to protect himself. The silence of the respectable press on cases involving sex between men had abetted this injustice, and, consequently, the *Times* especially seems to have noticeably increased its coverage of such cases subsequently.[79]

For Cobbett, the Bishop of Clogher affair came at a time of intensifying radicalism and precarious fortunes. Cobbett had difficulty reestablishing himself in Britain after his return from America in 1819. While in exile, he had lost his farm in Hampshire and had suffered a loss of credibility among radical leaders, including Hunt, who had faced imprisonment under the repressions of Lord Sidmouth while Cobbett was relatively safe abroad. Cobbett had brought Paine's bones back to Britain from America to make them a political rallying point, but this plan proved misguided. Other events growing directly out of the social and political conflict that had occurred in his absence, first and foremost the Peterloo Massacre, had instead become the focal points for popular politics and popular outrage. Cobbett's attempt to

Figure 3.5 William Cobbett returning from America with the bones of Tom Paine. *The Political Champion turned Resurrection Man!* by Isaac Robert Cruikshank, published by E. King, London, 1819. (© The Trustees of the British Museum.)

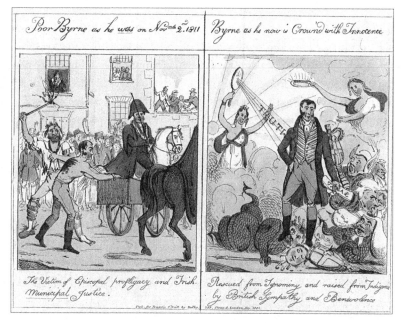

Figure 3.6 "The Victim of Episcopal profligacy and Irish <u>Municipal</u> Justice. Rescued from Ignominy and raised from Indigence by British Sympathy and Benevolence." *Poor Byrne as he <u>was</u> on Novmbr 2nd 1811/ Byrne as he now is Crown'd with Innocence*, published by Thomas Dolby, etching, hand-colored, London, 1822. (Rare Book Division, Special Collections, Princeton University Library.)

win election to Parliament in 1820 also misfired, although he still had the *Political Register*, which published continuously during his time abroad, as an outlet for his views.

The Queen Caroline affair provided a significant boost to Cobbett's fortunes, increasing the circulation and profits of the *Political Register* and providing a set of facts through which to critique the existing political system. The Bishop of Clogher incident provided another such opportunity, and when Cobbett learned that Byrne was still alive in Ireland, he brought him to London and gave him a hero's welcome, even presiding over a London banquet in Byrne's honor that was attended by more than two hundred individuals.[80] A public subscription was also set up for Byrne, raising more than £300. Advertisements for the banquet and subscription kept Byrne's name and his story before the public, as did the retelling of Byrne's story in a pamphlet with commentary by Cobbett.[81] In a way that he had tried but failed to do with the bones of Paine, Cobbett would invoke the name "James Byrne" for years to come as a way to succinctly sum up the immorality and economic exploitation that he claimed was endemic within the political class.[82]

William Benbow's Radical Politics

Allied with William Cobbett in the radical cause, and equally willing to use allegations of sex between men to undermine the legitimacy of established institutions, was William Benbow. Like his fellow radical Thomas Spence, Benbow was from the lowest ranks of English society. He was born in 1787, in Manchester, one of thirteen children of a shoemaker. He worked as a shoemaker himself for a time, although as a profession requiring a low level of training, it was swamped with displaced workers from other trades and thus provided him only a precarious living.[83] His early life was lived entirely in an era marked by steeply rising prices, ruinous taxes, and political repression caused by continuous warfare with France. He was married by the time he turned twenty, but, knowing nothing but a subsistence existence and seeing little hope of any positive change for those like him from within the existing political system, he began to actively resist the impossible terms on which he, his wife, and his two young sons were expected to live. He embraced radical revolutionary politics and became for a time a dissenting preacher, challenging the political and moral guidance of his social betters.[84]

Benbow was involved in a long list of revolutionary activities in his twenties. Shortly before the Spa Fields riots of 1816, he had been sent to London as a representative of Manchester's ultra-radicals to make contact with Spencean revolutionaries. In the following year, he was a representative of Manchester's Hampden Club to the convention called by Major Cartwright. He was one of the organizers of the "Blanketeers" march of 1817, designed to draw attention to the plight of Lancashire weavers, and, after a brief period of imprisonment after being linked to a plan for a revolutionary government, he became involved in a conspiracy to circulate forged banknotes to destabilize the government. It was only after this last plot that he fled to America, meeting up there with Cobbett, who was already in exile.[85] It was Benbow who dug up the bones of Paine from the unconsecrated ground in which they were buried in upstate New York so that Cobbett could bring them back to Britain.[86]

Benbow returned to London early in 1820 and was soon a major radical bookseller in the Strand. For a man of very limited education and economic resources, it was a dramatic change in circumstances, made possible, as McCalman explains in *Radical Underworld*, through the financial patronage of a more respectable middle-class radical, George Cannon. Cannon was a lawyer, "free-thinker," dissenting minister, and pornographer, and men like him formed alliances at this time with men like Benbow, offering the chance at an occupation vastly superior to the sweated trades Benbow and those of his class were born into, along with a chance to propagate, as well as sometimes author, radical publications that advanced causes that they believed in. Shortly after forming his alliance with Cannon, Benbow spent eight months in prison for producing a caricature of George IV in the context of supporting the cause of Caroline. The hardships during his imprisonment were severe, including the death of his wife and the near ruin of his fledgling business. After his release in early 1822, Benbow would be prosecuted by the Society for the Suppression of Vice for publishing "obscene libel" and forced to move from the Strand to less expensive premises in Leicester Square.[87]

These losses did not blunt his commitment to radical politics or his ability to hammer away at the Bishop of Clogher's abuses, which were just becoming known as Benbow was reestablishing himself in Leicester Square. The bishop's membership in the Society for the Suppression of Vice not only allowed Benbow some measure of personal revenge against that organization but also fed into the radical critique that "the Vice Society was 'a gang of reverend hypocrites' who confined their attention to the immorality of the labouring classes for political rather than religious reasons."[88] According to McCalman, Benbow had been collecting stories about abuses committed by clergymen from the time of the Queen Caroline affair. His goal was to highlight the hypocrisy of those bishops in the House of Lords and their supporting clergy in the Church of England who had cast doubt on Caroline's morality. But it was the 1822 Bishop of Clogher incident that shaped *Crimes of the Clergy*, the 1823 compendium in which most of those stories were first published.

The Politics of Sex between Men in Benbow's *Crimes of the Clergy*

The Bishop of Clogher incident "proved a godsend to the increasingly beleaguered radical press," and while many took advantage of it, Benbow went further than most.[89] In 1823, within a year of the bishop's arrest, Cobbett had published "The Parson and the Boy" as a stand-alone pamphlet and as most of the August 2 issue of the *Political Register*. But that work told only the story of the sexual advances made toward James Welsh, a twenty-year-old man in Cambridge, working as a gravel digger, by the Rev. Thomas Jephson, a doctor of divinity and college tutor at Cambridge.[90] Benbow's *The Crimes of the Clergy, or the Pillars of Priest-Craft Shaken* was a far more ambitious 240-page compendium indicting the clergy of England for abuse of the privilege, trust, and wealth that had been granted to them.

The Bishop of Clogher's story is given only four pages in *Crimes of the Clergy*, but he is mentioned by name in the descriptions of cases involving the Rev. Mr. Mills, the Bishop of Waterford, the Rev. Thomas Burgess, the Rev. John Fenwick, and Parson Eyre. He is also mentioned in the introduction and in the final paragraph before the start of the appendix.[91] Other case studies discussing clergymen who had sex with other men but without referencing the bishop include those on John Church, Parson Cooper, Dr. Sanders, Rev. Parson Walker, the Rev. V. P. Littlehales, and the Rev. Jephson.[92] Benbow focuses not just on the abuse of privilege by individual clergy but on the tendency of the upper class to protect its members from the laws that they enforced on others, perpetuating, in his view, their ability to live corrupt lives off the tithes and taxes of the majority.

The first example in Benbow's *Crimes of the Clergy*—and, at six-and-a-half pages, one of the most extensive—is only partially about sex between men, but examination of the narrative reveals much about Benbow's politics and how he used such stories to further his political goals.[93] John Fenwick is described as the second son of a gentleman whose income exceeded £4,000 per annum. If he was marked by anything at birth, it was by intelligence and the privileges of wealth. Starting at age fourteen, he spent seven years in Wadham College, Oxford, winning all three prizes for which he competed. His reputation suffered at Oxford, though, when he was discovered in bed with another man. Fenwick was a skilled musician, and he was known to have many "fiddlers and singers of the lowest class in Oxford" over to his apartments. It was "the washerwoman [who] surprised Mr. Fenwick and his musician in bed together, at mid-day, and immediately spread the tale over all the University."[94] But in Benbow's account, Fenwick was not punished for these actions; the woman who had walked in on him and the musician recanted her story, presumably under pressure, and so Fenwick remained at Wadham, although he was banned from the College Hall. According to Benbow, when Fenwick once later ventured into the hall to dine, "no one spoke to nor noticed him, but with looks of contempt," although this did not stop him from staying on to finish his degree.

Shortly after graduation, Fenwick came into his father's estate. He returned home after Oxford and took up a vicarage and a living worth £700 per annum, arranged by his father. He was extremely neglectful of his religious duties, though, almost always having his curate preach the sermon. According to Benbow, when he heard of the death of his brother, Fenwick only thought of his inheritance, and he "refused to have any thing to do with the funeral for his father, who was buried by his afflicted tenants, and on the same day his son attended a horse-race at Newcastle-upon-Tyne, and in the evening went to the theatre."[95]

Benbow presents Fenwick not as effeminate but instead as virile and aggressively masculine, regularly indulging in the habits, hobbies, and vices of athletic upper-class men. Fenwick was known for his love of hunting, horse racing, and gambling, willing to "risk hundreds" in a large bet "and taking small bets of five and ten shillings, and stripping to box for the decision of a wager." He was known to be good at all these activities, and "he became a complete hero of the turf, and rode supreme on every course."[96] He conspicuously enjoyed the luxury that his newfound fortune afforded him, but when the Bishop of Durham asked him to surrender his vicarage, Fenwick refused, wanting to keep the income while his curate did the work. Because "the Bishop was his very intimate friend, brother cock-fighter, and horse racer," he did not force the issue.[97] Thus it is shown that even when the authorities knew that the man at the head of the local spiritual community was of poor character, they did nothing.

This neglect of oversight only becomes clearer as John's abuses became criminal. Fenwick is depicted as preying on the young men of the area, as he "was at the time very active in procuring recruits for the army."[98] One young man "had to jump out of the Squire's library window, and escape through a pond, to avoid his nauseous embraces." Even worse, when the young male recruit tried to report the sexual assault to a magistrate, the "charge was treated with ridicule by the Magistrate (a brother fox hunter)." The young man, still hoping for justice, determined to go to the judge then presiding over the court of Assize. Before he could do so, however, he was seized by a press gang, most likely at the instigation of Fenwick, and was "hurried on board a Man of War, and fell in battle shortly after."[99] In another scene, Fenwick is shown sexually assaulting a girl who is below the age of consent. As long as his crimes were directed at those lower on the social scale, Fenwick was able to act with impunity. Indeed, Benbow observes, it was only when he cheated men of his own class in horse racing that he was finally turned out of local society.

Even after he was ultimately forced into exile, Fenwick was able to continue abusing his position. To keep the income from the vicarage, he agreed to marry the "cast off mistress" of another man as part of the bargain. But Fenwick "used her like a brute, and has been known, in a state of intoxication, to turn her out of his bedchamber, forcing her to arise at the hour of midnight, and then lock himself and his Curate inside, where they remained till morning, *tete-a-tete*."[100] This act was finally considered a bridge too far for the local elites, and magistrates issued an arrest warrant for Fenwick and his curate. Fenwick was able to escape to France unpunished, while the curate, Johnston, was kept in jail for a year before moving to Arbroath, Scotland, on a pension of £100 per annum, "settled on him by his paramour many years ago."[101]

As Benbow ends this first of many shocking narratives, he emphasizes its lessons. The first is that Fenwick was never prosecuted. Instead, like almost all men of rank, he was allowed to flee the country and escape justice. Those who worked on his estate, who had buried Fenwick's father with dignity, were shown to continue to pay the rents to Fenwick's wife. She in turn dutifully sent the money to Fenwick, who had settled in Naples, where "so far from having repented of his sins, that he glories in, and practices them in a country where such monsters are tolerated, and even esteemed."[102] Despite all this, Benbow notes that Fenwick "has never been publicly degraded from his dignities as a Clergyman of the Church of England," even though "the crimes of this miscreant were long known for *certain*."[103]

In Benbow's view, what makes Fenwick so dangerous to the parliamentary upper class is not that he seemed so different from them but that he seemed so similar. He was smart, educated, sporting, and well liked for much of his life by members of his own class, regardless of how he treated those below him. He might sexually violate a man's son or daughter and still retain his position as a county leader and as a clergyman in the Church of England. Because the upper class would not police its own, Benbow strongly implies, it was up to the rest of society to root out injustice. The image of Fenwick presented by Benbow is a figure expected to elicit disdain, not primarily as a man who had sex with other men but as an immoral abuser of the unchecked power that the current political environment vested in him and in those of his class.

Conclusion

The political contest of the 1810s and early 1820s between the supporters of the Tory Liverpool government and the radicals who wished to bring it down incorporated a battle over the meaning of "sodomite." Such works as *Crimes of the Clergy* and radical accusations of "unnatural crime" committed by the Duke of Cumberland endeavored to associate "sodomy" with the unchecked indulgences of the elite that left poorer men victimized. If the political and religious establishment that so harshly condemned sodomy in their public statements could be shown to practice it themselves with impunity, it became a powerful reason to reject that establishment wholesale.

The Tory Liverpool government and those who supported it, by contrast, benefited from having such images as the Vere Street raid in the public mind. The men of Vere Street were portrayed as wholly different from respectable loyal subjects. The sodomites of the Vere Street molly house were also plebian, and by secretly assembling in a public house, they resembled radical pressmen and tavern-based Spencean revolutionaries far more than they did members of the Tory government. In the judicial theater of a molly-house prosecution, the whole of society lined up behind church and king in a shared expression of outrage toward men who were considered different from pious and loyal Britons.

This type of polarization was prevalent in many aspects of parliamentary politics in the 1810s, leaving little space for compromise or reform. Sir Samuel Romilly's campaign, carried out between 1808 and 1818 to correct what he saw as a dangerous and growing misalignment between the frequent and arbitrary use of the death penalty and the public's increasing rejection of the practice, met with fierce resistance in Parliament. His proposal to end the death penalty for nonviolent thefts of small amounts from shops and houses was considered by opponents to be "very unadvisable and very unsafe" due to the "present depraved state of the domestic and other servants in the metropolis."[104] Opponents of reform even argued for the preservation of the law "by which it was ordained that the heart and bowels of a man convicted of treason shall be torn out of his body while he is yet alive," with the Attorney General stating that while "he would have never have voted for the old law if it were now to be enacted . . . since it had the sanction of centuries, he was against changing it."[105] This intransience would start to relax, opening an opportunity to reform at least some of the harshest aspects of the criminal law, but not until the early 1820s, when the economic and political crises that had extended through and beyond the French Revolutionary and Napoleonic Wars finally began to abate.

This was the political context when Peel, acting on behalf of the Tory Liverpool government, changed an aspect of the law in relation to sex between men in 1823 and again in 1825. He did so to protect upper-class men from blackmail involving sex between men, after his friend and cabinet colleague, Viscount Castlereagh, took his own life, days after telling others that he was being blackmailed for the same crime as the Bishop of Clogher. This legal change, though, was exactly the sort of privileging of upper-class men that brought the strongest public condemnation from such men as Cobbett and Benbow. It was also at this moment that Jeremy Bentham publicly intervened in the debate, publishing Part I of *Not Paul, but Jesus.* But Bentham never published Part II, and his liberal rationalist framework did not shape Peel's alteration of the law as it related to sex between men as it would Lord John Russell's under the reforming Whig government of the following decade. Also, while friendship between the main political protagonist (Peel) and a man associated with sex between men (Castlereagh) was a factor in the decision to change the law in 1823 and 1825, family ties (as between Fitzroy Kelly and Matthew Lewis) were not. The next chapter considers all these overlapping factors as it examines the Tory alterations of the law related to sex between men in the 1820s.

4

Secrets in High Politics

> Destroy [this letter] as soon as you have read it, unless you think
> it better to show it to the person whom we are to see, and I have
> some doubts whether it is not better to make an uncensored
> communication with that person, as any withholding might lead to
> an embarrassment in communication that may take place between
> the person to whom we are going to speak tomorrow morning, and
> the other person.[1]

The letter from which the above quote is taken was deliberately opaque. Its contents were considered so sensitive by its sender that it, like subsequent correspondence on the same topic, was vague to the point of being understandable only to someone already familiar with the issue under discussion. It concerned the second time in three years that Robert Peel was called upon to address allegations that a close parliamentary colleague had had sex with another man. Three years earlier, in 1822, the colleague had been Viscount Castlereagh, Peel's fellow cabinet minister. Now, in 1825, the colleague was Richard Heber, who by that point had served for four years as one of the two members of Parliament for Oxford, alongside Peel.

In the period in between, Peel had passed legislation directly related to sex between men, which had responded to Castlereagh's plight and contributed to Heber's. These changes in the law had made it easier for wealthier men to prevail in cases of blackmail related to sex between men, in part by spelling out, for the first time under statute law, that not only was the act of sodomy or its attempt illegal but so was, under certain circumstances, the "solicitation, persuasion, promise, or threat" of that act or its attempt. As with the Whig intervention regarding the law related to sex between men a decade later, the issue was first addressed in an omnibus bill, followed by more tailored legislation that more specifically addressed the issue of sex between men. Also similar to what would occur with the Whigs a decade later, sex between men was treated as a special case in the legislation, in a way that went against the general principles of the larger bill.

Addressing Peel's actions during this period involves working around the efforts taken at the time and since to hide, destroy, or make opaque written records relating to sex between men. Some secondary sources are currently an obstacle to understanding the sequence of events connecting the Bishop of Clogher affair, the Castlereagh suicide, and Peel's actions in Parliament. The first part of this chapter reexamines the current secondary literature in the process of placing these events in their proper relation to one another. The chapter then examines how Peel's work to repeal some elements of the Black Act, mostly in an effort to reduce the number of capital crimes, led to innovations in law related to blackmail and sex between men. The immediate impact of the 1825 amendment to the 1823 Threatening Letters Act and the wave of arrests that followed in the summer of 1825 are next analyzed. Peel's intentions are not always clear, but a series of private letters connecting Peel and Member of Parliament (MP) Heber, letters that directly discuss Heber's sexual relations with other men and his flight from Britain because of them, suggests some of Peel's motivations, foremost among them the preservation of secrets for the good of society.

The Strange Book on the Death of Lord Castlereagh

Viscount Castlereagh, also the second Marquess of Londonderry, was Foreign Secretary and leader of the House of Commons from 1812 to 1822. He was widely admired within the political class for his role in the diplomacy that had led to the defeat of Napoleon Bonaparte and the negotiated peace that followed.[2] He was at the War Office during the Peninsular War and was instrumental in giving Arthur Wellesley, the future Duke of Wellington, his first command in Portugal. Yet he was reviled among the radicals for his advocacy of the repressive domestic measures carried out to secure the victory against France, including his brutal policies in Ireland related to the suppression of the Irish uprising and the passage of the Act of Union. Castlereagh's wartime and postwar policies caused William Cobbett, William Godwin, and Lord Byron to despise him, and when the news spread in early August 1822 that he had taken his own life, "a stream of remarkably bitter obituaries and abusive epigrams found their way into the radical press."[3]

The most common explanation for Castlereagh's suicide in popular and scholarly works was that overwork, exhaustion, and the pressures of government had made him delusional. But Castlereagh had also made what were described as increasingly paranoid statements in his final days. Those state-

Figure 4.1 *Robert Stewart, second Marquess of Londonderry (Lord Castlereagh)*, by Sir Thomas Lawrence, oil on canvas, 1809–1810. (© National Portrait Gallery, London.)

ments included repeated confessions that he was being blackmailed for committing the same acts as the Bishop of Clogher. The first and only book devoted to the investigation of these claims was written in 1959. *The Strange Death of Lord Castlereagh* by H. Montgomery Hyde has shaped historians' views on the Castlereagh suicide ever since.

Hyde was uniquely positioned to carry out this historical investigation. He had a degree in history from Queen's University, Belfast, and a degree in jurisprudence from Magdalen College, Oxford. In 1933, he published his first book, *The Early Life of Castlereagh*, and two years later, he became librarian and then private secretary to Castlereagh's heir and descendant, the seventh Marquess of Londonderry. Hyde practiced law after being called to the bar in 1934 and served in counterespionage during World War II. After the war, he became an Ulster Unionist MP from 1950 to 1959, when he was best known for campaigning against capital punishment and for implementing the recommendations of the Wolfenden Committee, which called in 1957 for the decriminalization of private homosexual acts between consenting adults. He published more than a dozen books, including some of the earliest works on the history of homosexuality in Britain, such as the *Three Trials of Oscar Wilde* (1948) and an account of Wilde's imprisonment and final years, published in 1963. Hyde's work was well regarded. His access to the Castlereagh papers was unmatched due to his closeness with the Londonderry family; in addition to being the librarian and private secretary to the seventh marquess, he wrote several books with the Marchioness of Londonderry.[4]

Every scholar since Hyde has used *Strange Death* as the primary reference point when addressing the idea that blackmail played a part in Castlereagh's suicide, often mentioning the argument without fully embracing it. C. J. Bartlett's 1966 work mentions Hyde but then notes that "Wellington claimed to have made a careful investigation of the blackmail theory, and insisted there was nothing to it."[5] After summarizing Hyde's description of Castlereagh's entrapment, John Derry, writing in 1976, argues that "the evidence for such a sequence of events is far from conclusive, but it is possible that something of this sort happened."[6] In her 1981 work, Wendy Hinde gives a brief nod to Hyde's argument before asserting that overwork combined with the onset of mental illness is a more convincing explanation.[7] Giles Hunt's 2008 work gives more space to the suicide than most, taking ten pages to argue that syphilis, contracted while at Cambridge, was the real root of Castlereagh's decline in late July and early August.[8] The *Oxford Dictionary of National Biography* states that one of the anxieties leading to Castlereagh's breakdown and suicide "allegedly related to blackmail, after a chance encounter with a hostile transvestite male who deliberately attempted to compromise him, but no confirmation exists for the authenticity of this or of homosexual vagaries imputed to him."[9]

One of the reasons Castlereagh's biographers give so little interpretive weight to Hyde's version of events is that they find it incompatible with the majority of the available evidence and unimportant in explaining any of the broader political issues of the day. John Bew argues, "There is no evidence or hint that he had any homosexual inclinations at any point in his life."[10] Derry agrees with this sentiment and says that "Hyde [also] refutes suggestions that Castlereagh had actually committed a homosexual offence," noting that Hyde describes an encounter between Castlereagh and a cross-dressed man during which the two only talked and walked together to an assignation house, with Castlereagh thinking that he was with a woman.[11] Implicit in such biographies as Derry's is the idea that even if a chance encounter had occurred with a cross-dressed man, it would not really tell us that much about Castlereagh or the political climate within which he operated.

Such works fail to historicize the degree to which sex between men was a partisan issue at the time of Castlereagh's suicide and at the time that *Strange Death* was written. Hyde himself, in addition to being the employee and friend of Castlereagh's descendants, wrote *Strange Death* when sexual acts between men were still criminalized in Britain and he was actively campaigning as an MP to change that, efforts that have been cited as the reason he lost his seat in the 1959 election. Hyde was also a historian of talent and integrity known for being scrupulous in the pursuit and presentation of the facts and whose name is still honored annually at Queens's University, Belfast, where the top graduate in history is given the Dr. Harford Montgomery Hyde award. The tensions between these divergent loyalties are evident in *Strange Death* as well as in Hyde's brilliant reconciliation of them in a way that compromises none of them.

Hyde's book contains two wildly differing methodologies. Until the final chapter, Hyde is meticulous in his use of multiple corroborating sources. He uses several diaries as well as personal letters and other manuscripts written in the summer of 1822 to chart the deterioration of Castlereagh in the weeks before his suicide. With this same rigor, Hyde documents the occasions on which Castlereagh said he was being blackmailed for the same crime as the Bishop of Clogher. In its interrogations of the sources produced in July and August 1822, this work has not been equaled since, nor is it likely to be surpassed by anyone without the level of access to primary sources available to Hyde.

This scholarly rigor makes the methodology adopted in the last chapter all the more surprising. The final chapter is titled "The Mystery Explained," and it builds its argument from only one source, a third-hand account recorded more than thirty years after the death of Castlereagh. Only here is the story of the cross-dressing prostitute recounted. In a book that supports its claims with multiple contemporary sources, this is the most thinly sourced passage in the book, and yet the story of the cross-dressing prostitute is the one to which scholars have primarily responded. It is, therefore, worth closely examining the narrative presented in *Strange Death*, treating most of it as an unsurpassed authoritative analysis of the final days of Castlereagh's life while also offering alternatives to the narrative presented in the final chapter.

Castlereagh's Final Days

In *Strange Death*, Hyde expands the range of primary sources used by biographers to substantiate the story of Castlereagh's confessions (to George IV and others) that he was being blackmailed for the same crime as the Bishop of Clogher. Most valuable was the evidence from the diaries of Princess Lieven and Mrs. Harriet Arbuthnot, which Hyde interweaves throughout the text. The Lieven and Arbuthnot diaries are rich sources for information on the personal and political lives of the Regency-era cabinet. Dorothea Lieven had arrived in London in 1812 after her husband was appointed Russian ambassador to the Court of St. James. She was twenty-seven years old, witty,

Figure 4.2 *Harriet Arbuthnot (née Fane)*, by William Ensom, after Sir Thomas Lawrence, line engraving, published 1830. (© National Portrait Gallery, London.)

smart, and good at politics and diplomacy. She favored the Tories and was friends with Lord Liverpool and most of the cabinet as well as with George IV. Harriet Arbuthnot was married to Charles Arbuthnot, Chief Government Whip and Patronage Secretary. Castlereagh worked more closely with Charles than with perhaps any other cabinet minister, and Harriet was a close friend of Castlereagh's for eleven years.[12] The diaries of both women, widely used by diplomatic and political historians, provide detailed information on the last weeks of Castlereagh's life.

At the end of 1821, Castlereagh "appeared as complete master of himself and showed no sign of the burden which he had borne both as Foreign Minister and Leader of the House of Commons for nearly ten years." Signs that his memory might be starting to fail seem to have appeared in July 1822, but Castlereagh was also described as being cheerful at dinners on July 25 and 26 and clear in his last speech to the House of Commons on July 30.[13] It was eight to ten days before the suicide when the signs of Castlereagh's unusual agitation were noticed by most of those around him. Richard Meade, Lord Clanwilliam and the Undersecretary for Foreign Affairs, and George Hamilton Seymour, private secretary to Castlereagh, noticed paranoid behavior at this point.

On August 3, at a dinner party he gave for political friends, Castlereagh seemed agitated, as if expecting to be called out. At the party, Charles Arbuthnot told Castlereagh that he had for some time been receiving anonymous letters threatening to ruin many people in high office. Arbuthnot was surprised that Castlereagh suspected these letters were aimed at him, since the latest had accused Harriet of having an affair with the Duke of Wellington. On Monday, August 5, Castlereagh visited Harriet and asked her "whether she had ever heard anything against him." It was at this point that Castlereagh told her "that about three years before he had received an anonymous letter 'threatening to tell of his having been seen going into an improper house.'"[14] The letter writer asked for a job, a request that Castlereagh told Harriet he had ignored. He said he had taken no more notice of the matter until recently, when, she recalled him saying, "more anonymous letters began to reach him on the same subject."[15] Castlereagh met with the Attorney General and the Solicitor General to discuss the anonymous letters. One letter to Castlereagh threatened to reveal his conduct to his wife, and another threatened to accuse him of what Harriet euphemistically described as "a crime not to be named."[16]

On Friday, August 9, just days before his suicide, Castlereagh had an audience with George IV. Relying on the diary of Princess Lieven, who claimed to have gotten her information directly from the king, Hyde reports that as Castlereagh entered George IV's private apartments:

> He immediately seized the King by the arm.
> "Have you heard the terrible news?" asked Castlereagh looking wild-eyed.
> "No," replied the King. "What is it?"
> "Police officers are searching for me to arrest me."
> "Come, come," said the King, who thought at first that this was some kind of joke his Foreign Minister was playing on him. "What nonsense! Why should that be?"
> "Because I am accused of the same crime as the Bishop of Clogher."
> "You must be crazy."
> Castlereagh looked deadly serious. "There is no doubt a warrant has been issued and they are looking for me," he went on. "I have just had my horses come up from Cray. I shall leave by the little gate in your garden. I shall go to Portsmouth and there sail for France. I can no longer live in England."[17]

George IV reassured Castlereagh that he was not being pursued and insisted that he see a doctor right away. Castlereagh consented but first had the king swear to say nothing of this to his political colleagues. Princess Lieven, writing two days after Castlereagh's suicide, stated that on his last visit to

Carlton House, Castlereagh showed the king two anonymous letters, one threatening to reveal his conduct to his wife and the second concerning "a more terrible subject. This second letter sent him off his head." Lieven did not believe that there had been anything seriously wrong with Castlereagh before he received these letters.[18]

After this meeting with George IV, Castlereagh went to his house in St. James's Square, where he encountered the Duke of Wellington speaking to Lady Castlereagh outside. Castlereagh invited Wellington in and began speaking about the Bishop of Clogher, saying that he had been accused of a similar crime. After leaving Castlereagh's home, Wellington wrote two letters, one to Dr. Bankhead, Castlereagh's family physician, asking him to check on Castlereagh, and the other to Charles Arbuthnot. The letter to Arbuthnot indicated that Liverpool and the Duke of York had also heard Castlereagh say that he was being accused of the same crime as the Bishop of Clogher, and Wellington feared that Castlereagh was telling others also.[19]

Dr. Bankhead also received a letter from Castlereagh's wife that Friday afternoon and remained close to events until the suicide three days later. Lady Londonderry urged Dr. Bankhead to come to their London house; when the doctor arrived, finding Castlereagh to be "exceedingly ill," he had him cupped, taking several ounces of blood.[20] Lady Londonderry asked Dr. Bankhead to follow the couple to their house at North Cray, which he did the next day. When he arrived, Dr. Bankhead thought Castlereagh seemed "particularly grave" in his manner and was sure that "something must have happened amiss. He then asked me abruptly, whether I had anything unpleasant to tell him."[21] Over that weekend, Castlereagh repeatedly told individuals that "there was a conspiracy against him." Anne Robinson, Lady Londonderry's maid, added at the subsequent coroner's inquest that "during the last fortnight he repeatedly said some persons had conspired against him."[22] On the following Monday morning, as Dr. Bankhead entered Castlereagh's dressing room to speak with him, Castlereagh, "without turning his head, on the instant he heard my step . . . exclaimed, 'Bankhead, let me fall upon your arm,—'tis all over.'" Dr. Bankhead ran to him and caught him in his arms as "blood burst from him like a torrent from a watering-pot."[23] Eventually, Castlereagh fell from his arms.

Only in the following days did Dr. Bankhead begin to hint that Castlereagh may have been guilty of the same crime as the Bishop of Clogher. The doctor was accused of neglecting Castlereagh and misdiagnosing the seriousness of his condition. As recorded in Harriet's diary, "when Bankhead found that the whole world abused him for his neglect of Lord Londonderry, he immediately determined to endeavour to justify himself by saying that

DEATH of the MARQUIS of LONDONDERRY.
"Bankhead let me fall upon your Arm. 'Tis all over"

Figure 4.3 *Death of the Marquis of Londonderry (Charles Bankhead; Robert Stewart, second Marquess of Londonderry (Lord Castlereagh)),* by Unknown artist, hand-colored etching, 1822 or after. (© National Portrait Gallery, London.)

Londonderry was not mad, and that the crime of which he accused himself [to George IV] he had actually committed."[24] Hyde writes, "It was common knowledge that Castlereagh had accused himself of having committed a homosexual offence, since the King had repeated to a fairly wide circle of acquaintances what had passed at their last interview." Dr. Bankhead said that Castlereagh had confessed his guilt to him as well; that Castlereagh had been of sound mind; and that "his death was a mystery known only to himself and Lord Liverpool!" Harriet wrote that Dr. Bankhead told this to Wellington, "who was at first inclined to believe what he had heard but later revised his opinion."[25]

There were strong incentives for the government and Dr. Bankhead to take opposing positions on the issue of Castlereagh's insanity. If Castlereagh were sane, his act of suicide would have prevented him from being buried in a Christian churchyard, let alone in Westminster Abbey with an elaborate state funeral, as eventually occurred. This matter was raised in the press as well as on placards put up in London questioning whether someone who had died by suicide should be buried in Westminster.[26] But if Dr. Bankhead had failed to recognize that his patient was insane, he would have been guilty of incompetence as a doctor. His need to defend his professional reputation gave him cause to break the discretion that upper-class men usually exercised in relation to one another's private affairs.

Given that Hyde does so much throughout *Strange Death* to tell the story of Castlereagh's suicide by using multiple corroborating sources from the time the events occurred, it is surprising that at the end of his book, he places so much emphasis on a third-hand account remembered decades after the fact. Hyde uses a source written by the Rev. John Richardson as the critical piece of evidence, placing it in a chapter titled "The Mystery Explained." Only in the last eight pages of *Strange Death* does Hyde engage directly with Richardson's *Recollections, Political, Literary, Dramatic, and Miscellaneous*, privately printed in London in 1856. In this account, Richardson says that he was told the story by an informant, who in turn said he received it "from the mouth of a noble lord still living, with whom the Marquis [Castlereagh] was on terms of social intimacy, and with whom he was connected by political ties."[27] Hyde concludes that this person must have been Lord Clanwilliam, the parliamentary Undersecretary for Foreign Affairs and a close friend of Castlereagh's—the only man still alive in the 1850s fitting that description.

Richardson's narrative offers an account of the origin of the blackmail. It states that Castlereagh, in returning from the House of Commons to his abode in St. James's Square, would sometimes walk rather than ride in a carriage, and on these walks, it was said, he would occasionally speak to and sometimes walk with prostitutes who would accost men on the street. Richardson's account argues that this pattern of the marquis was discovered, "and advantage was taken of the discovery," by men who made their living off extortion.[28] Castlereagh was shown to an apartment by a person he thought to be a female prostitute, but then, when alone together in a room, discovered his companion to be a young man dressed as a girl. At this point, two men burst into the room, accused him "of being about to commit an act from which nature shrinks," and also made clear that they knew exactly who he was. The marquis gave up all his money and fled, but the men began to show up at his house, standing by the iron railing that surrounded St. James's Square, across from the windows of his residence, making it clear by their actions and gestures that they had not forgotten what they had seen. "Driven almost to distraction by this persecution, [Castlereagh] made known his case, with all the circumstances, to the late Duke of Wellington and to another nobleman."[29] He was advised by Wellington "to give the wretches into custody at once, avow the full facts, and extricate himself from further disgusting thralldom," but he apparently did not follow this advice. Hyde allows Richardson's account to be the final word in his book, offering no analysis of it and no conclusion. Before beginning the account of the cross-dressing prostitute, Hyde does include a sentence stating that he believes it to be the best explanation, but this comment does not alter the impression that *Strange Death* has a strange ending; an uncorroborated third-hand account written thirty years after the events in question is allowed to be the final word.[30]

Historians on Hyde and Alternative Explanations

As noted in the preceding pages, most Castlereagh biographers have reacted to Hyde's argument without examining it closely. Bew's 2012 *Castlereagh: A Life* is the primary exception. In his analysis, Bew cites two discrepancies in the account offered in *Strange Death*. The first stems from the fact that according to Castlereagh's statements just before his death, the incident that led to the blackmail occurred in 1819 rather than in 1822. "It is hard to countenance Richardson's claim that the blackmailers waited every day outside his house shortly before his death, in August 1822, three years after the original letters were sent," Bew writes.[31] Bew also questions Hyde's assertion that Clanwilliam was the source for Richardson's account. Bew agrees with Hyde that Clanwilliam best fits the description of Richardson's source, as the only one of Castlereagh's close associates still alive in 1855, but he remains skeptical of Clanwilliam as the originator of the story, given that he "never showed himself to be anything but a loyal lieutenant."[32] Bew concludes by saying that while "Hyde did not deal directly with these discrepancies in Richardson's account . . . his conclusion is broadly convincing: that while there was no plot against Castlereagh in 1822, the fact that there had once been one before played on his mind and exacerbated his mental breakdown."[33] Like other scholars before him, he points to the suicide of Sir Samuel Romilly, a leading Whig MP who cut his own jugular vein in 1818, to support the argument that "the pressures of personal and political life" were the decisive factors in Castlereagh's mental breakdown and suicide.[34]

Bew's assessment of Hyde is balanced and well researched, but it is formulated without knowledge of the degree to which sex between men had been politicized in July and August 1822, as discussed in the previous chapter, and it does not take into account that in the next parliamentary session, legislation would address the sort of blackmail to which Castlereagh told so many he had been subjected.

Castlereagh killed himself on August 12, 1822, just over two weeks after the *Times* declared that it could no longer keep silent about the Bishop of Clogher. Until then, like most respectable newspapers, the *Times* did not publish what might be shocking accusations against public figures. But now it was known that such a trusted public figure as a bishop had used the deference granted to him, and to members of his class, to subvert the legal system and use it to publicly torture, humiliate, and ruin an innocent man and his family. In the first days of August 1822, the *Times* and other "respectable" newspapers published reports and editorials almost as full of angry invective against this abuse of power as were those in the radical newspapers. If ever there was a moment when allegations that the Foreign Secretary had had a sexual encounter with another man might get a public hearing, this was it.

Among radicals, Castlereagh was one of the most hated political figures of the day, for the reasons discussed at the start of the chapter as well as for his long-standing opposition to parliamentary reform, his support for foreign autocratic regimes at the expense of liberal movements, his support of George IV in the Queen Caroline affair, and his support in Parliament of some of the most repressive legislation following the 1819 Peterloo Massacre. Those who hated Castlereagh, William Cobbett and William Benbow among them, were the same individuals who were most vehement in denouncing the Bishop of Clogher and were specifically drawing attention to how the press and the courts had allowed him to unjustly ruin James Byrne. Any defense Castlereagh would have mounted against a charge of having solicited sex from another man would have involved witnesses speaking to the good character of Castlereagh and against that of his accuser. Given the then-current uproar over just such a defense, Castlereagh may have felt trapped. According to one source, discussed below and on the following page, Castlereagh was told by a cabinet colleague that given the current political crisis, if such allegations were publicly made against him, he would have to face them on his own.

Bew cannot reconcile Clanwilliam's loyalty to Castlereagh with his circulation of the story of the cross-dressing prostitute, but that story is perhaps the most innocent interpretation of Castlereagh's statements to George IV and others. No source other than Richardson mentions a cross-dressing prostitute. According to Harriet Arbuthnot's journal, Castlereagh had asked her whether she "had ever heard anything against his honour or his character," and she wrote that "so strongly had business and fatigue upset his usually calm mind that he actually fancied the purport of the letter was to accuse him of a crime not to be named, and this notion could not be put out of his head."[35] Later, she wrote that "Dr. Bankhead was a very confidential friend as well as his physician and to him he talked in the most extraordinary manner, accused himself of the most horrid crimes, [and] thought that everybody was conspiring against him."[36] Still later in the entry, Harriet wrote that "there has been a disgusting story in all the newspapers about the Bishop of Clogher, and in his ravings Ld Londonderry actually accused himself to the King of the same crime, said everybody knew it, and that a warrant was out against him and that he must fly the country! This notion continued to haunt him to the last."[37] None of these sources, or any source save for Richardson, discussed only in the final eight pages of *Strange Death*, make any reference to a cross-dressing male prostitute.

Clanwilliam knew of such encounters in the park, though, because he had experienced one. In investigating Hyde's claim, Bew discovers that, in September 1821, Clanwilliam "confessed to Philipp von Neumann that he had been accosted in St. James's Park by a pretty young girl who turned out to have the voice of a man."[38] Bew speculates that Clanwilliam may have told this story to Castlereagh, who, when "in rapid mental decline . . . might easily have confused some of these details in his own mind." An equally plausible explanation, though, is that Clanwilliam used his own experiences to construct a relatively benign explanation for Castlereagh's confessions. William Toynbee alludes to other interpretations in *Glimpses of the Twenties* when he writes that "overwork had nothing whatever to do with it" and that Castlereagh "committed suicide because he believed himself to be confronted with the one thing which he, the coolest, and most courageous of men, could not bring himself to face: dishonour."[39]

Hyde cites Toynbee in *Strange Death*, but Toynbee's version of the reason for the suicide is very different from Richardson's. Toynbee depicts Castlereagh as subject to a much longer-term blackmail effort, although the situation was manageable until "London was convulsed by a stupendous scandal involving a nobly born and prominent ecclesiastic." Although Castlereagh occupied "a position that practically placed him 'above the law,' he saw in the doom of the wretched fugitive [Clogher] the realization of the disgrace with which he had been menaced for years." His blackmailers also "seized the opportunity for plying their threats more actively than ever." Toynbee's account adds that his cabinet colleagues "must have felt some degree of self-reproach [after the suicide], for it is said that [Castlereagh] sounded more than one of them as to whether, if matters came to a crisis, the Cabinet would stand by him; but he was informed that, considering the precarious condition of the Government, the scandal would be too great for them to connect themselves with by supporting him, and that he must fight his own battle."[40]

Shifting Attitudes toward Criminal Law Reform

Peel altered the law in the following parliamentary session in a way that would have helped Castlereagh face down his blackmailers, as resistance to criminal law reforms began to subside.[41] Romilly's 1808–1818 campaign to reduce the use of the death penalty had only brought about the revision of two capital statutes related to offenses against property, and only because the specific groups that those capital statutes were designed to benefit, the tanners in England and Ireland, lobbied with Romilly that the death penalty for petty thefts from their bleaching grounds was too harsh to work as an effective deterrent.[42] When prosecutions for this type of theft went up after the end of the death penalty in this area, Romilly "looked upon it as the vindication of the reformers' claim that the Bill fulfilled its main purpose, which was to enhance the certainty of punishment by relaxing its severity."[43] Further alterations in the capital statutes did not follow in Romilly's lifetime, but the example was later used to refute the idea that any softening of the legal code might pose a threat "to the preservation of social stability."[44]

In emphasizing the increase in prosecutions as an indication of success, Romilly's statements also draw attention to the coercive aspects of liberal reform. From the beginning, liberal reforms to the legal code "not only repealed the death penalty but also broadened the definition of the offence . . . increasing the number of acts which could be tried under it."[45] In this way, the process of criminal law reform followed a pattern associated with other liberal freedoms, which were often combined with requirements for greater individual discipline.[46] In two of the three instances where the elimination of the death penalty for sodomy was proposed in Parliament, in 1835 and in 1861, the reform was coupled with provisions that would have increased the certainty or severity of punishment; only in 1840–1841 was this not the case, highlighting the uniqueness of what happened at that point.

A Petition from the Corporation of London in 1818, calling on Parliament to examine the use of the death penalty within the criminal law, was one of the most influential elements within the growing public campaign for reform. That petition focused on "the inordinate number of statutes imposing capital punishment . . . the widespread disinclination to put these statutes fully into effect and to the rapid increase in crime which, it stated, was at least in part due to these two factors."[47] Phil Handler has argued that 1818 was a crisis moment, as juries refused to convict ever-increasing numbers of individuals lest they be put to death for forging low-denomination banknotes.[48] To mitigate the use of the death penalty as capital crimes increased, legislation in the eighteenth century had given judges the right to commute death sentences to terms of transportation. The frequent use of the royal pardon also reduced the number of executions, but at the price of making the enforcement of the law seem capricious and arbitrary. Between 1770 and 1830, an estimated thirty-five thousand death sentences were handed down in England and Wales, but only seven thousand executions were carried out.[49] As many as twelve thousand petitions were received by Parliament at this time calling for criminal law reform, leading one observer to argue that "public opinion" had "pronounced upon the penal code . . . a sentence of indignant condemnation."[50]

In this charged atmosphere, Sir James Mackintosh and Sir Thomas Fowell Buxton, leaders of the reform movement in Parliament after the death of Romilly, facilitated the creation of a Committee of Inquiry into the Criminal Laws, which passed over the objections of the government. The committee collected statistical and anecdotal evidence of "a dangerous discrepancy between the feelings of the people and the state of the criminal law," examined the arguments for consolidating certain areas of the criminal law, and explored what secondary punishments might replace the death penalty.[51] The 1819 Committee Report set forth a plan for far-reaching reform, calling for a division of offenses according to their gravity, with a corresponding scale of punishments that would be made certain, proportionate, and in harmony with public sentiment. In the area of capital punishment, the 1819 Committee Report limited the capital statues that it recommended for repeal, including only those passed as emergency acts, such as the Black Act, or covering offenses that had long been acknowledged as not serious enough to warrant the imposition of the death penalty.[52]

Although the committee had been formed over the objections of the Tory administration, its recommendations were taken up by later Tory as well as

Whig governments. In an 1820 letter to a government minister, Peel asked whether "that great compound of folly, weakness, prejudice, wrong feeling, right feeling, obstinacy, and newspaper paragraphs, which is called public opinion—is more liberal, to use an odious but intelligible phrase—than the policy of the Government?" Peel went on to say that "there is a feeling, becoming daily more general and more confirmed . . . in favor of some undefined change in the mode of governing the country." Peel asked whether the government, in the face of this movement, was going to continue to act as it had been or "w[ould] they carry into action moderate Whig measures of reform?" The alternative to this change, he argued, was to give up the government to the Whigs, which would result in their enacting more far-reaching reforms.[53]

Not long after Peel expressed these views, in January 1822, Liverpool's administration was reconstituted, in a move that has been described as the first "parliamentary recognition of the steady rise of that liberal tide which reached its flood in 1830."[54] Viscount Sidmouth, responsible for some of the most repressive domestic legislation in the wake of the 1819 Peterloo Massacre, was replaced as Home Secretary by Peel. Mackintosh's attempt at that moment to bind the government to certain goals of the 1819 Committee was defeated, but "Peel made known the decision of the Government to consider the whole question of the criminal law."[55] Mackintosh and Buxton welcomed this pledge and added that under these circumstances, "officially sponsored reforms would cease to be regarded as Party measures."[56]

Jeremy Bentham's Contributions to the Public Debate

As the most promising conditions for criminal law reform in his lifetime began to coalesce, Jeremy Bentham published two works in 1823, both of which he had described in his letter to William Beckford as supporting his efforts to decriminalize sex between men. The first was a republication of *An Introduction to the Principles of Morals and Legislation*, in which all the passages relating to sex between men and why it should not be criminalized remain intact from the 1789 edition.[57] The second was Part I of *Not Paul, but Jesus*.[58]

As early as 1817, Bentham had planned to break *Not Paul, but Jesus* into two parts, with the first part demonstrating that the ascetic tradition was not inherent in the teachings of Jesus. Bentham anticipated some resistance to the arguments in Part I, but he believed that such resistance would be manageable and would help the work garner attention while also preparing readers for the more controversial ideas of Part II. In Part II, as described in Chapter 1, Bentham intended to make the argument that the state should not punish most pleasures of sense, including consensual sexual acts. Part II was to have chapters devoted to why "the Attic taste" should be regulated no more harshly than other indulgences of other senses, such as taste, hearing, or sight.[59] Bentham had hoped to secure Beckford as a powerful patron for *Not Paul, but Jesus*, but when Part I was published in 1823, no prominent name was associated with the work—not even Bentham's—for he published it under the name "Gamaliel Smith."

The published version of *Not Paul, but Jesus* broadly follows the plan that Bentham had set out in the 1817 prospectus. Bentham opens by citing the work of the famous Church of England theologian the Rev. Dr. Conyers Middleton, who, in the early eighteenth century, by his "bold, though reverend hand . . . cleared up many a heap of pernicious rubbish" that had made its way into Christian doctrine. Bentham claims that *Not Paul, but Jesus* continues that work, which was necessary, since "one thorn still remained, to be plucked out of the side of this so much injured religion,—and that was, the addition made to it by Saul of Tarsus."[60]

Bentham begins Part I of *Not Paul, but Jesus* by questioning aspects of the five "different, and in many respects discordant," accounts given of Paul's conversion. Bentham works through evidence to argue that Paul was not a convert before his arrival in Rome and that "no proof, of his alleged supernatural commission from the Almighty, is deducible, from any account we have." Later chapters describe how some statements of Paul contradicted more authoritative accounts by Matthew and Luke. The book culminates, in its sixteenth chapter, with an analysis of "the self-declared oppositeness of Paul's Gospel, as he calls it, to that of the Apostles." At this point, Bentham, writing as Gamaliel Smith, goes so far as to call Paul's doctrines "Antichrist" and more of a real threat than "the fabulous [Antichrist], created by Paul, and nursed by the episcopal authors and editors of the Church of England."[61]

The advertisements that appeared for *Not Paul, but Jesus* in September and October 1823 were confrontational. One, announcing that the book would be published in a few days, stated that it would show "that Paul had no such commission as he professed to have"; that "his enterprize was a scheme of personal ambition, and nothing more"; and that "it has no warrant in anything that, as far as appears from the four gospels, was ever said or done by Jesus."[62] Other advertisements indicated that the work was an "examination of the question, How far we are warranted in considering that which Paul calls 'his Gospel,' as forming part and parcel of the Religion of Jesus."[63] Bentham had written to Beckford that his intent was to excite the feelings of the advocates of religious orthodoxy, confident that if controversy spread his ideas, their logic would win over the individuals exposed to them. Bentham had selected the title *Not Paul, but Jesus* in 1817 because of its provocative qualities, and the advertisements taken out for the work made clear that the goal of courting controversy had, along with much of the previously planned content, been retained from Bentham's 1817 proposal.

Some of the initial reactions to *Not Paul, but Jesus* were what Bentham might have hoped for. One of the early reports on the book, printed in the *Examiner* of September 28, 1823, echoed many of Bentham's reservations about Paul, noting "the character, writings, and conduct of St. Paul have produced much difference of opinion and discussion, even among persons who . . . are neither infidels nor skeptics." The author of the *Examiner* article did not endorse the argument of *Not Paul, but Jesus* but created room for it to be debated, arguing that "without pronouncing any opinion upon his particular merits, it may be contended, that as a teacher of the Christian Religion, Paul was essentially distinguished from the more immediate disciples of Christ . . . and that under his interpretation the Gospel received modifications which, had the evangelical records formed the only scripture, no uninspired human being would have deduced from them." But the author of the *Examiner* piece was uncomfortable with Bentham's depiction of Paul as "a corruptor of the simplicity of the Gospel" and "a bold, ambitious, and assuming innovator." The *Examiner* also observed that while others might choose to hide such challenging ideas behind "the half-mask of irony," this approach was "studiously rejected" in *Not Paul, but Jesus.*

But Bentham had overestimated the power that his argument would have to sway opinion and underestimated the backlash that it would provoke among religious leaders. By the first week of January 1824, the Rev. T. S. Hughes, Christian advocate for Cambridge, had published a defense of the apostle Paul.[64] By the end of January, Edward William Greenfield, Minister of Laura Chapel, Bath, had published *The Doctrinal Harmony of the New Testament Exemplified*, which offers "a comparison of the Epistles of St. Paul, with the Gospels, Acts, and Epistles of the other Apostles," proving the harmony between them.[65] A few months later, Ben David published *A Reply to Two Deistical Works*, one of which is *Not Paul, but Jesus.*[66] Almost two years after *Not Paul, but Jesus* first appeared, the *Cambridge Quarterly Review* published a further refutation of it, along with reviews of three earlier refutations.[67]

Not Paul, but Jesus remained a touchstone in public debate throughout the 1820s. The Rev. David Bowker Wells advertised the fact that he was the author of *The Vindication of St. Paul*, "in answer to the work of Mr. Gamaliel Smith, *Not Paul, but Jesus*," when he ran for the office of Christian advocate for Cambridge University in 1828.[68] In the same year, a letter writer, commenting on a local controversy stemming from a Church of England minister's repeated use of the word "Non-cons" to refer to members of other denominations, described himself as someone who tried "on all occasions, even the most trifling, to overthrow the impertinent assumption of bigots of every sect, and especially of sects who have contrived to link themselves to the State, who meddle with the religious opinions of their neighbors." The author then identified himself as being "of the sect of NOT PAUL BUT JESUS."[69]

Bentham wrote but never published the remainder of *Not Paul, but Jesus*. The part that he did publish was one of a series of radical works that appeared between 1817 and 1825. Fear of prosecution had kept him from publishing some of these works earlier, and some friends had continued to advise him against doing so in the late 1810s and early 1820s.[70] Bentham published an *Analysis of the Influence of Natural Religion on the Temporal Happiness of Mankind*, also under a pseudonym, in 1822, and a less radical work on religion, *Church of Englandism and Its Catechism Examined*, in 1818, under his own name. Bentham was thus airing his oppositional views to established Christian doctrine long before the Bishop of Clogher incident. Yet given what he wrote to Beckford in 1817, there might be reason to suspect that the 1822 uproar surrounding the Bishop of Clogher and the unjust persecution of Byrne, combined with the real chance of law reform that Peel's appointment as Home Secretary represented, influenced him to publish the first part of *Not Paul, but Jesus* in 1823.

Bentham may have also been influenced by what was written in the papers in September 1822 about John Holland, a forty-two-year-old bricklayer who was supporting a wife, children, and aged parents; William King, a thirty-two-year-old laborer; and William North, a former navy man, age fifty-four.[71] These men had met together in a secluded part of Moorfields, just north of London's city wall, which had been known since the eighteenth century as a location for highwaymen, brothels, sexual liaisons between men, and other marginalized activities.[72] There had not been a sodomy execution in London for consensual sex between men since at least 1816, and yet for engaging in an act that Bentham had argued since the 1780s was no crime at all, these three men were told by the judge who sentenced them to death that their "abominations" had "disgraced human nature, and dishonored the country in which you live."[73] They were also told that in the "earlier ages of the world, the Almighty destroyed whole cities through the commission of crimes like yours; you have polluted the world" and that other criminals sentenced to death would feel "repugnance to ascending the same scaffold with you." North had tried to address the court, after the judge had excoriated him on religious and legal grounds, "but was taken away by the turnkey" before he could.[74] Perhaps Bentham, in the guise of Gamaliel Smith, spoke for him instead, attempting to bring to light a Jesus and a Christian religion that would have been tolerant of North and his compatriots.

Robert Peel and the Threatening Letters Act

Peel made the office of Home Secretary more powerful than it had ever been, although he did so largely through the coordinated implementation of a range of reform plans already developed by others. A plan for reforming the police had been developed by Patrick Colquhoun, "an active and enlightened London magistrate."[75] The 1819 Committee had largely set out the plan for the revision of the criminal law. The reform of the rules for criminal procedure had already been developed by Bentham, with such procedures seen by Bentham as "a bulwark against the arbitrary tendencies of the state and a means of reducing the uncertainty of punishment" and therefore deterring crime.[76]

Peel also gave greater discretion to judges to curtail the use of capital punishment. The 1823 Punishment of Death Act (4 Geo. 4, c. 48) authorized a court "to abstain from pronouncing Judgment of Death, whenever such Court shall be of Opinion that, under the particular Circumstances of any Case, the Offender . . . is . . . a fit and proper Subject . . . to be recommended for the Royal Mercy." In such cases, the court was "authorized to enter Judgment of Death on Record against such Offender." Such judgments were to "be followed by all the same Consequences, as if such Judgment had actually been pronounced in open Court, and the Offender had been reprieved by the Court." Enacted at a time when more than two hundred crimes still carried the death penalty, "Death Recorded" appears in the record of verdicts in 1823 and later, associated early on with cases related to theft and robbery, and later, after 1835, as a verdict in cases of rape or sodomy.[77]

Also passed in the 1823 parliamentary session, the first since Castlereagh's suicide, was a law that addressed the type of blackmail that Castlereagh had said he had faced. This passage was done within the context of a larger effort to repeal the Black Act, one of the early landmark struggles in the process of reforming England's "Bloody Code."[78] As Leon Radzinowicz observes, "No other single statute passed during the eighteenth century equaled [the Black Act] in severity, and none appointed the punishment of death in so many cases."[79] The act made the simple appearance with face blackened or otherwise disguised on high roads, in open heaths, in commons, or in a range of other places liable to a sentence of execution. It also made liable to execution anyone who was an accessory to such a disguised individual, either at the time or even, in certain instances, after the fact. Under the Black Act, the death penalty was extended to killing or taking deer, hares, conies, or fish; killing or maiming cattle; cutting down trees; setting fire to a range of property, from a house to a haystack; willfully shooting at another person; extorting money by sending anonymous threatening letters demanding payment of some sort; and forcefully rescuing any person in custody for any other offense against the Black Act. In total, the Black Act added more than fifty new capital crimes to the statute books and greatly expanded the power of local authorities to harshly punish what had been accepted forms of popular protest.[80] Scholars have connected the Black Act to other draconian policies enacted by Sir Robert Walpole in the wake of the economic dislocations caused by the South Sea Bubble of 1720, with such emergency legislation used to sustain the Whig oligarchy during that period.[81]

In relation to the sending of threatening letters, the provisions of the Black Act in this area were combined with two later acts, ostensibly to equalize punishments. Peel stated in the debate that "sending threatening letters was another case in which the law was anomalous. A man might charge another with the grossest crimes, to extort money, and it was only a transportable offence; whilst sending directly for money, or venison, offences made capital by the Black act, was made punishable with death. There could be no reason for this, and the law should be equally applicable to both."[82] The punishment for an extortion attempt became transportation for life, although if money was actually exchanged, the offender was "deemed guilty of robbery" which was subject to the death penalty.[83] In addition to rationalizing punishments, the bill was amended as it passed through successive readings in the Commons, so that in the final act, the "threat to accuse" no longer needed to be in writing, significantly increasing the circumstances under which the law could be applied.[84]

The applicability of this law specifically to incidents involving accusations of sex between men was greatly enhanced when the Threatening Letters Act was amended in 1825. That amending bill only added one clause to the Threatening Letters Act, designed to address a shortcoming in the new law that had become evident the year before. The law had been used in a court case where one man accused another of making "overtures" to commit sodomy. The initial conviction had been thrown out, though, because the letter only accused the other man of attempting a sexual advance, which did not constitute an "infamous crime" under the law. Consequently, in the year following the court decision, Peel amended the Threatening Letters Act to expand the definition of what constituted an infamous crime within the 1823 act. The definition now included

> every assault with intent to commit any Rape, or the abominable Crimes of Sodomy or Buggery, or either of those crimes, and every attempt or endeavour to commit any Rape, or the said abominable Crimes, or either of them; and also every solicitation, persuasion, promise, threat or menace, offered or made to any person, whereby to move or induce such person to commit or to permit the said abominable Crimes.[85]

With these changes, it was now illegal to accuse a man of showing sexual interest in another man, provided that there had been some offer to exchange anything of value in return for silence. While parts of the 1825 amendment applied to rape and sodomy, the provisions related to making illegal the "solicitation, persuasion, promise, threat or menace . . . to move or induce such a person" only applied to "the said abominable crimes," which were sodomy and buggery, but not rape. Because it would always be assumed that the poorer man would be the one to request some form of payment, this advantaged wealthier men in situations where each accused the other of a sexual advance.

The work of Anthony Simpson shows that the eighteenth-century laws related to threatening letters only had limited effectiveness when they were used to defend against accusations of "the grossest crimes," as Peel phrased it in parliamentary debate. But the 1825 amendment to the 1823 Threatening Letters Act made a difference. The strongest evidence for this change is the wave of prosecutions that immediately followed, with the newspapers and courtroom officials citing the new law as the catalyst.

Arrests in the Summer of 1825

The summer of 1825 has not been considered significant in the history of sexuality in Britain, but it should be. In one of the unusually large number of extortion cases brought that summer, "the Judge, in summing up, remarked upon the increase of crimes of this nature since the passing of the act of the 4th Geo. IV."[86] No fewer than thirty-four separate reports related to sex between men appeared in the *Times* in 1825, and no fewer than twenty-four appeared in the *Weekly Dispatch*. The largest single category of reported cases in this year involved extortion with threats to accuse of an infamous crime. One of the first was described as "deserving the particular attention of the jury, from its being the first instance of a prosecution under the late statute (4 George IV)."[87] In this case, Frederick Denman and Joseph Mould were put on trial for threatening to accuse Thomas Cozens of an infamous crime; Charles Houlder and David Gardener were indicted on 4 Geo. IV for feloniously sending a letter to the Rev. Edmund Cartwright; James Dovey and Roger Adams were charged with threatening to accuse another man of an infamous crime; Thomas Dunkley, a journeyman baker, and Samuel Bird, a butcher, were indicted for extorting John Axx; and George Kelly, a carpenter, was accused of extorting money from Edward Turner. These and other cases involving extortions related to an infamous crime were extensively reported in the summer of 1825. Sexual assaults in front of picture shop windows, cases involving soldiers and sailors, and one molly-house raid were also reported that summer.[88]

Multiple comments were made in the press regarding the perceived increase in prosecutions. The *Times* noted that "scarcely a week passes but the magistrates of this office have individuals brought before them, (and those of most respectable connexions in society), charged with indecent assaults on the sentries in the park." Less than two weeks later, a report from a different police court noted that "the disgusting propensity to practices at which human nature revolts, and which were formerly seldom or ever heard of among Englishmen, is again evidently upon the increase in the metropolis." The report went on to say that "in addition to the instances that have recently transpired at Bow-street and other public offices, two charges for offences of similar descriptions have occurred at this Justice-room within the course of the present week." One week later, at another police court, "the Magistrate was occupied for a considerable time in the investigation of one of those revolting and unnatural cases, so many of which have recently been heard at the different police offices in town."[89] Three weeks later, a man was acquitted on a charge related to "this horrible and increasing crime," while yet another court a few weeks later also dealt with "disgusting charges of human depravity, which has unhappily, in so many recent instances, engaged the attention of police magistrates."[90] A few days later, at the end of a trial centered on sex between men, the *Age* noted that at "this particular moment . . . the town has been deluged by an explosion of so many horrors of the precise nature which this outcast stands guilty."[91] Finding even one such statement that these cases were on the increase in any given year is rare, and so the fact that so many can be recovered for the summer of 1825 strongly indicates that such comments reflected actual change.

The August 23 raid on the Barley Mow was the most publicized attack on a molly house since the 1810 Vere Street arrests, yet on the same day, newspaper readers also learned of the techniques that John Grossett Muirhead, esq., a member of the Society for the Suppression of Vice, vice president of the Auxiliary Bible Society, and brother-in-law of the Duke of Athol, had been using to pick up young men for the better part of two decades. Several such encounters were described in detail, including his three meetings with Charles Lane, age sixteen, who was first approached by Muirhead as he stood in front of a picture shop window.[92] Muirhead's pursuit of young men had not gone unnoticed, and he was well known to many in the neighborhood, including the owner of the picture shop, who attempted "to shame him away from the place, by holding up to his face a print of the Bishop of Clogher; but instead of going away in consequence, he stood and looked at it with the utmost unconcern." In years past, the shop owner had approached two magistrates about having Muirhead arrested but had been informed that his evidence alone was not enough.[93] Once Muirhead was arrested, though, multiple other witnesses provided similar stories going back twenty years, while one elderly gentleman, Muirhead's former steward, said that he had left Muirhead's service after witnessing similar practices.

Other stories from the summer of 1825 showed that the picture shop where Muirhead approached men was not unique. A different picture shop was described in another trial as having "for a long time been the nightly resort of wretches of this description."[94] At that location, it was said that "several persons had been similarly assaulted, but fearful of having their names connected in any manner with such disgusting transactions, had declined taking any notice publicly." The same story included an account of the arresting constable who had been sexually assaulted in the same location by a "country gentleman" but had declined to prosecute after the gentleman begged to be let go. The story of another man was recounted, who had "knocked [a similar] fellow down, and contenting himself with that summary punishment, suffered him to make his escape."[95]

Also by the end of the summer of 1825, two MPs were in exile after being accused of having sex with other men. One of them, Richard Heber, fled England for the continent in late July 1825, on the eve of being publicly accused. The second, Henry Grey Bennet, was also in exile in August 1825, as his "public reputation at home was ruined by the threat, albeit averted, of criminal prosecution for importuning a young male servant."[96]

When measured against the frequency of prosecutions involving sex between men for the whole of the eighteenth and nineteenth centuries, a comparison that we can now perform with confidence, the summer of 1825 was clearly extraordinary. The actions taken against Muirhead, Heber, and Bennet, plus the dozens of prosecutions brought against less prominent men, seem to have been instigated independently. A significant number of the prosecutions that summer can be directly linked to the implementation of the amended version of the Threatening Letters Act, but others cannot. Many of these events may have been unconnected in any meaningful way, but it might also be, as so often was the case when sex between men was involved, that records of what motivated the actions have been destroyed. Supporting this latter supposition—and documenting a link between Peel and Heber's resignation from Parliament—is a series of letters that survives only because one of the first instructions in the letters was ignored, and they were not destroyed after being read.

Robert Peel behind the Scenes

In late July 1825, Peel received a letter dated only "Sunday Evening, ¼ past 10," with "Confidential" written across the top. It was addressed to "My Dear Peel" and began with its author, Sir Robert John Wilmot-Horton, informing Peel that he was "very anxious to have half an hour's conversation . . . upon a very painful subject."[97] Wilmot-Horton had been an MP for seven years, serving much of that time as Undersecretary of State for War and the Colonies, and was known as an energetic reformer who strongly supported humanitarian causes.[98] He was a close friend of Reginald Heber, the Bishop of Calcutta. Reginald was the half-brother of Richard Heber, who then served along with Peel as an MP for Oxford, and Wilmot-Horton at that point considered himself to be a close friend of both Heber brothers. Wilmot-Horton, Lord Byron's cousin, was one of the three men responsible for burning Byron's memoirs when Byron died in 1824.

Wilmot-Horton knew of Richard Heber's affairs with men, and as he wrote in a later letter, he had "the strongest suspicions that the brother [Reginald] left England [accepting the post of Bishop of Calcutta in late 1822] in consequence of his having obtained some sort of knowledge upon this subject."[99] This was approximately when Richard Heber's relationship with Charles Henry Hartshorne began. Hartshorne, a middle-class aspiring antiquary, had first approached Heber in July 1821, when Hartshorne was nineteen and Heber forty-eight. From the time of their first acquaintance, they were known to spend extended periods together. At least as early as 1824, after Heber took Hartshorne to a Roxburghe Club dinner, rumors of a sexual relationship between them circulated in upper-class London society.[100] But while the possible affair between Heber and Hartshorne would become the focus of public discussion of Heber's sexuality, Heber's alleged sexual interest in two other men, one from his own social class, is what concerned the Home Secretary and his assistant.

The next letter, also dated "Sunday Night" but penned at least one week later, suggested that plans to force Heber's resignation from Parliament and his exile from Britain were being formulated. Wilmot-Horton referred to "the *precise course* which is now agreed upon." To ensure secrecy, Wilmot-Horton wrote that Peel should "destroy [the letter] as soon as you have read it, unless you think it better to show it to the person whom we are to see."[101] Wilmot-Horton did not mention anyone by name or disclose the issue that was sparking these meetings. Yet even such a vague letter, Wilmot-Horton believed, contained material too sensitive to be allowed to survive.

Wilmot-Horton referenced a separate letter, dated "Downing St., Friday," that is also preserved in the Peel Papers. It described how a system of intermediaries was created between Peel and Heber to facilitate communication between them while allowing Peel to maintain deniability. In the letter, Heber was advised that "every man has some confidential friend in whose entire honor and secrecy he can . . . confide, and if you will name such a person to me, and authorize him to communicate with me upon the subject, it is my earnest wish to make such explanations to him."[102] Wilmot-Horton then wrote that "if—which I should *deeply regret* on your own account—you were to answer this letter by stating that you do *not understand* what I mean—you will compel me most reluctantly to adopt a course, which would be painful to me, and the consequences of which I could not attempt to predict."[103] In another letter, Wilmot-Horton asked whether Peel had any objection to the above letter being sent as it was and indicated that it was important for Heber to "see the case in its *true* light, which as yet he does not *appear* to me to do."[104] This, again, was done without ever mentioning Heber by name. A version of this letter was sent to Heber, and he was asked to respond without delay.

The next significant letter from Wilmot-Horton to Peel was dated "Tuesday Morning." It indicated that on the previous night, Wilmot-Horton had gone to "the house of _____," but instead of going inside had "Mr. _____" come to him outside, at which point they walked "to his Partner's house (to whom he had communicated everything, having no [reserve] from him)." It took a very long conversation, but eventually it was agreed that they would proceed in the manner that Wilmot-Horton had requested. After this agreement, "the consequence was the *instantaneous* and *complete* confession of the _____. This confession stopped *only short* of _____, and I am inclined to believe. There was not intentional concealment on the part of _____." The letter ended by saying that "the most prudent and the kindest course has been taken towards _____," and otherwise it would have brought "ruin to himself, and leaving an almost [illegible] stain upon his own 'CASTE' in society."[105] As has been shown in the preceding chapters, this protection of the collective reputation of upper-class men by suppressing evidence of same-sex desire within their "caste" was a recurring theme and often a more important goal for the men involved than the punishment of any individual.

When Henry Hobhouse, the Undersecretary of State at the Home Office, became involved in the discussions with Heber, the questions over Heber's sexual relations with men became more pointed.[106] At first, Heber was defiant, with Hobhouse informing Peel in a letter that he had "seen H_____ who firmly denies the imputation and expresses his determination not to budge an inch, and to abide the result." Heber challenged Hobhouse's right to negotiate with him and asked Hobhouse where he had gotten his information. When Hobhouse indicated that the source was connected to the Athenaeum Club, Heber "remarked that most of the waiters there were boys." To this comment, Hobhouse replied that it was not the waiters who had made the complaint but "a gentleman's son" whose name was not passed on to Hobhouse, and another man named Fisher. Heber then retorted that Fisher was the son of his agent, and while the two had met several times at the Athenaeum, "he denied having ever taken liberties with his person." The other individual who had accused Heber, as the son of the gentleman, would have to have been someone other than Hartshorne, because the Hartshornes were a middle-class Shropshire family, and neither father nor son was a member of the Athenaeum. While asking how they should proceed, Hobhouse stressed that "H. has *admitted* enough to justify all that has been done, but struggled against departure. I have strenuously enforced the necessity of that measure, but do not yet know whether I have prevailed."[107]

What persuaded Heber to finally leave the country is not recorded, but his decision to do so was made within a week of Hobhouse's entreaty. On Thursday, August 4, Richard Heber himself wrote from Calais. In the letter, he asked permission to return to either London or one of his two country residences at some point within the next two months, to attend to unspecified matters that he could not address from the continent. Heber wrote, "Of course I should keep in that case very private on all accounts," and "I should not think of doing so, without the fact being known . . . in the present state of affairs." The letter specified no recipient and was not addressed to anyone or signed by Heber, making its contents understandable only to those already familiar with the events under discussion.[108] Hobhouse's reply, dated five days later, addressed the core issue, but again obliquely. Hobhouse wrote that it was the goal of those he wrote for "to prevent your retaining the place you have filled in English society, and that if that object can be attained without recourse to legal proceedings, there is no disposition to take those steps." Hobhouse then wrote that it was up to Heber to decide whether, under those circumstances, he should reenter the country, but whatever the decision, he did not want to know of it. In response, Heber thanked Hobhouse for the information and wrote, "At present I shall certainly not think of returning to England" just before outlining how he would keep to his properties and avoid company if he did.[109]

Not long after, Heber sent Hobhouse a letter of resignation, to be given to his constituents in case of a dissolution of Parliament. Heber said in the letter that he was resigning because he needed more time for his literary pursuits. The dissolution did not come until June 1826, though, with Heber remaining an MP for Oxford until February 1826.[110] Shortly after Heber's resignation, on May 14, 1826, the *John Bull* published a short observation strongly implying a sexual relationship between Heber and Hartshorne, sparking the libel case that drew wider public attention to accusations against Heber, but also masking the fact that he had begun his exile from the continent almost a year before, after accusations that he had made sexual advances toward a man of his own class. Accurately dating the start of Heber's exile places it within the cluster of events occurring in the summer of 1825, as recorded in newspapers, court records, the poem *Don Leon*, and other sources.

Conclusion

Given that Peel's negotiation of the terms of Heber's resignation from Parliament can be proven, despite the efforts that were made at the time to obscure them, it seems prudent to document the cluster of events involving sex between men in the summer of 1825, even if causal links cannot be established between a substantial number of them. Near the end of his exchange with Peel about Heber, Hobhouse "expressed [his] hope that this state of things w[ould] not only justify us in keeping our resolution of secrecy, which is so important for the good of society."[111]

But not everyone agreed that the actions of the government in this area, or the secrecy in which those actions were cloaked, were for the good of society. Bentham disagreed, as did the authors of the text and notes of the poem *Don Leon*. That poem directly addresses the parliamentary debate at which Peel amended the Threatening Letters Act, excoriating him for actions that made laws related to sex between men more draconian. The poem is a strident defense of the idea that an individual might sexually desire men and women and that such feelings might be inborn and natural. The poem draws on a range of literary examples and examples from the ancient world, echoing the suggestions that Bentham provided to Beckford when he asked for the production of just such a work to be released in conjunction with *Not Paul, but Jesus*. As in Part II of *Not Paul, but Jesus*, the original version of the argument in *Don Leon* focuses on ending government regulation of sexuality in general and contains arguments for the right of married couples to engage in sodomy if they so desire. It also follows Bentham's lead in not attacking Christianity but finding ways to reconcile it and a liberal approach to sexuality. The next chapter examines the poem *Don Leon* and its links to the summer of 1825, placing that work into the context of its time.

5

"Silence Now Were Tantamount to Crime"

Oh! Peel, for this nefarious deed alone,
Do what thou wilt, thou never canst atone.
Why blow the bubble of thy own repute
For laws amended, and on this be mute?
Mute! No, not mute; for heretofore there lay
A stumbling block in every jury's way;
But, Draco like, thou (gainsay who that can)
Did add a clause to drown the sinking man
Why were the listening Commons silent then?
Martin has mercy—yes, for beasts, not men;
And Brogden's modesty his voice impedes,
Who, when the sections of a bill he reads,
With furs of coneys, to a gentle hush
Subdues his tone, and feigns a maiden's blush.
But answer, Mackintosh; wert thou asleep?
Or was the tide of feeling at its neap?[1]

At least a few individuals watching Robert Peel's work on the Threatening Letters Act were angry over what they saw. We know their feelings because they wrote about them, with one of them composing the above verse not long after the 1825 parliamentary session it describes. The original text he worked from as well as the updates are tied to the novelist and poet William Beckford, who was likely inspired by the philosopher

Jeremy Bentham. The portions most likely written by Beckford construct an argument against the sodomy law based on its interference in the lives of not only same-sex but also opposite-sex couples. These sections downplay the importance of the physical sexual act and instead emphasize the importance of interpersonal relationships built on love and commitment as requiring protection from the intrusion of the sodomy law. The contribution likely by Beckford is elegant and sophisticated; it embraces rather than refutes Christianity, and it seems designed to appeal to an educated Anglican elite.[2]

Over the years, the work passed through the hands of radical pressmen, the heirs of William Cobbett and William Benbow, who by the 1840s and 1850s were better known for publishing pornography than political tracts, even as they blurred the boundary between the two.[3] One of these pressmen, William Dugdale, in 1866 published the earliest surviving edition of the work: a 1,465-line poem titled *Don Leon*, sixty-three additional pages of endnotes titled "Notes to *Don Leon*," and "Leon to Annabella," a 330-line poem without notes. In its final form, *Don Leon* culminates with bawdy puns and coarse verses describing sexual acts.[4] Yet these ribald and impassioned additions are also directed at ending the state's punishment of sodomy. Some of the later passages also contain the most detailed information about the actions of specific members of Parliament who might have facilitated such a reform.

Scholars have made important discoveries about *Don Leon*, but the degree to which it was a part of a political reform process has not been understood.[5] No previous work has explored the links between *Don Leon* and the events in Parliament in 1825, 1835, 1840, and 1841 related to the regulation of sex between men. Beckford has not previously been considered a candidate for the authorship of *Don Leon*, nor has Bentham's 1817 invitation to Beckford been linked to *Don Leon*. Most importantly, previous scholarship emphasizes 1833 as the most likely origin date for the poem rather than the years just before and after 1825, a mistake that has obscured much of the poem's meaning.[6]

While providing new insights into *Don Leon*, this chapter leaves many of the mysteries associated with it untouched. Page DuBois, in *Sappho Is Burning*, cautions us in relation to "the desire of the scholar confronted by fragments" and asks us to "think again about our will to make the broken material evidence of the past whole."[7] Any reading of *Don Leon* that makes all the surviving pieces fit a single argument should be suspect, given that even the authorship of all or most of it cannot be known with certainty. Openness to indeterminacy, however, should not preclude efforts at knowing what can be established with a greater degree of certainty. Our ability to follow the recommendations of such scholars as John Vincent and to create meaningful analysis based on methodologies that refuse a reassuring "fantasy of sheer lucidity" does not invalidate new answers to the questions of when the poem was written, by whom, and for what purpose.[8]

Love and Family in *Don Leon*

The first six hundred lines of *Don Leon* seem remarkably similar to what Bentham suggested that Beckford write in 1817. This portion of the larger work focuses on the acceptance of acts involving same-sex desire that were accepted within ancient Mediterranean cultures. It is not a dry catalogue of examples from antiquity but instead a contemporary telling of one man's discovery of his own inborn sexual tastes. The poem is written as if it were by Lord Byron and presented as his sexual awakening, put forward regardless of the cost to his reputation, to bring about necessary reform.

The poem opens by asking a judge to take off the black cap that he wears when imposing a sentence of death and to look out the window at the man hanging from the gallows for committing sodomy. The poet asks whether that man could not have been spared, because he had hurt no one and had done what he did privately, exposed only because the state "did'st send thy myrmidons to prowl."[9] The poet then asks how he could stay silent in the face of such injustice. Even if the laurels that this poet wears around his head are "destined to wither, when these lines are read," the poet is determined to face the consequences of speaking out. If those who engage in financial fraud escape the hangman's noose, then mercy should be extended to those only guilty of venial crimes, "e'en to Clogher." The poet explains that "sheer indignation quickens into rhyme," because *"silence now were tantamount to crime."*[10]

The poet next addresses the warrant of inborn feelings. What, he asks, if "in man some inborn passions reign, which, spite of careful pruning, sprout again." A tree, it is argued, "will, when its boughs are grown, produce no other blossoms than its own." The poet ends this series of questions by asking "was I or nature in the wrong, If, yet a boy, one inclination, strong In wayward fancies, domineered my soul."[11] What then follows is an account of an individual's sexual coming of age. Education, for a time, directed his desires exclusively toward women, and his "youthful instincts . . . seemed awhile subdued."[12] The poet speaks first of his infatuation with a young woman who did not return his affections, and so his passions turned elsewhere in his teens, to another woman and to a young man, because "sex caused no qualms where beauty lured the eye. Such were my notions ere my teens began, And such their progress till I grew a man."[13]

The poet is described as feeling a similar love at this time for two individuals, Margaret Parker and Robert Rushton, paralleling Byron's own recorded experiences.[14] Parker's company made him "forget my task, my play, my books," and his feelings for her "soared above The frigid systems of Platonic love." As they lay together under the shade of trees, it was only the poet's inexperience and innocence that limited the scope of their embraces. It was the same with Rushton, although the true nature of the feelings only became clear in retrospect, since "though decency forbad The same caresses to a rustic lad; Love, love it was, that made my eyes delight to have his person in my sight."[15] The poet writes that "to unobserving eyes," the time he and Rushton spent together might seem like lordly benevolence, "yet something then would inwardly presage The predilections of my riper age." The poet describes his feelings in the presence of Rushton, stating, "Thus passed my boyhood: and though proofs were none / What path my future course of life would run / Like *sympathetic ink*, [meaning invisible ink] if then unclear, / The test applied soon made the trace appear."[16]

The poet is drawing on individuals and incidents from Byron's real life, but the story is edited to better align those details to the poet's case for law reform. Margaret Parker was Byron's cousin with whom he fell in love when he was twelve, and Robert Rushton was a young man who had grown up on Byron's estate, whom Byron later made his page.[17] Traumatic early experiences, such as Byron's suffering repeated sexual abuse at age nine from his Scottish nursemaid, May Gray, are not addressed, although "Byron speculated that this early introduction to sex had influenced him negatively."[18] Also left out of the *Don Leon* poet's retelling of Byron's early life is Henry Edward Yelverton, Lord Grey de Ruthyn, the older man with whom some scholars believe Byron had his first same-sex sexual experience.[19] Byron subsequently broke with Grey, expressing deep animosity toward him, and some have argued that what happened between the twenty-four-year-old Grey and the fifteen-year-old Byron was not consensual. Byron may thus have had unwanted sexual experiences forced on him by two adults before he reached his later teens. The *Don Leon* poet, however, does not include these traumatic events in his telling of Byron's early years.[20] What is presented instead is the beginning of an idealized sexual awakening, where the internal desires of the individual are the truth of the self, and physical force or trauma is not allowed to play a part in the process of sexual self-understanding.[21] If this portion of *Don Leon* was meant to be a companion piece to *Not Paul, but Jesus*, arguing against laws related to pleasures of sense, then this was precisely the sort of subject needed to justify such a reform: an idealized subject, who came by his feelings naturally.[22]

Finding Yourself at University

The next step in the poet's process of sexual and spiritual self-discovery occurs at university. Like the real-life Byron, the poet is shown attending Cambridge and forming a friendship with John Cam Hobhouse. Others in Byron's close circle of Cambridge friends, including William Bankes, Scrope Berdmore Davies, and Charles Skinner Matthews, are not discussed.[23] The poet is described as engaged in revels at Cambridge, but as he grows into manhood, he begins to long for a "kindred mind," someone who might meet and return his intense feelings.[24]

One fateful night, he is pulled from his "drunkard's bowl" by the evening bell to vespers and then drawn into the chapel by the sound of the choir. While attending services, he sees and became captivated by Eddleston, a young man in the choir. Of the relationship that ensues, the poet writes, "His friendship and his tenderness I wooed. Oh! how I loved to press his cheek to mine; How fondly would my arms his waist entwine! Another feeling borrowed friendship's name, And took its mantle to conceal my shame."[25] The poet argues that it is difficult to discern where friendship ends and love begins but then postulates that "friendship's the chrysalis, which seems to die, But throws its coil to give love wing to fly." The poet's passion for Eddleston is "so violent, yet pure," and it is significant that this love relationship is first recognized at a religious service.[26] The tension (but also the reconciliation) between Christianity and love for another man is a theme of the first six hundred lines of *Don Leon*.

But the feelings he experiences in the chapel give the poet pause, because he knows that to love another man is "illicit." The conflict makes him angry, and he begins to ask, "What prompts nature then to set the trap" and "Whence spring these inclinations, rank and strong? And harming no one, wherefore call them wrong?"[27] The poet observes that this love does not violate the Golden Rule, does not violate anyone's marriage vows, and does not lead to illegitimate children. Unable to understand why such love is nevertheless condemned, the poet begins searching for answers "from volumes of the dead."[28]

The poet finds ancient writers who can justify his love. He enjoys Plato's "honeyed talk," reads Mantuan, drinks "from wisdom's cup with Socrates," and strolls with Bion of Smyrna in a shady grove.[29] The poet is heartened by these examples but plagued by the contradiction between his situation and theirs. The crux of the dilemma for him is that "I love a youth; but Horace did the same; If he's absolved, say, why am I to blame?"[30] The poet goes on, writing that Virgil told the world that he loved Alexis and that every schoolmaster's pen extols him. Plutarch lauded Epaminondas, the Theban general statesman who broke Thebes from Sparta's control, and his "love for his young catamite," Cephidorus, who was buried with him. This is just the sort of compendium of examples from ancient literature that Bentham had asked Beckford to produce. But the poet does not simply extol pagan values; he acknowledges that the present age has a purer religious code, that "a Saviour had redeemed the world," and that pagan gods had been overthrown.[31] For that reason, he begins a search in more modern times for positive examples of the love he feels and concludes that human nature is unchanged and that examples of men loving youths can be found among popes, kings, scholars, jurists, poets, and military leaders, all of whom were pious Christians as well. Like Bentham, he believes that the prohibitions on these desires have recently become more severe, noting that William Shakespeare's love sonnets to young men "would damn a poet now-a-days."[32]

The poet then seriously questions whether these ancient texts and more contemporary examples of love between men might be leading him astray, and even to damnation, regardless of how well they seem to justify his inner desires. The poet wonders whether "the great, the wise, the pious, and the good, Have what they sought not rightly understood."[33] Rather than attacking Christianity, the poet struggles to reconcile ancient practice and Christian belief, much as Bentham does in *Not Paul, but Jesus.* The poet describes himself at this point as full of doubt, desire, and "feverish fancies," on the verge of revealing his feelings to Eddleston, so that "upon the brink of infamy I stand, Now half resolved to plunge, now half afraid."[34] In the end, though, the decision is taken out of his hands: his beloved Eddleston, the object of his desires, dies tragically, of causes not disclosed in the poem. After Eddleston's death, neither drunken revelry nor ardent study seems to cure the poet's restlessness, and he determines to leave Cambridge, declaring, "I'll ramble, and investigate mankind."[35]

Gap Year

The ensuing trip reveals wonders, but not, at first, what the poet most desires: a spiritual and physical connection with another. He travels with his friend from Cambridge, Hobhouse, just as Byron had done, and sees "splendid cities," feasts, revels, and princely courts, even though pleasure and excess are "foreign to my theme: Love, love, clandestine love, was still my dream."[36] The first city described in detail is Istanbul. The poet has heard that young men can be found in the brothels of Istanbul, along with women, and he and Hobhouse visit such a place together. The youths he encounters there, though, performing a "lewd dance," leave him cold. The poet writes that he "found no kindred leaning in the breast Of those around me, and I felt opprest."[37] Unwilling to admit to Hobhouse his real reason for wanting to come to such a place, the poet feigns a "mask of horror" at the presence of a dancing boy and his potential clients and calls on Hobhouse to leave the "monstrous" establishment with him. The poet is still "Resolved to do what yet I feared to tell," but a brothel is not the place in which to do it.[38]

In Athens, the next stop, the poet has his first sexual encounter with a man that is built on the spiritual connection that he hopes for. Hobhouse soon returns to England to take up a career in Parliament. Alone in Greece, the poet wonders whether he is not a "wicked Childe" and thinks that perhaps his impulse to find "another Phaedrus," in the land where Plato found his, is nothing more than a "Satanic force" driving him to his undoing. "Retrieve the moment lost, ([the demonic voice] whispered)—Haste, and pleasure's cup exhaust."[39] Satan counsels the immediate satisfaction of lust, but the poet holds out for love.

The poet takes the time to absorb his surroundings. He contemplates a landscape of ruined temples and lawless bandits, but also of olive groves and myrtle blossoms, and he thinks about those who had lived there before, "virtuous dead, whose names shall never die." He spends time reflecting on the greatness still present in the landscape and the fragrance of the life still ongoing, writing that "Ne'er till this body in corruption rot, Shall those loved moments ever be forgot."[40] There is no discussion of sexual contact or even the desire for it at this point. Instead, the spiritual and emotional connection to place is established, preparing the poet for the meeting to come.

The poet attempts to reconcile the ancient world with the less doctrinaire aspects of Christianity, spending time in Athens with an order of monks, an offshoot of the Franciscans, who have built a monastery around the Choragic Monument of Lysicrates, near the Acropolis. The monks have literally formed their successful Christian community around one of the great markers of the ancient world, and in harmony with it. The Choragic Monument is also known as the Lantern of Demosthenes, where that prominent Athenian statesmen and orator, known to have had pederastic relationships, had written many of his speeches.[41] It is only after a long and contemplative stay in this space that symbolically reconciles ancient and Christian values that the poet meets the young man with whom he achieves a spiritual and physical connection.

Pausing to look more closely at a heap of broken marble statuary and pediments, carelessly piled in the street, the poet at first attracts the attention of "boorish men," who are kept back when the poet's Muslim servant (not mentioned before in the poem) brandishes a sword at them. This rejection of the attentions of some rough Athenians establishes the poet as selective, so that when a man appears in a doorway adjacent to the artifacts, standing at the threshold of a "Grecian dwelling," the poet's acceptance of his invitation to enter can be read as an act of discernment. The poet enters the house and speaks with the man, while his son, "as Eastern usage demand[s]," stands silently and serves them food and drink as needed.[42] The poet is captivated by the son's androgynous features and pays many subsequent visits to the father, bringing gifts for the young man. Eventually, the father, seeing it as a path to possible advancement, offers his son to the poet as a page.[43]

The poet idealizes the relationship between himself and the young man, Giraud. He obtains permission from the young man's father to form a relationship with the son, and the poet in turn is shown to take responsibility for the education of the young man. The relationship is also shown to be a caring and compassionate one before it becomes physical, with the poet writing, "How many hours I've sat in pensive guise, To watch the mild expression of his eyes." The poet at times has "gazed unsated at his naked charms" and contented himself with caring gestures, rather than sexual acts.[44] When they do finally consummate their relationship, it is understood as a natural progression. Education is mixed with physical passions, so that each day is spent with poetry and each evening in physical embraces.

Given that the poet has recently left Cambridge, the age difference between the two would not have been more than a few years. However, the economic power imbalance between the poet and Giraud is great. Giraud's voice is never heard in the poem; he is presented as object rather than subject. Nonetheless, the relationship between the two men is depicted as companionate, mutually respectful, and compatible with family and community values.

Nothing that follows in the next eight hundred lines of the *Don Leon* poem itself is nearly so well crafted. After this scene, the language becomes coarse, and the description of sex grows more graphic. Sex, rather than love and spiritual connection, becomes the focus. The examples become more contemporary, and most are given only cursory treatment. The narrative voice also becomes more polemical and didactic, often dropping entirely the pretense that it is Byron narrating the poem. While the poem still has large blocks of classical allusion, it presents religion in a more negative light. Commentary on specific contemporary political events begins to appear. This commentary is extremely telling, as it conclusively ties the poem to the events of the summer of 1825 and to key individuals who would factor into subsequent efforts to end the death penalty for sodomy. Some of this material may still be by Beckford, because many of the events referenced in this section are also documented in his collection of newspaper clippings. But its author is angrier than the author of the first six hundred lines, more directly critical of the sodomy law and its supporters, perhaps in reaction to developments that warranted a forceful response. This is perhaps why "Leon to Annabella" is presented as a separate poem instead of as a continuation of *Don Leon*, which closely tracks Bentham's request to Beckford.

Understanding "Leon to Annabella"

In the first surviving edition of *Don Leon*, "Leon to Annabella" appears as a ten-page appended poem. It has often been neglected by scholars of *Don Leon*, but in its consistent focus on telling a single personal narrative without vulgarity or digressions, emphasizing love rather than lust in a way that strengthens arguments for ending the sodomy law, "Leon to Annabella" is more like the first six hundred lines of *Don Leon* than the eight hundred lines that follow. If the first six hundred lines of *Don Leon* demonstrate that sex between men can be companionate, mutually beneficial, and compatible with family and social networks, "Leon to Annabella" lays out an equally strong and beautifully told case for the privacy of marriage and for the principle that what a husband and wife consent to do with each other is no business of the state's. Building on the well-known story of Lord and Lady Byron's separation, it makes a more widely applicable argument against the sodomy law, in which, it suggests, all married couples have a stake.[45]

It seems logical that someone fulfilling Bentham's request might argue that opposite-sex couples, like same-sex couples, have a stake in overturning the sodomy law and that Byron's life history provides a narrative device for doing so. Bentham's work discusses sexuality in general, even if he acknowledges that the execution of men for having sex with men is the primary factor adding urgency to his need to publish.[46] Samuel Chew argues that "Leon to Annabella" is associated with *Don Leon* and "belongs, I believe, to 1817 or 1818," which would have it originating just after Bentham's letter to Beckford, as discussed in Chapter 1.[47] In his twenties, Byron (like Beckford) had affairs with younger men, and (again, like Beckford) he later married, with Byron having one daughter, and Beckford having two.[48] According to some accounts, it was Byron's sodomy with his wife Annabella that Stephen Lushington used as leverage in the custody dispute between Annabella and Byron.[49] *Don Leon* is told in the voice of Byron because Byron's life story includes two arguments against the sodomy law, one relevant to same-sex couples and one to opposite-sex couples. Like the first six hundred lines of *Don*

Leon, "Leon to Annabella" is set in the context of a loving and companionate relationship, this time between a man and a woman.

"Leon to Annabella" opens with the poet bereft. His love, Annabella, has left him and refuses to answer his letters. He states that there had been no issue between them before she left home to visit her parents, but then suddenly, after a few kind letters, she had written to say that he was now dead to her and that he should take back his wedding ring. The poet writes that he does not know why his love has forsaken him, as all his vices, which he admits are many, were known to her before their marriage and therefore should not have sparked such a strong new reaction. He had, in fact, given up the pursuit of other sexual partners to devote himself to her. Distraught at this seemingly inexplicable change in his wife's affections, the poet laments the precariousness of founding happiness on a marriage and investing so many hopes in another person who cannot really be known before the decision to marry is made. He does not question his love for Annabella, but only its fragility as a structure for a life.

As he spends time alone, thinking about what might possibly have happened, his mind drifts back over the intimacies they had shared, as his "memory portrayed . . . the tender pastimes of the night."[50] The poet then has a sudden revelation of the possible cause of Annabella's anger:

> *What! if, by thoughtless indiscretion led,*
> *Thou couldst betray the secrets of our bed?*[51]

The poet has always been faithful to his wife, even as over time he had felt the need to move beyond their standard sexual practices. The poet writes, "Thy charms were still my refuge—only this, I hoped to find variety in bliss."[52] This is as sexually explicit as "Leon to Annabella" ever gets, and that approach is consistent with the author's argument. The sexual act is not described, because marital privacy is a right, protected by Church of England sacrament. If, to keep that sacrament, he and his wife choose to perform certain consensual acts together to reduce the temptation to seek sexual partners outside their marriage, that is their business and no one else's.

Then, mirroring the poet's quest in the first six hundred lines of *Don Leon* to find examples of others who feels the way he does, the poet wishes for "some goblin take thee pick-a-pack From house to house, and draw the curtains back."[53] If this were to happen, it would be seen that "loving couples play Lampsacian games, In postures more than Elephantis names." No one's virtue is stained by these adventurous sexual acts, just as no harm would have come from what he and Annabella have done in private, if no one has brought attention to their actions and called "scoffers . . . to mock what we had done."[54]

The poet then documents the deterioration of his life in the following weeks. His "Friends and relations left me one by one, And like a plague my presence seemed to shun." He suspects that Annabella's trusting nature was played on and that another woman, seeking gossip, has coaxed out of her a story that Annabella should probably have known not to tell. He does not think it is his mother-in-law who has done this, because she, as a wife, is "too wise" to tell others of "these Eleusinian mysteries."[55] Although he assumes that Annabella's innocence was manipulated in her initial confession, the poet still feels some anger toward her for her subsequent decision to "hang thy conscience on a lawyer's peg." Here, Lushington is described as a "lisping fool" whose "empty dictums" are forcing their way into the poet's marriage. The poet's anger at this infringement on marital privacy is made clear when he writes, "Shall dolts like him a husband's rights define, Say wives may grant him this, must that decline."[56] The poet laments that his and his wife's reputations are now ruined forever.

At this point, the poet, paralleling the first six hundred lines of *Don Leon*, directly addresses the role of the sodomy law in creating injustice. Of mixing love and Themis (the Greek personification of law, fairness, and order), the poet writes:

> *Fools! take her balance and her sword away;*
> *The sighs of lovers were not made to weigh.*
> *Ah! would you with those manacles repress*
> *The fitful aestus of a warm caress?*
> *Or try Young Hymen's inoffensive sports*
> *By blood-stained statutes and in penal courts?*
> *Hang up the glaive,—Love does not kill or steal;*
> *He forms no plot against the common-weal*[57]

The call to married individuals to protect the sanctity and the privacy of their marital beds is reinforced at the end of the poem, when the poet asserts that so long as the sodomy law stands, "no couple can in safety lie, [since] Between the sheets salacious lawyers pry."[58]

Just as the first six hundred lines of *Don Leon* make an innovative argument for how Christian ethics and sex between men could be reconciled under certain circumstances, "Leon to Annabella" is as ambitious in positing that eliminating the sodomy law is more aligned with Christianity than is keeping it. The sodomy law itself violates Christian principles. The poet argues that in the name of upholding a biblical sanction against sodomy, the state presumes to intrude on the far more important religious sacrament of marriage. Whatever the poet and Annabella—and, by extension, any woman and her husband—might do to help them preserve fidelity to each other and therefore maintain the sacramental space of their marriage is of greater religious import than the church's proscription of sodomy. Here is an early-nineteenth-century Anglican argument that eliminating the sodomy law would advance a more important Christian principle.[59] This is a subtle, erudite, and ruthlessly logical syllogism that might have reached and appealed to upper-class members of Parliament. It is an argument that upholds Anglican and Christian ethics and doctrine, even as it undermines the religious rationale for the sodomy law.

The vows exchanged and sanctified by the church give a permanence to the marriages formed by men and women, but the poet's understanding of marriage in the first six hundred lines of *Don Leon* and in "Leon to Annabella" emphasizes the equivalency of same-sex and opposite-sex love. This understanding becomes clear when the poet describes his wedding day. As he leaves the ceremony, the poet accidently calls Annabella by her maiden name. Others would later say that this implies a lack of commitment to her from the start, but the poet explains that he did not yet feel, even after the ceremony, that he and Annabella were truly united. Only after they first had sexual intercourse, grounded in love and mutual commitment, did it become automatic for the poet to think of Annabella as his wife.[60] The connecting of individuals through love, compassion, and caring in conjunction with a physical union of bodies make a marriage. The implication is that the poet and Giraud, too, have been married, their relationship grounded in love and mutual support, albeit in a way that does not come with the same expectations of permanence.

The reason "Leon to Annabella" is appended to the end of *Don Leon* is that it is a part of the original work that Bentham asked Beckford to write. In addition, many items in Beckford's newspaper clippings collection align with the material in the final eight hundred lines of the *Don Leon* poem and with the material in the "Notes to *Don Leon*." The notes seem to have been updated by multiple individuals, at least some of whom were unaware of the intent of the author in the corresponding portions of the poem. The "Notes to *Don Leon*" and the final eight hundred lines of *Don Leon*, written between the mid-1820s and the early 1850s, also seem to follow the trajectory identified by Iain McCalman, where the publications of radical pressmen, such as Benbow, evolved from primarily political in the 1820s to more pornographic by the 1840s.[61]

This trajectory is illustrated by contrasting the scene between Leon and Annabella in the final eight hundred lines of *Don Leon* with what is presented in "Leon to Annabella." In *Don Leon*, after the parliamentary material (described later in this chapter), Leon and Annabella are seen lying in bed after a session of "amorous play."[62] Annabella asks her husband about his trip to the East, wanting him to describe the "strange and jealous men" there, with their "secret harems." Annabella is presented as jealous and insecure, believing that some "Eastern maid has heard thy plighted vows, She was thy love, I'm nothing but the spouse."[63] This sparks the poet's statement that women in the East must serve their husband's whim and that men in the East also seduce youths. He then tells her that some admired ancients, including Virgil, Anacreon, and Catullus, loved youths. This conversation prompts the poet to discuss anal sex with Annabella and suggest, because she is then eight months pregnant, that they could try it together. The poet invokes arguments from ancient and contemporary medicine, including Galen, Celsus, and Hippocrates, as to why this act would be safe, and Annabella consents.[64] What then follows is more than thirty lines of pithy panegyrics to the physical act of anal sex, including such verses as "How many view this grotto from afar, While fear and prejudice the entrance bar!" or the use of such phrases as "as the dildo slides, Besmeared" to describe an anal penetration.[65]

In "Leon to Annabella," marriage is sacred, the love between husband and wife is paramount, and what they do in bed is kept private. In this version of the scene between Leon and Annabella in the final eight hundred lines of *Don Leon*, by contrast, Annabella assumes that she as a wife is lesser in her husband's affections than is his mistress. This version offers no argument for marital privacy, and Leon recounts the details of his sex life with his wife for all to see. In these passages, sex is only about the physical pleasure it might give, in contrast to the treatment of the subject in the first six hundred lines of *Don Leon*, in "Leon to Annabella," or in *Not Paul, but Jesus*. Such arguments, too, had a place in creating a larger argument supporting sodomy-law reform, but they were not what Bentham originally asked for or what Beckford, most likely, originally wrote.

Later Additions to *Don Leon*: Grubb Street, Politics, and the Beckford Clippings

Much of the content in the final eight hundred lines of *Don Leon* and in the "Notes to *Don Leon*" seems informed by a different sensibility, even as many elements of it reference events recorded in Beckford's newspaper clippings.[66] As shown in the remainder of this chapter, some of these later additions directly reference specific parliamentary actions related to altering the laws pertaining to sodomy and sex between men in the 1820s and after.

The tone of the poem seems to shift in the final passages set in Greece, as themes become coarser and less well developed. Following the section on Greece, the poet draws on the work of Thomas Malthus to argue that the taste for males provides a solution to overpopulation and then asserts that "God, like the potter, when the clay is damp, Gives every man, in birth, a different stamp" that determines their particular tastes.[67] Next comes a rapid-fire listing of transgressive sexual tastes, including exhibitionism, incest, voyeurism, flogging, pederasty, lesbianism, and the employment of courtesans.[68] Before transitioning to the parliamentary material, the poet addresses themes and stories related to sex between men that were then long addressed in the British newspapers. References are made to the Vere Street and Barley Mow molly-house raids, followed by the sexual practices and same-sex desires of soldiers, sailors, and clergymen. Reports of such activities were not rare in the early nineteenth century, but it is still noteworthy that a significant number of articles discussing them are present among Beckford's clippings.[69]

The poet then asks, "Are you a senator?" and takes the reader into the House of Commons, naming specific members of Parliament who share the taste for sex with men and noting that what they decide "hangs the penny-less and spares the lord."[70] The first man described is Richard Heber. The poet writes:

> *Alas! The time shall come, when he, like me,*
> *Shall fall victim to foul calumny.*
> *Then all his love of learning, all his worth,*
> *The seat he holds by talent and by birth,*
> *Shall count as dross; whilst basest rumors, spread*
> *Folks care not how, shall light upon his head.*[71]

Heber had fled the country in the summer of 1825, although he would quietly return in 1831 to lead a secluded private life until his death two years later.[72] His obituary in the *Annual Register* indicated that he had not been welcomed back into his previous social circles, as "rumors had been circulating degrading to his moral character."[73] The newspaper stories that Beckford collected on Heber contained all the information needed to write what appears about Heber in the poem and in the explanatory "Notes to *Don Leon*."[74]

Another Member of Parliament (MP) referenced in this section of the poem is Henry Gray Bennet, who was publicly accused of having sex with another man in August 1825. Bennet was "one of the most active and promi-

Figure 5.1 *Richard Heber*, by John Harris, pencil, circa 1830. (© National Portrait Gallery, London.)

nent radical Whigs of his time," making more than five hundred speeches in Parliament and opposing the government on almost every vote.[75] He was a constant campaigner for criminal-law and prison reform, and he was one of the strongest supporters of Caroline. His parliamentary biography indicates that he was one of a group of about twenty members more concerned with cultivating extra-parliamentary support than with obtaining office and used that support to work toward desired reforms.[76] Of Bennet's work in Parliament, the poet writes:

In vain the negro's cause he nightly pleads;
Tells how the gangrened back with lashes bleeds;
Delights with philanthropic zeal to rail,
And paint the horrors of the felon's jail;
But let some knave vituperate his name,
Adieu to all his former well-earned fame!
An exile to a foreign land he'll fly,
Neglected live, and broken-hearted die.[77]

The "Notes to *Don Leon*" indicate that Bennet was "maligned in *The Age* newspaper . . . with gross insinuations of an improper intimacy between" him and a Brussels servant.[78] The *John Bull* also published veiled accusations against Bennet, writing that "Mr. Grey Bennett would jump for joy at the hopes of a snug game of back-gammon," and that "this mode of attacking men behind their backs may do very well for Mr. Bennett." These accusations led the *London Evening Standard* to later observe that "the *John Bull* has incurred punishment by impugning the chastity of Queen Caroline and the MANHOOD of Mr. Henry Grey Bennett."[79] When Bennet, according to his parliamentary biography, "could not deny that the allega-

Figure 5.2
Henry Grey Bennet, by William Holl Sr, after Abraham Wivell, stipple engraving, published 1823. (© National Portrait Gallery, London.)

tion was partly true . . . his reputation as a 'moral patriot' was destroyed."[80] He chose Florence as his place of exile, remaining there until his death in 1836.[81]

Beckford saved a newspaper story from the *Age* that contained a series of future obituaries of public figures not yet dead, with the first three separately mocking Bennet, the Duke of Cumberland, and the Bishop of Clogher, each disparaged primarily for his sexual interest in other men. The epithet on Bennet's imagined tombstone was:

> *Turn not your BACK upon this sod,*
> *For here GREY BENNETT lies,*
> *Who's gone the path which others trod,*
> *And once again may rise!*[82]

A third MP, James Stanhope, is also alluded to in this section of the poem, and in a way that highlights the stylistic differences between sections of *Don Leon*. Stanhope is identified by name in the "Notes to *Don Leon*," but charges related to his sexual interest in men cannot be confirmed through other sources as they can for Heber and Bennet. Stanhope had served in Sicily and Spain during the Napoleonic Wars and had been severely wounded at the Siege of Saint Sebastian in 1813. He had an undistinguished career in Parliament, holding seats for three separate constituencies between 1817 and 1825, and he suffered the loss of his wife in childbirth in 1823.[83] The section that deals with Stanhope in the poem begins:

> *Look at that row where elder Bankes is placed,*
> *There sits a youth with courtly manners graced.*
> *He fought his country's wars, and fixed a tent*
> *Where Etna burns with fuel never spent.*
> *'Twas there, where summer suns eternal beam,*
> *And life's the doze of one delicious dream . . .*
> *There, nursed by heated sap, new blossoms shot,*
> *And the rich soil exotic fruit begot . . .*
> *Not face to face his stream with hers combined,*
> *But mixed his nasty waters from behind.*[84]

Stanhope is described in the endnote associated with this passage as "the intimate friend of Mr. Heber, [who] soon after the disclosures made concerning the latter gentleman, hung himself in an outhouse in Caen Wood, the residence of his father-in-law, Lord Mansfield."[85] The text of the poem, though, associates Stanhope with opposite-sex sodomy only. This tension between the poem and the note is in keeping with the idea that the argument of the poem has been reshaped over time, with the later additions placing greater emphasis on same-sex desire and less on the threat that the criminalization of sodomy posed to married couples.[86]

It is worth noting that the "elder Bankes" is mentioned here without a discussion of the scandal that overtook his son. It is not until the last hundred lines of the 1,465-line poem, in a passage that was almost certainly added quite late, that Bankes and his father are discussed together, in relation to the son's 1833 arrest for having sex with a soldier. Beckford kept multiple newspaper clippings about Bankes, and everything needed to write what appears in *Don Leon* and in the "Notes to *Don Leon*" about Bankes can be found in that collection.[87]

"Oh Peel!" and Further Tension between the Notes and the Text

After describing the MPs who ran afoul of the laws prohibiting sodomy and sex between men in the spring and summer of 1825, the poet then singles out for attack Peel, in the passage quoted at the opening of the chapter, for making the laws against sex between men harsher than they had been.[88] This passage and the related material in the "Notes to *Don Leon*" provide further evidence that later contributors were not always aware of the intent of the earlier *Don Leon* poet or poets.

Peel is faulted in the poem for removing the "stumbling block in every jury's way" and for adding "a clause to drown the sinking man." The poet then names three MPs—Richard Martin, James Brogden, and Sir James Mackintosh—who were known for supporting humanitarian causes and asks why they do not do something to block Peel's efforts. It is one of the most dramatic sections of *Don Leon*, although the author of note 69 seems to indicate that he does not understand what the poem refers to. In the comment on this section of the poem, the "Notes to *Don Leon*" author writes:

> These strictures are not altogether just. It was in May 1828, that Mr. Peel in revising the criminal code, introduced some changes respecting the punishment of sodomy. Before this time the punishment was death, but then it was necessary that the witness should swear to having seen the actual perpetration; now the punishment is not capital but the conviction is rendered consequently easier. The reader must decide upon the amendment.[89]

The note does not accurately summarize what Peel did in 1828. The rules for proof of sodomy and rape were changed in 1828, making convictions for sodomy and rape easier by dropping the previous requirement of proof of ejaculation as well as anal or vaginal penetration for a conviction.[90] Sodomy and rape remained capital crimes after this 1828 change, though, with proof of penetration alone being enough for a conviction. In 1828, Peel did not add a clause to a bill making this change; rather, it happened in the context of his consolidation of the criminal law in relation to Offences against the Person, as a part of his consolidation of the criminal law more broadly. To facilitate the passage of an omnibus bill that consolidated dozens of previous statutes, the criminal statutes were not to be altered in the process of consolidation, although the law in relation to sodomy and rape was.[91]

The text in the poem is a much better fit with the events of 1825. In that year, Peel added a clause to an existing piece of legislation, the Threatening Letters Act. Also, the poet's invocation of Martin, Brogden, and Mackintosh is significant. Martin left Parliament in April 1827.[92] The three men were in Parliament together in March 1825, and on March 24, Martin had given a speech related to cruelty to animals just before Peel started the only substantial debate related to his 1825 amendment of the Threatening Letters Act. It was therefore likely that Martin was in the chamber when Peel spoke.[93] Division lists do not exist that can speak to the physical presence of Brogden and Mackintosh, but this, combined with the fact that Heber, Stanhope, and Bennet were all also in Parliament in March 1825 but out before the end of the summer, seems to indicate that the political argument in *Don Leon* centers on the parliamentary session of the summer of 1825. While only a passing knowledge of Martin was needed to write what is included about him in *Don Leon*, Beckford kept multiple newspaper stories about him and his efforts to strengthen the law against cruelty to animals.[94]

Neither Martin, Brogden, nor Mackintosh spoke out against Peel's alteration of the law related to sex between men, but another politician mentioned in *Don Leon*, the "Notes to *Don Leon*," and "Leon to Annabella" eventually did—Stephen Lushington. Almost at the end of the *Don Leon* poem, after the scene in which Leon and Annabella are depicted having anal sex, the poet tells Annabella, "Divulge it not, lest Lushington should know."[95] The "Notes to *Don Leon*" state that "Lord Byron's rage against Sir. S. Romilly and Dr. Lushington, for the advice they gave to Lady Byron, seems to have known no bounds."[96] In Thomas Moore's *Life of Byron*, Byron is recorded as saying, "Do you suppose I have forgotten or forgiven it? It has comparatively swallowed up in me every other feeling."[97] Other sources confirm that Byron's anger at Lushington was public and intense. The title page of "Leon to

Annabella" includes a statement attributed to Lushington to the effect that "Lady Byron can never cohabit with her noble husband again. He has given cause for a separation which can never be revealed; but the honour due to the female sex forbids all further intercourse for ever." In addition to this statement, Lushington is described in detail in the body of "Leon to Annabella."[98]

Did Lushington know that he is mentioned in *Don Leon*? Did he know just how much Byron hated him for destroying his marriage and his reputation? Did he, as a religious man, have reservations over the right of the state to intrude on the private decisions between a husband and wife? Was one of his many motivations for joining Fitzroy Kelly in 1840 and 1841, in addition to his general support for humanitarian causes, his general opposition to the death penalty, and his family tie to Matthew Gregory Lewis, his regret for taking advantage of the sodomy law in the case of Byron?[99] The sodomy law's potential to damage married couples was not abstract or theoretical in the early nineteenth century; it was a story that Byron had lived out publicly, and a story in which Lushington had played more than a minor role.[100] We cannot know what motivated Lushington, but he is one of the few individuals mentioned by name in the text of the poem *Don Leon*, in the "Notes to *Don Leon*," and in the text of "Leon to Annabella." Beckford kept at least one substantial newspaper story describing debates over Kelly and Lushington's bill that would have ended the death penalty for sodomy and several other articles about Lushington's work to end the death penalty in general.[101]

The William Beckford Reflected in His Clippings

There is a great deal in Beckford's clippings collection that links him to *Don Leon*. True, Beckford also kept numerous newspaper stories about high society, the monarchy, Horace Walpole, the Thames Tunnel, balloon ascents, and a comet then appearing in the sky. He kept many reviews of his own literary efforts and dozens of reports on recently published biographies of Byron as well as many articles related to Byron's life, reputation, and influence. He also collected many stories related to gender nonconformity that are not drawn on in the "Notes to *Don Leon*," including several about a young woman who, on her death, was found to have the body of a man.[102] Beckford also kept far more articles about court cases involving sex between men than are referenced in *Don Leon*. He seems to have had a fondness for accounts of upper-class men running afoul of the law, such as when a "well-dressed lad, of sixteen, who is said to be the second son of an Irish Peer, was brought up to Marlborough-street office, on Saturday, on a charge of having made indecent proposals to a sentry on duty at Knightsbridge barracks."[103] He also saved a story from

1822, a few months after the Bishop of Clogher's arrest, stating that "there are no less than six English *Noblemen* and *Dignitaries* of the *Established Church*, now resident in Paris, who have left this country *for ever*, because the climate is not congenial to *their tastes*."[104] There are stories of incest, sexual crimes committed by men against women, and gruesome murders, but these have been more difficult than the material related to same-sex desire to match with discussions in *Don Leon*.

Religion and same-sex desire are also themes that intersect in *Don Leon* and in the Beckford newspaper clippings. Beckford saved many reports of clergymen abusing the trust placed in them by sexually assaulting men and boys, and some of these clippings may have provided source material for *Don Leon* and the "Notes to *Don Leon*." That Beckford might have collected these stories out of a distaste for hypocrisy rather than an anticlerical impulse is suggested by another clipping, one that mocks Americans for taking "the fanaticism of temperance" so far that in some of the Protestant sects, "communicants have refused to use wine even in the sacrament of the Lord's supper, and have substituted buttermilk or lemonade instead of it!" The article called this "a most revolting and profane abuse of a valuable principle."[105] Perhaps there is a similarity between the man who decided to save this article and the man who argued that the puritanical zeal to police sodomy should not be allowed to infringe on the sacrament of marriage.

Expecting More from Robert Peel

By the end of the 1820s, Peel had implemented a number of the reforms called for in the 1819 Committee Report. He had eliminated capital punishment for a small number of offenses and readjusted the scale of punishments for lesser offenses against property.[106] Peel's four most important statutes consolidated the criminal law in relation to larceny and allied offenses (1827), malicious injuries to property (1827), offenses against the person (1828), and forgery (1830).[107] Together, these acts consolidated hundreds of previous statutes and covered more than three-quarters of all criminal offenses.[108] Peel did not consider it advisable to modify the criminal law any further, though. The severity of the law could not be additionally relaxed, he believed, without an effective police force throughout the country.[109] Unlike those running the 1819 Committee, Peel consulted with judges on all his bills, and the most prominent among them, including the Lord Chancellor, by 1830 "considered it unsafe to go beyond what Peel had already accomplished."[110] While he made extensive reforms, Peel wanted "no rash subversion of ancient institutions, no relinquishment of what is practically good, for the chance of speculative and uncertain improvement."[111] At least two men, though, one associated with *Don Leon* and one not, appealed to him to go further and extend his reforms to the laws against sodomy and its attempt.

At the very end of *Don Leon*, in a passage added after 1833, an abrupt transition brings the reader back to Parliament. The poet then describes a man seated in the Commons chamber, "rich in classic lore, Who roamed, like me, in strange countries." This man is Bankes, an MP, collector, and Egyptologist, and the poet laments that he cannot act as an oracle, warning Bankes away from the path that would lead to his 1833 arrest and trial for having sex with a soldier. The trial was extensively covered in the press, which reported on the shame evident in the demeanor of Bankes's father, also an MP, as he stood by his son.[112] The Bankes family had been in Parliament for decades, controlling the parliamentary seats for Corfe Castle for the Tories; the father had been friends with William Pitt and William Wilberforce since their time together at Cambridge. Because of this, the poet asked:

> *Then Peel, if conscience be not wholly dumb,*
> *Within thy bosom shall compunction come.*
> *How shalt thou sorrow for the moment, when*
> *A single scratch of thy reforming pen,*
> *Had from our code erased a peccant lust,*
> *And left its punishment to men's disgust.*[113]

No such broad reform was attempted by Peel in the later 1820s, when his consolidation of the criminal law could have provided an opportunity to make such a change, following the process by which sodomy laws had been quietly dropped on the continent.[114]

A military officer who was not associated with *Don Leon* also thought Peel's reforms in the 1820s provided an opportunity to decriminalize sex between men, and he wrote to Peel repeatedly to make this argument. Most men in the British military were almost by definition better traveled than those in the civilian population and therefore had been exposed to a range of cultural practices.[115] Such men could not help but notice that the British prohibition against sex between men was perhaps the strictest in the world. As a surgeon in the 10th L. Cavalry, stationed in India in the 1820s and 1830s, Thomas Baker had been exposed to attitudes unlike those at home, and while still serving in the military, he wrote multiple letters to the British Home Secretary, arguing for the decriminalization of sex between men.[116]

In his correspondence with Peel, Baker wrote that "in all climates to the East, and in China, I believe it is of the most constant and common occurrence . . . and it is not by them considered as a crime, or in any way disgraceful." He cited examples from Lucknow and added that "in Italy and other parts of the continent the crime is equally common" and "as we know there are many nations who think lightly of it, we may question the justice of our own laws regarding it," because it did no injury to the "peace and happiness" of civil society. To address the religious objection, this military surgeon conceded that sodomy was "pronounced capital by the law of Moses, but as we do not in all cases act up to the Mosaic law, I do not see any particular reason for acting up to it in this instance." He further argued that "the Koran is chiefly founded on this law, yet in two or three passages where this crime is alluded to, the punishment, if any, is very slight, for it says 'if they repent and amend, let them both alone, for God is easy to be reconciled and merciful.'"[117]

Baker made the argument against the criminalization of sodomy by putting it into the context of the recently passed Catholic Emancipation and the recent improvements in the criminal laws, stating that this further reform was "suitable to the times, and agreeable to the spirit of the age we live in." Baker argued that the punishment of the crime "greatly exceeds the offence," and he quoted William Blackstone on the ease with which someone could be accused of the crime for the purposes of extorting money and the difficulty of refuting such a charge. "If no notice were taken of this crime in our civil courts and newspapers, it would in my opinion become less frequent, for thousands would then never know the present existence of this unnatural offence."[118]

Baker ended by writing that although his previous letters on this subject were anonymous, he was putting his name on this one, to remove any doubt as to the character of the writer, because he was well known within the Bengal presidency and acquainted with several generals. Baker even stated that he "should have no objection publicly to express the sentiments contained in this letter, for I think they are in strict accordance with justice, reason, and humanity; *and that they are the real sentiments of the very great majority of the public.*"[119] Baker did acknowledge that there might be an "affected and foolish" outcry against the softening of these laws, but that response should not stop officials from doing "what they know to be right and proper." Baker's views did not change British policy, but they also do not seem to have hurt his career. The *Calcutta Monthly Journal and General Register* of 1838 records that Baker retired with rank in that year.[120]

Conclusion

Baker's arguments did not have long to work on Peel. The Roman Catholic Relief Act received royal assent in April 1829. After November 1830, when the Tory government fell and Charles Grey became the head of the first Whig administration in two generations, Peel was no longer in a position to shape legislation. Factoring in the time it would have taken for news of the Catholic Emancipation to reach India, and for Baker's letter to make the return journey, there would have been only a few months at the most for Peel to heed Baker's words, and there is little evidence that he would have done so. Peel's intervention into the law as it related to sex between men in 1823 and 1825 seemed designed to protect men of his class as well as his "CASTE," to borrow Robert John Wilmot-Horton's phrase, not to lessen the stigma against men who sexually desired other men. His intervention into the law in 1828 actually made convictions for sodomy more likely by lowering the required standard of proof. Peel was willing to embrace some liberal reforms of the law, but he did not seem sympathetic to the ethical proposition, put forward by Bentham and others, that either the punishment or the execution of men for consensual sex was wrong. This attitude was not shared, though, by the next great reforming Home Secretary, Lord John Russell.

Don Leon outlasted Peel. Some of it was written in the 1820s, when Peel was still shaping the political agenda, but it was expanded and elaborated upon in the 1830s, when the Whigs were in control and a torrent of liberal and humanitarian reforms was being enacted.[121] Those reforms, especially the radical reduction in the number of crimes subject to the death penalty, drew attention to the injustice of retaining the death penalty for sodomy. In these years, the key governmental figure shaping legal reform was Russell. Unlike Peel, Russell directly expressed his support for ending the death penalty for sodomy at least twice: once in a speech to Parliament and once in a bill that he drafted and planned to put forward in case the efforts of Stephen Lushington and Fitzroy Kelly failed. But, like so many others, Russell also actively obscured his involvement with this issue, letting other MPs, including Kelly and Lushington, take most of the initiatives in this area, even as he helped the process along at key moments. The story of Russell, Kelly, Lushington, and how their actions led, in 1835 and 1841, to bills ending the death penalty for sodomy passing in the Commons is told in the following two chapters.

6

"Finding Any One Hardy Enough" in the 1830s

I am convinced that the only reason why the punishment of death
has been retained in this case is the difficulty of finding any one
hardy enough to undertake what might be represented as the
defense of such a crime.[1]

—Hensleigh Wedgwood to Lord John Russell, 1835

The efforts to end the death penalty for sodomy the 1830s were marked
by missed opportunities and tragic consequences. At two points, the
broad reformist tendency of the era aligned with the actions of individuals who started processes in the British Parliament that could have ended
the death penalty for sodomy. But in each case, when faced with resistance,
the supporters of the reform seemed unwilling to press forward. They were
reluctant to risk their personal reputations, or their ability to bring about
other reforms was deemed more pressing. There were strong advocates for this
reform in the 1830s, their views recorded most forcefully in *Don Leon* and
one other source, and while they were connected to Parliament, their role in
getting the first bill ending the death penalty for sodomy passed in the House
of Commons in 1835 remains ambiguous.

The most tragic episode in this period of potential without progress unfolded in the summer of 1835, when a bill that would have ended the death
penalty for sodomy, having passed in the Commons in July and August, lan-
guished in the House of Lords as two men faced execution for sodomy under
circumstances that seemed to highlight all the cruelty and injustice of the
then-current law. The condemned were two men who, in private, behind a
locked door, had held each other with "a great deal of fondness and kissing."[2]
It was a situation that had gotten the attention of Charles Dickens and forced
itself onto the agenda of Lord John Russell. What these and other men did—
and did not do—when, over the course of the 1830s, opportunities arose to

make the British sodomy law more "suitable to the times, and agreeable to the spirit of the age we live in" is the subject of this chapter.[3]

Coming of the Whigs and the Age of Reform

The term "reform" had been a key political slogan and an aspiration since the 1780s.[4] It was first adopted by extra-parliamentary movements to redress abuses within the political system, with different reform agendas voiced by a range of groups, many working independently of one another and often at cross purposes. Reform of institutions was largely disparaged by the Tory governments in light of the turmoil caused by the French Revolution, even as the period of Tory dominance saw the abolition of the slave trade in 1807, the criminal law reforms of the 1820s, and Catholic Emancipation in 1829. It was in November 1830, though, with the first Whig government in nearly two generations, that the real torrent of change came.[5] Led by Earl Grey, the Whigs brought about franchise reform in 1832, the abolition of slavery in 1833, factory regulation in 1833, poor law reform in 1834, and municipal government reform in 1835.[6] In addition to these most far-reaching and well-known changes were sustained reform efforts directed at a broader range of institutions, including the Church of England, the high courts, the universities, the medical colleges, the theatrical patent system, the Bank of England, the East India Company, and the Royal Academy, among many others. Together, as Arthur Burns and Joanna Innes note, these reforms "began to bring about major changes in the political and cultural landscape."[7]

The Whigs and Criminal Law Reform

The Whig government did not make reforming the capital laws a priority in the first years of their administration; private member initiatives, led by individuals including William Ewart, Stephen Lushington, and Henry Aglionby, brought about the first Whig repeals of particular capital statutes. These reformers drew on statistics that showed that conviction rates had increased in those areas where the death penalty had been repealed, and they cited evidence that public opinion agreed with the principle that the death penalty should not apply to crimes against property alone.[8] Early initiatives abolished the death penalty for offenses related to housebreaking, robbery, and larceny. The 1832 Punishment of Death, Etc. Act reduced the number of capital crimes significantly, eliminating the death penalty in areas of theft, counterfeiting, and most instances of forgery, except the forgery of wills and certain powers of attorney.

Resistance began to build to this piecemeal approach to reforming the criminal law, and calls were made for a more general and fundamental review that would establish an overall scale of punishments and determine exactly where the line should be drawn between capital and noncapital offenses.[9] Under Lord Melbourne, as Home Secretary, and Lord Brougham, as Lord Chancellor, the Royal Commission on Criminal Law was initiated in 1833.[10] The Criminal Law Commission was unique in that never before had a committee of legal experts been brought together for a long-term investigation of the feasibility of creating a code or digest of the criminal law, combining common and statutory law.[11] Like Brougham, all the commissioners were followers of Jeremy Bentham. They published seven reports between 1834 and 1843, in which they classified offenses based on their gravity, graduated penalties accordingly, and proposed limiting judicial discretion in sentencing. The *First Report* of the Royal Commission, issued in July 1834, described the general principles that guided its work, while the *Seventh Report*, issued in 1843, contained a compete draft of a new criminal-law code for England and Wales, consolidating the work of the earlier reports.[12]

These reform efforts were carried out in the early 1830s, when approximately five hundred individuals were sentenced to death in England and Wales each year. On average, though, only around thirty of these individuals were executed, and those primarily for murder.[13] The discrepancy between the number of those capitally convicted and those executed had been justified by the doctrine of "discretionary selection." Central to this doctrine were three interrelated principles: that capital punishment would only need to be applied in a few select instances to have the desired deterrent effect, that it would not be possible to set in advance which circumstances might most warrant its application, and that such decisions were best made according to the circumstances described at a specific trial. The courts and the executive (through the Privy Council) were expected to use their respective powers of commutation "to prevent any unduly harsh enforcement of the law."[14] Russell, among many others, critiqued the effectiveness of this doctrine, arguing that it could hardly serve as a deterrent if "no one know what specific features or aggravation led to offenders being selected for execution." Russell also argued that "judges and Home Secretaries could differ widely in their decisions," adding to the arbitrariness of decisions on which life and death turned.[15]

Societies for the Abolition of
Capital Punishment

Although not on the same scale as with franchise reform or the abolition of slavery, organized pressure groups formed outside Parliament to advocate against the death penalty. The Society for the Diffusion of Knowledge Respecting the Punishment of Death and the Improvement of Prison Discipline (SDKPDIPD), established in 1808, and the later Society for the Diffusion of Information on the Subject of Capital Punishment (SDISCP), established in 1820, saw their roles as publishing facts about capital punishment, promoting petitions to Parliament and letters to Members of Parliament (MPs), and obtaining funds to carry out this work.[16] Subscriptions were never robust, and the cost of even moderate publications drove the SDKPDIPD to bankruptcy by 1815, with the SDISCP also facing financial problems. The SDISCP lapsed for a few years in the 1820s but was revived in 1829 and renamed the Society for the Abolition of Capital Punishment (SACP) in 1846. It was only in the 1840s that "abolitionists," such as John Thomas Barry, "became familiar gliding quietly through the corridors" of Parliament.[17]

An Argument against the Death Penalty:
A Free Examination

While not a publication of the SDISCP, *A Free Examination into the Penal Statutes*, published most likely in 1833, was very similar to the materials that that group produced. It lays out a series of rational, moral, and historical arguments against the death penalty. *A Free Examination*, however, makes these arguments specifically about executions for sodomy; it goes so far as to argue against the criminalization of sex between men in general. According to the subtitle of the book, it is addressed to both houses of Parliament at a time when the debate over criminal law reform was accelerating with the founding of the Royal Commission.[18]

Only fragments of *A Free Examination* survive, some as quoted material in the "Notes to *Don Leon*" and some in the *Index Librorum Prohibitorum*, with the earliest surviving copy of each work dating from 1866 and 1877, respectively. The fragments indicate that many of its passages were similar to Bentham's unpublished arguments against the criminalization of sex between men.[19] The wording of some of the quoted passages indicates that the work was written and endorsed by more than one person, and authorship is attributed to "A. Pilgrim, &c."[20]

Like Bentham's writings, *A Free Examination* argues that the religious injunction against sex between men was an inadequate basis for a legal prohibition. It observes that "in an affair which involves reputation and life, a verse or two, worded so vaguely that it would be impossible to cite them as an authority from a book of law precedents (had they been found there instead of being found in Bible), are made to decide upon *our* very destiny and existence."[21] To allow such an ambiguous warrant to go unquestioned, the authors argue, is in effect "yielding up the exercise of our judgment, the distinctive privilege of reasonable beings" and forgoing "the right of demanding the proofs, which in other cases we require."[22] That the law must be based on reason rather than tradition (religious or otherwise) is a central idea in Bentham's legal writing.

Like the earliest sections of *Don Leon*, *A Free Examination* contrasts the then-current prejudice against sex between men with the attitudes in the ancient world. According to the authors, their contemporaries tended to discuss "antiphysical propensities" only in relation to "the vices of a Tiberius, a Nero, a Caligula, or a Heliogabalus, endeavoring to disguise or conceal from their readers this important truth, that the virtuous, the brave, the generous and the temperate, have equally sympathized in the same predilection."[23] Examples from the ancient world are used to show that noble and praiseworthy individuals shared this taste and that in those instances when sanctions were placed on it, they were mild. This theme from *A Free Examination* is also quoted by Henry Spencer Ashbee, in the *Index Librorum Prohibitorum*, where he writes that he is "inclined to agree with the author of '*A Free Examination* . . . ' that the taste has been in all ages that of the most distinguished individuals, and that we might count perhaps as many delinquents in the great continental cities now, as there were in Athens, or in ancient Rome."[24]

Sodomy between men and women is also a theme in *A Free Examination*, as it is in Bentham's writings on sexuality. After citing Malthus on overpopulation, the authors tell the story of an ancient ruler of Crete who tried to limit the population by discouraging reproductive sex between men and women, while "the same law permitted arsenerasty as an equivalent for the privations which it imposed."[25] In another passage, techniques then employed in Switzerland between husbands and wives to limit family size are hinted at, recalling the "Leon to Annabella" section of *Don Leon*.[26]

Ashbee and the authors of *A Free Examination* take up the issue of the present-day punishment for sex between men. Ashbee attributes the prevalence of cases among the lower classes to "their using less precaution against discovery" and lists "[William] Beckford, Richard Heber, Grey Bennet, [Percy] Jocelyn, Bishop of Clogher, [William] Bankes, and [Charles] Baring

Wall; and . . . many others which were well known in society" who also ran afoul of the law.[27] The *Free Examination* authors express more emotion when addressing contemporary punishments, writing that the essence of the argument in this area "may be summed up in a paragraph extracted from a French newspaper of July 18, 1833."[28] The account of the translated newspaper story relates that a "noble marquis was recently fined for an indecent attempt upon a gendarme; the laugh went amazingly against the Marquis." The authors then say that another, humbler man had made an "indecent assault" on a city sergeant and was sentenced to fifteen days' imprisonment. The *Free Examination* authors then write, "We have the fine and the laugh for the Marquis, and the fortnight's prison for the humbler individual. Will Mr. Peel please to say that this is not better than death warrants and gibbets; not to mention the distress of innocent families rendered miserable for ever."[29] Why the author of this passage is still chastising Robert Peel in 1833 (or sometime thereafter), years after he had left the government, seems to suggest a possible author for the passage, when understood in the context of other events of 1833.

William Bankes in 1833

The year 1833 saw the formation of the Royal Commission on Criminal Law, the publication of *A Free Examination*, substantial updates to *Don Leon*, and the prosecution of two MPs, William Bankes and Charles Baring Wall, on charges of having sex with men. Bankes was close friends with Lord Byron, connected to William Beckford, and, as an ultra-Tory with considerable independence, alternately a political ally and a political adversary of Peel. Bankes never won an election after his 1833 arrest, in contrast to Wall, who had not been so connected to Byron and Beckford and who continued to win elections through the 1830s and beyond, even after being arrested and as the veiled public statements disparaging his masculinity continued.

After Lushington, Bankes is the most widely discussed politician in *Don Leon* and the "Notes to *Don Leon*." Bankes's family had controlled the rotten borough of Corfe Castle for generations, and Bankes's father, Henry Bankes, had become friends with William Pitt and William Wilberforce at Cambridge, after which all three men entered Parliament together in the 1780s.[30] William Bankes grew up with the most important politicians in the country as regular presences in his home. As a second son, he was freer to set his own course, until he reached his early twenties, when his elder brother died.

The greatest evidence for Bankes's sexual interest in men, before his arrests in 1833 and 1841, comes from his time at Cambridge. According to Fiona MacCarthy, at Cambridge, "Byron discovered an already thriving sub-

WILLIAM JOHN BANKES
1786 - 1855
PAINTED BY SANDARS, 1812.

Figure 6.1 *W. J. Bankes in 1812 miniature* by George Sandars from the Drawing Room at Kingston Lacy, Dorset, watercolor on ivory. (© National Trust Images / Derrick E. Witty.)

culture of sodomy, with its own rituals and codes, into which he was indoctrinated by William Bankes, later defined by Byron as 'his collegiate pastor, and master,' and the 'father of all mischiefs.'"[31] In her detailed analysis of Bankes's college years, Dorothy Seyler shows that Bankes was in the same social circle as Byron, Charles Skinner Matthews, and Scrope Berdmore Davies.[32] Byron, Matthews, and Davies, as MacCarthy has shown, wrote to one another in coded language when describing their sexual interest in younger men, and their acting on such impulses, in Britain and when traveling abroad.[33] Seyler documents especially well the closeness between Byron and Bankes and the jealousy that John Cam Hobhouse, also at Cambridge at this time, exhibited toward Bankes because of it.

The surviving evidence suggests that Bankes attempted to discipline himself in conformity with his understanding of Greek love, as had Byron and Beckford.[34] His same-sex attachments seem to have been to younger men while he himself was still relatively young; later in life, he had flirtations and affairs with women. Bankes courted Anne Isabella "Annabella" Noel Byron (then Milbanke) at the same time as Byron, but he was also known to have visited Fonthill Abbey in 1811, when a visit to Beckford's residence endangered one's reputation.[35]

After graduating from Cambridge, he traveled to the continent to join the Duke of Wellington, a family friend, as an aide de camp during the Peninsular War. Following the defeat of Napoleon Bonaparte, Bankes, then twenty-nine years old, went to Egypt, venturing further into that country than had any other European in modern times. Bankes remained in Egypt from 1815 to 1819, amassing notes, sketches, and artifacts that at the time and since have been considered a significant contribution to the scholarship on ancient Egypt.[36] On his way back to England, he paused in Ravenna and Venice, where he spent time with Byron, then in exile because of rumors surrounding the reason for his separation from Annabella. Byron thought that Bankes had "done *miracles* of research" and that he had already done more with his life than most men.[37] Later, back in London, Bankes, known for having "good looks, easy charm, and independent wealth," moved into the highest social and political circles.[38]

In 1822, Bankes won a competitive three-way contest to represent Cambridge University in Parliament, despite not being the favored candidate of the Tory government.[39] He was unseated in 1826; Bankes and his family suspected that the government had conspired to remove him. After unsuccessful efforts, he was returned to Parliament in 1829 (for the pocket borough of Marlborough) to continue his advocacy against Catholic Emancipation. That issue, and opposition to the Reform Act of 1832, dominated his parliamentary legacy. In what was considered one of his best speeches in the Commons, Bankes condemned Catholic Emancipation as "plain, unqualified, unconditional surrender," and he "damned Wellington and Peel for their betrayal of the Protestant constitution: 'they have stolen upon us in the night, and thrown a firebrand into the body of the church.'"[40]

Bankes, then forty-seven years old, had just been returned as a member for Dorset in the 1832 general election when he was arrested on June 6, 1833. He had been apprehended with Thomas Flowers, a private in the Coldstream Guards, as the two men lingered together in a public urinal in the church-yard of St. Margaret, Westminster. It was reported that "at least 2,000 persons had assembled in front of the office" when word spread that an MP had been arrested on this charge.[41] The presiding magistrate cleared the court to limit newspaper coverage, although many newspapers reported that outside the courtroom, Bankes's father, who provided bail and a carriage ride home for his son, could not bring himself to look at him even once.[42] Both Bankes and the soldier faced two years of imprisonment, and because multiple witnesses had seen them acting suspiciously, both before and after they had entered the urinal, their defense would be difficult.

These events seemed to have sparked work on *A Free Examination, Don Leon,* and the "Notes to *Don Leon,*" in part, perhaps, by Bankes himself. Six weeks after his arrest and release on bail, and months before the December trial, someone saved the newspaper story used in *A Free Examination*, as quoted on page 145, from a French-language newspaper describing the same sort of situation that Bankes and Flowers found themselves in, with the comment that In France, conviction would yield at most two weeks imprisonment and more likely a fine and a bit of public humiliation. The person who comments on this clipping in *A Free Examination* asks Peel by name whether this was not a better punishment for the crime and invokes the ruin of a family. The scene involving Bankes added to the end of *Don Leon*, discussed at the end of Chapter 5, expresses similar anger toward Peel personally and also invokes the ruin of a family. It is worth remembering that in the main Parliament scene in *Don Leon*, the poet makes it a point to demonstrate that Bankes's father is publicly associating with a sodomite, sitting next to the man who had acquired a taste for sodomy with women in Sicily.[43] Could this be a plea for a father to recognize that his son's transgression was not so bad and the same as a sin that the father tolerated in others? Perhaps this is the work of a disinterested party commenting on Bankes's plight, but it seems more emotional than that.

If this evidence points to Bankes's authorship, it also points to someone in France in the summer of 1833. In addition to the French-language newspaper story from July 18, 1833, cited on page 145, eight of the twenty-five newspaper citations in the "Notes to *Don Leon*" are from 1833; are from a Paris newspaper, *Galignani's Messenger*; and are used to demonstrate that "it will not be difficult, within the compass of a single year, to select from police reports cases enough to force from the strongest stickler at the morality of this churchgoing generation," an admission that such acts were common.[44] Bentham's argument against the criminalization of such situations as Bankes was arrested for is directly quoted in the "Notes to *Don Leon*," where it is observed that "such delinquents are sufficiently punished by the shame and infamy of a discovery."[45] This quotation is taken from a French translation of Bentham's work, *Theorie des Peines et des Récompenses*. The summer of 1833 sparked updates to *Don Leon*, the "Notes to *Don Leon*," and *A Free Examination*, most likely by Bankes or someone very close to him who was then in France. Bankes was acquitted at his trial when it was finally held in December 1833, but he never won another election.

Charles Baring Wall in 1833

Being put on trial for attempting sex with a man in uniform did not have to end a political career. Charles Baring Wall, an MP for Wareham, was arrested only three months before Bankes and charged with the same offense with a police officer. Evidence for his interest in other men in the years just before his 1833 arrest, and the disparaging comments that others made because of that interest, are easier to document for Wall than for Bankes. Examples include the time Wall was recorded as saying, "I wish I lived in a disturbed district" after meeting "two good looking soldiers" in August 1828, when he was in his early thirties.[46] In October 1829, weeks after the new uniformed Metropolitan Police first began to appear on the streets of London, Wall wrote, "I delight in them all."[47]

Wall's willingness to occasionally hint at his admiration for men was only one indication of the independence evident in his personal life and political career. His father had married Harriet Baring, an evangelical religious activist and daughter of the founder of Baring's Bank.[48] Wall inherited a large fortune when his father died in 1815; he was only twenty. He used his vast wealth to support his political career and to pursue his interests in the fine arts. He was a supporter of Catholic relief, the repeal of the Test Acts, and Jewish Emancipation, and he favored Russell's early-1820s plan for parliamentary reform. Grey's later plan, he thought, went too far.[49] Wall's speech against Grey's bill "was widely hailed as one of the best from the opposition side," although his statement within it, that the loss of one of the parliamentary seats for Guilford, which he represented, would leave him "but half a man," was met by a later chide from Lord Auckland that "he overstates it very much."[50]

Statements about Wall's masculinity also surfaced in his social circle. The novelist Emily Eden was friendly with Wall and his mother, Harriet, and an occasional guest at Wall's estate. She once wrote to a friend, "I am glad you are more just to little Mr. Wall. I tried to be so unjust to him myself that I do not like to find anybody else so. After all, he makes one laugh, which is a merit, and he is a warm friend, and if he is a little ridiculous, it is no business of ours. Heaven help Mrs. Wall—if there ever should be such a person. But there never will."[51] Wall most likely would not have appreciated these comments, but such observations, from either politically powerful men or socially powerful women, did not stop him from having a long and distinguished career.

The above statements about Wall were recorded before the question of what he asked a police officer on the street became national news. In March 1833, Wall saw John Palmer, a young constable, on an otherwise deserted street south of Regent's Park around 1:00 A.M.[52] Wall went up to him and engaged in conversation, which was probably flirtatious and may have led to an unwanted physical advance. As reported in the *Evening Mail* and other newspapers, Palmer asked Wall, "Do you think I am a _____, or what?" Wall then followed up his verbal proposition with physical contact that Palmer considered to be a sexual advance.[53] Palmer arrested Wall, despite Wall's offers of money to forget the whole thing.

Wall faced far less serious consequences for his actions than did Bankes for his. The reporting of the initial stages of Wall's case was limited to stories of only a few lines noting that high bail had been set and that the case would be moved to the Court of King's Bench.[54] When Wall's trial was held in mid-May, it received extensive coverage in the newspapers, with reports continuing over multiple columns.[55] Wall was described in the press as "a Gentleman of rank, fortune and fashion, moving in the highest and best circles of society," which gave him a decided advantage, especially as no one had witnessed the incident.[56] As the case was framed by Wall's defense, there "were two things for consideration, one of which must inevitably be the result—either the defendant was unworthy to hold that station in society which he had hitherto held, or that the prosecutor was a base slanderer and calumniator."[57] Given this framing, and the fact that "a great number of witnesses (amongst whom were several members of the House of Commons) were called, and the defendant received from all the most unexceptionable character for morality," the case seemed likely to go Wall's way.[58]

It did, and by November of that year, Wall was attending state functions and leading toasts to the character of the mayor of Guildford. He also saw such works as "Charles Baring Wall, Esq., MP, and the Reporters" published, which promised "A VINDICATION of the REPORTERS concerning the CASE . . . and several interesting and highly amusing Anecdotes."[59] Snide remarks were made about him in print in subsequent years, linking him to Bankes and to sexual interest in men in general. Wall, however, remained in Parliament for another twenty years, and, like Hobhouse, he would be in Parliament for the 1835 vote to end the death penalty for sodomy and for the more contentious effort to bring about the same reform in 1840–1841.

The First Attempt: Charles Law and Lord John Russell

Among those who, in the early 1830s, believed that change was happening too rapidly was William IV. Fearful of the pace of innovation under the Whigs, William declared that he had lost confidence in the government. He invited the Tories to form a minority ministry in November 1834, with new elections to be held in January 1835. In the space of a few months, Wellington and then Peel responded to William's requests to head a minority government, but that government failed to win a majority in the election, as the king had hoped. Whig power was diminished after the election, but

Figure 6.2 *Charles Ewan Law (1792–1850)*, by Henry William Pickersgill, oil on canvas, early nineteenth century. (Used by permission of the Master and Fellows of St. John's College, Cambridge.)

the Whigs were able to command a majority in the Commons through an alliance with Radicals and Daniel O'Connell's Irish Repeal Association, and Peel stepped down in April 1835.[60] It was the last time a monarch would ever try to impose a government on the Commons that did not have majority support in that house. Lord Melbourne formed a new Whig ministry, which would last until August 1841. Importantly for the effort to end the death penalty for sodomy, Russell then became Home Secretary, a position he would hold until August 1839. It was Russell who made criminal law reform a government priority, having been a long-time supporter of Sir Samuel Romilly and having served on the 1819 Criminal Law Committee.[61]

The 1835 election also brought Charles Law into Parliament; he put forward the first legislation to end the death penalty for sodomy only a few months later. Law had been the Recorder of London since 1833; he had previously served as a judge of the sheriff's court, as King's Counsel, and as the assistant to the Recorder of London, known as the Common Sergeant.[62] He became a Tory MP for Cambridge University in early 1835, holding that seat along with the office of the Recorder of London until his death in 1850. As Recorder, Law was the senior circuit judge at the Old Bailey, renamed the Central Criminal Court by Parliament in 1834. In this position, he heard cases and assigned cases to the other judges at the Central Criminal Court. He came from a prominent family, with his elder brother serving as governor-general of India, although Charles himself was considered to have only moderate abilities as a parliamentarian.

Two months after the Whigs were back in power, Law proposed an amendment to a bill already making its way through Parliament that would have ended the death penalty for sodomy. That bill would have addressed what some saw as a shortcoming of Peel's Offences against the Person Act. As the law then stood, an aggravated assault that might eventually result in death could not be prosecuted as manslaughter if manslaughter was not in the original indictment. The bill would have made it possible to prosecute such crimes as manslaughter if death had resulted from the injury between the indictment and the trial.[63]

Law proposed two clauses to be added to the bill that bore some relationship to its intent. The first made buggery, rape, sex with a girl under ten years of age, and attempted murder all no longer punishable by death but instead subject to no fewer than seven years' transportation or four years' imprisonment with or without hard labor. The second paragraph allowed juries to find individuals charged with any of the sexual offenses covered by the law guilty of the attempted act, if they considered the evidence insufficient to prove the act itself.[64] Like the bill it was attached to, this clause would have allowed juries to find an individual guilty of a crime not explicitly mentioned in the indictment. This would have ended the death penalty for sodomy, but it also would have likely increased the number of individuals subject to punishment for attempting the act. In a pattern that would be repeated in 1861, but not in 1840 or 1841, the effort to end the death penalty for sodomy was coupled with other legislation that would have likely resulted in an increase in the number of convictions involving sex between men. Also, as in 1861, but not in 1840 or 1841, the sodomy provision was never voted on separately from the law relating to other sexual offenses. Additionally, as in 1861, but not in 1840 or 1841, no significant debates or official division lists have been preserved related to this legislation, making it impossible to know which MPs supported the change. In all these ways, 1835 follows the pattern of 1825 and 1828 (and presages that of 1861 and 1885), when the British Parliament addressed the law pertaining to sex between men but did so in a way that avoided most discussion of it and often conflated it with other issues. This record highlights the uniqueness of what occurred in 1840 and 1841, when events did not follow these patterns.

The 1835 bill with Law's clauses added passed in the House of Commons, but it leaves very little trace in the official records. The *Journals of the House of Commons* record that on June 5, 1835, a bill "amending the Law relating to Offences against the Person in certain cases" was read for the first time.[65] None of the twelve *Hansard* entries for Law for 1835 are related to the clauses he proposed for this bill, nor is there any related entry for George Pryme or Sir John Jervis, the two men who presented the initial bill that Law hoped to amend. The bill was read for a second time on June 15, 1835, but this is only mentioned in the preamble to the records of the day's proceeding. The bill incorporating Law's two clauses as he had initially written them was printed on July 1. On July 13, "the ingrossed Bill for amending the Law relating to Offences against the Person in certain cases, was, according to Order, read the third time" and sent on to the House of Lords.[66] Whether Wall was in the room for this vote, we do not know. He did, however, appear in a partisan newspaper at this moment. The *Age* decided to publicly mock Wall on August 16, 1835, reporting:

> That respectable personage, Baring Wall, gave a picnic party at Beulah Spa on Wednesday. The company was "highly distinguished," and Banks, the learned co-traveller of Wall, was present by special invitation. The hon. giver of the feast enlarged eloquently on the convenience and usefulness of the *new police*; whilst Banks, whose taste in *flowers* is unexceptionable, dwelt much on the surrounding beauties of nature. The entertainment passed off exceedingly well.[67]

Beckford saw this article and kept the clipping, but without comment.

The House of Lords—August 28, 1835

There was almost as little discussion of the bill with Law's amendment in the House of Lords. The bill was presented with two others, also related to the criminal law, by Lord Denman, the Lord Chief Justice of England. One of the three bills, which would have ended the death penalty for stealing letters and for committing certain acts of sacrilege, was uncontroversial. Denman and the assembled lords agreed that "no reasonable objection could be made" to that bill, and it was recommended for a second reading.[68]

The other two bills were controversial. One would have given "persons indicted for felony the power of making a full defence to the jury by counsel," and there was concern that this might mean that "a gentleman could be compelled by the Court to undertake that office" and have unwanted clients forced on him.[69] The other bill, the one with Law's amendment, was described as "making offences against the person punishable more severely than at present," ignoring the part of the bill that would have ended the death penalty for sodomy and rape. Denman remarked that these two bills should be considered together, although there were "strong differences of opinion as to the propriety of any new enactment at all."[70]

The specific objections to the bill with Law's amendment, and any discussions in the Lords regarding those objections, are not recorded. What is recorded was that consideration of the bill with Law's amendment as well as the Prisoners' Counsel Bill should be suspended for six months. On August 29, 1835, the day after this decision was made in the Lords, the Commons ordered that "a Select Committee be appointed to inspect the Journals of the House of Lords, with relation to proceedings upon the Prisoners' Counsel Bill; and, Capital Punishments Bill, and to make Report thereof to the House."[71]

At this point, Russell interrupted the main work of the Royal Commission and asked it to consider which offenses should continue to be subject to capital punishment and whether counsel for a prisoner should have the right to address the jury in felony cases. The *Second Report* of the Royal Commission, issued in 1836, considers both of these issues, the two reforms that Denman had objected to in the House of Lords debate on August 28, 1835.[72] This report would form the basis of Russell's subsequent legislation on both of these matters, and it is the last report that John Austin, who was aware of Bentham's arguments against the criminalization of sex between men, helped draft, before repeated clashes with the other commission members led to his resignation.

The Tragic Fates of William, John, and James

On August 29, 1835, the same day that Russell reoriented the work of the Royal Commission, John Smith and James Pratt would be transformed into desperate men with a tragic stake in the commission's recommendations. That had not been the case at the start of the day, when John and James had planned to meet William Bonell, a sixty-eight-year-old former gentleman's servant, then out of place. William shared several traits with Charles Baring Wall, if nothing of his social status or the protections that came with it. Like Wall, he seems to have had a taste for handsome men, and he, too, was not so careful as he might have been about who knew it. William liked to invite men—often couples—back to the room he rented in central London.[73]

John Smith, forty years old and an unmarried laborer, who had also at one time been a gentleman's servant, had been to William's room before.[74] John was supporting his mother, and so William's room most likely gave him more privacy than he had at home. He came by again that afternoon. William's landlords, George and Jane Berkshire, who ran the shop John had to walk through to get to William's room, did not like John and discouraged his visit, with George telling John that he did not think that William was in. But John had already seen William at his window, and he walked past George and Jane and down the hallway to the stairs leading to William's room. Before reaching the room, John surreptitiously opened a back door, letting in James Pratt, a thirty-year-old servant. James did not greet George and Jane in the shop but went upstairs with John to William's room. The three men sat there "laughing together in conversation" and sharing gestures of affection and camaraderie. After a time, William stepped out to get some alcohol, and in his absence, John and James became more affectionate. This time was marked by "a great deal of fondness and kissing," before the men, James "laying on his back . . . with his body curled up" and John "upon him," engaged in consensual sex.[75]

They did not know that they were being watched. George stood on a shed to peer through a window at them, and then he and Jane took turns contorting themselves to peer through a keyhole.[76] When William came back to his room, he found policemen present and his comrades distraught. The three men were roughly taken to the nearby police station. Because they were poor men, they could not make bail. John and James spent what remained of their lives incarcerated, facing a series of unwanted observations and vindictive judgments from judges, assembled mobs, clergymen, and journalists. In this process, they lost the power to represent themselves, becoming only the points around which other people anchored stories.

Some of those who engaged with John and James at this point were more interested in their souls than in their lives. These religious men tried to get them to repent, to save their souls and to be able to broadcast the message of repentance to the nation.[77] In the early nineteenth century, the comportment of men facing execution was a matter of public interest. If they cried or otherwise showed what they were feeling, that became the focus of the narrative. Whether this final pressure of the unalterable judgment of man might act as the catalyst for bringing the condemned to repent was a story of vital interest to the church and the nation.[78] Many of those who spoke with John and James in their final days likely felt no compunction over carrying out a ministry that accepted the loss of these men's lives as inevitable. These religious individuals, though, at least engaged with John and James according to the tenets of their belief system. The death penalty abolitionist movement, at other times "sensitive to current affairs, such as scandals involving bungled executions or controversial sentences," made no issue over the arrest, conviction, and eventual execution of these two men for private, consensual, nonviolent acts.[79]

There was apparent consensus regarding their punishment among the judges, reporters, clergymen, and other officials in these cases. And yet we know that, even as John and James were being prepared for execution, that unity had broken down in the British Parliament, and that only months before, a majority in the Commons had voted to end the death penalty for sodomy. For Law in particular, the case of John and James led to an especially direct confrontation between his personal beliefs and his public actions.

Just months after he had proposed ending the death penalty for sodomy, Law, as the Recorder of London, had a role to play in the execution of John and James. Shortly after the defendants' September 21 trial, Law met with two aldermen to review the capital cases from the previous court session.[80] Law prepared the documents that would be sent to the Privy Council regarding the fourteen death sentences handed down by the Central Criminal Court in that session. As he was preparing the documents, Law wrote to Russell that "the cases of John Smith, James Pratt, and Robert Swan will, I regret to say, require a detailed statement to his Majesty."[81] The contents of that detailed statement, though, seem to have helped only Swan, who had been convicted of extorting another man by threatening to accuse him of an unnatural assault. At the Privy Council meeting, held in Brighton on November 20 and attended by Russell, Swan's sentence was reduced to transportation for life, in part because doubts had begun to surface over the trustworthiness of his accuser. Of the other individuals sentenced to death at that session of the Central Criminal Court, all were reprieved except for John and James.[82]

The degree to which this decision may or may not have posed a moral crisis for Law cannot be known, but it was a recognized dilemma during the process of criminal law reform. One of the arguments made for not soliciting judges' opinions on criminal law reform in 1819 and at other points was that they might subsequently have to enforce laws that they had publicly argued against. As Anna Clark notes in *Alternative Histories of the Self,* men like Law who served in official capacities often compartmentalized their ethics, carrying out directives that they personally disagreed with as a necessary part of their participation in larger governing structures.[83]

The question of enforcing a law that had been voted down by the Commons but upheld by the Lords had already surfaced in the process of reforming the use of the death penalty. In 1830, in Peel's last year as Home Secretary, radicals in Parliament had forced through a provision that would have ended executions for many forms of forgery. Peel had expressed frustration at this turn of events, as he feared that "after the vote in the House of Commons no verdicts w[ould] be obtained" in forgery trials, even though the measure was rejected by the Lords. As Peel had expected, "after 1830 no offender was put to death in England for this offence."[84] Peel had assumed that the vote in the Commons would affect juries, who, along with judges and the executive, through the Privy Council, had the power to ensure that executions would not occur as the result of a specific criminal act, even if the Lords upheld executions for that crime.

No general rules governed the granting of a royal pardon.[85] The Crown generally followed the recommendation of the judges as the Privy Council reviewed capital sentences, and in most cases little or no information was introduced to these discussions beyond the judges' reports.[86] Because these reviews were not judicial procedures, though, they were not bound by the technical rules of evidence, and the Home Secretary "could obtain knowledge of facts which necessarily remained unknown to the court," such as the opinion of Hensleigh Wedgwood, the magistrate at the Union Hall Police Office quoted at the start of this chapter, who wrote that he firmly believed that the death penalty should no longer apply to sodomy and that the only reason it still did was that no one had yet mustered the moral courage to champion that change.[87] As a general practice, the "royal prerogative of mercy helped to redress the balance between the antiquated criminal law and the modern notions of guilt and punishment then beginning to take shape. As such it performed a valuable and markedly humanizing function."[88]

Those Who Were Not Silent

Multiple petitions came to the Home Office on behalf of James. His wife, Elizabeth Pratt, pleaded her husband's case to Russell, "however suspicious the appearance might have been."[89] Mary Monihan, a family friend of the Pratts for eighteen years, did the same. John Wilson, a baker in the neighborhood, had "known James Pratt and his family for many years" and wrote that James was "respected by all his neighbours and acquaintances."[90] More than fifty residents of Deptford and Greenwich came forward, including ironmongers, coal-sellers, physicians, butchers, a fishmonger, publicans, tailors, grocers, a draper, an upholsterer, and individuals of many other professions.[91] Regardless of whether they believed the charge against their friend and neighbor, they were still willing to stand with him. All these petitions passed though the hands of Russell, who had been Home Secretary for only few months at this point.

William Scott Preston, one of the petitioners on James's behalf, wrote that "as a member of the English Bar I am aware of the integrity of a jury and the mercy of our judges," and he expressed hope that some legitimate grounds might be found for preventing the execution, such as evidence of falsehood in the story of James's accusers.[92] Judges usually granted a reprieve when "it seemed possible that the offence was included in some general act of grace," when there was doubt regarding the prisoner's guilt, or when the judge intended to recommend mercy due to the circumstances of the case, following the doctrine of discretionary selection.[93] When considering why discretionary selection might not have benefited John and James, it is worth reviewing why other individuals in the eighteenth and nineteenth centuries had death sentences for sodomy commuted to sentences of transportation. For those instances where evidence survives, the "aggravating circumstances" that seem to have led to an execution often involved the use of violence or habitual engagements in the act of sodomy. William's room did seem to be the site of regular sexual encounters between men, but the frequency with which John and especially James were involved in other encounters there is less clear. Also, no other examples of habitual sodomy from eighteenth- or early-nineteenth-century capital cases seem so domestic, so private, and so conventionally companionate. Might this fact, also, have given pause to someone already inclined to see sodomy as undeserving of the death penalty? Russell disagreed with executing men for sodomy, but he was also aware of the criticism that some magistrates faced for not more fully enforcing the death penalty and "preferring their own *feelings as men*, to the duty which they owe to the public."[94]

Dickens faced no such strictures. His first collection of essays, *Sketches by "Boz,"* published in 1836, includes a piece titled "A Visit to Newgate."[95] At the end of his description of the room at the prison where most of the men condemned to die were kept, Dickens then turns to a much smaller room, "where three men, the nature of whose offence rendered it necessary to separate them," are being held. He describes John and James:

> One of them, who was imperfectly seen in the dim light, had his back towards us, and was stooping over the fire with his right arm on the mantle-piece, and his head sunk upon it. The other was leaning on the sill of the furthest window. The light fell full upon him, and communicated to his pale, haggard face, and distorted hair, an appearance which, at that distance, was perfectly ghastly. His cheek rested upon his hand; and, with his face a little raised, and his eyes widely staring before him.[96]

When Dickens passes by their room again some time later, John and James "still remained in the positions we have described, and were motionless as statues."

Dickens describes John and James with a hint of sympathy, but his description of the other man in the room complicates matters. This man is a soldier convicted for threatening to accuse a wealthier man of an infamous crime (mentioned in Law's letter, described on page 156. Since his trial, new reasons to believe that the wealthier man had falsely accused the soldier have come to light. The soldier is said to have kept as far away from John and James as the small room would allow and to have put up a front of "courageous indifference; his face was purposely averted towards the window, and he stirred not an inch while we were present."[97] It is in many ways the same stance that John and James take, but it is given a very different meaning.

Dickens would become prominent in the campaign against the death penalty in later years, and scholars have pointed to characters and plotlines in his works that seem to reference same-sex desire and associated nonnormative gendered behaviors.[98] There is no evidence that Dickens worked to end the death penalty for sodomy, but one of his closest friends from the 1830s, Thomas Talfourd, did take a public stand on the matter in 1841, if not earlier. Talfourd had been brought into Parliament in the same 1835 election as Law, and he was known as an impassioned supporter of humanitarian causes. Dickens modeled one of his most virtuous characters after him, and in 1841, Talfourd would join Fitzroy Kelly and Stephen Lushington in sponsoring the final version of the bill that would have ended the death penalty for sodomy.[99]

Like Kelly, Talfourd was also a stranger to many of the masculine privileges of the parliamentary class. He was a playwright and poet, with a strong sense of morality and social justice, which he had expressed in publications starting in his teenage years. He excelled at his grammar school in Reading, but he was prevented by his family's poverty from attending university. Instead, he pursued a legal apprenticeship and was called to the bar in 1821.[100] In this decade and the next, he supported himself with low-level legal work and continued to write poems, plays, pamphlets, and tracts that highlighted humanitarian and philanthropic causes, such as his 1815 plea for the abolition of the pillory. His first great political speech was made in October 1819, to protest the Peterloo massacre.[101]

From the time he entered Parliament in 1835, Talfourd was a radical who supported universal male suffrage "and campaigned ardently for black emancipation."[102] The lawyer and diarist Henry Crabb Robinson "observed with surprised approval . . . in 1836 that this provincial brewer's impoverished son was now dining with Lord Melbourne."[103] Talfourd was responsible for the Infant Custody Act (1839), which was the first check on the power that fathers had over their minor children, giving courts the power to award custody of children under age seven to their mothers in cases of divorce or separation.[104] Talfourd also did much of the work to secure the passage of the Copyright Act of 1842, something that Dickens greatly appreciated, although by this point their friendship had been long established.

In the early 1830s, when Dickens was in his early twenties and writing for the *Morning Chronicle*, Talfourd, who was in his late thirties, was supplementing his income by reporting on legal cases for the *Times* and writing on theater and literature for the *Edinburgh Review*. By the late 1830s, Dickens and Talfourd were close friends. In John Foster's biography of Dickens, he describes the intense final weeks of Dickens's work on *Oliver Twist*, when he was deciding the fates of some of the main characters. Dickens is described as having said, "How well I remember that evening! and our talk of what should be the fate of Charley Bates, on behalf of whom (as indeed for the Dodger too) Talfourd had pleaded as earnestly in mitigation of judgment as ever at the bar for any client he most respected."[105] Did two such close friends, who passionately debated the fate of fictional characters, also discuss the fate of two nonviolent offenders, caught in circumstances that seem likely to have evoked the sympathies of anyone capable of feeling sympathy for such men? A few months before, Talfourd had been called on to vote on whether executions for sodomy should continue. We cannot know Talfourd's vote in 1835, but we do know that he was willing to sponsor legislation to end the death penalty for sodomy in 1841.

Endgame of the 1830s Effort

The *Second Report* from His Majesty's Commissioners on Criminal Laws, completed in June 1836, came far too late to influence the fates of John and James.[106] The report is not as bold as Bentham's *Principles of Morals and Legislation* in how it positions the sodomy law in relation to the rest of the criminal law, but it has features in common with that late-eighteenth-century treatise. The report focuses on two issues: the defense of prisoners by counsel and the examination of punishments, "particularly that of death." Evidence is presented to show that ending capital punishment would not increase the number of criminal offenses overall and that more consistent sentencing would likely decrease that number.[107] When considering what crimes should remain capital offenses, a series of factors, including a jury's willingness to condemn someone to death for the crime, are systematically assessed. As in Bentham's *Principles of Morals and Legislation*, objective criteria are established by which judgments could be rationally made as to which crimes should carry a death sentence. After conducting that assessment, the commissioners write, "We think that the punishment of death ought to be confined to the crime of High Treason (happily one of rare occurrence) and (with perhaps some particular exceptions) to offences which consist in, or are aggravated by, acts of violence to the person, or which tend directly to endanger human life."[108]

The authors do not reject the implications of their logic, but neither do they follow it to its conclusion and recommend ending the death penalty for sodomy. Following the list of the crimes that were to remain capital, the report states that "a nameless offence of great enormity we, at present, exclude from consideration."[109] Thus, ending the death penalty for sodomy is not recommended as it is, however obliquely, by Bentham in one of his most widely read works of legal theory. The authors of the *Second Report* put forward an argument that undercuts the rationale for executions in that area, but they do not defend that position. As noted in Chapter 1, Austin was a member of the Royal Commission when the *Second Report* was written. In his copy of Bentham's *Principles of Morals and Legislation*, the arguments as to why the state should not punish consensual sexual acts between men are among the more heavily underlined.

By education, personality, and connections, Austin was well placed to advance a controversial reform. He was described as a decisive man of action, "'offensive,' 'confident,' 'dictatorial,' 'presumptuous,' and a 'loud talker,'" but also as someone with a passion for the writings of John Locke and a strong desire "to study and elucidate the principles of Law."[110] He chose another ambitious intellectual as his wife; Sarah Austin acted as John's literary agent while also working as a reviewer and translator, with her income vital to their household. Although never wealthy, John Austin became an important and well-connected legal theorist. He and Sarah were neighbors as well as close friends with Bentham and James Mill during the years they were living at their Queen's Square address.

In his *Lectures on Jurisprudence*, Austin acknowledges that he is "prone to follow" Bentham's ideas, and Bentham "probably had a heavier impact on Austin's ethical and legal philosophy than any other person."[111] Austin argued throughout his career that there were no necessary connections between law and morality. Human legal systems, he claimed, could and should be structured in an empirical, value-free way.[112] Largely through Bentham's influence, Austin was appointed professor of jurisprudence at the newly founded London University in 1826, and his personal friendship with Bentham was the closest of any of the original Royal Commission members.

Drawing on the *Second Report* of the Royal Commission, between April and July 1837, Russell passed ten bills for the reform of the criminal law, seven of which were directly concerned with the reduction of capital punishment.[113] Russell had told the commissioners that alterations were needed at once and could not wait for the general work of consolidation, and he argued in Parliament that the "awful punishment of death should not be left long in debate or dispute."[114] These bills established the principle that no offense only against property should carry the death penalty and marked an "abandonment of the idea that crime could only be kept in check by the threat of death even though capital punishment should in practice rarely be inflicted."[115] These bills did not end the death penalty for sodomy, although they did end it for robberies stemming from extortions involving a threat to accuse of sodomy, which had been made a capital crime by Peel in 1823.[116] Russell's bills reduced the number of capital crimes to sixteen, but, as with the *Second Report* of the Royal Commission, his 1837 reforms left the question of the death penalty for sodomy unconsidered.[117]

The Royal Commission, in turn, followed Russell's lead in avoiding the issue of sodomy again in 1839. The commission's mandate was to move through the criminal law systematically, and each successive report after the *First Report* of 1834, which outlines general principles of criminal law reform, and the *Second Report* of 1836, begun at the special request of Russell, would take on another portion of the law. Further reports from the Royal Commission were issued in 1837, 1839, 1840, and 1841, with the *Fourth Report* expected to address the sodomy law.[118] But the report that was presented in March 1839 includes no analysis of the sodomy law. Instead, it notes that "rape and unnatural crimes have been already noticed in the *Second Report* of the Commissioners on Criminal Law, which treated of the punishment of death. We then stated that it was our intention to resume the consideration of the subject; but as, since that Report was made, the mitigation of capital punishments has been maturely considered by Parliament, without leading to any alteration of the law relating to these offences, we for the present think it unnecessary to make any remarks upon them, and merely present the law as it now stands."[119]

This final statement on the sodomy law in the 1830s, made in March 1839, seems a fitting end to the decade. The logic that was used to assess every other portion of the law was not applied to sodomy, for no reason that the Royal Commission was willing to articulate or defend. To say that Russell's not addressing sodomy in his 1837 legislation was a warrant for the Royal Commission's own neglect of the issue ignores the fact that Russell's mandate, as Home Secretary and a politician, was different from theirs, as unelected legal experts brought in to assess the logic and coherence of the legal system. A reform that the commissioners must have known received majority support in the House of Commons three years before, and that seems clearly implied by the logic of the reports that they generated over the better part of a decade, would remain unarticulated by the commissioners. It was a choice that, by the moral and ethical standards of the time, was an indefensible sidestepping of their responsibility.[120]

Conclusion

The 1830s were marked by several such lost opportunities, but that did not mean that the landscape had not changed in relation to the death penalty for sodomy. The Whigs remained in power, after carrying out a torrent of reforms that overturned long-standing precedents. The *Second Report* of the Royal Commission undermines the logic by which the death penalty was prescribed for sodomy, even if the *Fourth Report* fails to follow through on that logic. Sodomy executions had been abolished on the continent for more than a generation, and the evidence from other world regions and from Europe's past, as described in *Don Leon* and *A Free Examination*, showed the anomalous nature of the British sodomy law.[121] Bentham's arguments against the sodomy law had helped inform the debate. Law had proven that a man could propose ending the death penalty for sodomy and win reelection. Charles Baring Wall had shown that a man could be put on trial for propositioning another man and still be returned to Parliament. The 1830s also proved that majorities in the Commons could be secured for ending the death penalty for sodomy, albeit in a way that linked that change to increasing the chances that a man who had had sex with a man might be successfully prosecuted on lesser charges.

The events of 1835 seem to have unfolded without the participation of individuals in the Commons who advocated for the end of the death penalty for sodomy, but that would not be the case in 1840 and 1841. After 1837, most of the reforms that Russell proposed in relation to the death penalty had been achieved. Moving forward on the sodomy law would no longer endanger other reforms, and because it was an area that had not yet been addressed by him, he could do so without revisiting previous decisions (a principle that was important to him and that he reiterated in 1840 and 1841). It is unknown whether his experience facilitating the execution of John and James had an impact on Russell, but they were the last men to be executed for sodomy in Britain. Russell would never again sign off on executions for sodomy after knowing that a majority in the Commons had voted to end the practice. For the remainder of the 1830s, executions were avoided by commuting individual sentences through the process described here, but that was not the permanent solution. In *Bureaucratic Mercy*, Roger Chadwick describes the Royal Prerogative as "a mechanism for accommodating moral change," and he draws on Sir Henry Maine's view, stated in 1861, of "the role of the royal conscience as a flexible link between an evolving social perception of justice and the less elastic progress" of the law.[122] As such, it was a temporary fix, and Russell prepared legislation that would make the change permanent. As shown in the next chapter, though, Russell held his bill in reserve. He was not the individual who was "hardy enough to undertake what might be represented as the defense of such a crime."

The man who was brave enough to do this was Fitzroy Kelly, the son of a single mother who had made herself into a successful novelist to rescue her family from poverty, and the brother of a man who was the "absorbing passion" of Matthew Gregory Lewis's life. The debates that occurred in 1840 and 1841 in relation to the bill to end the death penalty for sodomy that Kelly proposed were still conducted in veiled and vague language, but they were far more extensive than any other debates related to sex between men in the British Parliament in the nineteenth century. The bill Kelly proposed bundled together several reforms, but the importance of the sodomy reform became clear as the bill worked its way through the legislative process. Lushington and eventually Talfourd would stand with Kelly, cosponsoring the bill, but Kelly's actions time and again kept the issue on the agenda. Without private papers to draw on, his motivations for specific actions cannot be known, but his public actions on the floor of the Commons are documented well enough to answer many questions about his reasoning, determination, and motivations. The next chapter tells that story for the first time.

7

The Parliamentary Debates

July 1840 to June 1841

The account that follows is drawn primarily from the parliamentary debates and focuses on an eleven-month period during which Fitzroy Kelly led the efforts to pass his Punishment of Death Bill. These records demonstrate ways in which sex between men was debated in the British Parliament in the mid-nineteenth century and how that discussion was interlaced with consideration of other issues. The word "sodomy" appears only at the end of the recorded debates, in the last exchanges before the final vote in the House of Lords. But it had been the topic of conversation over the previous eleven months, even as the members of Parliament and those recording their discussions made numerous efforts to conceal this.[1] By looking at all the clauses of Fitzroy Kelly and Stephen Lushington's bill and the debates that they elicited, it is possible to understand how the issue was framed to garner votes for the reform.

No other work on the abolition of the death penalty in Britain examines these debates. Brian Block and John Hostettler's *Hanging in the Balance* describes them in a single sentence, arguing that "like [Robert] Peel before him, [John] Russell had gone as far as he felt the majority in the country wanted, and he continued to oppose Bills introduced later by Fitzroy Kelly and others for abolition in regard to serious offences against the person, although he conceded it for rape at the suggestion of the judges."[2] Close attention to the debates, the votes, and the different iterations of the bill, though, indicates that Lord Melbourne's government and Kelly were in agreement over ending the death penalty for sodomy, even as the government worked to retain the death penalty in other areas where it still applied.[3]

Stephen Lushington, Capital Punishment, and Sodomy

Lushington had long supported abolishing capital punishment, using arguments against state-supported violence and cruelty that paralleled his arguments for the abolition of slavery, but this attitude does not seem sufficient to explain his cosponsorship of the 1840–1841 Punishment of Death Bill.[4] As the previous chapters have demonstrated, sodomy was treated as an exception to most rules. In the work of the Criminal Law Commission, it disrupted the logic otherwise applied, and, as Jeremy Bentham observed, men were held suspect if they did not reject the concept with anger and indignation.[5] As the following examination of the 1840–1841 Punishment of Death Bill demonstrates, the sodomy and rape provisions were its main and most controversial aspects, with the former significantly more controversial than the latter. Even William Ewart, the most prominent campaigner against capital punishment at the time, had declined to join Kelly in presenting the bill. Yet Lushington had agreed. Not only did Lushington have a family tie to Kelly through Matthew Gregory Lewis; he was also already publicly associated with what some considered to be the questionable use of a sodomy allegation.

Lushington had been introduced to Anne Isabella "Annabella" Noel Byron after she and her parents had sought legal advice from others regarding her failing marriage to Lord Byron. Long before her marriage, Annabella had already built a reputation for outreach to her local community, following the example of her father, a baronet, who was known for his strenuous efforts on behalf of local charities. She was also well educated, having studied mathematics, astronomy, and magnetism, among other subjects, with a Cambridge tutor. During her social debut in the 1810 season, she had attracted the interests of several suitors, including William Bankes and Lord Byron, perhaps being drawn in turn to these unconventional men as ones who would be more receptive to her intellectual pursuits and community involvement. She refused Byron's first proposal of marriage in 1812, the year he published the work that made him famous, but accepted a renewed offer two years later.[6]

The marriage deteriorated quickly, and the couple lived together for only slightly more than a year. In that time, Annabella gave birth to the couple's only child. Over the course of that year, Byron's sister Augusta came to stay with them, and Augusta and Annabella became deeply concerned about By-

Figure 7.1 *Stephen Lushington*, by and published by William Walker; after Sir William John Newton, mezzotint, published 1834. (© National Portrait Gallery, London.)

ron's heavy alcohol consumption and signs of mental instability, which included threats directed against Annabella. On January 15, 1815, Annabella took her newborn daughter to visit her parents and never returned.

Lushington drafted the first letter that Byron received from his father-in-law, asking him to separate from Annabella. Any such separation, though, would have given custody of their infant daughter, Ada, to Byron if he so requested it. This request was made more than two decades before Thomas Talfourd would propose the 1839 Infant Custody Act, which would change this law and allow courts to grant custody of children under seven years of age to mothers in cases of separation or divorce. Talfourd, perhaps coincidentally, joined the sponsorship, along with Lushington and Kelly, of the 1841 version of the bill to end the death penalty for sodomy. But in 1815, however, Annabella had no legal right to custody of Ada. A sodomy accusation, however, could change that.

Three main charges circulated publicly and privately regarding Byron in the early months of 1816: that he had committed sodomy with men, that he had committed incest with his sister, and that he had committed sodomy with his wife. John Cam Hobhouse recorded in his diary that he had heard rumors "in the streets," spread by Lady Caroline Lamb, that accused Byron of sodomy with men. Byron had years before confessed to her some of his sexual affairs with men, occurring in Britain and in the Eastern Mediterranean. Fiona MacCarthy demonstrates how fear of losing her child sparked Annabella's discussions with Lushington of incest between Byron and Augusta and the "suggestion of marital sodomy."⁷ While, again according to MacCarthy, the "possibility of anal intercourse between Byron and his wife was to paralyse some of Byron's best-known twentieth century biographers," such as Harold Nicolson and Doris Langley Moore, MacCarthy finds the evidence for it compelling. She notes that in his copy of Thomas Moore's biography of Byron, "Hobhouse penciled in the margin: 'Something of this sort certainly, as Lord Holland told me, he tried to _____ her.'"⁸ Any one of these three accusations might have been enough to destroy Byron's reputation. Having all three in circulation, publicly and privately, was too much to face, and on April 25, 1816, just over three months since Annabella left home with their newborn daughter, Byron fled England, never to return.

The marriage between Annabella and Byron might have failed of its own accord, due either to the behavior of Byron or the irreconcilable differences between the spouses, but whether that would have happened without outside intervention will never be known. Byron wished to reconcile with Annabella and, as might be expected, had a much more benign understanding of how he had treated her. Annabella has been described as conflicted over the separation; she did not wish to leave her husband if he were actually sick, which for her would constitute abandonment of him on her part. Annabella was told by several individuals not to speak personally with Byron; they feared that she might reconcile with him if she did.⁹ Also contributing to the permanence of the separation was Lushington, whom MacCarthy characterizes as an "ambitious young barrister whose cool professional zeal in pursuing the case as the Noels' chief legal adviser was to have the effect of ruling out all prospect of reconciliation between Byron and his wife."¹⁰

Annabella remained grateful to Lushington for the rest of her life, but others had a far more negative view of his interventions in the case. The authors of "Leon to Annabella" and *Don Leon* excoriate Lushington for prying into the private matters between a husband and wife. A sodomy accusation may have been an effective tool in keeping Annabella and Ada together, but the consequences—the exile and early death of the greatest poet of his generation—were significant. Were they significant enough to weigh on Lushington's mind in later years? It is remarkable that the man who made the most significant use of the sodomy law in the case of an opposite-sex couple in the early nineteenth century also became one of the cosponsors of the most important bill up to that point to reduce the penalty for sodomy.

Debating the 1840 Bill

The formidable political alliance of Kelly and Lushington faced government resistance to their 1840 bill, which would have had the effect of ending
capital punishment in all cases except treason and murder. The Attorney
General, John Campbell, attempted to get Kelly to withdraw the measure,
on the grounds that the acts passed in 1837 had the effect of eliminating
the death penalty for all but fourteen crimes and had only fully come into
effect in 1839. The Attorney General believed that enough time should be
allowed to see the impact of the previous legislation before further reforms
were attempted. He also objected to the fact that Kelly and Lushington's
legislation (described in the following paragraphs) did not treat each capital
crime separately but rather "lumped them together, and said that they should
be punished by transportation for life, or for any term not less than seven
years, or by imprisonment in England for five years, with or without hard
labour."[11] He noted that doing this would give a large degree of sentencing
discretion to judges and that Kelly and Lushington could not have consulted
the judges on this, as the judges were then out on the circuit.

At this point, the Attorney General ventured an explanation for the strange
way in which Kelly and Lushington's legislation was framed. In the context of
inquiring about the opinions of the judges, the Attorney General asked:

> Was it not desirable that their opinions should at least be known with
> respect to a certain offence which he could only glance at? His hon.
> and learned Friend would know what he meant.[12]

And then, in a rare occurrence when the sodomy law was under discussion
in the British Parliament, the Attorney General spelled out in more detail
what he meant:

> In a bill which had passed through the House of Commons, a clause
> was introduced to take away the punishment of death for those of-
> fences, but in the House of Lords that clause was struck out upon the
> suggestion, he believed, of a noble and learned judge. Was his hon.
> and learned Friend aware that that objection had since been removed
> in that quarter, and did he think it possible that such a bill as this
> could pass without discussion in the other House?[13]

This is almost certainly a reference to Charles Law's 1835 amendment, discussed in the previous chapter. But this time, unlike in 1835, individuals

Figure 7.2 *Sir Fitzroy Edward Kelly*, by Sydney Marks, after A. Lucas, mezzotint, (1845–1852). (© National Portrait Gallery, London.)

were willing to defend the clause in debate, and those debates were recorded in *Hansard* and reported to a lesser extent in some newspapers. Kelly, for his part, gave no ground and defended his actions against the Attorney General's objections, because, as he said, "He should not act as his strong sense of duty prompted him, if he acceded upon that occasion to the proposition of his hon. and learned Friend."[14]

In responding to the Attorney General's points, Kelly observed that there was no more discretion given to judges in his bill than in the 1837 legislation that the government itself had written. He specifically referenced the support that he was receiving from Ewart, Parliament's most prominent campaigner for the abolition of the death penalty, and Lushington, and said that he had asked them to take the lead on this measure before doing so himself. He said that he had asked the government repeatedly whether they planned to put forward such a measure and only did so himself upon learning that they did not, despite the fact that he "understood, too, that her Majesty's Government had no objection to the principles of the bill," including the sodomy provision. Finally, Kelly said, in relation to judges, that he had had "common conversation" with them on this matter and "could venture to say, that if this bill passed with the sanction of the Legislature, the judges as a body would be found among the last of her Majesty's subjects to complain of it."[15]

Russell then joined the debate. While Russell's tenure as Home Secretary had ended in August 1839, he continued to serve in the government as Secretary of State for War and the Colonies and remained the primary representative for the Melbourne Ministry in the Commons. He agreed with the Attorney General that it would be better for the bill to not go forward that session, for the reasons that the Attorney General had already given. He said that because Kelly had already determined that capital punishment should be abolished in all cases, then it was easy for Kelly to dismiss the government's desire to proceed more slowly. Nevertheless, Russell stated, because Kelly "wished to persist in going into Committee, he certainly should not oppose the Speaker's leaving the chair."[16] This being the case, the Commons moved into committee and began debating the merits of the individual clauses of the bill.

To evaluate the government's stance on the sodomy provision, it is necessary to be familiar with other significant aspects of the bill.

The differences between the supporters of Kelly and Lushington and the supporters of Russell and the government came out in the first debate and division. The issue was whether the death penalty should be preserved for individuals who set fire to Royal Navy ships. For Kelly, this was a crime against property alone, and that settled the matter. For Russell and his supporters, the crime was close enough to treason, and rare enough in practice, that the death penalty could remain in place. Russell allowed that he had previously believed that the death penalty should not apply in this instance, but he had since been convinced by the arguments of others. Individuals spoke on both sides of the issue, but the government lost, with the final vote forty-eight to thirty.[17]

The next division, and the only other held in that committee session, was over the provision to end the death penalty for rape and sodomy. Almost all the discussion focused on the rape provision and whether what were described as extremely aggravated cases warranted execution. As before, the government supporters, led by Russell, argued against Kelly, Ewart, and their supporters. Among the issues discussed were whether retaining the death penalty for rape made it more likely that a female victim would be murdered (to eliminate the witness to the crime), the degree to which rape could be proven, and the question of false accusations made by a woman "for the mere purpose of forcing a marriage."[18]

One of the individuals participating in the debate, though, seems to have spoken about the sodomy provision. The record in *Hansard* shows the committee working through the clauses of the bill in order, with this particular debate under the heading of "On the seventh paragraph of the preamble referring to the crime of rape." In the printed bill itself, though, the seventh paragraph of the preamble is on the rape *and sodomy* provision of the legislation, confirming that *Hansard* might have elided the mention of sodomy even when compiling an official record.[19] For this reason, it seems worth pausing over this statement:

> Mr. Hobhouse hoped the clause would be allowed to stand without any alteration. Charges of this nature *were often preferred from conspiracy.* He objected to keeping the punishment of death for this offence on our statute-book, when the punishment was virtually repealed; for in every instance where persons had been found guilty of this offence the punishment had been commuted; and this commutation of the punishment was calculated upon by the criminals as much as if there were no capital punishment for the offence.[20]

This statement is emblematic of the ways in which sodomy sometimes seems to have been the topic under discussion, even when it cannot be proven. Conspiracy was more often associated with charges of sodomy than with charges of rape. Thomas Benjamin Hobhouse had two brothers who have figured in previous chapters. One of his brothers, John Cam Hobhouse, had close friends and acquaintances who faced accusations related to sex between men. John Cam Hobhouse's papers are also one of the best sources for evidence of the same-sex desires of Byron, Bankes, and others.[21] Thomas's other brother, Henry Hobhouse, had been asked by Peel in 1825 to help with the secret negotiations between Peel and Richard Heber after Heber had been accused of sexual advances toward the son of a social equal. The meaning of Thomas's statement remains enigmatic, although his support for the reform was not. When it came to the vote, Thomas Hobhouse voted to retain the rape and sodomy provisions of Kelly and Lushington's bill.

Also voting with Lushington and Kelly was Charles Baring Wall. In a session during which six out of seven members were absent, in what was later described as "a very thin House," the only sitting member to have been tried for attempting sex with another man was present.[22] Fifty Members of Parliament (MPs) voted to keep the clause in the bill, while only twenty-five voted against; the bill would move out of committee with the clause intact. However, just before the end of the debate, one man asked Kelly how he could be certain of success. The man strongly suggested that Kelly incorporate some of the changes that Russell had suggested, because "he believed that it would be acknowledged by all acquainted with the other House of Parliament, that in its present state it would not pass that House."[23]

Kelly reiterated his belief that "the punishment of death should be taken away in all cases except high treason and murder." As to the opinion of the House of Lords, which had stripped the clause that would have ended the death penalty for sodomy and rape from an earlier bill, he had reason to be confident. As Fox Maule stated when the bill came up for its third reading, it "was so ingeniously drawn, as to make it necessary either to accept it wholly, or reject it wholly," with the preamble of the bill containing a list of all the crimes to be changed, followed by a clause that gave the new penalty for everything in the preamble.[24] Kelly "firmly believed that if the sanction of the House [of Commons] should be given to the bill, it would not meet with any serious opposition in the other House."[25]

When the report on the bill was brought up in preparation for its third and final reading in the Commons, the Attorney General objected that "many offences of more or less magnitude were included in the same category," bundled together simply because they had all, until now, been punished by death. He argued that this approach was not "that mature and deliberate manner in which such a subject ought to be dealt with."[26] Russell then gave a speech explaining why he wanted the measure put off for at least three months. Because of the systematic way in which he discussed Kelly and Lushington's "Abolition Bill" (as he called it), it is possible to identify his position on each of its clauses. Although Russell did not explicitly say when he was addressing the sodomy provision of the bill, a simple process of reading his statements along with the clauses of the bill itself can determine which of his comments referenced that provision.[27]

Russell first made clear that anything covered by the 1837 legislation should not be revisited so soon. Those bills, it was said, were based "upon the principle that it was not desirable to affix the punishment of death to minor offences against the person, but that it was just and proper to retain it for serious offences against the person." The latter included attempts at murder, robberies committed with blows and violence, burglary accompanied by violence to persons, setting fire to a house in which persons were at the time, or setting fire to ships, which might destroy life.[28] Of the twelve clauses of Kelly and Lushington's bill, the final five did not rise to this level, according to Russell, and thus were opposed by the government.

Russell also addressed the issue of rape. He expressed a desire to preserve the death penalty for the most aggravated cases of rape, including cases where two or more men assaulted a woman. He left open the possibility that the government might eventually support the clause written by Kelly and Lushington related to rape but suggested that the trial returns must be studied first to see how many such extreme cases had occurred and what their judicial outcomes had been.

And then Russell made a statement about what the government did not object to in the bill. According to *Hansard*:

> He thought that with regard to offences against property, upon the point to which he had alluded, the filing of the dock-yards, *and perhaps with respect to some other offences*, there might be an alteration of the law in the approaching Session; but he could not say that for attempts at murder, or for violence against the person.[29]

The first six clauses of the bill were such offenses against property, and so the only offense left unaddressed, which might be what was meant by "some other offences," was sodomy. As discussed in the previous chapter, revisions to the sodomy law had been left out of Russell's 1837 legislation, and therefore altering it in 1840 would have been consistent with his desire not to revisit any law altered in 1837. This speech also predicted the government's voting pattern in 1841: the government would vote for the first six clauses as they appeared in the redrafted 1841 legislation, and, as discussed later in this chapter, its representatives would also vote to end the death penalty for sodomy and rape on May 3, 1841. Kelly later referred to this statement and others by Russell, suggesting that he intended to put forward a government bill, and Kelly offered to withdraw his and Lushington's bill if Russell proposed one of his own.[30] The government did not support Kelly and Lushington's 1840 bill, but it was not the sodomy provision that the government rejected. On May 3, 1841, in fact, the government would reshape the Punishment of Death Bill, making the end of the death penalty for sodomy, arguably, its most prominent feature.

If Russell and Kelly as well as their respective supporters were speaking circumspectly, it was in part because of the opinions held by such men as Henry Vane, the Earl of Darlington.[31] In all the 1840 debates in the Commons on the Punishment of Death Bill, Darlington alone launched into a vitriolic denunciation of sex between men. On July 29, 1840, he said:

> There was another horrid crime which was revolting to the general feelings of mankind. We had had, certainly, but very few instances of it, and God forbid that it should ever become less rare in this country. However, we had had instances of persons being fully convicted of this crime, and executed for it, and would any Member now get up in his place and say that those persons had not been properly executed.[32]

Darlington ended his speech by arguing that Kelly, Lushington, and their supporters "were influenced by a sentiment of false humanity" and that if their measure passed, "so far from being a public benefit, it would be found fraught with infinite mischief."[33]

When Joseph Hume spoke next, he did not dispute Darlington's central premise, as the authors of *Don Leon* might have hoped. Instead, he asked whether "that sacrifice of life [would] prevent the crime and protect society? Did it guard against the evil they now sought to avoid?" He argued that the same principles that invalidated the use of the death penalty in general should be extended to sodomy cases. Hume ended his statement by saying that "the sacrifice of a single life by the law ought not to be sanctioned unless there was a prospect of doing good to society."[34] It was not much, but it was more public support than was usually given for the position articulated in *Don Leon*.

Kelly's final statements on the 1840 bill reiterated many of his previous positions while also reinforcing the idea that the issue of rape and the protection of women were central to the debate. He lamented that those opposed to his bill "seemed to rest upon a few extreme examples," and he offered statistical evidence that in all cases for which data were available, conviction rates increased when the death penalty was removed, and often the number of reported instances of that type of crime dropped. Severe punishments were still applied to the crimes for which the death penalty would be abolished, Kelly argued, and "in asking them to pass this bill, he only asked them to make a law according to a practice which had for some time prevailed," for in many of the instances covered by Kelly and Lushington's bill, death sentences had been commuted to lesser penalties in recent years. Kelly ended with the argument that the principles of the bill "had obtained the support of the majority of the country."[35]

Lushington also offered further arguments regarding the rape provisions of the bill, including why ending the death penalty for rape would protect women rather than lessen their security. Lushington was in command of a great deal of statistical information, using it to show that the proportion of convictions for rape fluctuated between 5 and 11 percent when the death penalty was regularly applied in such cases, with the conviction rate rising to 23 percent after the de facto end of the death penalty for rape in 1834.[36] Thus, Lushington argued, ending the death penalty was about supporting the victims of crime and not the criminals. Drawing his speech to a close, Lushington added that "whatever might be the fate of this bill let . . . no hon. Gentleman get up to waste the time of the House by taunting the advocates of this bill with false humanity."[37] Lushington's speech thus offered strong arguments about how his and Kelly's bill would enhance the protection of women, but he was willing to link those greater protections for women to the willingness of the Commons to also end the death penalty for sodomy.

When the final vote on the 1840 version of the bill came, though, Kelly, Lushington, Ewart, and Hume were on the losing side. Forty-seven individuals voted with them, including the Conservative Frederick William Robert Castlereagh, the nephew of the previous Viscount Castlereagh, while seventy-six voted with Russell and the government, including Peel.[38] The bill was then put off for three months, and over that time Kelly and Lushington reworked it, acquiescing to the pressure to allow for voting on the crimes individually by placing them into separate clauses. The subsequent votes in 1841 would give a further indication, although still not the clearest offered in the 1841 session, that Russell and the government supported the end of the death penalty for rape and sodomy.

The Kelly–Lushington–Talfourd Bill of 1841

Kelly introduced his and Lushington's revised bill to the Commons on February 9, 1841, with Talfourd now also listed as a sponsor of the legislation. Kelly said in a speech that the previous bill "had been read a first and second time, passed through a committee, and only thrown out upon the third reading by a very small majority."[39] Based on this experience, he felt confident in reintroducing a very similar measure in this session. The greatest difference in the legislation was that his current bill placed each of the separate offenses in a different clause, so that each could be debated, and perhaps altered, separately. This change, Kelly argued, would give the committee reviewing the bill greater scope to set the secondary punishments for each offense. He added that if the government wished to put its own bill forward, to accomplish the same ends, "which the enlightened spirit of the age imperiously and unanimously called for," he would at once withdraw his version.[40]

A few weeks later, when the bill came up again, a curious thing occurred: Russell gave his longest speech associated with the 1841 Punishment of Death Bill, systematically addressing each of its provisions.[41] Russell explained his thoughts on each, starting with why he supported the elimination of the death penalty for embezzlement and forgery, and next giving the reasons why he did not support the end of the death penalty for arson in the Royal Dockyards. The next provision he addressed was the one on rape and sodomy, and while reviewing arguments for eliminating the death penalty for rape, he continued without always naming the provision to which he was referring, but with comments that mirrored arguments previously articulated by Bentham and others for ending the death penalty for sodomy.[42] Russell stated:

> They could not make a criminal law, and they did not profess to make one, that could reach every moral offence, according to the degree of its moral guilt, and punish it in proportion to its enormity. They could not assume to themselves the Divine power, and affix to every moral crime the penalty that ought to be attached to it. This was beyond their power; but if it were not, in this instance, they would find that there were other offences to which they could not attach such penalties as would be adequate for the offences that had been perpetrated. . . . [I]t was because the offence was beyond the law and above the law. It was an offence that could only find its punishment in the feelings of mankind, its punishment must be in the conscience of the offender—its punishment was in the retribution of an eternity; but they, as men, could not attempt to assign to it its adequate punishment.[43]

This is how a cabinet minister and spokesman for the government in the early 1840s could publicly argue against the death penalty for sodomy. He did not name the crime directly, and he did not draw on the more positive arguments found in *Don Leon* and "Leon to Annabella." Instead, he argued that some issues were outside the scope of the law, in keeping with the arguments of Bentham, as published in the 1780s in one of his most widely read works on legal reform.[44] While Bentham concluded that the state should not regulate sex between men at all, Russell was not willing to go that far. Russell thought that "the punishment of death ought to be retained for certain great offences," but sodomy was not such an offense for him, even if it still warranted ten years' imprisonment.[45]

While there is ambiguity associated with Russell's meaning in the quoted passage above, we know Russell's attitude on the death penalty for sodomy with some certainty because even though Kelly, Lushington, and Talfourd's bill continued to be the focus of parliamentary debate, Russell separately drafted three bills that would have ended the death penalty in those three areas where he agreed with these men. One of Russell's three bills had as its sole purpose the elimination of the death penalty for sodomy and rape.[46] Russell's bill would never be debated in the Parliament—it was withdrawn by the Attorney General after its first reading in the Commons—but it does provide unambiguous evidence that Russell, like Lushington and Kelly, believed that it was time to end the death penalty for sodomy and rape.[47]

Outside Parliament

By this point, newspapers had covered the debates regarding the Punishment of Death Bill, but most were vague regarding the effect that the legislation would have had on the sodomy law. On July 9, 1840, the *Morning Chronicle* printed a list of the clauses in the bill but did not indicate that sodomy was also covered in the clause addressing rape.[48] The most important parliamentary debates on the Punishment of Death Bill in 1840 took place on July 15 and July 29 and were covered by many newspapers in reports that extended over multiple columns. Russell's attempt on July 15 to retain the death penalty for aggravated cases of rape was recounted in many of those reports, drawing attention to a clause that would have ended the death penalty for rape and "certain other crimes against the person."[49] Many reports described Lushington and Hobhouse as strongly urging the Commons to keep the clause without alteration, but without any mention of the sodomy provision.[50] Darlington's July 29 speech, quoted on page 174, was given only a truncated paraphrasing in the *Times*. It reported that Darlington said that he "could not allow that [for] attempts to murder . . . all cases of rape, *and other crimes revolting to human nature*, the power should be wholly taken away from the judges to pronounce, and the Secretary of State to inflict, the capital punishment."[51] At least until reports would emerge of the debate in the Lords in July 1841, when more clear and explicit language would be used in Parliament and in the press, it would take a careful reader, or one with another source of information, to understand that Kelly and Lushington's bill would eliminate the death penalty for sodomy.

One of these newspaper stories, describing the efforts of Kelly and Lushington up to the second week of February 1841, was saved by William Beckford in his newspaper-clippings collection.[52] The report gave a brief history of what had happened with the Punishment of Death Bill in 1840 and recounted some of Kelly's and Ewart's arguments in favor of the measure. The saved story also recorded that "Lord J. Russell was favourable to the abolition of the punishment of death in certain cases" and would not block the introduction of the bill, although he did not approve of its elimination in all cases. As with so much other evidence, though, there is ambiguity in this link between Beckford and the Punishment of Death Bill. Unlike many of the other Beckford clippings, which contained just one article, this clipping contained several stories from the page, with no indication of which article he was primarily interested in. It is a piece of evidence that is suggestive but not conclusive.

An event that seems similarly suggestive involved three men connected to Parliament and mentioned in *Don Leon*. Charles Baring Wall surprised at least one of his dinner party guests, John Cam Hobhouse, in April 1841 by also inviting William Bankes to attend.[53] Many friends had dropped Bankes after his 1833 arrest for soliciting sex from a man, although the Duke of Wellington had continued to correspond with him and extend invitations to him. Wellington had written within several months of Bankes's trial that "if I had a party of persons . . . with whom [Bankes] had been on terms of intimacy I should ask him to meet them. If Bankes is wise, however, he will not expose himself to the world for some time. He might be formally or coldly received by some, which would make a lasting impression upon him. . . . A little patience will set everything right."[54] Perhaps Wellington was right, but for Hobhouse, who had been close friends with Byron and his Cambridge circle, the invitation extended by Wall to Bankes in April 1841, as Kelly, Lushington, and Talfourd's bill was working its way through the Commons, was still surprising.

Reshaping the Bill: May 3, 1841

After passing its second reading in the Commons without incident, the 1841 Punishment of Death Bill moved to committee, where the individual clauses of the proposed legislation could be debated. Unlike the "very thin House" of the 1840 committee votes, the 1841 divisions drew more than 230 MPs.[55] Of the six individual clauses that would eliminate the use of capital punishment, four, including the one concerning sodomy and rape, were debated and voted on separately, with the division lists preserved for each of those four votes. Russell spoke first in three of the four debates, and he was in the majority in all four divisions, to the frustration of Kelly, who by the end of the night thought the government was purposely trying to undermine his efforts.[56]

The greatest participation, with 232 MPs voting, concerned the clause that would have ended the death penalty for setting fire to royal ships or dockyards. As he had in 1840, Russell argued to retain the death penalty in this case, because even though it was a crime against property alone, it was a crime that might compromise national security.[57] Against this tack, the argument was made that if a harsher punishment were to be handed out for a crime against property, it ought to be "for those who destroyed the property of poor and helpless individuals," while another added that capital punishments were "generally regarded as too severe, according to the calculations of men of humanity, and this feeling was now becoming universal with the public."[58] When the vote came, Russell prevailed in retaining the death penalty in this area, although with only 122 votes in favor of his position, and 110 against.[59]

The next debate was on the fourth clause, which would have ended the death penalty for rape and sodomy. Sir Charles Douglas began by attempting to add a provision that would have preserved the death penalty for rape if the victim were under ten years old or if two or more individuals had perpetrated the rape.[60] The vote, however, did not address these issues, because Capt. Frederick Polhill changed the subject. Polhill, a Conservative, a former captain in the King's Dragoons Guards, and a successful playwright, declared that he "was altogether opposed to the clause" itself and that "he advised his hon. Friend to withdraw his amendment, [related to the rape provision] and the question could be taken on the clause itself."[61] This suggestion was agreed to, the amendment was then withdrawn, and the division was held as to whether to keep the clause that would have eliminated the death penalty in cases of rape and sodomy.[62] There could have been little confusion about what was being decided, with 123 members voting to keep the clause and only 61 voting against doing so.

The final two clauses to be debated covered executions for certain attempts to murder. It was argued by Kelly's supporters that the death penalty made juries less likely to convict and that "sacred precepts as strongly condemned the executioner as the murderer."[63] One supporter emphasized that he "was actuated by no false philanthropy—but he was convinced that, by making men accustomed to blood, they also made them more regardless of shedding it; they made them brutes."[64] Russell, in turn, argued against these measures by stating that his 1837 legislation had already considered one of these issues and that the statistical evidence offered in relation to the other could not be taken as definitive proof "that the fear of death was not likely to deter men from the commission of crime." When votes were taken on these measures, they both went Russell's way.

The bill that moved forward contained only three clauses that would have eliminated the death penalty. The first would have repealed it for five crimes related to embezzlement and forgery. The second would have ended it for the destruction of churches or other property in the course of a riot. The third would have ended it for rape and sodomy, replacing it with a sentence of transportation for life. In the Lords, where the final debates on this bill would shortly take place, the most controversial aspect of the bill was the proposed elimination of the death penalty for sodomy—and yet the clause that did this was the only one that united Kelly's principal supporters with Russell's in the votes taken on May 3.[65] There was more bipartisan consensus over ending the death penalty for rape and sodomy than on any other issue debated that night.

All the MPs voting on the fourth clause that night knew that they were voting to lessen the punishment for sodomy, and they did so by a margin of two to one, the largest majority for any of the votes taken that night.[66] Given the widely held view at the time and since any association with sex between men would taint a man's reputation, it is worth considering what can be said about the 123 men as a group who were willing to be associated in the public record with this reform.

Members of Parliament Voting to End the Death Penalty for Sodomy

Data collected from official parliamentary sources show few significant differences between those who voted for and against the end of the death penalty for sodomy.[67] In absolute and proportional terms, more Liberals than Conservatives voted for the reform, but in only one other area does there seem to have been a significant divergence between those who favored ending the death penalty for rape and sodomy and those who were against the proposal.

Eighty-six Liberals voted to end the death penalty for rape and sodomy, along with eleven Conservatives and twenty-six other individuals who did not list party affiliations. They included sixteen barristers or advocates, eleven company directors, nine landowners, eight men supported by private income, seven bankers, four writers or journalists, four army officers, one naval officer, one cotton spinner, one newspaper proprietor, and one colonial administrator. Daniel O'Connell was one of the members who voted along with Russell for the abolition of the death penalty for sodomy. Wall was not present for this vote.

The group voting against the elimination of the death penalty for sodomy included twenty-eight Conservatives, seventeen Liberals, and sixteen other individuals who did not give party affiliations. They included ten landowners, eight army officers, six barristers or advocates, six company directors, five men with private income, three naval officers, two private secretaries, one civil servant, and one judicial officer. Peel and Gladstone voted to retain the death penalty for rape and sodomy.

The average age of those voting for or against the reform was almost exactly the same: 48.9 versus 48.7. The educational background was listed for fifty-nine of those voting for the reform and thirty-three of those voting against it, and there did not seem to be significant differences here, either. Of those voting for the reform, fourteen went to Oxford, five went to Cambridge, and twenty-three had received "private tuition." Of those voting against the reform, ten went to Oxford, four went to Cambridge, and eleven listed "private tuition."

The more pronounced difference between those who voted for or against the reform was their participation in government. Six of the individuals voting against the reform held a total of fifty-four parliamentary offices over the course of their careers. Twenty-nine of these parliamentary positions, though, were held by one man, Gladstone, with another eleven held by Peel. Together, Gladstone and Peel accounted for more than two-thirds of all the parliamentary offices held by those voting against the reform. By contrast, eighteen such individuals voted to end the death penalty for sodomy, and between them they held a total of ninety-two parliamentary offices during their careers. While twenty of these positions were held by Russell, and ten by Sir George Grey, together they make up less than one-third of the total.

This last comparison strongly implies that those men most politically attuned to the demands of government, and most capable of meeting those demands, disproportionately favored ending the death penalty for rape and sodomy. This is reminiscent of Linda Colley's finding that Catholic Emancipation was supported by the most capable MPs.[68] As Colley demonstrates, many MPs believed that discrimination against Catholics was an outdated and unsupportable prejudice, but they were unwilling to face the popular anger that most believed would accompany any attempt to change the law. As shown in Chapter 5, at least some in the 1820s saw a connection between Catholic Emancipation and ending state punishment for sex between men. A parliamentary majority for ending the death penalty for sodomy was achieved in the Commons in 1841, but the results were different when the debate shifted to the Lords.

The Final Debate in the House of Lords

There was significant discussion of the elimination of the death penalty for sodomy in the House of Lords, which was reported in the newspapers. As in the Commons, explicit terminology was often avoided; it was recorded, for instance, that "the Earl of Winchilsea intimated, that it was his intention to propose an amendment, by striking out the two last lines of clause 3, and if the amendment was rejected, he should propose, that the third clause be struck out altogether."[69] The *Times* made it clear that "this part of the bill refers to crimen non nominandum inter Christianos." Also in the *Times* was Winchilsea's assertion that the "crime to which the words he wished to have omitted referred ought never to have been included in the bill, and he was of the opinion that persons convicted of such a heinous offence ought not to be exempted from just punishment."[70] It was the first time in the months-long process that it was suggested that the fates of the rape and sodomy provisions should be separated, and this proposal was made clear to the public as well as debated in Parliament.

In support of Winchilsea's position, the Earl of Wicklow argued that "this bill had been carried this Session by the House of Commons; but it had been rejected Session after Session in former years." He went on to argue that the bill had only passed in "the very last days of the Session, when the House was hurrying to terminate its business, and when it could not give due consideration to any subject of importance, much less to one of such vast magnitude as this."[71] He stated that if the Lords passed this law, "they would lower themselves in public opinion; for as the organ of the public voice, they would sanction what the people of this country would never confirm—that sodomy and rape were not crimes of so heinous a character as to deserve death."[72]

In defense of the bill as it was written, the Earl of Radnor made arguments that aligned with Russell's statements, Bentham's work, and the reports of the Royal Commission on Criminal Law. Radnor argued that "the question was not what crimes were worthy of death, but what were the punishments which would be effectual in repressing crime." This was supplemented by the argument that punishments must have a logical consistency, which the bill in its present form maintained.

The debate resumed the next day with the third reading of the bill. Winchilsea argued that sodomy ought to carry "the heaviest punishment" and that "the crime to which the first part of the clause related [sodomy], was one which he thought ought especially to remain a subject for capital punishment. He implored their Lordships not to withdraw the punishment of death from a crime so utterly abhorrent to the feelings of human nature." The *Morning Chronicle* and other newspapers reported this argument along with Winchilsea's statement that "the abolition of the punishment of death in such cases would shock the moral and religious feelings of the community."[73] He then moved "that all the words of the 3rd clause from the word 'that' in the fifth line to the word 'felon' in the seventh line be omitted."[74]

The Home Secretary, the Marquess of Normanby, responded by saying that he "was glad that the noble Earl had proposed his amendment with so much brevity, because one of the worst things their Lordships could do was to enter into a discussion on an amendment of this kind."[75] If a powerful argument might have been able to sway the Lords and preserve the intent of Kelly, Lushington, and Talfourd's bill, Normanby was ill-suited to make it. He had become Home Secretary in August 1839, exchanging jobs with Russell, who took over Normanby's position as Secretary of State for War and the Colonies. Russell had been a passionate advocate for criminal law reform, while Normanby had no such commitment. He was transferred to the Home

Office in 1839 due to his lack of aptitude for colonial affairs, something Wellington considered "a 'very bad and very foolish' appointment."[76] Rather than making an argument for the legal principles that underpinned the Punishment of Death Bill as it had been drafted, Normanby decided that "he should be ready to bow to the opinion of the House in this matter," and Winchilsea's amendment was agreed to without a division.[77] This was reported in the press, with the *Morning Post* observing that "much of the third clause as took away capital punishment from the commission of an unnatural offence [was] expunged from the Bill. The . . . result, therefore, is that persons guilty of this offence will still be liable, as at present, to be punished with death."[78]

It was likely that the personality of the Home Secretary played a role in retaining the death penalty for sodomy in 1841. But at least equally important was the personality of the man who chose to make an issue of it. Winchilsea was not the typical member of the House of Lords but known as "a very frequent speaker [who] vigorously defended the protestant tory cause." He had gone so far as to challenge Wellington to a duel over Catholic Emancipation in 1829, and in 1830, he had led the ultra-Tory rebellion that precipitated the fall of Wellington's government. He had strongly opposed the 1832 Reform Act and most subsequent Whig reforms. He was almost alone among English noblemen in supporting the Orange party in Ireland, and he regularly denounced O'Connell.[79] Winchilsea labeled sodomy "abominable," but he was one of the few to do so in all the debates over the 1840–1841 Punishment of Death Bill. Most men in both houses of Parliament, based on the votes on this issue in the Commons and the earlier readings of the bill in the Lords, seem to have been willing to let the provision pass into law, so long as it could be done quietly. But Winchilsea made an issue of it, and without defenders, it was struck from the bill in its final reading in the House of Lords.

A general election was held shortly after this debate, between June 29 and July 22. Kelly and Talfourd lost their seats; Lushington did not run. The Melbourne ministry decisively lost its majority, falling on August 30, 1841, to be replaced by Peel's Tory government. On the following day, August 31, Bankes was again arrested for having sex with a soldier, soon fleeing to Venice rather than face trial for the second time. The chance to end the death penalty for sodomy based on ethical arguments passed.[80]

Conclusion

A Different Dynamic

1861 and 1885

The year 1861 was not the culmination of the process to end the death penalty for sodomy that almost succeeded in 1841. Fitzroy Kelly was a key player in both instances, but very little else carried over from 1841 to 1861. No parliamentary discussion related to the sodomy law was recorded in relation to the 1861 Offences against the Person Act, and division lists were not kept on critical votes. Nobody of Lord John Russell's stature argued in favor of ending the death penalty for sodomy in the House of Commons or prepared a government bill, even one held in reserve, to bring it about. There was no equivalent of *Don Leon* or *A Free Examination* produced in the 1850s or anyone of Jeremy Bentham's stature who seemed to be informing the debate. After the failure of the 1841 Punishment of Death Act to eliminate the death penalty for sodomy, many of the threads indicating parliamentary activity by individuals with reasoned or emotional reservations over the practice seem to end.

There was not the same moral crisis in 1861. Just over twenty-five years had passed since the last man had been executed for sodomy; lives of men were no longer at stake. The makeup of Parliament had also changed. While the Reform Act of 1832 seemed to improve the chances of ending the death penalty for sodomy by increasing the momentum toward liberalization of the criminal law, it also seemed to have led to a reduction in the number of men in Parliament who were associated with certain tastes. Protected seats and rotten boroughs had helped bring such men as William Beckford, Matthew Gregory Lewis, Richard Heber, William Bankes, and Charles Baring

Wall to the Commons. The number of such men seemed to shrink with each election, and new men, less devoted to art, theater, and travel in the Mediterranean, took their place.[1]

The broader cultural context had also changed. Throughout British society, fear of innovation in relation to institutional arrangements was overtaking reformist optimism. The Indian Rebellion of 1857 was thought by many to have been sparked in part by rapid institutional innovations. Doubts over the abolition of slavery in the British Caribbean, made evident in the debates over the Morant Bay uprising, also precipitated a retreat from the belief in the power of institutional reform to benefit society. If in the early nineteenth century many Britons believed in the ability of legislation to bring about desired changes in Jamaica, in India, and within Britain itself, the national mood by the 1860s was far more defensive, reactionary, and pessimistic.[2]

The issue at the heart of the debates culminating in the 1861 Offences against the Person Act was also different from what it had been in 1840 and 1841. The later debate focused on whether legal experts in Parliament had a greater right than other members to change the law. The acts resulting from these debates (based on bills bundled together) did take the death penalty for sodomy off the statute books of Britain, but at the high price of *quintupling* the potential maximum sentence for acts short of sodomy and an increase in the arbitrariness of the application of the law as it related to sex between men. After 1861, a man could receive up to ten years' imprisonment for attempted sodomy or an "indecent assault" on a man. Because no one had been executed for sodomy since 1835 and far more men had been charged with attempted sodomy and indecent assault than with sodomy itself, the 1861 changes made the situation far worse for men who had sex with men, perhaps indicating the perils of attempting an ethical reform without making an ethical argument for it.[3]

If an arbitrary and punitive quintupling of the maximum sentence for attempted sodomy and "indecent assault" between men was part of the price to be paid for ending the death penalty for sodomy, then the story of the end of the death penalty for sodomy continues until 1885, when the arbitrary increase was effectively undone. The process by which that happened has parallels in the events of 1840–1841 in that in both instances, the reform was supported by the government, even as its author was a Member of Parliament (MP) outside the government.[4] The change brought about by what is commonly referred to as the Labouchere Amendment can be found in proposed legislation of the Liberal government years before.

Seeing the Labouchere Amendment to the Criminal Law Amendment Act of 1885 as a liberalization of the law would constitute a significant reinterpretation of it. It is most often represented as toughening the laws against sex between men, even as scholars have puzzled over Henry Du Pré Labouchere's reasons for proposing it, noting how his radical Liberal politics and bohemian choices throughout his life made him a strange candidate for doing so and recognizing that very little in the surviving archive speaks to his motivations in this regard.[5] This chapter concludes the book by exploring how this understanding of Labouchere's actions became established, arguing for the need for greater attention in queer scholarship to the period before the late nineteenth century.

From Criminal to Statute Law Reform

After 1841, only eight capital statutes remained in England and Wales, and they would not be further reduced until 1861.[6] The remaining capital crimes included murder, attempts to murder, burglary with violence, robbery with wounding, arson of occupied dwellings, high treason, and sodomy. From 1842 to 1849, there were nearly as many convictions for sodomy as there were for murder, even if in the decade after 1841 only murderers were actually executed, with between nine and sixteen hanged in a given year.[7] In the early 1840s, Russell believed that reforms in the capital laws had "gone as far as was possible in the existing state of society," and in 1847, a Select Committee of the House of Lords found that nearly half of the judges consulted thought it necessary to retain the death penalty for all eight crimes to which it then applied, while only one-third would have restricted it to murder alone.[8] While many literary figures, including Charles Dickens, William Thackeray, William and Mary Howitt, and others, still opposed capital punishment, the support for the movement would wane in the decade that followed.[9] Given the low numbers of actual executions, combined with the rise of more pressing issues related to incarceration and the approaching end of transportation as a secondary punishment, public and parliamentary interest and pressure for further reductions in the capital laws began to decline significantly.[10]

Despite this shift, the work of consolidation of the criminal law continued. Robert Peel and the Tories had begun the work of consolidating the criminal law in the late 1820s, and the feasibility of further consolidation had been examined under the Whigs, starting with the Royal Commission on Criminal Law in 1833.[11] The reports generated by the Royal Commission embraced the whole of the criminal law, with the *Seventh Report*, produced in 1843, offering a model for a consolidated criminal code.[12] In 1845, a Commission of Revision was given the power to revise the work of the commissioners who had preceded it, producing five reports, between 1845 and 1849, intended to form the basis of new laws.[13] In 1848, Lord Brougham used these reports to attempt a consolidation of statute and common law, but it did not pass. After this, a new Offences against the Person Bill was drawn up in the House of Lords, under the direction of the Lord Chancellor, incorporating some of the changes that had been in the failed bill. When serious disagreements arose over fundamental points related to codifying common law, the Lord Chancellor decided to work toward consolidating statute law only.[14] The Statute Law Commission was established in 1853 to build on this earlier work but also had a mandate to move beyond the criminal law and consider the consolidation of statute law more broadly.[15] The work of the commission was to be reviewed by "eminent and competent authorities," including Kelly.[16]

Initially, the commission was to confine itself to consolidation, without any attempt at amendment, but after a time, as with Peel's efforts in the 1820s, it was decided that "admitted imperfections and omissions should be remedied." This change was to be a focus of controversy for the next four years, raising the question of who had the right to alter criminal statutes. Did experts in the law have a greater right to do this than other representatives did, or should all elected representatives fully exercise their oversight authority?[17] Many in Parliament objected to putting the power to draft legislation in the hands of experts, especially when those experts tended to tie disparate reforms together in bundles that had to be accepted or rejected as a whole, as was the case with these reform efforts. This broader revision of the criminal statutes also provided an opportunity for those who wanted to further reduce the use of capital punishment. Russell, among others, made the argument that this review should be taken as an opportunity to limit the use of capital punishment to only murder and high treason.[18]

The First Liberal Bills of 1857

In July 1857, the Lord Chancellor introduced eight bills based on the work of the Statute Law Commission. These bills, the Lord Chancellor said, would consolidate "the whole of the law relating to an important portion of the Criminal Law," and they were to be the first of a series of bills directed at different portions of the law.[19] One of these, the Offences against the Person Bill, covered the death penalty for sodomy. The Lord Chancellor said that the bills had "been gone through with the utmost care by those members of the Commission best qualified to judge of their merits," and among those listed as reviewing the bills was Kelly.[20] The Solicitor General made clear that there were amendments to existing laws in the bills, but that only the amendments that "had been suggested by the Criminal Law Commissioners, and which had met with universal approval" were included; at this time, the death penalty for sodomy remained in the bills.[21]

At this point, events across the Channel intervened. Before the bill could be considered, an assassination attempt on Napoleon III raised the question of whether Britain had been used as a base to plan the attack. The government fell in the wake of the ensuing controversy, and Lord Derby formed his second administration. He appointed Kelly to the post of Attorney General.

The Bills of Attorney General Fitzroy Kelly

Within a few months of becoming Attorney General, Kelly redrafted the bills that had come out of the Statute Law Commission.[22] A revised and reprinted version of the 1857 Offences against the Person Bill was prepared and brought in by Kelly and the Attorney General for Ireland, James Whiteside, in April 1859. While most of it was unchanged from 1857, the 1859 bill would have replaced the death penalty for sodomy with penal servitude for life.[23] The 1859 legislation also contained a new clause. Rather than relying on the principle that made any attempted felony a misdemeanor under English law, the new legislation made separate provision for the crime of attempted sodomy:

> LXI. Whosoever shall be convicted of the abominable Crime of Buggery, committed either with Mankind or with any Animal, shall be liable to be kept in Penal Servitude for Life.
>
> LXII. Whosoever shall attempt to commit the said abominable Crime, or shall be guilty of any Assault with Intent to commit the same, or of any Indecent Assault upon any Male Person, shall be guilty of a Misdemeanor, and, being convicted thereof, shall be liable to be *kept in Penal Servitude for the Term of Three Years.*[24]

In this form, as redrafted by Kelly and Whiteside, the Offences against the Person Bill had its first reading in the Commons in April 1859. Kelly stated that this work was an outgrowth of the Statute Law Commission and built on the work of "some of the first lawyers and statesmen of the country." Whiteside, who followed Kelly, emphasized that the bill would end the death penalty in most cases "in which it was now legal, reserving it only for treason and murder."[25] Within two months, though, Kelly and Whiteside lost their posts with the fall of the Derby ministry.

Debate resumed on the Offences against the Person Bill (as drafted by Kelly and Whiteside) several weeks later, under the new Palmerston ministry.

Explaining why they had chosen to alter the work of the Statute Law Commission on the subject of the death penalty (by exceeding the commission's recommendations for the reduction in the number of capital crimes), Whiteside stated that when "the subject was considered by the late Cabinet . . . it was thought that it would be a very proper thing to propose to Parliament to abolish the punishment of death in all cases except those of high treason and murder."[26] Kelly then emphasized the bipartisan nature of the process up to that point. He had inherited those bills, he said, and put them forward "with some alterations and amendments," perhaps understating the importance of the alterations he had made.[27]

In his response to Kelly and Whiteside, the new Attorney General stated that "putting the criminal law of this country on a sound and rational basis" was the government's responsibility. Although he "entirely concurred in the suggestion of humanity, and, he would add, of justice, that had been brought forward for the purpose of inducing the House to consent to a change of the criminal law," he also invoked "the peril of altering the law by accepting an enactment which it took on trust and credit from some other quarter."[28] The current bills were, the Attorney General argued, "being brought into the House on the mere authority—however great that might be—of individual Members of the House," and he therefore withdrew them from consideration.[29]

Final Passage: The Liberal Bills in 1861

The process then began again, with the Liberals creating new bills that built on the work of the Statute Law Commission and contained the additions of Kelly and Whiteside in relation to sodomy and attempted sodomy. The Lord Chancellor presented eight of those new bills to the House of Lords in February 1860, and promised that if the Lords approved the bills, they would be sent to a Select Committee for further examination and possible revision.[30] That committee then added the possibility of hard labor to the three-year sentence for attempted sodomy, but it did not attempt to reinstate the death penalty for sodomy, an action it did take in the case of attempted murder.[31]

The most significant change to the bills as they pertained to sex between men came out of the Select Committee of the House of Commons, which did not meet until almost a year after the bills had been reintroduced in the Commons from the Lords.[32] That committee was formed to review the changes to the Offences against the Person Bill along with six other criminal law reform bills. The committee's thirty members included Kelly. The Offences against the Person Bill contained eighty clauses at this point, including three dealing with sex between men. Thirteen different votes were taken on proposed changes to the clauses of the bill.[33] The penalty for sodomy had previously been set at "Penal Servitude for Life"; the committee amended the clause to define the period of servitude as "any Term not less than Ten Years," to be decided at the discretion of the court.[34]

For the crime of attempted sodomy or "indecent assault" between men, the Select Committee made far more extensive changes. The clause as amended by the Commons stated:

> Whosoever shall attempt to commit the said abominable Crime, or shall be guilty of any Assault with Intent to commit the same, or of any indecent Assault upon any Male Person, shall be guilty of Misdemeanor, and being convicted thereof shall be liable, at the Discretion of the Court, to be kept in Penal Servitude for *any Term not exceeding Ten Years and not less than Three Years, or to be imprisoned for any Term not exceeding Two Years, with or without Hard Labour.*[35]

At this very late stage, the possibility of tripling the previously proposed sentence for attempted sodomy or "indecent assault" on another man was introduced. On April 22, 1861, the day on which this change was agreed to, Kelly was not present, although sixteen other members of the committee were.[36] No discussion was recorded as to why the change was made.

No debates occurred over this change in the weeks before the bill became law. The Offences against the Person Bill and six other bills were brought up and discussed together in the committee of the whole House, passing quickly with only minor adjustments. It and the other bills then went back to the Lords, where Brougham observed that they had already been debated in a previous session and had also been thoroughly considered by the Select Committee. He now believed that they should be passed "with as little discussion as possible in the two Houses," which they were.[37] It was stated in one of the last Lords debates that "great mitigations had been made in the punishments attached to various offences" by the Committee.[38] He then listed many of the mitigations but made no mention of the change to the punishment for attempted sodomy and indecent assault between men. The closest anyone came to such a statement was Lord Chelmsford's objection to the bills' being brought to the Lords so late in the session, because

> most of the alterations were so trifling that they might be accepted as matters of course; but there were others of a somewhat important

character, to which it was impossible at that period of the Session to give due consideration. As it was the House had no alternative but to pass the Bills as they had come up to them.[39]

Two other Lords echoed this reservation.[40] But these bills were tied together, and a majority of the Lords was ready to see them into law. These were the last objections made, and an end to the death penalty for sodomy passed the Lords, bundled with seventy-seven other clauses in the Offences against the Person Act, which was bundled with the Accessories and Abettors Bill; the Criminal Statutes Repeal Bill; the Larceny, &c. Bill; the Malicious Injuries to Property Bill; the Forgery Bill; and the Coinage Offences Bill. In bills that had been scrutinized for years, the sentence for attempted sodomy and "indecent assault" between men was more than tripled in the final weeks before passage, in a way that seems to have occurred without significant debate or review.

The Opposite of Progress

This late-stage change in the law had devastating consequences for some men, in the short and long terms. John Griffiths, a well-educated thirty-five-year-old warehouseman, was found guilty at the Central Criminal Court in November 1861 of attempted sodomy with William Harrold, for which he was sentenced to ten years' penal servitude.[41] William Smith, a thirty-three-year-old unmarried laborer from Dublin, was convicted of an assault "with sodomitical intent" on William Curtis in June 1875, and he was sentenced to five years' penal servitude.[42] Pierre Frongier, a forty-eight-year-old unmarried Frenchman with a "dark complexion" was given a five-year sentence for an assault "with a sodomitical intent" on Thomas Humphreys in June 1878.[43] These men would have likely gotten a sentence of two years at most before 1861.

Some court officials were still learning of the implications of the 1861 modification of the law years later. This was the case in 1863, when Charles Morrison, a clerk employed by a respectable legal firm in Gray's Inn, was arrested and brought into the Hammersmith Police Court, "charged with committing various 'indecent assaults.'"[44] He was to be released on a modest bail, but then the prosecutor reminded the presiding magistrate that "under the new Act such an assault was made liable to penal servitude for a term of ten years." It was reported that the magistrate, after "having read the Act, increased the amount of bail to 500*l.*" for each of the two required sureties.[45] Morrison was unable to raise that much and remained imprisoned until his trial just over a month later at the Central Criminal Court. He lost his case, and it was reported that he was sentenced to six years' imprisonment.[46]

After 1861, most sentences for attempted sodomy and "indecent assault" between men continued to be set at no more than two years. Sentences of more than two years seemed to be handed down in cases that officials saw as more aggravated examples of the crime. George Brown, a forty-nine-year-old laborer of "imperfect education," was found guilty of attempted buggery of Maria Brown and sentenced to ten years' penal servitude for his attack.[47] George Grant and William Mahoney were found guilty of attempted sodomy with each other in 1871, but their sentences varied widely, most likely because of their ages. Grant was a fifty-year-old servant of "imperfect education," while Mahoney was a seventeen-year-old laborer of only "remedial education." Grant was imprisoned for five years for his actions, while Mahoney received only two months' imprisonment despite evidence that the sex between them was consensual.[48] Acts that involved coercion, whether through violence or by taking advantage of someone's youth and inexperience, seemed to garner longer sentences, but nothing in the law stipulated this consideration as the basis for decision making.

Discretion rested with judges, and sex between men short of sodomy could now be punished with anything from only a few months' to ten years' imprisonment.[49] That the punishment should be closely calibrated to the crime had been a cornerstone of legal reform since the 1819 Select Committee on Criminal Laws had laid out that principle.[50] The *First Report* of the Criminal Law Commission in 1833 had also proposed to end "the high maxima of sentences and the wide discretion allowed to judges" in sentences.[51] Almost all the reforms carried out over the previous four decades had moved the law in the direction of standardization, but for the law as it related to sex between men, 1861 saw a significant step in the opposite direction. It made the law as it related to attempted sodomy and "indecent assault" between men not only more severe but also far more arbitrary.

The end of the death penalty for sodomy came in 1861, but only in the context of bills that were designed to consolidate statute law, to which were later added the goal of ending the death penalty for all crimes short of murder.[52] No one in 1861 publicly presented a moral argument in favor of ending the death penalty for sodomy. Such arguments had been made earlier in the century by Bentham in his published and unpublished writings, by Russell and others on the floor of the House of Commons, by the authors of *A Free Examination*, and by the authors of *Don Leon* and "Leon to Annabella." While it might seem that there was a connection to the events leading to the 1861 Offences against the Person Act and *Don Leon*, given that the oldest surviving copy was published in 1866, an examination of the text does not seem to indicate that it was connected to the events leading to the 1861 Act.

The Final Updates to *Don Leon*

A reference to *Don Leon* appeared in print in the early 1850s, but the oldest surviving copy was published in 1866.[53] The changes to the text datable to the two decades before 1866 seem to have little to do with politics. The last material added to the "Notes to *Don Leon*" dates from 1853 and 1858; it references Byron's authorship of a poetic fragment and a dispute involving his estate. All the notes that quote newspaper material published after 1836, eleven in total, also seem to have little to do with politics and were added after the first version of the endnotes had been set. This material is either appended to the end of existing notes or assigned the same numbers as earlier notes, as there are two Note 24s, two Note 26s, two Note 51s, and two Note 76s.[54] The fact that in a work about ending the death penalty for sodomy published in 1866 there is no discussion of the occurrence of that event in 1861 supports the theory that pornographers rather than radical pressmen published the final version of *Don Leon*.

The Society for the Abolition of Capital Punishment

Also absent in 1861 was the Society for the Abolition of Capital Punishment (SACP). William Ewart had founded the SACP in 1846, inspired by the success of the Anti-Corn-Law League in using an organized and informed middle class to pressure Parliament on a specific issue. Similar organizations, including the Anti-Gold-Law League, the Anti-Land-Law League, the Anti-Bribery League, and the Electoral League, were also founded around this time.[55] By the late 1850s, the SACP was a well-organized if still small group, deploying the traditional tools of "pressure from without," which included public meetings, pamphlet distribution, petitions to the Home Secretary and Parliament, and the lobbying of individual MPs. The SACP cause was considered to be aligned with other philanthropic concerns, including antislavery, temperance, peace, and vegetarianism.

While public statements that could be construed as a defense of sodomy would have been difficult to make, it is still worth noting that the SACP did not take a stand on this question.[56] Writing decades ago, Walter Houghton describes how one of the most admirable traits of the Victorians was their willingness to grapple with the sometimes-devastating consequences of clashes between two deeply held beliefs, as when religion was first confronted by the science of evolution. Rather than retreat into denial or hypocrisy, Houghton demonstrates, many Victorians struggled with the challenge and earnestly worked to resolve the conflict.[57] Had such a struggle confronted those who believed in the end of capital punishment, even for murder, while the same penalty was still on the books for a private consensual sexual act? If SACP members felt this way, they did not build a campaign around it.

Restoring the Two-Year Sentence: 1878 to 1885

It seems likely that the increase in the penalty for "indecent assault" and attempted sodomy in 1861 was linked to the end of the death penalty for sodomy. An effort to reestablish a criminal offense with a two-year cap on sentences for the punishment of sex between men seems evident in an 1879 Royal Commission Report and the 1880 Criminal Code Bill.[58] The 1879 Royal Commission Report lists "indecent acts" after "attempt to commit unnatural offence," as does the later 1880 Criminal Code Bill. It was not an entirely new law, but it had not previously been grouped with the other laws related to sex between men before. Per the 1880 Criminal Code Bill:

PART XIII: CRIMES AGAINST MORALITY.
140. UNNATURAL OFFENCE.
> Every one is guilty of a crime, and liable to penal servitude for life, who commits buggery either with a human being or with any other living creature.
> This offence is complete upon penetration.
141. ATTEMPT TO COMMIT UNNATURAL OFFENCE.
> Every one is guilty of a crime, and liable to ten years' penal servitude, who attempts to commit buggery, or assaults any person with intent to commit buggery, or who being a male indecently assaults any other male.
142. INDECENT ACTS.
> Every one is guilty of a crime, and liable to two years' imprisonment with hard labour, who wilfully (a) Does any indecent act in *any place to which the public have* or are permitted to have *access*; or (b) *Does any indecent act in any place*, intending thereby to insult or offend any person.[59]

A memorandum published in the parliamentary papers explained the principal changes in the law proposed by the 1880 Criminal Code Bill. In relation to "indecent acts," it stated that "acts of indecency are at present in-dictable only if committed in a public place. By Sub-section (b) of this Section they are made punishable if they are done with intent to insult or offend any person anywhere."[60] The Royal Commission had also emphasized the importance of clause (b) in the original 1879 report, writing in the margin beside it, where earlier versions of laws or clauses were listed, "This is new."[61]

This Criminal Code Bill did not become law, but this precedent for the government's attempting to reestablish a category for the punishment of sex between men that did not allow for ten years' imprisonment helps explain at least some of the events that unfolded on the night in 1885 when Labouch-ere proposed an amendment criminalizing "gross indecency" between men. The debate directly related to this issue was short, and Labouchere was chal-lenged by another member that it had nothing to do with the current bill, before the Speaker advised that anything could be introduced at that stage, with the consent of the House. Labouchere then introduced his amendment, which read:

> Any male person who, in public or private, commits, or is a party to the commission of, or procures or attempts to procure the com-mission by any male person of, any act of gross indecency with another male person, shall be guilty of a misdemeanour, and, being convicted thereof, shall be liable, at the discretion of the Court, to be imprisoned for any term not exceeding *one year* with or without hard labour.[62]

The aspect of the amendment that Labouchere felt the need to explain was related to the age of consent. Labouchere stated:

> The meaning of it was that at present any person on whom an assault of the kind here dealt with was committed must be under the age of 13, and the object with which he had brought forward this clause was to make the law applicable to any person, whether under the age of 13 or over that age. He did not think it necessary to discuss the proposal at any length, as *he understood Her Majesty's Government were willing to accept it.*[63]

Labouchere then stated that he would leave the matter for the House and the government to deal with. Only two MPs spoke after that. The first "point[ed] out that under the law as it stood at the present moment the kind of offence indicated could not be an offence in the case of any person above the age of 13, and in the case of any person under the age of 13 there could be no consent."[64] The second speaker suggested that the sentence be raised from one year to two years, to which Labouchere did not object.[65]

The term "gross indecency" was used in the nineteenth century in reference to a range of sexual and nonsexual acts, but in the late 1870s, it began to be used most frequently in the parliamentary papers in relation to sexuality among boys. "Gross indecency" was the term used in a case at Harrow in 1827, in the context of dismissing boys having sex with one another at that institution.[66] It appeared in government reports on the education of pauper children, in relation to the issue of sex involving boys.[67] Although it has always sounded harsh to contemporary ears, at least one individual quoted in these reports from the 1860s spoke of "the enormity of his offence, which, to use *the mildest term* that can be applied to it, was one of gross indecency towards the younger boys in the school."[68] In 1880, during debates regarding the age of consent in the context of the Assaults on Young Persons Bill, it was stated that "the term 'indecent assault,' was by common consent applied to cases of gross indecency."[69] The 1880 law established that it "shall be no defense to a charge or indictment for an indecent assault on a young person under the age of thirteen to prove that he or she consented to the act of indecency."[70] Given his discussion of the age of consent in relation to his proposal, Labouchere seems to have had these associations in mind.

Given the effort of the government years before to establish something like what Labouchere proposed in 1885, and Labouchere's own statements at the time that the government supported his effort, there may be room to reassess his personal role in passing the amendment that is often referred to by using his name. As early as 1976, F. B. Smith was commenting that Labouchere "was an unlikely instigator of such a law. He was a witty, worldly-wise Radical and a knowing journalist."[71] Jeffrey Weeks observes that Labouchere's "ultimate intentions have never been fully clarified" and that "in fact, he offered several explanations" for why he proposed his amendment, all of which were put forward years afterward.[72] Morris Kaplan notes that his "aim in proposing the amendment remains unclear."[73]

The *Dictionary of National Biography* notes that for "all his life Labouchere was a rebel against constituted authority."[74] He went to Eton and Cambridge, but at the age of twenty-one, he traveled to South America and Mexico, where he "wandered about for a year or two, fell in love with a circus lady, and joined the troupe. For six months he lived in a camp of Ojibwe Indians."[75] His family arranged a diplomatic career for him, and he served as an attaché in Washington and in a series of European capitals, at which point he was best known for his gambling and "insubordinate and indolent" behavior. Leaving the diplomatic service after a falling out with Russell, Labouchere returned to England, where he briefly held a seat in Parliament for Middlesex before enmeshing himself in the worlds of journalism and theater.[76] He invested in and helped run the Queen's Theater in London, and in 1868, he formed a relationship with Henrietta Hodson, an actress who was then separated from her husband. The couple lived together throughout the 1870s, had a daughter in 1884, and married in 1887, after Henrietta was widowed.[77]

Labouchere established a weekly journal, *Truth*, in 1874, with part of the fortune he had inherited a few years before. He "wrote with candour about his own adventurous life and the follies and failings of his contemporaries," according to Herbert Sidebotham, who adds, "Above all, *Truth* won admiration and gratitude by its fearless exposure of fraudulent enterprises of all sorts."[78] Smith describes *Truth* as not endorsing overzealous purity campaigns and as chastising rural magistrates for not holding men to account who physically abused their wives or children. In 1880, Labouchere returned to Parliament. He held a seat for Northampton for the next twenty-five years, soon becoming "one of the most powerful radicals in the Commons." Smith notes that Labouchere was not on record as expressing negative views about sex between men before 1885 and goes on to say that Labouchere's "active engagement with the theatrical world, and frequenting of the Haymarket, ought to have made him more tolerant than most."[79]

The existing primary sources did not help Smith understand Labouchere's motivations for introducing his amendment. Speculation was called for, Smith states, since the "question can never be settled convincingly. Labouchere's personal papers mostly seem to have been destroyed and the few that are known have no bearing on this episode."[80] Moreover, the papers of the Attorney General, Sir Henry James, and the other members of the government who saw the bill through committee "are all devoid of evidence about the amendment."[81] Smith comments on the fact that "despite the incongruities in the story of the amendment and the paucity of evidence about Labouchere's intentions, biographers and commentators have shown remarkable confidence in declaring that Labby intended the clause to mean what it said and have the results that it had."[82]

The year 1885 was more than forty years after the period of study central to this book, in a period examined far more comprehensively by other scholars, and so no definitive statement will be given as to Labouchere's motivations for helping facilitate this policy that had long-standing government support. Other scholars have found statements made by Labouchere years later, wherein he indicated that his intent was to ensure that some men who had previously escaped prosecution would no longer be able to do so.[83] Even taken at face value, these statements by Labouchere would not be incompatible with the idea that his efforts of 1885 might be considered liberal reform in relation to sex between men. Charles Law did something similar in 1835, tying the elimination of the harshest penalty for sex between men to a clause that would have made prosecutions for lesser offenses more likely.[84] Improving the certainty of punishment for a crime while making the resulting punishment less draconian was a hallmark of nineteenth-century British legal reform as well as a succinct description of what was achieved with the amendment that Labouchere proposed.

Conclusion

The point of reviewing these events is not to rehabilitate the reputation of Labouchere or to overinflate the importance of a point of interpretation but instead to argue for the value of more thoroughly pursuing queer history into the period before the late nineteenth century, where we might gain a perspective that makes current assumptions, such as those about Labouchere's motivations, or the nature of the unspeakable in the nineteenth century, begin to look different from how they do currently. Assumptions made on the edges of periods of investigation are usually less accurate than those made closer to the core of a field.

Some of the earliest work in lesbian, gay, bisexual, transgender, and queer (LGBTQ) history focuses on events of the eighteenth century, where sources documenting sex between men seem abundant.[85] Scholars, led by Randolph Trumbach, have argued for an eighteenth-century "sodomite" identity, but that project atrophied from the 1990s forward, as more theoretical approaches to questions of sexuality and identity demonstrated that such categories as "homosexual," "lesbian," "straight," "bisexual," "trans," and other identity categories related to sexuality are relatively recent creations, stemming from the late nineteenth century.[86] David Halperin argues that evidence of same-sex sexual acts, or even forms of same-sex desire, before the late nineteenth century might be components of what later became modern sexual identities, while Alan Bray, Martha Vicinus, Richard Godbeer, and others argue that different customs within homosocial communities, or different understandings of friendship, might account for evidence that others had read as synonymous with modern sexual identities.[87] In light of this work, consensus built among scholars that while there is abundant evidence for a cultural category of "sodomite" in the eighteenth century, that evidence is most often insufficient to speak to issues of individual identity.

Where sources permit, some scholars have been able to show that in the late eighteenth and early nineteenth centuries, a few individuals placed same-sex desire at the center of their self-understandings. As argued by Anna Clark, this does not mean that scholars should push the origin of modern sexual identities back in time but should instead focus on the role of intellectual frameworks from earlier periods, such as the idea of the unique or "expressivist" self, as developed in the work of Rousseau, to explain these self-understandings.[88] Such individuals as Anne Lister and the Chevalièr/e d'Éon were able to fashion identities that reconciled inner feelings of same-sex desire or nonnormative gender identity expression with their cultural contexts. They were unique individuals, although as unique individuals, their synthesis of sexuality, self-understanding, and gender performance seems to have not outlived them or been the basis of a shared identity within a community.[89] Theirs are important stories to recover, but a field of queer scholarship before the late nineteenth century centered on understanding such individuals would soon be starved for sources and exhaust its archive.[90]

If sources of information on such individuals before the late nineteenth century are rare and difficult to locate, sources of information on the institutions and texts that shaped such individuals are not. As queer scholarship has increasingly shifted over the past two decades to demonstrating how identity categories are constructed, attention has been redirected to the institutions and mechanisms of power that made those identities possible. Margot Canaday's study of how the U.S. federal government played a role in fashioning the category of the homosexual in the twentieth century is only one of the most prominent of these studies.[91] Her methodology is similar to that deployed by Patrick Joyce in *The Rule of Freedom*, which investigates how the liberal state shaped the behavior and perceptions of citizens in nineteenth-century Britain.[92] Increasingly, a new generation of scholars is also focusing on the coercive nature of those institutions, demonstrating not how they built up liberal subjects but instead how they attempted to tear down and strip away the humanity of individuals, especially in systems of slavery, incarceration, and systemic discrimination.[93]

The focus on how institutions shaped subjectivities allows us to apply a queer methodology (and the methodology of critical history more broadly) to events before the late nineteenth century and before the late-nineteenth-century development of the modern subject defined by sexuality.[94] Scholars are already pursuing this method, focusing on a range of institutions, but there seems to be an untapped opportunity to use parliaments as a site for this sort of analysis as well.

The preceding chapters have demonstrated that the structured nature of parliamentary debate and the copious amounts of evidence preserved within and around the British Parliament can help us derive greater meanings from even small amounts of surviving evidence related to same-sex desire. Following Kelly, a backbench individual, has led to uncovering unexpected actions by Russell and to realizing that a majority in the House of Commons as early as 1835 voted to end the death penalty for sodomy, qualifying this reform to rank as one of the classic early reforms in Britain's "Age of Reform."[95] If Russell's role in ending the death penalty for sodomy has not been better known, it is because most previous Russell biographies and "high politics" narratives ignore his actions in this area. Other unexpected insights of value to queer scholars might be in the debates over the Infant Custody Act, the Marriage Act, or smaller backbench bills unknown today.

Queer history never had its "high politics" moment, and high politics has never been successfully queered. Including Parliament as an institutional site for queer history in the eighteenth and nineteenth centuries can help in a number of ways, especially if the focus is placed on the issues that challenged the hegemonic values of British society, if politics is considered as intersecting with parliamentary debate rather than being contained by it, and if a focus is placed on the ethical arguments made and the ways in which diverse coalitions were brought together to bring about common goals. If we keep the focus on issues of sexuality, especially as they intersect with issues of race, class, and gender, and make the subject the discovery of how issues played out in politics to create ethical subjects, more ethical social interactions, and greater justice, this might open avenues to a queer analysis focused on issues of power, rather than issues of identity. As Laura Doan observes, gender history transformed the whole of historical scholarship when it made this transition from issues of identity to issues of power in the 1980s, and, she argues, if sexuality as a category has not yet had such a transformative effect, it is in part because it has not yet fully embraced this transition.[96] The parliamentary archive, accessible as never before due to advances in digitization, can enhance the explanatory power of the evidence of sexuality and help us place issues of power and ethics, rather than issues of identity, at the center of more of our studies set before the late nineteenth century.

A focus on ethics, and on the issues arising from the field of queer studies in general, not only helps establish a different set of questions from those used by scholars who previously engaged with the parliamentary record but also prevents us from too quickly or uncritically placing at the center of analysis every past identity incorporating same-sex desire that might be discovered. There does seem to have been, after all, an attempt in the early nineteenth century to employ inside and outside Parliament something very closely approximating a shared identity category to argue for greater rights for men who had sex with men. But it was a significantly compromised synthesis when considered from the perspective of the ethics of its own time and place as well as in relation to our own.

Such men as Lord Byron, Beckford, Bankes, and others were not "queer" in the sense of resisting identity categories. They were not attempting to fundamentally disrupt societal norms, and they were not letting their passions be the unmediated guide for their actions. Instead, in a process similar to what Clark describes for Lister and the Chevalièr/e d'Éon, they were using wealth and the high-value cultural texts to which they had access to fashion an identity that helped them reconcile their internal desires with their understanding of themselves as deserving the privileged place they held in society, despite their sexual tastes. They disciplined themselves in alignment with how they understood sex between men to operate in the ancient world, aspiring to control and conform themselves to this model that allowed for physical expressions of same-sex desire toward younger men at a certain stage of life, followed by marriage and family. A related cultural resource from the ancient world for these men was the Roman concept of the "vir," the full Roman citizen, equal to other citizens and dominant over others. So long as the vir was the dominant partner in the sexual relationship, the sex of whomever he subordinated would not affect his masculine status. Byron, Bankes, and some of their college friends seem to have shared an identity drawing on these Greek and Roman cultural forms, with these same ideas at the core of the argument in the first six hundred lines of *Don Leon*.

But there was a potential ethical problem at the center of these self-understandings taken wholesale from the slave societies of the ancient world. In those societies, slaves, women, children, and other dependents in a household were considered to be of an inferior status. They could be sexually violated at any time, for any reason, by the male head of their household. What mattered was the dominance and pleasure of the "vir," and the objects of his desire were not considered fully human in the same way he was.[97]

The younger partner in the pederastic relationship was extremely vulnerable to domination. He might be loved, he might be adored, and he might even be respected, as Giraud is in the *Don Leon* poem, but the relationship was predicated on a power imbalance, deemed necessary by the older man for no other reason than to preserve a certain understanding of his masculine status. Throughout this study, the age of consent, as it was understood by British society at the time, has been considered when determining whether a relationship under examination might be consensual or whether it could not be (because of the age of one of the participants) and was therefore a crime by today's standards as well as those of the nineteenth century. Significant age differences between sexual partners who are both above the age of consent are not in some inherent way problematic, but it does seem concerning that the voice and the desires of the younger partner are almost always absent from the historical record of such relationships. These younger men are the objects of desire and the objects of the narrative, but never the subjects.

Don Leon grapples with reconciling Christian ethics and same-sex desire but does not fully resolve the issue. We see the protagonist of the first six hundred lines of the poem struggling to reconcile his passions for other men, which he wishes to express in the ways that Virgil, Socrates, and Epaminondas did, with "a purer code [that] the Christian law revealed."[98] Central to the Christian ethical code, though, is the fundamental equality of souls. That idea carried over into Enlightenment philosophy, so much so that from the perspective of scholars steeped in non-Western ethical traditions, such as Uday Singh Mehta, the autonomous individual at the center of much enlightenment philosophy reads as a secularized version of the Christian soul.[99] Enlightenment and Christian ethics posited the value of the individual, even as the practitioners of each ethical system and the institutions built on those ideas have often fallen far short of this ideal. Even so, the Christian and Enlightenment traditions in the eighteenth century gave rise to individuals and movements that challenged slavery, women's subordinate status, and other forms of subjugation. Bentham achieved an ethical reconciliation of Enlightenment philosophy and same-sex desire in the late eighteenth century, and such an ethical reconciliation between Christianity and same-sex desire was also achievable, but not based on a system that predicated the erasure of one individual for the desires of another.

Stronger ethical arguments for same-sex desire in the Western tradition would grow out of different discourses. The most famous of these was the medical discourse of the late nineteenth century, which, as Harry Oosterhuis has shown, evolved in response to the correspondence between physicians, such as Richard von Krafft-Ebing, author of *Psychopathia Sexualis*, and individuals from across Europe who saw something of themselves in the case studies he presented, but who also claimed the right to argue for alterations in those representations so that they would better fit their self-understandings.[100] More recently, works by Harry Cocks on religion and Matt Cook on family have shown how these belief systems and social contexts could support positive understandings of same-sex desire, while Sheila Rowbotham has shown how these same themes, along with other economic and social frameworks, including socialism and feminism, helped underpin Edward Carpenter's public arguments for the positive value of love between men.[101]

Rather than seeing the creation of *Don Leon* as an unproblematic first step toward the gay identity of a later period, it is better understood as one of many fascinating responses to the conditions of its time, containing ethical arguments and assertions of identity that are both positive and problematic. Like the self-understandings of Lister and Chevalièr/e d'Éon, the synthesis these men created was also relatively short-lived and yet still valuable for revealing the ways of thinking about the self in their time. As remarkable as the identities fashioned by Lister, the Chevalièr/e d'Éon, or the authors of *Don Leon* were, they were only open to those with significant wealth, significant education, and significant leisure. They were most often tied up with guaranteeing class privilege rather than challenging it. They may have been appealing to some but were available to only a few.

Identity categories based on elite texts were not necessary for such individuals as John Smith and James Pratt. They held, they kissed—adult men, behind a closed door. Perhaps the purity and clarity of what they did, and their ethical right to do so, by the standards of the best version of the values of Victorian society, were what made their deaths so shocking. Perhaps far more Victorians actually understood the moral wrong of what happened to John and James than we have previously allowed ourselves to imagine. Russell easily could have not known about the arguments in *Don Leon* or *A Free Examination*. It is far less likely that he did not know about the rational arguments in Bentham's writing against the punishment of sex between men. But there is no way that he did not know about John and James. One of his earliest actions as Cabinet Minister was to facilitate their execution for a private consensual act. He did not record his emotional response on having to do this, but he never did it again, and he took the opportunity a few years later to try to make it no longer legal for anyone to do so. Perhaps Russell, and an unknown number within the majority in Parliament who had voted in 1835 that men should no longer be executed for a private consensual act, felt ashamed for letting John and James die without raising any objection. Perhaps more of the nation they represented shared this view than we have suspected, and shared the shame at letting something they knew to be immoral continue. Perhaps that, too, is what they found so unspeakable.

Notes

INTRODUCTION

1. Roger Chadwick, *Bureaucratic Mercy: The Home Office and the Treatment of Capital Cases in Victorian Britain* (New York: Garland Publishing, 1992), 12–13.

2. Leon Radzinowicz, *A History of English Criminal Law and Its Administration from 1750*, vol. 1, *The Movement for Reform 1750–1833* (New York: Macmillan, 1948), 231–267.

3. *Hansard*, Commons Sitting, vol. 55, July 15, 1840, 735; "Punishment of Death: A Bill for taking away the Punishment of Death in certain Cases, and substituting other Punishments in lieu thereof. Prepared and brought in by Mr. Fitzroy Kelly and Dr. Lushington," June 23, 1840—4 Vict.

4. HO 17/120/60, Petition for James Pratt and John Smith, sentenced to death for sodomy. Letter of Hensleigh Wedgwood, magistrate at the Union Hall Police Office, to Lord John Russell, explaining why he has dismissed similar cases in the past rather than commit individuals for trial on sodomy charges.

5. C. J. W. Allen, 2004, "Kelly, Sir Fitzroy Edward (1796–1880), judge," *Oxford Dictionary of National Biography*, April 2019; Richard Greene, 2016, "Kelly [née Fordyce; other married name Hedgeland], Isabella (bap. 1759, d. 1857), poet and novelist," *Oxford Dictionary of National Biography*, April 2019; Joanne Shattock, *The Oxford Guide to British Women Writers* (Oxford: Oxford University Press, 1993).

6. Montague Summers, *The Gothic Quest: A History of the Gothic Novel* (New York: Russell and Russell, 1964), 263; Louis F. Peck, *A Life of Matthew G. Lewis* (Cambridge, MA: Harvard University Press, 1961), 103.

7. S. M. Waddams, *Law, Politics, and the Church of England: The Career of Stephen Lushington, 1782–1873* (Cambridge: Cambridge University Press, 1992), 90–91; S. M. Waddams, 2004, "Lushington, Stephen (1782–1873), judge," *Oxford Dictionary of National Biography*, April 2019; Terry Jenkins, "Lushington, Stephen (1782–1873),"

Member Biographies, in *The History of Parliament: The House of Commons 1820–1832*, ed. D. R. Fisher (Cambridge: Cambridge University Press, 2009).

8. Louis Crompton, *Byron and Greek Love: Homophobia in 19th-Century England* (Berkeley: University of California Press, 1985), 353n, 378n; Leslie A. Marchand, *Byron: A Biography* (New York: Knopf, 1957), 2:587n; George Wilson Knight, *Lord Byron's Marriage: The Evidence of Asterisks* (New York: Macmillan, 1957), 74–76, 237–240.

9. *Don Leon; A Poem by the Late Lord Byron . . . to Which Is Added Leon to Annabella: An Epistle from Lord Byron to Lady Byron* (London: Printed for the Booksellers, 1866).

10. *Hansard*, Commons Sitting, vol. 55, July 15, 1840, 744–746; *Hansard*, Commons Sitting, vol. 57, "Punishment of Death," May 3, 1841, 1415–1421; *Hansard*, Commons Sitting, vol. 57, March 8, 1841, 54.

11. The Earl of Winchilsea had previously challenged and fought the Duke of Wellington in a duel over the Catholic Emancipation in 1829. *Hansard*, Lords Sitting, vol. 58, June 17, 1841, 1557; G. C. Boase, 2004, "Hatton, George William Finch-, tenth earl of Winchilsea and fifth earl of Nottingham (1791–1858), politician," *Oxford Dictionary of National Biography*, May 2019.

12. Arthur Burns and Joanna Innes, eds., *Rethinking the Age of Reform: Britain, 1780–1850* (New York: Cambridge University Press, 2003); Randolph Trumbach, "The Birth of the Queen: Sodomy and the Emergence of Gender Equality in Modern Culture, 1660–1750," in *Hidden from History: Reclaiming the Gay and Lesbian Past*, ed. Martin Duberman, Martha Vicinus, and George Chauncey (New York: Penguin, 1990); Randolph Trumbach, "London's Sodomites: Homosexual Behavior and Western Culture in the 18th Century," *Journal of Social History* 11, no. 1 (Fall 1977); Faramerz Dabhoiwala, *The Origins of Sex: A History of the First Sexual Revolution* (New York: Oxford University Press, 2012); Catherine Hall, Keith McClelland, and Jane Rendall, eds., *Defining the Victorian Nation: Class, Race, Gender and the Reform Act of 1867* (Cambridge: Cambridge University Press, 2000).

13. This focus on parliamentary politics (broadly defined) and culture captures perspectives and opinions not found in sources used by legal historians who have examined sodomy law. The approach taken here builds on that earlier work and is meant to complement rather than replace it.

14. Louis Crompton, *Homosexuality and Civilization* (Cambridge, MA: Belknap Press of Harvard University Press, 2003), 366, 533; Morris B. Kaplan, *Sodom on the Thames: Sex, Love, and Scandal in Wilde Times* (Ithaca, NY: Cornell University Press, 2005), 24, 186; Angus McLaren, *Sexual Blackmail: A Modern History* (Cambridge, MA: Harvard University Press, 2002), 17–18; H. Montgomery Hyde, *The Other Love: A History and Contemporary Survey of Homosexuality in Britain* (London: Heinemann, 1970), 92; "The capital charge for sodomy was quietly dropped in 1861, attracting no comment from *The Times* or other newspapers": Sean Brady, *Masculinity and Male Homosexuality in Britain, 1861–1913* (New York: Palgrave Macmillan, 2005), 61; Ed Cohen, *Talk on the Wilde Side: Towards a Genealogy of a Discourse on Male Sexualities* (New York: Routledge, 1993), 92, 118.

15. H. G. Cocks, *Nameless Offences: Speaking of Male Homosexual Desire in Nineteenth-Century England* (London: I. B. Tauris, 2003).

16. In 1977, Jeffrey Weeks, drawing on the Leon Radzinowicz passage discussed on page 5, observed that "when Lord John Russell attempted to remove 'unnatural offences' from the list of capital crimes in 1841, he was forced to withdraw through lack of parliamentary support." Jeffrey Weeks, *Coming Out: Homosexual Politics in Britain from the Nineteenth Century to the Present* (London: Quartet Books, 1977), 13.

17. Leon Radzinowicz, *A History of English Criminal Law and Its Administration from 1750*, vol. 4, *Grappling for Control* (London: Stevens and Sons, 1968), 322, 328–329.

18. Ibid., 328–329.

19. James Gregory, *Victorians against the Gallows: Capital Punishment and the Abolitionist Movement in Nineteenth-Century Britain* (London: I. B. Tauris, 2012), 21, 22; Richard Clark, *Capital Punishment in Britain* (Hersham, UK: Ian Allan, 2009); Brian P. Block and John Hostettler, *Hanging in the Balance: A History of the Abolition of Capital Punishment in Britain* (Winchester, UK: Waterside Press, 1997); John Laurence, *A History of Capital Punishment, with Special Reference to Capital Punishment in Great Britain* (Port Washington, NY: Kennikat Press, 1971); Elizabeth Orman Tuttle, *The Crusade against Capital Punishment in Great Britain* (London: Stevens, 1961); Chadwick, *Bureaucratic Mercy*; James E. Crimmins, *Origins of the Death Penalty Debate in Britain and the U.S., 1725–1868* (Bristol, UK: Thoemmes, 2003).

20. Joan Scott, "Gender: A Useful Category of Historical Analysis," *American Historical Review* 91, no. 5 (1986); C. Riley Snorton, *Black on Both Sides, a Racial History of Trans Identity* (Minneapolis: University of Minnesota Press, 2017); Joanne Meyerowitz, Heidi Tinsman, Maria Bucur, Dyan Elliott, Gail Hershatter, Wang Zheng, and Joan W. Scott, "AHR Forum: Revisiting 'Gender: A Useful Category of Historical Analysis,'" *American Historical Review* 113, no. 5 (December 2008); Partha Chatterjee, *The Black Hole of Empire: History of a Global Practice of Power* (Princeton, NJ: Princeton University Press, 2012).

21. Modern homosexual identity is characterized by an individual's having sexual desires that are fixed, exclusively focused on members of the same sex, and seen as central to that person's identity. Michel Foucault, *The History of Sexuality*, vol. 1, *An Introduction* (New York: Vintage Books, 1990).

22. Laura Doan, *Disturbing Practices: History, Sexuality, and Women's Experience of Modern War* (Chicago: University of Chicago Press, 2013). For an example of Doan's methodology applied to historical actors across the long nineteenth century, see Anna Clark, *Alternative Histories of the Self: A Cultural History of Sexuality and Secrets, 1762–1917* (New York: Bloomsbury Academic, 2017), 51–75.

23. Doan, *Disturbing Practices*; Michel Foucault, *The Archaeology of Knowledge* (New York: Pantheon Books, 1972).

24. Jeremy Bentham, *An Introduction to the Principles of Morals and Legislation. Printed in the Year 1780, and Now First Published* (London: T. Payne and Son, 1789); Jeremy Bentham and Louis Crompton, "Offences against One's Self," *Journal of Homosexuality* 3, no. 4 (1978); Jeremy Bentham and Louis Crompton, "Jeremy Bentham's Essay on 'Paederasty,'" *Journal of Homosexuality* 4, no. 1 (1978); Louis Crompton, "Jeremy Bentham's Essay on 'Paederasty,'" *Journal of Homosexuality* 3, no. 4 (1978).

25. *Don Leon*; "Leon to Annabella."

26. John Hostettler, *The Politics of Criminal Law Reform in the Nineteenth Century* (Chichester: Barry Rose Law Publishers, 1992), 59–75; Michael A. Rustigan, "A Reinterpretation of Criminal Law Reform in Nineteenth Century England," *Journal of Criminal Justice* 8, no. 4 (1980); J. R. Dinwiddy, *Radicalism and Reform in Britain, 1780–1850* (London: Hambledon Press, 1992); Burns and Innes, *Rethinking the Age of Reform*, 1–70.

27. Michael T. Davis and Paul A. Pickering, *Unrespectable Radicals? Popular Politics in the Age of Reform* (Aldershot, UK: Ashgate, 2008); Iorwerth Prothero, "William Benbow and the Concept of the 'General Strike,'" *Past and Present* 63 (1974); William Benbow, *The Crimes of the Clergy; or, the Pillars of the Priest-Craft Shaken* (London: Benbow, 1823); "The Parson and the Boy, or, the Fire-Shovel Hats in a Bustle: Being an Account of the Trial of the Reverend Thomas Jepson, Doctor of Divinity, and Tutor at Cambridge, on a Charge of Attempting to commit an Unnatural Crime on James Welsh, a labourer," *Cobbett's Weekly Political Register*, August 2, 1823.

28. Cocks, *Nameless Offences*.

29. Charles Upchurch, *Before Wilde: Sex between Men in Britain's Age of Reform* (Berkeley: University of California Press, 2009).

30. *Hansard*, Commons Sitting, vol. 57, March 8, 1841, 54.

31. Matt Cook, *Queer Domesticities: Homosexuality and Home Life in Twentieth-Century London* (London: Palgrave Macmillan, 2014); Emma Rothschild, *The Inner Life of Empires: An Eighteenth-Century History* (Princeton, NJ: Princeton University Press, 2011). For the role of family in shaping self-understandings in relation to cultural forms, see John R. Gillis, *A World of Their Own Making: Myth, Ritual, and the Quest for Family Values* (New York: Basic Books, 1996).

32. E. P. Thompson, *Customs in Common* (New York: New Press, 1991); James Vernon, *Politics and the People: A Study in English Political Culture, c. 1815–1867* (New York: Cambridge University Press, 1993).

33. Iain McCalman, *Radical Underworld: Prophets, Revolutionaries, and Pornographers in London, 1795–1840* (Cambridge: Cambridge University Press, 1988). Digitized works used include Violet Dickinson, ed., *Miss Eden's Letters* (London: Macmillan, 1919); William Toynbee, *Glimpses of the Twenties* (London: A. Constable, 1909); and R. G. Thorne, ed., *The House of Commons, 1790–1820*, 5 vols. (London: Published for the History of Parliament Trust by Secker and Warburg, 1986), and also available online at http://www.historyofparliamentonline.org/research/members.

34. Knight, *Lord Byron's Marriage*; Leslie Alexis Marchand, *Byron: A Portrait* (New York: Knopf, 1970); Doris Langley Moore, *Lord Byron: Accounts Rendered* (New York: Harper and Row, 1974); Crompton, *Byron and Greek Love*; Fiona MacCarthy, *Byron: Life and Legend* (New York: Farrar, Straus and Giroux, 2002), xii–xiii.

35. Bentham, *Introduction to the Principles of Morals and Legislation*, xii.

36. Chapter 1 demonstrates how John Austin, one of six men on the Royal Commission tasked by Lord John Russell to recommend which crimes should no longer carry the death penalty, knew about these ideas in Bentham. Chapter 6 illustrates how these ideas of Bentham seem evident in the final report produced by the Royal Commission. Chapter 5 shows how these ideas of Bentham were quoted in a political argument over ending the death penalty for sodomy.

37. For the first substantial discussion of this 1772 event in a secondary source, see

Rictor Norton, *Mother Clap's Molly House: The Gay Subculture in England, 1700–1830*, rev. 2nd ed. (Stroud, Gloucestershire: Chalfont Press, 2006).

38. Seth Koven, *The Match Girl and the Heiress* (Princeton, NJ: Princeton University Press, 2014).

39. Matthew Gregory Lewis, *Journal of a West Indian Proprietor: Kept during a Residence in the Island of Jamaica* (London: John Murray, 1834).

40. McCalman, *Radical Underworld*, 34–39, 225–227; H. T. Dickinson, *British Radicalism and the French Revolution, 1789–1815* (New York: Blackwell, 1985); Gary Dyer, *British Satire and the Politics of Style, 1789–1832* (Cambridge: Cambridge University Press, 1997). "Sodomite" is addressed here as a cultural category rather than as an identity category. The debate over a sodomite identity in the eighteenth century is addressed in the Conclusion.

41. James Byrne, Percy Jocelyn, and William Cobbett, *The Trial of Unfortunate Byrne (Late Coachman to the Hon. John Jocelyn,) . . . Which Is Annexed the Opinion of That Great Political Writer Mr. Cobbett on the Late Abominable and Disgusting Transaction* (Dublin: Published at No. 1 Princes Street, 1811); Norton, *Mother Clap's Molly House*; Brian Lacey, *Terrible Queer Creatures: Homosexuality in Irish History* (Dublin: Wordwell Books, 2008).

42. H. Montgomery Hyde, *The Strange Death of Lord Castlereagh* (London: Heinemann, 1959), 40–41, 50–52; Harriet Arbuthnot, *The Journal of Mrs. Arbuthnot, 1820–1832*, ed. Gerald Wellesley Wellington and Francis Bamford (London: Macmillan, 1950), 176–178.

43. Letter to Beckford and Part II Prospectus, BENTHAM, 161a, ff. 1–19.

44. Burns and Innes, *Rethinking the Age of Reform*, 46–47; Peter Mandler, *Aristocratic Government in the Age of Reform: Whigs and Liberals, 1830–1852* (Oxford: Clarendon Press, 1990).

45. Offences Against the Person Bill, Clauses to be Proposed in Committee, by Mr. Law. June 1835; 6 Will. IV.—Sess. 1835. A Bill [As Amended by the Committee] For Amending the Law Relating to Offenses Against the Person in Certain Cases, Prepared and brought in by Mr. Jervis and Mr. Pryme, July 1, 1835.

46. Fr. Frank Ryan, OMI, "The Execution of James Pratt and John Smith . . . Redeeming Our Past, Securing Our Future," unpublished manuscript, 2014. Cocks, *Nameless Offences*, 38.

47. *Hansard*, Commons Sitting, vol. 56, February 9, 1841, 463; *Hansard*, Commons Sitting, vol. 57, March 8, 1841, 54.

48. *Royal Commission to Consider Law Relating to Indictable Offences*. Report, Appendix (Draft Code) Command Papers: Reports of Commissioners Parliament: 1878–1879; Criminal Code Bill, 43 Vict., 1880.

CHAPTER 1

1. *Report of the Select Committee on Criminal Laws*, 1819, 139–140. Figures are given in this report for London and Middlesex from 1689 onward and checked against the full-text *Old Bailey Proceedings Online* (version 8.0) and *Ordinary of Newgate's Accounts* for accuracy.

2. Letter to Beckford and Part II Prospectus, BENTHAM, 161a, ff. 1–19.

3. Lewis Melville, *The Life and Letters of William Beckford of Fonthill* (London: William Heinemann, 1970), 185–188, 283–287; Harold Alfred Nelson Brockman, *The Caliph of Fonthill* (London: Werner Laurie, 1956), 165–173, 31–43; Anita McConnell, 2009, "Beckford, William Thomas (1760–1844), writer and art collector," *Oxford Dictionary of National Biography*, April 2019.

4. Harry Cocks, *Visions of Sodom: Religion, Homoerotic Desire, and the End of the World in England, c. 1550–1850* (Chicago: University of Chicago Press, 2017).

5. Letter to Beckford, 4, BENTHAM, 161a, ff. 14.

6. Leon Radzinowicz, *A History of English Criminal Law and Its Administration from 1750*, vol. 1, *The Movement for Reform 1750–1833* (London: Stevens, 1948), 1:355–357.

7. Jeremy Bentham, *An Introduction to the Principles of Morals and Legislation. Printed in the Year 1780, and Now First Published* (London: T. Payne, and Son, 1789).

8. Louis Crompton, *Homosexuality and Civilization* (Cambridge, MA: Belknap Press of Harvard University Press, 2003), 530.

9. F. Rosen, 2014, "Bentham, Jeremy (1748–1832), philosopher, jurist, and reformer," *Oxford Dictionary of National Biography*, May 2014.

10. Jeremy Bentham and Louis Crompton, "Offences against One's Self," *Journal of Homosexuality* 3, no. 4 (1978); Jeremy Bentham and Louis Crompton, "Jeremy Bentham's Essay on 'Paederasty,'" *Journal of Homosexuality* 4, no. 1 (1978); Louis Crompton, "Jeremy Bentham's Essay on 'Paederasty,'" *Journal of Homosexuality* 3, no. 4 (1978).

11. Crompton, "Bentham's Essay on 'Paederasty,'" 383.

12. Ibid., 384–385. Emphasis added by Crompton, to emphasize Bentham's editing of the text. The italicized phrase was later changed to "betrayed."

13. Louis Crompton, *Byron and Greek Love: Homophobia in 19th-Century England* (Berkeley: University of California Press, 1985), 30–31; "It is notable of course that Bentham never published these proposals, though he repeatedly considered doing so. He was intensely aware of the odium they would bring upon his philosophy and his personal character in a climate in which, as he himself analysed so acutely, hatred of sodomy had become a touchstone of respectability." Faramerz Dabhoiwala, "Lust and Liberty," *Past and Present* 207, no. 1 (May 2010): 172–173.

14. Bentham, *Principles of Morals and Legislation*, xii.

15. Ibid., xv.

16. Ibid.

17. Crompton, "Bentham's Essay on 'Paederasty,'" 383–388.

18. Bentham, *Principles of Morals and Legislation*, ccciv.

19. Ibid., ccciii–ccciv.

20. The quote continues, "Except in as far as in virtue of some connection he may have with the offender, either in point of sympathy or of interest,' a mischief of the derivative kind" may happen to devolve upon him." * See ch. vi [Sensibility], xxv, xxvi. ** See ch. xii [Consequences], iv. Bentham, *Principles of Morals and Legislation*, ccciv.

21. Bentham, *Principles of Morals and Legislation*, ccciv.

22. Ibid.

23. Crompton, "Bentham's Essay on 'Paederasty,'" 386.

24. Emphasis added. Bentham, *Principles of Morals and Legislation*, ccciv.

25. Ibid., ccxviii.

26. Only six items appear in this list. Ibid., cclxxxviii.

27. This seems similar to Montesquieu's belief that for crimes against morals, "fines, public infamy, expulsion from home and society and other corrective measures should be sufficient." Radzinowicz, *History of English Criminal Law*, 1:273.

28. Hal Gladfelder, "In Search of Lost Texts: Thomas Cannon's *Ancient and Modern Pederasty Investigated and Exemplify'd*," *Eighteenth-Century Life* 31, no. 1 (Winter 2007): 22–38; Hal Gladfelder, "The Indictment of John Purser, Containing Thomas Cannon's *Ancient and Modern Pederasty Investigated and Exemplify'd*," *Eighteenth-Century Life* 31, no. 1 (Winter 2007).

29. *Report of the Select Committee on Criminal Laws*, 148–155. Checked against *Old Bailey Proceedings Online* and *Ordinary of Newgate's Account* for case details and to determine whether sentences were carried out. The 1730 execution stemmed from the rape of a fourteen-year-old, Paul Oliver, by a man.

30. *British Newspaper Archive*, the *17th-18th Century Burney Collection Newspapers* database, and the *Times Digital Archive*. For the methods used in the survey, see Charles Upchurch, "Full-Text Databases and Historical Research: Cautionary Results from a Ten-Year Study," *Journal of Social History* 45 (Fall 2012).

31. Although his rank was lieutenant, Robert Jones was known in society and referred to in the press most often as "Captain Jones."

32. Rictor Norton, *Mother Clap's Molly House: The Gay Subculture in England, 1700–1830*, rev. 2nd ed. (Stroud, Gloucestershire: Chalfont Press, 2006); Anna Clark, "The Chevalier d'Eon and Wilkes: Masculinity and Politics in the Eighteenth Century," *Eighteenth-Century Studies* 32, no. 1 (1998): 34.

33. As Hannah Barker has argued, in the 1770s, new power was infused into the idea "that the press could act as a public tribunal in which the behaviour of the country's rulers could be judged, criticized, and ultimately kept in check." Hannah Barker, *Newspapers, Politics, and Public Opinion in Late Eighteenth-Century England* (Oxford: Clarendon Press, 1998), 12; Bob Harris, *A Patriot Press: National Politics and the London Press in the 1740s* (New York: Oxford University Press, 1993); Kathleen Wilson, *The Sense of the People: Politics, Culture and Imperialism in England, 1715–1785* (Cambridge: Cambridge University Press, 1995).

34. *Public Ledger*, August 5, 1772. Norton, *Mother Clap's Molly House*, 1st ed., 170–171. "The notion of the brave hero defying the effeminate aristocrat deployed a notion of masculine independence that cut across class, as historian Kathleen Wilson observes." Anna Clark, *Scandal: The Sexual Politics of the British Constitution* (Princeton, NJ: Princeton University Press, 2004), 15; Wilson, *Sense of the People*, 185–205.

35. "To the King," *London Evening Post*, August 6–8, 1772; "To the Printer of the *London Evening Post*," *London Evening Post*, August 8–11, 1772.

36. "To the Printer of the *Morning Chronicle*," *Morning Chronicle*, August 11, 1772.

37. "To the Printer of the *Morning Chronicle*," *Morning Chronicle*, August 13, 1772.

38. "To the Printer of the *Morning Chronicle*," *Morning Chronicle*, August 20, 1772.

39. "To the Printer of the *Morning Chronicle*," *Morning Chronicle*, August 21, 1772.

40. "To the Printer of the *Morning Chronicle*," *Morning Chronicle*, August 13, 1772.

41. Ibid.

42. "To the Printer of the *Morning Chronicle*," *Morning Chronicle*, August 17, 1772.

43. Ibid.

44. Ibid.

45. "But it may be a question, whether the public prosecution thereof be founded in wisdom." "To the Printer of the *Morning Chronicle*," *Morning Chronicle*, August 20, 1772.

46. Bentham and Crompton, "Offences against One's Self," 403.

47. Ibid., 400.

48. Ibid., 403.

49. For a resonant argument over the power of the law and prohibitions to shape desire and identity, see Michel Foucault, *The History of Sexuality*, vol. 1, *An Introduction* (New York: Vintage Books, 1990).

50. BENTHAM, Box 74a, folio 3; Crompton, *Byron and Greek Love*, 27. In 1774, Bentham wrote that he would not abandon these views in relation to sex between men, despite public opinion. BENTHAM, Box 74a, folio 4; Crompton, *Byron and Greek Love*, 30.

51. For William Courtenay, see Brockman, *Caliph of Fonthill*, 29–42; Laurent Châtel, *William Beckford: The Elusive Orientalist* (Oxford: Voltaire Foundation, 2016); H. Montgomery Hyde, *The Other Love: A History and Contemporary Survey of Homosexuality in Britain* (London: Heinemann, 1970), 72–75.

52. For other examples of individuals associated with same-sex desire who continued to function at least for a time in upper-class society, see Martha Vicinus, *Intimate Friends: Women Who Loved Women, 1778–1928* (Chicago: University of Chicago Press, 2004), 7–28; Harry Cocks, "Safeguarding Civility: Sodomy, Class and Moral Reform in Early Nineteenth-Century England," *Past and Present* 190, no. 1 (2006); H. G. Cocks, *Nameless Offences: Speaking of Male Homosexual Desire in Nineteenth-Century England* (London: I. B. Tauris, 2003); Charles Upchurch, *Before Wilde: Sex between Men in Britain's Age of Reform* (Berkeley: University of California Press, 2009), 30–41; Crompton, *Homosexuality and Civilization*, 483–488; Alan Bray, *Homosexuality in Renaissance England* (New York: Columbia University Press, 1995).

53. Radzinowicz, *History of English Criminal Law*, 1:282, 1:285.

54. Ibid., 1:240.

55. Ibid., 1:406, 1:410.

56. Ibid., 1:406.

57. Ibid., 1:248, 1:254.

58. Ibid., 1:422–423.

59. Ibid., 1:430, 1:445, 1:475.

60. Ibid., 1:447.

61. Ibid.

62. Ibid., 1:422.

63. Arthur Gilbert, "Buggery and the British Navy, 1700–1861," *Journal of Social History* 10 (1976); Arthur Gilbert, "Sodomy and the Law in Eighteenth- and Early Nineteenth-Century Britain," *Societas* 8, no. 3 (1978); Seth Stein LeJacq, "Buggery's Travels: Royal Navy Sodomy on Ship and Shore in the Long Eighteenth Century," *Journal for Maritime Research* 17, no. 2 (2015).

64. Three-quarters of these executions were the result of convictions in civilian courts, while the rest resulted from military judicial proceedings. Crompton, "Bentham's Essay on 'Paederasty,'" 384.

65. One of the executed men was a keeper of the house, and one had lived on the premises for two years. *Old Bailey Proceedings Online* (version 8.0), April 20, 1726, trials of Gabriel Lawrence, William Griffin, and Thomas Wright. Another man was convicted and sentenced to death for sodomy with an eighteen-year-old on the same day, but the incident involved only two men and was not connected to the molly house, and he was reprieved. *Old Bailey Proceedings Online*, April 20, 1726, trial of George Redear.

66. *Old Bailey Proceedings Online*, December 4, 1776, trial of Thomas Burrows.

67. *Old Bailey Proceedings Online*, February 15, 1797, trial of William Winklin.

68. *Report of the Select Committee on Criminal Laws*, 5.

69. Letter to Beckford and Part II Prospectus, BENTHAM, 161a, ff. 1–19.

70. Part II Prospectus, 2, 7, BENTHAM, 161a, ff. 15–16.

71. Emphasis original. Letter to Beckford, 1, BENTHAM, 161a, ff. 14.

72. Ibid., 2.

73. Ibid., 1.

74. Ibid.

75. Ibid., 2.

76. Ibid., 3.

77. Part II Prospectus, 1, BENTHAM, 161a, ff. 15.

78. Ibid.

79. It is indicated here that historical references would be used to anchor arguments, with a reference mentioning that "for James Ist . . . as inferred from practices, pleasure of sexuality in the Attic mode not too great for a King." Ibid., 2.

80. "By the Law of Moses, (Leviticus, xx. 18.) in case of conjunction under that circumstance, death was the punishment of the male." Ibid., 4.

81. Ibid., 5–6.

82. Emphasis original. Ibid., 6.

83. Emphasis original. Ibid., 7. This is a possible reference to a translator of ancient texts working in England in the fifteenth century, Antoyne de Beccara.

84. Emphasis original. Ibid., 7–8.

85. Ibid., 8.

86. Ibid., 8–9.

87. Ibid., 10.

88. Ibid.

89. Ibid.

90. Ibid., 12–14.

91. Ibid., 12.

92. Ibid., 14.

93. Letter to Beckford, 3, BENTHAM, 161a, ff. 14.

94. Ibid.

95. Ibid., 4; Patrick Woodland, 2004, "Meredith, Sir William, third baronet (bap. 1724, d. 1790), politician," *Oxford Dictionary of National Biography*, April 2019; John Brooke, "Meredith, Sir William, 3rd Bt. (1725–90)," Member Biographies, in *The History of Parliament: The House of Commons 1754–1790*, ed. L. Namier and J. Brooke (Cambridge: Cambridge University Press, 1964).

96. Letter to Beckford, 4, BENTHAM, 161a, ff. 14.

97. Ibid.

Chapter 2

1. Isabella Hedgeland (née Kelly) to the Committee of the Literary Fund, British Library, Western Manuscripts, Loan 96 RLF 1/632/9, 1832.

2. On the question of whether the relationship was romantic, see Louis F. Peck, *A Life of Matthew G. Lewis* (Cambridge, MA: Harvard University Press, 1961), 63–66, 220, 236, 268; David Lorne Macdonald, *Monk Lewis: A Critical Biography* (Toronto: University of Toronto Press, 2000), 15, 60–63; Mrs. Cornwell Baron-Wilson, *The Life and Correspondence of M. G. Lewis: With Many Pieces in Prose and Verse, Never before Published* (London: H. Colburn, 1839), 1:271–276, 1:362, 2:94–105, 2:382–387; Montague Summers, *The Gothic Quest: A History of the Gothic Novel* (New York: Russell and Russell, 1964), 263–267, 290, 305; George E. Haggerty, *Queer Gothic* (Urbana: University of Illinois Press, 2006), 263–267. This question is also addressed in the following chapter.

3. In a similar way, Baron-Wilson writes that after an incident that led to their parting of ways, "Lewis no longer recognized his unworthy protégé as a member of his family." Baron-Wilson, *Life and Correspondence of M. G. Lewis*, 2:95.

4. "A Bill: for taking away the Punishment of Death in certain Cases . . . Prepared and brought in by Mr. Kelly and Dr. Lushington." June 23, 1840—4 Vict., and "A Bill [As Amended by the Committee] For taking away the Punishment of Death in certain Cases . . . Prepared and brought in by Mr. Kelly, Dr. Lushington, and Mr. Serjeant Talfourd." May 24, 1841—4 Vict. For an example of such a denunciation in the Lords, see *Hansard*, Lords Sitting, vol. 58, June 17, 1841, 1557.

5. Matthew requested that Sir Henry Lushington "burn all such as he may judge improper to be seen. If there are any which he wishes to keep for himself or for my sister, he is at liberty to do so." Baron-Wilson, *Life and Correspondence of M. G. Lewis*, 2:384.

6. "It was by far the most important of his spheres of activity outside his professional career." S. M. Waddams, *Law, Politics, and the Church of England: The Career of Stephen Lushington, 1782–1873* (Cambridge: Cambridge University Press, 1992), 63–99.

7. Macdonald, *Monk Lewis*, 60; Ernest Lovell, ed., *His Very Self and Voice: Collected Conversations of Lord Byron* (New York: Macmillan, 1954), 133.

8. George Mosse, *The Image of Man: The Creation of Modern Masculinity* (New York: Oxford University Press, 1996); Henry French and Mark Rothery, *Man's Es-*

tate: Landed Gentry Masculinities 1660–1900 (Oxford: Oxford University Press, 2012); Sean Brady, *Masculinity and Male Homosexuality in Britain, 1861–1913* (New York: Palgrave Macmillan, 2005).

9. For an analysis of the term "Attic taste," see Chapter 1.

10. Harry Cocks, *Visions of Sodom: Religion, Homoerotic Desire, and the End of the World in England, c. 1550–1850* (Chicago: University of Chicago Press, 2017); George Mosse, *Nationalism and Sexuality: Respectability and Abnormal Sexuality in Modern Europe* (New York: H. Fertig, 1985), 37–40, 181–188.

11. James Gregory, *Victorians against the Gallows: Capital Punishment and the Abolitionist Movement in Nineteenth-Century Britain* (London: I. B. Tauris, 2012); Elizabeth Orman Tuttle, *The Crusade against Capital Punishment in Great Britain* (London: Stevens, 1961); Vic Gatrell, *The Hanging Tree: Execution and the English People, 1770–1868* (Oxford: Oxford University Press, 1994); Harry Potter, *Hanging in Judgment: Religion and the Death Penalty in England from the Bloody Code to Abolition* (London: SCM Press, 1993); John Laurence, *A History of Capital Punishment, with Special Reference to Capital Punishment in Great Britain* (Port Washington, NY: Kennikat Press, 1971); Roger Chadwick, *Bureaucratic Mercy: The Home Office and the Treatment of Capital Cases in Victorian Britain* (New York: Garland Publishing, 1992); M. J. Wiener, *Men of Blood: Violence, Manliness and Criminal Justice in Victorian England* (Cambridge: Cambridge University Press, 2004); Randall McGowen, "A Powerful Sympathy: Terror, the Prison, and Humanitarian Reform in Early Nineteenth-Century Britain," *Journal of British Studies* 25, no. 3 (July 1986). Fitzroy Kelly is not mentioned in the main biography of Stephen Lushington, by S. M. Waddams. For Lushington's work on the abolition of capital punishment in general, see Waddams, *Law, Politics, and the Church*, 26–30.

12. Contradictory information for Isabella Kelly is found in the handful of short secondary sources on her life. Where conflicts exist over otherwise unverifiable details of her personal life, the information she provided to the Literary Fund in 1828 and 1832 is given precedence. Other sources include Roger Lonsdale, ed., *Eighteenth Century Women Poets: An Oxford Anthology* (New York: Oxford University Press, 1989); Joanne Shattock, *The Oxford Guide to British Women Writers* (Oxford: Oxford University Press, 1993); Janet Todd, ed., *A Dictionary of British and American Women Writers, 1660–1800* (Totowa, NJ: Rowman and Allanheld, 1985), 183; Virginia Blain, Patricia Clements, and Isobel Grundy, eds., *The Feminist Companion to Literature in English: Women Writers from the Middle Ages to the Present* (New Haven: Yale University Press, 1990), 602–603.

13. Isabella Hedgeland (née Kelly) to the Committee of the Literary Fund, letter dated October 25, 1832.

14. Kelly "may have been the natural son who had joined Col. Kelly in Madras in 1786 but eventually failed to inherit his wealth." Lonsdale, *Eighteenth Century Women Poets*, 481.

15. Edward Hawke, the First Baron Hawke, served as First Lord of the Admiralty from 1766 to 1771 and died in 1781. Martin Hawke, the Second Baron Hawke, died in 1805.

16. Baron-Wilson, *Life and Correspondence of M. G. Lewis*, 1:271.

17. Isabella Hedgeland (née Kelly) to the Committee of the Literary Fund, letter dated October 25, 1832.

18. Richard Greene, 2016, "Kelly [née Fordyce; other married name Hedgeland], Isabella (bap. 1759, d. 1857), poet and novelist," *Oxford Dictionary of National Biography*, April 2019.

19. There is conflicting information in secondary sources. The information given here is based on the parish birth registers for William Henry Martin Dillon Kelly, Fitzroy Edward Kelly, and Amel Rosa Eliza Charlotte Souter Johnson Kelly. *England Births and Baptisms*, available at https://www.findmypast.co.uk.

20. Dorothy Blakey, *The Minerva Press, 1790–1820* (London: Printed for the Bibliographical Society at the University Press, Oxford, 1939).

21. Isabella Hedgeland (née Kelly) to the Committee of the Literary Fund, letter dated October 25, 1832.

22. Summers, *Gothic Quest*, 263.

23. Peck, *Life of Matthew G. Lewis*, 24–29.

24. Byron gave up his Hindon seat to represent another rotten borough adjacent to Fonthill Abbey.

25. Nigel Leask, 2015, "Lewis, Matthew Gregory [called Monk Lewis] (1775–1818), novelist and playwright," *Oxford Dictionary of National Biography*, April 2019.

26. Baron-Wilson, *Life and Correspondence of M. G. Lewis*, 1:272.

27. Ibid., 1:362.

28. Ibid., 1:275.

29. Matthew wrote to his mother that "it would be in the bookseller's interest to have your name known . . . and then would follow paragraph after paragraph, with all our family affairs ripped up, till every one of us would be ready to go mad with vexation." This debate between Matthew and Frances occurred in 1804. Ibid., 1:276.

30. Ibid., 2:383.

31. Ibid.

32. Matthew seemed to be quoting that phrase back to his mother from a letter she had written to him. Ibid., 2:382.

33. Baron-Wilson, *Life and Correspondence of M. G. Lewis*, 1:284. Some sources indicate that Matthew's earliest efforts to publish his work were inspired by the desire to have an independent income with which he could assist his mother. Leask, "Lewis, Matthew Gregory [called Monk Lewis]," *Oxford Dictionary of National Biography*.

34. Summers, *Gothic Quest*, 266.

35. Baron-Wilson, *Life and Correspondence of M. G. Lewis*, 1:272–274; Summers, *Gothic Quest*, 265. From a letter dated August 11, 1802; Macdonald, *Monk Lewis*, 60–61.

36. Isabella Hedgeland (née Kelly) to the Committee of the Literary Fund. The *Oxford Dictionary of National Biography* entry for Isabella lists Robert Hawke Kelly as "apparently" dying in Madras in 1807. Greene, "Kelly [née Fordyce; other married name Hedgeland], Isabella," *Oxford Dictionary of National Biography*.

37. *Oxford Dictionary of National Biography* has Isabella marrying Hedgeland in 1809 and his dying in 1812, contradicting Isabella's statements to the Literary Fund in

1828 and 1832 that they were married for only one year. Greene, "Kelly [née Fordyce; other married name Hedgeland], Isabella," *Oxford Dictionary of National Biography*; Isabella Hedgeland (née Kelly) to the Committee of the Literary Fund, letters dated October 25, 1832, and July 25, 1828.

38. Summers, *Gothic Quest*, 266.

39. Matthew's mother, Frances, was described as "taking a deep interest in the lad's welfare." Ibid.

40. Ibid.

41. Baron-Wilson, *Life and Correspondence of M. G. Lewis*, 2:96.

42. Ibid., 2:94.

43. Summers, *Gothic Quest*, 263; Peck, *Life of Matthew G. Lewis*, 103.

44. Macdonald, *Monk Lewis*, 63; Peck, *Life of Matthew G. Lewis*, 66.

45. George Haggerty, "Literature and Homosexuality in the Late Eighteenth Century: Walpole, Beckford, and Lewis," *Studies in the Novel* 18, no. 4 (Winter 1986): 349.

46. Macdonald, *Monk Lewis*, 60; Thomas Medwin, *Conversations of Lord Byron: Noted during a Residence with his Lordship at Pisa, in the Years 1821 and 1822* (London: Printed for Henry Colburn, New Burlington Street, 1824), 235; Peck, *Life of Matthew G. Lewis*, 65, 302n104.

47. Macdonald, *Monk Lewis*, 63.

48. Ibid., 61; Baron-Wilson, *Life and Correspondence of M. G. Lewis*, 2:384–385; Peck, *Life of Matthew G. Lewis*, 65.

49. Macdonald, *Monk Lewis*, 62; Baron-Wilson, *Life and Correspondence of M. G. Lewis*, 2:99–102; Summers, *Gothic Quest*, 266.

50. Baron-Wilson, *Life and Correspondence of M. G. Lewis*, 2:100, 2:102–103.

51. Ibid., 2:101.

52. Macdonald, *Monk Lewis*, 62; Baron-Wilson, *Life and Correspondence of M. G. Lewis*, 2:95, 2:103.

53. Macdonald, *Monk Lewis*, 62; Baron-Wilson, *Life and Correspondence of M. G. Lewis*, 2:99–101; Summers, *Gothic Quest*, 267.

54. Three speeches by Hassan expressing antislavery sentiments were marked by the licenser. These speeches were included in the printed version of the play without significant alterations. Peck, *Life of Matthew G. Lewis*, 75.

55. Leask, "Lewis, Matthew Gregory [called Monk Lewis]," *Oxford Dictionary of National Biography*; Peck, *Life of Matthew G. Lewis*, 158.

56. Macdonald, *Monk Lewis*, 15.

57. Lewis canceled the £1,500 that was to be left to William in his will once this annuity was set up. Macdonald, *Monk Lewis*, 63; Baron-Wilson, *Life and Correspondence of M. G. Lewis*, 2:103–105, 2:387.

58. Isabella wrote that Jerdan had "always acted in a polite and friendly way" toward her. Isabella Hedgeland (née Kelly) to the Committee of the Literary Fund, letter dated October 25, 1832.

59. According to Jerdan, these observations were made after William's death and while Fitzroy Kelly was Solicitor General, which places them in either 1845 or 1846. William performed in New York for the first time on November 17, 1831. William

Jerdan, *Autobiography, with His Literary, Political, and Social Reminiscences and Correspondence during the Last Fifty Years* (London: A. Hall, Virtue, 1852–1853), 1:102–103.

60. *Harper's New Monthly Magazine* 79 (November 1889): 882. William died in 1843.

61. *Times*, September 20, 1880. His obituary in the *Times* indicated that he "often lamented" this lack of public school or university education. For the role of public schools and universities in shaping masculinity in this period, see Paul Deslandes, *Oxbridge Men: British Masculinity and the Undergraduate Experience, 1850–1920* (Bloomington: Indiana University Press, 2005).

62. C. J. W. Allen, 2004, "Kelly, Sir Fitzroy Edward (1796–1880), judge," *Oxford Dictionary of National Biography*, April 2019.

63. Mrs. Isabella Hedgeland, late Mrs. Kelly, 1828–32: Registered Case—No. 632—vol. 19. Isabella Hedgeland (née Kelly) to the Committee of the Literary Fund, letter dated July 30, 1828. A note on the back of the letter mentions that Isabella is the mother to Fitzroy Kelly, the barrister.

64. Isabella Hedgeland (née Kelly) to the Committee of the Literary Fund, letter dated July 25, 1828.

65. *Wiltshire Marriages Index, 1538–1933, Parish marriages, England*, available at https://www.findmypast.co.uk.

66. Isabella Hedgeland (née Kelly) to the Committee of the Literary Fund, letter dated October 25, 1832.

67. Allen, "Kelly, Sir Fitzroy Edward," *Oxford Dictionary of National Biography*.

68. Ibid.

69. *Times*, September 20, 1880.

70. Kelly first became Solicitor General in the reconstituted government that Peel formed near the end of 1845. Press cuttings on Isabella Hedgeland and the success and death of her son, Sir Edward Fitzroy Kelly, British Library, Western Manuscripts, Loan 96 RLF 1/632/14, 1848.

71. *Hansard*, Commons Sitting, vol. 55, July 15, 1840, 737. For William Ewart's efforts in the area of capital punishment, see W. A. Munford, *William Ewart, M.P., 1798–1869: Portrait of a Radical* (London: Grafton, 1960).

72. Waddams, *Law, Politics, and the Church of England*, 181–188.

73. Ibid., 24.

74. Ibid., 181–183; S. M. Waddams, 2004, "Lushington, Stephen (1782–1873), judge," *Oxford Dictionary of National Biography*, April 2019.

75. Charles Buxton, ed., *Memoirs of Sir Thomas Fowell Buxton, Baronet. With Selections from His Correspondence* (London: John Murray, 1860), 133; Waddams, "Lushington, Stephen," *Oxford Dictionary of National Biography*.

76. Waddams, "Lushington, Stephen," *Oxford Dictionary of National Biography*.

77. Among other things, Coleridge called the book "a poison for youth, and a provocative for the debauchee." Peck, *Life of Matthew G. Lewis*, 25; Waddams, *Law, Politics, and the Church of England*, 52, 55–57.

78. Peck, *Life of Matthew G. Lewis*, 168. Letter of January 24, 1819, Sophia Shedden to Walter Scott, W, IX, fol. 10. Published in part in Wilfred Partington, ed., *The*

Private Letter-Books of Sir Walter Scott: Selections from the Abbotsford Manuscripts (New York: Frederick A. Stokes, 1930), 228–230.

79. "Journal of a West India Proprietor; kept during a Residence in the Island of Jamaica," *Literary Gazette: A Weekly Journal of Literature, Science, and the Fine Arts* 893 (March 1834): 150–152; "Journal of a West India Proprietor," *Metropolitan Magazine* 9, no. 36 (April 1834): 103–104; "Journal of a West India Proprietor," *Gentleman's Magazine* 159 (February 1836): 161–164; "Journals of a West India Proprietor," *Select Journal of Foreign Periodical Literature* 4, no. 2 (October 1834): 38–49; "Journal of a West India Proprietor," *Quarterly Review* 50, no. 100 (January 1834): 374.

80. "Journal of a West India Proprietor," *Edinburgh Review* 59 (April 1834): 74.

81. Peck, *Life of Matthew G. Lewis*, 169.

82. Boyd Hilton, *The Age of Atonement: The Influence of Evangelicalism on Social and Economic Thought, 1795–1865* (New York: Oxford University Press, 1987), 144–145. See the discussion of John Church in Anna Clark, *The Struggle for the Breeches: Gender and the Making of the British Working Class* (Berkeley: University of California Press, 1995), 113–117, 153.

83. See especially Matthew Gregory Lewis, *Journal of a West Indian Proprietor: Kept during a Residence in the Island of Jamaica* (London: John Murray, 1834), 118, 119, 166.

84. For a discussion of the *Legacies of British Slave-Ownership* project and the research that has stemmed from it, see Catherine Hall, Nicholas Draper, Keith McClelland, Katie Donington, and Rachel Lang, *Legacies of British Slave-Ownership: Colonial Slavery and the Formation of Victorian Britain* (Cambridge: Cambridge University Press, 2014).

85. Lewis, *Journal of a West Indian Proprietor*. Current secondary works analyzing the journal include Maureen Harkin, "Matthew Lewis's Journal of a West India Proprietor: Surveillance and Space on the Plantation," *Nineteenth-Century Contexts* 24, no. 2 (June 2002); Ellen Malenas, "Reform Ideology and Generic Structure in Matthew Lewis's 'Journal of a West India Proprietor,'" *Studies in Eighteenth Century Culture* 35 (January 2006); Lisa Ann Robertson, "'Sensible' Slavery," *Prose Studies* 29, no. 2 (August 2007).

86. Lewis, *Journal of a West Indian Proprietor*, 30–31.

87. Ibid., 150. There are only the occasional comments, such as "certainly, if this star be really Lucifer, that 'Son of the Morning,' the Devil must be 'an extremely pretty fellow.'" Ibid., 59–60.

88. Ibid., 47.

89. Ibid.

90. For an analysis of pirate ships specifically and eighteenth-century Atlantic maritime crews in general as sources of multiracial resistance to systems of imperialism, see Peter Linebaugh and Marcus Rediker, *The Many-Headed Hydra: Sailors, Slaves, Commoners, and the Hidden History of the Revolutionary Atlantic* (Boston: Beacon Press, 2000); Marcus Rediker, *Villains of All Nations: Atlantic Pirates in the Golden Age* (Boston: Beacon Press, 2004); Lewis, *Journal of a West Indian Proprietor*, 59.

91. Lewis, *Journal of a West Indian Proprietor*, 61.

92. First emphasis added, second original. Ibid., 60–61.

93. Ibid., 61. A similar sentiment is expressed later in the work, when, after individuals who had formerly been enslaved on the estate came to a festival Matthew held and paid their respects to him, Matthew writes, "All this may be palaver; but certainly they at least play their parts." Ibid., 90.

94. Ibid., 62.

95. Ibid., 108. For an analysis of paternalist sentiments expressed by slaveholders, see Trevor Burnard, *Mastery, Tyranny, and Desire: Thomas Thistlewood and His Slaves in the Anglo-Jamaican World* (Chapel Hill: University of North Carolina Press, 2004); Eugene D. Genovese, *Fatal Self-Deception: Slaveholding Paternalism in the Old South* (New York: Cambridge University Press, 2011); Caitlin Rosenthal, *Accounting for Slavery: Masters and Management* (Cambridge, MA: Harvard University Press, 2018).

96. Lewis, *Journal of a West Indian Proprietor*, 102. For comparisons between enslaved individuals in the Caribbean and factory workers in Britain, see Seymour Drescher, "Cart Whip and Billy Roller: Antislavery and Reform Symbolism in Industrializing Britain," *Journal of Social History* 15, no. 11 (September 1981); David Brion Davis, "Capitalism, Abolitionism, and Hegemony," in *British Capitalism and Caribbean Slavery: The Legacy of Eric Williams, Studies in Interdisciplinary History*, ed. Barbara Solow and Stanley Engerman (New York: Cambridge University Press, 1987), 209–277.

97. Lewis, *Journal of a West Indian Proprietor*, 133–139.

98. Ibid., 100.

99. Ibid., 95, 115.

100. James Epstein, *Scandal of Colonial Rule: Power and Subversion in the British Atlantic during the Age of Revolution* (New York: Cambridge University Press, 2012).

101. Lewis, *Journal of a West Indian Proprietor*, 118. Matthew had earlier written that it had been twenty years since an owner of these estates had visited from England, and "agents and overseers . . . for the last twenty years, have been reigning in my dominions with despotic authority." Ibid., 47.

102. Epstein, *Scandal of Colonial Rule*, 15–35.

103. Lewis, *Journal of a West Indian Proprietor*, 119. For the use of the lash on British soldiers, see Linda Colley, *Captives: Britain, Empire and the World, 1600–1850* (New York: Pantheon Books, 2002); Jonathan Shipe, "The Cost of a Moral Army: Masculinity and the Construction of a Respectable British Army, 1850–1885," Ph.D. diss., Florida State University, 2016.

104. Lewis, *Journal of a West Indian Proprietor*, 119.

105. Ibid., 119.

106. Ibid., 83, 192, 237; Deborah Gray White, *Ar'n't I a Woman? Female Slaves in the Plantation South* (New York: W. W. Norton, 1999), 152–153, 174–177, 187–189.

107. Lewis, *Journal of a West Indian Proprietor*, 149–150; Diana Paton, "Witchcraft, Poison, Law, and Atlantic Slavery," *William and Mary Quarterly* 69, no. 2 (April 2012).

108. Lewis, *Journal of a West Indian Proprietor*, 179.

109. Ibid., 173–174; Catherine Hall, *Civilising Subjects: Metropole and Colony in the English Imagination, 1830–1867* (Chicago: University of Chicago Press, 2002).

110. Emphasis original. Lewis, *Journal of a West Indian Proprietor*, 173–174, 227; Christopher Leslie Brown, *Moral Capital: Foundations of British Abolitionism* (Chapel Hill: University of North Carolina Press, 2006), 55–78; C. L. R. James, *The Black Jacobins: Toussaint L'Ouverture and the San Domingo Revolution* (New York: Vintage Books, 1963); Gelien Matthews, *Caribbean Slave Revolts and the British Abolitionist Movement* (Baton Rouge: Louisiana State University Press, 2006).

111. Lewis, *Journal of a West Indian Proprietor*, 173–174, 224–225, 234.

112. Ibid., 234.

113. Brown, *Moral Capital*, 75–88; Epstein, *Scandal of Colonial Rule*, 226–245; Matthews, *Caribbean Slave Revolts*; Seymour Drescher, *Abolition: A History of Slavery and Antislavery* (New York: Cambridge University Press, 2009).

114. Lewis, *Journal of a West Indian Proprietor*, 166. Conversion of his slaves to Christianity is not a major theme of Matthew's reforms. He does make some efforts in this direction but states that he does so hoping that "nobody will be able to accuse me of neglecting the religious education of my negroes." Ibid., 83.

115. Ibid., 392.

116. Ibid., 402.

117. Ibid., 220–223. Matthew also writes of enslaved individuals on other estates coming to ask him to protect them from mistreatment from their overseers and drivers, once his reforms become known. Ibid., 144.

118. For methodology, see Seth Koven, *The Match Girl and the Heiress* (Princeton, NJ: Princeton University Press, 2014).

CHAPTER 3

1. M. J. D. Roberts, "The Society for the Suppression of Vice and Its Early Critics, 1802–1812," *Historical Journal* 26, no. 1 (March 1983): 164.

2. *Part the First, of an Address to the Public, from the Society for the Suppression of Vice, Instituted, in London, 1802* (London: Printed for the Society, 1803), 27–31.

3. Seymour Drescher, *Abolition: A History of Slavery and Antislavery* (New York: Cambridge University Press, 2009); Seymour Drescher, *The Mighty Experiment: Free Labor vs. Slavery in British Emancipation* (New York: Oxford University Press, 2002), 115–145; Boyd Hilton, *The Age of Atonement: The Influence of Evangelicalism on Social and Economic Thought, 1795–1865* (New York: Oxford University Press, 1987), 203–251.

4. Iorwerth Prothero, "William Benbow and the Concept of the 'General Strike,'" *Past and Present* 63 (1974); Iorwerth Prothero, "Benbow, William," in *Dictionary of Labour Biography*, vol. 6, ed. Joyce M. Bellamy and John Saville (London: Macmillan, 1972–2010); Malcolm Chase, 2015, "Benbow, William (1787–1864), radical and publisher," *Oxford Dictionary of National Biography*, April 2019.

5. Iain McCalman, *Radical Underworld: Prophets, Revolutionaries, and Pornographers in London, 1795–1840* (Cambridge: Cambridge University Press, 1988), 161, 34–39, 225–227; Hannah Barker, *Newspapers, Politics and English Society, 1695–1855* (Harlow, UK: Longman, 2000); Kevin Gilmartin, *Print Politics: The Press and Radi-*

cal Opposition in Early Nineteenth-Century England (New York: Cambridge University Press, 1996); Kevin Gilmartin, *Writing against Revolution: Literary Conservatism in Britain, 1790–1832* (Cambridge: Cambridge University Press, 2007).

6. Prothero, "Benbow and the 'General Strike'"; Prothero, "Benbow, William," *Dictionary of Labour Biography*; Chase, "Benbow, William," *Oxford Dictionary of National Biography*.

7. McCalman, *Radical Underworld*, 34–39, 225–227; Barker, *Newspapers, Politics and English Society*; Gilmartin, *Print Politics*; Gilmartin, *Writing against Revolution*.

8. *Morning Chronicle*, August 27, 1825.

9. Ibid.

10. McCalman, *Radical Underworld*, 34–39. For reports in the days immediately after the incident, see *Evening Mail*, June 1, 1810; *Morning Post*, June 1, 1810; *Morning Chronicle*, June 2, 1810; *Morning Post*, June 2, 1810; *Morning Advertiser*, June 2, 1810; *Bell's Weekly Messenger*, June 3, 1810; *Examiner*, June 3, 1810; *Hampshire Chronicle*, June 4, 1810; *Morning Chronicle*, June 4, 1810; *Morning Post*, June 4, 1810; *Morning Advertiser*, June 5, 1810; *Kentish Gazette*, June 5, 1810.

11. For reports on the 1813 libel trial, see *London Courier and Evening Gazette*, March 6, 1813; *Leeds Intelligencer*, March 8, 1813; *Bury and Norwich Post*, March 10, 1813; *Saunders's News-Letter*, March 10, 1813; *Saunders's News-Letter*, March 11, 1813; *Stamford Mercury*, March 12, 1813; *Kentish Weekly Post or Canterbury Journal*, March 12, 1813; *Manchester Mercury*, March 16, 1813; *Suffolk Chronicle; or Weekly General Advertiser and County Express*, May 15, 1813; *Lancaster Gazette*, May 22, 1813; *Liverpool Mercury*, May 28, 1813; *Northampton Mercury*, May 29, 1813; *Bath Chronicle and Weekly Gazette*, November 11, 1813. One of the most graphic and sensationalized accounts of the Vere Street arrests was also published in this year. See Robert Holloway, *The Phoenix of Sodom, or, the Vere Street Coterie: Being an Exhibition of the Gambols Practised by the Ancient Lechers of Sodom and Gomorrah, Embellished and Improved with the Modern Refinements in Sodomitical Practices, by the Members of the Vere Street Coterie, of Detestable Memory* (London: J. Cook, . . . to be had of all the booksellers, 1813).

12. Emphasis added. The text is a summary from the published book that sparked the libel trial, reprinted in the *Morning Chronicle*. *Morning Chronicle*, April 19, 1832.

13. *Annual Register*, 1833, 90.

14. Place's participation was mentioned prominently in accounts of the coroner's inquest, although Iain McCalman has concluded that it is "not unreasonable to suspect Place of collusion with the government, particularly in view of his dominance of the 1810 jury proceedings, his contingent rise to prosperity and his penchant for backroom manipulation. Burdett and [Henry] Hunt never ceased to believe that he had been bribed by the government in 1810." McCalman, *Radical Underworld*, 41.

15. *Morning Chronicle*, June 2, 1810.

16. *Evening Mail*, June 1, 1810.

17. *Morning Chronicle*, June 2, 1810.

18. *Evening Mail*, June 1, 1810. Another witness confirmed that he was "so great a favorite of his master, that he and his family were accommodated with lodgings over the gate-way, leading into the Kitchen-court from Cleveland Row; from which there was a communication with the Duke's suite of apartments."

19. *Morning Chronicle*, June 2, 1810.

20. Emphasis added. *Evening Mail*, June 1, 1810; *Morning Chronicle*, June 2, 1810.

21. *Morning Chronicle*, March 6, 1813; *Saunders's News-Letter*, March 10, 1813; *Saunders's News-Letter*, March 11, 1813; *London Courier and Evening Gazette*, March 6, 1813; *Leeds Intelligencer*, March 8, 1813; *Bury and Norwich Post*, March 10, 1813; *Stamford Mercury*, March 12, 1813; *Kentish Weekly Post or Canterbury Journal*, March 12, 1813; *Manchester Mercury*, March 16, 1813.

22. Sellis's body was to be buried at a crossroads at midnight on a Saturday, at Charing Cross. "The curiosity of some people was so great, that they actually waited in the yard till 3 o'clock," but the body was "not taken away till about twelve o'clock yesterday, when a hearse drove up close to the settling-house, and immediately after four men brought the body out of the Duke's house in a shell, and put it into the hearse, which drove furiously away with it." *Morning Chronicle*, June 4, 1810.

23. Emphasis added. *Saunders's News-Letter and Daily Advertiser*, March 11, 1813.

24. *Annual Register*, 1833, 92.

25. "London hummed with sensational murder rumors: that the Duke had been surprised in a 'shirt dance' (homosexual act) with Sellis, or had aroused Sellis's jealousy by taking a new manservant-lover; that Cumberland had fathered a bastard child by Sellis's wife; and, fascinatingly, that Sellis had been an ardent Jacobin who was blackmailing the Duke." McCalman, *Radical Underworld*, 34.

26. The text is a summary from the published book that sparked the libel trial, reprinted in the *Morning Chronicle*. *Morning Chronicle*, April 19, 1832. For accusations against the Duke of Cumberland, see John Wardroper, *Wicked Ernest: The Truth about the Man Who Was Almost Britain's King: An Extraordinary Royal Life Revealed* (London: Shelfmark Books, 2002); Alan Palmer, 2009, "Ernest Augustus (1771–1851), king of Hanover," *Oxford Dictionary of National Biography*, April 2019; Cecil Woodham-Smith, *Queen Victoria: Her Life and Times*, vol. 1, *1819–1861* (London: Cardinal, 1975).

27. Anna Clark, *Scandal: The Sexual Politics of the British Constitution* (Princeton, NJ: Princeton University Press, 2004), 154–155, 160.

28. "Throughout the eighteenth-century, scandals erupted concerning the role of the monarchy, the aristocracy, and public opinion, but until 1763 they failed to pose a serious threat to the political order." Ibid., 12.

29. *Times*, July 5, 1810.

30. Cobbett was in King's Bench Prison in relation to a prosecution he had faced before the Court of King's Bench over an incident that had occurred a year before. The Attorney General who conducted this state prosecution directed his first opening statement to the jury, explaining the delay in bringing the case forward. The trial began on June 15, 1810, and Cobbett was placed in King's Bench Prison on July 6, 1810, with the depositions published by Cobbett on July 7, 1810. *Times*, June 16, 1810; *Cobbett's Weekly Political Register*, July 7, 1810. Cobbett published the depositions of the Duke of Cumberland; Cornelius Neale, valet to the Duke of Cumberland; Ann Neale, wife of Cornelius Neale; Benjamin Smith, porter to the duke; Matthew Henry Graslen, servant to the duke; Joseph Creighton, sergeant in the Coldstream Guards; Thomas Strickland, under butler to the duke; Sarah Valley, housemaid to the duke; Antonio

Panzer, former valet to the duke; Ferdinand Burzio, a jeweler who had known Joseph Sellis for fourteen years; Mary Ann Sellis, widow of Joseph Sellis; Ann Hill, servant to Mrs. Sellis; Samuel Thomas Adams, esq., who presented two letters found among Sellis's possessions; James Paulet, page to the duke; and multiple other individuals.

31. Ian Dyck, *William Cobbett and Rural Popular Culture* (New York: Cambridge University Press, 1992); Leonora Nattrass, *William Cobbett: The Politics of Style* (New York: Cambridge University Press, 1995); James Sambrook, *William Cobbett* (London: Routledge and Kegan Paul, 1973); Daniel Green, *Great Cobbett: The Noblest Agitator* (London: Hodder and Stoughton, 1983); Morris Leonard Pearl, *William Cobbett, a Bibliographical Account of His Life and Time* (London: Oxford University Press, 1953).

32. Cobbett did accept some financial help from the New Opposition, a parliamentary group that opposed seeking peace with France.

33. Green, *Great Cobbett*; Dyck, *William Cobbett*.

34. On July 5, the *Morning Chronicle* published the deposition of Mary Ann Sellis. *Morning Chronicle*, July 5, 1810.

35. The Duke of Cumberland stated that "in the closet at the foot of his bed was found the scabbard with a pair of slippers belonging to Sellis." *Cobbett's Weekly Political Register*, July 7, 1810. Cornelia Knight, companion to Princess Charlotte, recorded in her journal that "there were some circumstances that threw a doubt upon his guilt. The slippers were old, and the name written in them appeared to be in French, whereas Sellis was a Piedmontese." Rictor Norton, ed., "Scandal Involving the Duke of Cumberland, 1832," *Homosexuality in Nineteenth-Century England: A Sourcebook*, May 27, 2012. Mary Ann Sellis's deposition, published in that same issue, indicated that "he scarcely ever wore slippers at home." *Cobbett's Weekly Political Register*, July 7, 1810.

36. Among the many works discussing the Vere Street molly-house raid in this way, see H. Montgomery Hyde, *The Other Love: A History and Contemporary Survey of Homosexuality in Britain* (London: Heinemann, 1970), 79–82; Rictor Norton, *Mother Clap's Molly House: The Gay Subculture in England, 1700–1830*, 1st ed. (London: GMP, 1992), 204–226; Dominic Janes, *Oscar Wilde Prefigured: Queer Fashioning and British Caricature, 1750–1900* (Chicago: University of Chicago Press, 2016), 105; Morris B. Kaplan, *Sodom on the Thames: Sex, Love, and Scandal in Wilde Times* (Ithaca, NY: Cornell University Press, 2005), 20–24; Ed Cohen, *Talk on the Wilde Side: Towards a Genealogy of a Discourse on Male Sexualities* (New York: Routledge, 1993), 116–117; Louis Crompton, *Byron and Greek Love: Homophobia in 19th-Century England* (Berkeley: University of California Press, 1985), 163–169; Dominic Janes, *Picturing the Closet: Male Secrecy and Homosexual Visibility in Britain* (New York: Oxford University Press, 2015), 41; Christopher Hobson, *Blake and Homosexuality* (New York: Palgrave, 2001), 213–227; Dorothy U. Seyler, *The Obelisk and the Englishman: The Pioneering Discoveries of Egyptologist William Bankes* (Amherst, NY: Prometheus Books, 2015), 56, 58; Graham Robb, *Strangers: Homosexual Love in the Nineteenth Century* (New York: W. W. Norton, 2004), 19–20; H. G. Cocks, *Nameless Offences: Speaking of Male Homosexual Desire in Nineteenth-Century England* (London: I. B. Tauris, 2003), 122–123; Matt Cook, *London and the Culture of Homosexuality, 1885–1914* (New York: Cambridge University Press, 2003), 8–14.

37. *Morning Chronicle*, July 10, 1810.

38. For some of the most inflammatory accounts of what men did at Vere Street, see Holloway, *Phoenix of Sodom*. This work was published in the same year as the first major libel trial relating to the Duke of Cumberland and Sellis, which concluded in March of that year.

39. *Morning Chronicle*, September 28, 1810; *Morning Post*, September 28, 1810; *Evening Mail*, September 28, 1810; *Saunders's News-Letter*, October 3, 1810; *Hampshire Chronicle*, October 1, 1810; *Bell's Weekly Messenger*, September 30, 1810; *Kentish Weekly Post or Canterbury Journal*, October 2, 1810.

40. Emphasis added. Quoted from the *Star*, September 28, 1810. Most of the twenty-seven men arrested were acquitted or released without charge. The six sentenced to stand in the pillory for an hour also served prison sentences of two to three years. Norton, *Mother Clap's Molly House*, 1st ed., 187–198.

41. For some of the many works discussing the Vere Street molly-house raid without discussing the Duke of Cumberland affair, see footnote 36 on the previous page.

42. This quoted phrasing is repeated in many of the newspaper accounts listed in footnote 39.

43. That later scandal was the 1822 Bishop of Clogher affair, discussed in detail later in this chapter. Emphasis added. *Bell's Life in London and Sporting Chronicle*, July 28, 1822.

44. Emphasis added. *Bell's Life in London and Sporting Chronicle*, July 28, 1822.

45. For an analysis of using scenes of punishment or other artificially constructed spaces to enact performances of "natural" reactions or traits as a way of disseminating norms in society, see Judith Butler, *Undoing Gender* (New York: Routledge, 2004). For a concise application of this theoretical model, see Conrad Brunstrom and Tanya Cassidy, "'Scorn Eunuch Sports': Class, Gender and the Context of Early Cricket," *Journal for Eighteenth-Century Studies* 35, no. 2 (2012).

46. The following papers published only one short paragraph noting the execution and the presence of the duke. "Thursday J. Hepburn, late an ensign in a vet. batt. and White, the drummer, only 16 years of age, for an abominable offense, were executed in front of Newgate. The Duke of Cumberland, Lords Sefton, Yarmouth, and other noblemen, were in the yard." *Bath Chronicle and Weekly Gazette*, March 14, 1811; *Sussex Advertiser*, March 11, 1811; *Morning Post*, March 9, 1811; *Kentish Gazette*, March 12, 1811; *Salisbury and Winchester Journal*, March 11, 1811; *Cheltenham Chronicle*, March 14, 1811; *Norfolk Chronicle*, March 16, 1811; *Carlisle Journal*, March 16, 1811.

47. *Carlisle Journal*, March 16, 1811.

48. Dyck, *William Cobbett*; Nattrass, *William Cobbett*.

49. G. C. Boase, 2009, "Stoddart, Sir John (1773–1856), writer and lawyer," *Oxford Dictionary of National Biography*, April 2019.

50. Ibid.; *The History of the Times*, vol. 1, *"The Thunderer" in the Making, 1781–1841* (New York: Macmillan, 1935).

51. For some of the reporting on the libel trial, see *Morning Post*, February 24, 1819; *Globe*, April 15, 1820; *Morning Chronicle*, April 15, 1820; *Morning Post*, April 15, 1820; *Public Ledger and Daily Advertiser*, April 15, 1820; *Evening Mail*, April 17, 1820;

Norfolk Chronicle, April 22, 1820; *Sheffield Independent*, April 22, 1820; *Inverness Courier*, April 27, 1820.

52. The defendants were John Stoddart, proprietor; Edward Quin, esq., editor; and Andrew Mitchell, printer (of the *New Times*). *Morning Chronicle*, April 15, 1820; *Public Ledger and Daily Advertiser*, April 15, 1820.

53. For the use of the term "man-mistress" to mean a man kept by a woman for her sexual pleasure, see *Scots Magazine*, September 1, 1823. The term "man-mistress" was also used to describe a male servant of Percy Jocelyn, who was thought to also be his sexual partner. See William Benbow, *The Crimes of the Clergy; or, the Pillars of the Priest-Craft Shaken* (London: Benbow, 1823), 43. For the use of the term "master-mistress" in relation to William Shakespeare's Sonnet 20 and in a published critique of Alfred, Lord Tennyson's poetry, see Crompton, *Byron and Greek Love*, 189–190.

54. McCalman, *Radical Underworld*, 213.

55. Ibid., 155–161.

56. *Examiner*, 1822, 475.

57. David Huddleston, 2008, "Jocelyn, Percy (1764–1843), bishop of Clogher," *Oxford Dictionary of National Biography*, April 2019.

58. Benbow, *Crimes of the Clergy*, 42; James Byrne, *Sketch of the Life and Unparalleled Sufferings of James Byrne: Late Coachman to the Honourable John Jocelyn . . . Together with Some Observations on the Conduct of the Jocelyn Family . . .* (London: Printed and pub. for F. O'Neill by T. Dolby, 1822).

59. *Bell's Life in London*, August 4, 1822; *Times*, August 3, 1822.

60. *Bell's Life in London*, August 4, 1822; *Times*, August 3, 1822.

61. Emphasis original. *Bell's Life in London*, August 11, 1822.

62. "In Dublin his chariots stood at livery, and he had only one servant to attend him, and that a wretch like himself, his man-mistress, of whose villainy much is said in the account of Byrne's case." Benbow, *Crimes of the Clergy*, 43.

63. Matthew Parris and Nick Angel, *The Great Unfrocked: Two Thousand Years of Church Scandal* (London: Robson Books, 1998), 146–148.

64. Ibid., 144; Brian Lacey, *Terrible Queer Creatures: Homosexuality in Irish History* (Dublin: Wordwell Books, 2008); Norton, *Mother Clap's Molly House*, 1st ed., 216–221; John Fairburn, *The Bishop!! Particulars of the Charge against the Hon. Percy Jocelyn, Bishop of Clogher, for an Abominable Offence with John Movelley, a Soldier of the First Regiment of Foot Guards: Including the Evidence before the Magistrate at Marlborough-Street* (London: Printed and pub. by John Fairburn, 1822).

65. First emphasis original, second emphasis added. *Cobbett's Weekly Political Register*, July 27, 1822.

66. Emphasis original. Ibid.

67. Cobbett then drew a connection to this unequal application of the law and the practices in Virginia, where "it was, until of late years, *not murder to kill a black*, which was punished with a *fine*." Emphasis original. Ibid.

68. Ibid.

69. Ibid.

70. Ibid.

71. Ibid.

72. *Bell's Life in London and Sporting Chronicle*, July 28, 1822.

73. Emphasis original. *Bell's Life in London and Sporting Chronicle*, July 28, 1822.

74. In a later issue, *Bell's* observed that the case "cannot but be viewed as a most important lesson to judges, magistrates, and counsellors." *Bell's Life in London and Sporting Chronicle*, August 4, 1822.

75. *Times*, July 25, 1822.

76. Emphasis added. *Times*, July 26, 1822. The *Times* argued that part of Jocelyn's property should be seized and given in compensation to Byrne. *Times*, July 26, 1822.

77. Charles Upchurch, "Politics and the Reporting of Sex between Men in the 1820s," in *British Queer History: New Approaches and Perspectives*, ed. Brian Lewis (New York: University of Manchester Press, 2013), 17–38; *Times*, September 4, 1826. For just some of the stories appearing in only two newspapers for the remainder of 1822 related to the Bishop of Clogher incident, see *Times*, July 26, 1822; *Times*, July 30, 1822; *Times*, July 31, 1822; *Times*, August 3, 1822; *Bell's Life in London and Sporting Chronicle*, August 4, 1822; *Times*, August 8, 1822; *Bell's Life in London*, August 11, 1822; *Times*, August 27, 1822; *Times*, August 31, 1822; *Bell's Life in London*, September 1, 1822; *Times*, September 6, 1822; *Times*, September 10, 1822; *Times*, September 20, 1822; *Bell's Life in London*, September 29, 1822; *Times*, October 2, 1822; *Times*, October 8, 1822; *Times*, October 11, 1822; *Bell's Life in London*, October 13, 1822; *Times*, October 14, 1822; *Times*, October 24, 1822; *Times*, October 29, 1822; *Times*, October 30, 1822; *Times*, November 2, 1822; *Bell's Life in London*, November 3, 1822; *Times*, November 5, 1822; *Times*, November 8, 1822; *Bell's Life in London*, November 10, 1822; *Times*, November 12, 1822; *Times*, November 13, 1822; *Bell's Life in London*, November 17, 1822.

78. Emphasis original. *Bell's Life in London*, August 4, 1822.

79. Upchurch, "Politics and the Reporting," 22–24, 33.

80. Charles Upchurch, "Full-Text Databases and Historical Research: Cautionary Results from a Ten-Year Study," *Journal of Social History* 45 (Fall 2012), 100–101; John Brown, *The Historical Gallery of Criminal Portraitures, Foreign and Domestic Containing a Selection of the Most Impressive Cases of Guilt and Misfortune to Be Found in Modern History* (Manchester: J. Gleave, 1823), 598.

81. Benbow, *Crimes of the Clergy*; James Byrne, Percy Jocelyn, and William Cobbett, *The Trial of Unfortunate Byrne (Late Coachman to the Hon. John Jocelyn,) . . . Which Is Annexed the Opinion of That Great Political Writer Mr. Cobbett on the Late Abominable and Disgusting Transaction* (Dublin: Published at No. 1 Princes Street, 1811).

82. Upchurch, "Full-Text Databases," 100–102.

83. Prothero, "Benbow and the 'General Strike'"; Prothero, "Benbow, William," *Dictionary of Labour Biography*; Chase, "Benbow, William," *Oxford Dictionary of National Biography*; McCalman, *Radical Underworld*, 67, 89, 152–158.

84. Prothero, "Benbow and the 'General Strike,'" 147; Prothero, "Benbow, William," *Dictionary of Labour Biography*.

85. Chase, "Benbow, William," *Oxford Dictionary of National Biography*.

86. Gary Kent, "Tom Paine's Grave-Robber Ends His Days in Sydney," *History* [Magazine of the Royal Australian Historical Society] 123 (March 2015): 11–14.

87. Benbow called his new shop in Leicester Square "The Byron's Head." Mc-Calman, *Radical Underworld*, 205.

88. Ibid., 213.

89. Ibid., 206.

90. "The Parson and the Boy," *Cobbett's Weekly Political Register*, August 2, 1823.

91. Benbow, *Crimes of the Clergy*, 7; the Rev. Mr. Mills, 40; the Rev. Thomas Burgess, 197; the Rev. Richard Milles, 138; the Rev. John Fenwick, 11; Parson Eyre, 133; and "Notes by the Editor" final paragraph, 240. The Bishop of Clogher is mentioned three times in relation to the 1640 example of the Bishop of Waterford, 25.

92. See Benbow, *Crimes of the Clergy*, John Church, 19–21; Parson Cooper, 118–121; Dr. Sanders, 124–127; Rev. Parson Walker, 229–230; the Rev. V. P. Littlehales, 238; and the Rev. Thomas Jephson, 239–240.

93. In note 156 in Chapter 7, William Gibson and Joanne Begiato state that there is "no record of a John Fenwick as incumbent or assistant curate of either St. Peter or St. Andrew Byall (which is presumably Bywell, Northumberland) so there may have been some misinformation or some event invention." William Gibson and Joanne Begiato, *Sex and the Church in the Long Eighteenth Century: Religion, Enlightenment and the Sexual Revolution* (New York: I. B. Tauris, 2017).

94. Benbow, *Crimes of the Clergy*, 9.

95. Ibid.

96. Ibid., 10.

97. Ibid.

98. Ibid., 11.

99. Ibid.

100. Ibid., 12.

101. Ibid.

102. Ibid.

103. Emphasis original. Ibid., 14.

104. Leon Radzinowicz, *A History of English Criminal Law and Its Administration from 1750: The Movement for Reform 1750–1833* (London: Macmillan, 1948), 1:516.

105. One year later, the law was successfully changed, replacing disemboweling with quartering of the body. Ibid., 519.

CHAPTER 4

1. Emphasis original. Add. MS 40380, ff. 229–30.

2. H. Montgomery Hyde, *The Strange Death of Lord Castlereagh* (London: Heinemann, 1959), 2; John Bew, *Castlereagh: A Life* (Oxford: Oxford University Press, 2012), 362.

3. Hyde, *Strange Death*, 35; Bew, *Castlereagh*, 547; *Cobbett's Weekly Political Register*, August 17, 1822; *Black Dwarf*, August 14, 1822.

4. R. B. McDowell, 2004, "Hyde, Harford Montgomery (1907–1989)," *Oxford Dictionary of National Biography*, July 2018.

5. C. J. Bartlett, *Castlereagh* (New York: Charles Scribner's Sons, 1966), 262–263.

6. John W. Derry, *Castlereagh* (London: A. Lane, 1976), 277–278.

7. Wendy Hinde, *Castlereagh* (London: Collins, 1981), 280.

8. Giles Hunt, *The Duel: Castlereagh, Canning and Deadly Cabinet Rivalry* (New York: I. B. Tauris, 2008), 177–186. Other works more focused on diplomacy do not mention the issue of the suicide. See Henry Kissinger, *A World Restored: Metternich, Castlereagh, and the Problems of Peace, 1812–22* (New York: Grosset and Dunlap, 1964).

9. Roland Thorne, 2004, "Stewart, Robert, Viscount Castlereagh and second Marquess of Londonderry (1769–1822)," *Oxford Dictionary of National Biography*, July 2018.

10. Bew, *Castlereagh*, 552.

11. Derry, *Castlereagh*, 227–228.

12. Hyde, *Strange Death*, 98; Harriett Arbuthnot, *The Journal of Mrs. Arbuthnot, 1820–1832*, ed. Gerald Wellesley Wellington and Francis Bamford (London: Macmillan, 1950), 176; Dorothea Lieven, Peter Quennell, and Dilys Powell, *The Private Letters of Princess Lieven to Prince Metternich, 1820–1826* (New York: E. P. Dutton, 1937).

13. Hyde, *Strange Death*, 168, 171, 174; Arbuthnot did write that Castlereagh seemed exhausted and "completely knocked up" by the parliamentary session. Arbuthnot, *Journal of Mrs. Arbuthnot*, 177.

14. Hyde, *Strange Death*, 40.

15. Arbuthnot, *Journal of Mrs. Arbuthnot*, 178; Hyde, *Strange Death*, 40.

16. Arbuthnot, *Journal of Mrs. Arbuthnot*, 178; Hyde, *Strange Death*, 41.

17. Hyde, *Strange Death*, 51–52.

18. Lieven, Quennell, and Powell, *Private Letters of Princess Lieven*, 193–194; Hyde, *Strange Death*, 189; Bew, *Castlereagh*, 552.

19. Hyde, *Strange Death*, 64. Hyde states that the original manuscript of this letter to Arbuthnot is in the possession of the current Duke of Wellington.

20. *Annual Register*, 1822, 432–437; John Richardson, *Recollections, Political, Literary, Dramatic, and Miscellaneous: Of the Last Half-Century* (London: C. Mitchell, 1856), 289.

21. Richardson, *Recollections*, 297.

22. Anne Robinson testified that "in my opinion he has not been well during the last fortnight, and particularly so since Monday week." Ibid., 293–294. For an account of the August 9, 1822, conversation in which Castlereagh told Wellington that his colleagues conspired against him, see Sir Herbert Maxwell, *The Life of Wellington: The Restoration of the Martial Power of Great Britain* (London: S. Low, Marston, 1899), 2:164. In this work from 1899, Maxwell acknowledges that it "is known that Lord Castlereagh fell into a nefarious stratagem, which exposed him to a peculiar cruel system of blackmail." Maxwell, *Life of Wellington*, 2:164.

23. Richardson, *Recollections*, 299; *Annual Register*, 1822, 432–437.

24. Hyde, *Strange Death*, 179.

25. Dr. Bankhead told Wellington "a long story of what Lord Londonderry had himself told him and stated to him *two facts* and told it all so plausibly that he actually made the Duke believe there was some truth in what he said." Emphasis original. Ibid.

26. Ibid., 10, 29–30.

27. Richardson, *Recollections*, 283.

28. Ibid., 286.

29. Ibid., 287.

30. Hyde, *Strange Death*, 182.

31. Bew, *Castlereagh*, 553.

32. Ibid.

33. Ibid.

34. Ibid., 537, 541. Hyde also cites the 1815 suicide of MP Samuel Whitbread, who also cut his own throat with a razor. Hyde, *Strange Death*, 4.

35. Arbuthnot, *Journal of Mrs. Arbuthnot*, 178.

36. Ibid., 180.

37. Ibid., 183.

38. Philipp Neumann and E. Beresford Chancellor, *The Diary of Philipp Von Neumann*, vol. 1, *1819 to 1850* (Boston: Houghton Mifflin, 1928), 41; Bew, *Castlereagh*, 554–555.

39. William Toynbee, *Glimpses of the Twenties* (London: A. Constable, 1909), 126, 127–128; Hyde, *Strange Death*, 184. Cobbett was convinced that there was something more to Castlereagh's death that the government was trying to cover up. "What makes the bankers, money-jobbers, and merchants, cut their throats so gallantly? The dread of humiliation." *Cobbett's Weekly Political Register*, August 17, 1822.

40. Toynbee, *Glimpses of the Twenties*, 127, 130, 132.

41. Leon Radzinowicz, *A History of English Criminal Law and Its Administration from 1750*, vol. 1, *The Movement for Reform 1750–1833* (New York: Macmillan, 1948), 525; Sir Samuel Romilly, *Memoirs of the Life of Sir Samuel Romilly: Written by Himself; with a Selection from His Correspondence*, ed. by his sons (London: J. Murray, 1840), 2:247; R. Melikan, 2008, "Romilly, Sir Samuel (1757–1818), lawyer and politician," *Oxford Dictionary of National Biography*, June 2018.

42. Radzinowicz, *History of English Criminal Law*, 1:527, 1:311.

43. Ibid., 1:503.

44. Ibid., 1:504.

45. Ibid., 1:502.

46. Patrick Joyce, *The Rule of Freedom: Liberalism and the Modern City* (London: Verso, 2003), 105.

47. Radzinowicz, *History of English Criminal Law*, 1:526.

48. Phil Handler, "Forging the Agenda: The 1819 Select Committee on the Criminal Laws Revisited," *Journal of Legal History* 25, no. 3 (December 2004): 254.

49. Vic Gatrell, *The Hanging Tree: Execution and the English People, 1770–1868* (Oxford: Oxford University Press, 1994).

50. Radzinowicz, *History of English Criminal Law*, 1:527–528.

51. Handler, "Forging the Agenda," 249–250. The 1819 report does not make recommendations in relation to sexual crimes. *Report of the Select Committee on Criminal Laws*, 1819.

52. Radzinowicz, *History of English Criminal Law*, 1:547.

53. Ibid., 1:562.

54. Ibid.

55. Ibid., 1:566.

56. Ibid., 1:563.

57. Jeremy Bentham, *An Introduction to the Principles of Morals and Legislation* (London: Printed for W. Pickering and E. Wilson, 1823).

58. Gamaliel Smith, esq., pseudonym of Jeremy Bentham, *Not Paul, but Jesus* (London: Printed for John Hunt, Old Bond Street, 1823).

59. See Chapter 1.

60. Smith/Bentham, *Not Paul, but Jesus*, iii–iv.

61. Ibid., 371–373, xii.

62. *Examiner*, September 21, 1823; *Morning Post*, September 24, 1823.

63. *Morning Chronicle*, September 26, 1823; *Examiner*, September 28, 1823; *Morning Post*, October 2, 1823; *Examiner*, October 5, 1823.

64. *Cambridge Chronicle and Journal*, January 2, 1824; *Morning Chronicle*, December 25, 1823; *Cambridge Chronicle and Journal*, October 22, 1824.

65. *Morning Post*, January 26, 1824; *London Courier and Evening Gazette*, February 9, 1824.

66. *Examiner*, May 2, 1824.

67. *Morning Chronicle*, July 9, 1824.

68. *Bury and Norwich Post*, September 3, 1828.

69. *Liverpool Mercury*, February 29, 1828.

70. F. Rosen, 2014, "Bentham, Jeremy (1748–1832), philosopher, jurist, and reformer," *Oxford Dictionary of National Biography*, May 2014; Bhikhu Parekh, *Jeremy Bentham: Critical Assessments*, vol. 3, *Law and Politics* (London: Routledge, 1993); J. R. Dinwiddy, *Radicalism and Reform in Britain, 1780–1850* (London: Hambledon Press, 1992).

71. *Digital Panopticon*, *Times*, September 25, 1822.

72. "Old Bailey, Tuesday, September 17," *Times*, September 18, 1822.

73. "Old Bailey, Tuesday, September 24," *Times*, September 25, 1822. The one London sodomy execution that occurred between 1816 and 1822, in 1819, involved John Markham, a pauper in St. Giles's workhouse, who seems to have raped a man, and therefore his punishment would not have been unjust in Bentham's estimation, because it was sexual violence. *Kentish Weekly Post or Canterbury Journal*, December 31, 1819. Although more than two dozen newspaper reports and court records have been recovered for the 1816 execution of Robert Yandell, they give no indication as to the circumstances of the sex he engaged in and whether it was consensual. There would not be another sodomy execution in London until 1835.

74. *Times*, September 25, 1822.

75. Radzinowicz, *History of English Criminal Law*, 1:567.

76. Ibid.

77. "A Bill For enabling the Judges to abstain from pronouncing Sentence of Death, in certain Capital Felonies (Ordered by The House of Commons to be Printed, 27 May 1823)," 4 Geo. IV.—Sess. 1823. 1823 Judgment of Death Act, 4 George 4 c. 48.

78. E. P. Thompson, *Whigs and Hunters: The Origin of the Black Act* (New York: Pantheon Books, 1975); John Broad, "Whigs and Deer-Stealers in Other Guises: A Return to the Origins of the Black Act," *Past and Present* 119 (May 1988); Eveline Cruickshanks and Howard Erskine-Hill, "The Waltham Black Act and Jacobitism," *Journal of British Studies* 24, no. 3 (July 1985).

79. L. Radzinowicz, "The Waltham Black Act: A Study of the Legislative Attitude towards Crime in the Eighteenth Century," *Cambridge Law Journal* 9, no. 56 (1945): 57.

80. E. P. Thompson, *Customs in Common* (New York: New Press, W. W. Norton, 1991).

81. "An Act for the more effectual punishing wicked and evil disposed Persons going armed in Disguise, and doing Injuries and Violences to the Persons and Properties of His Majesty's Subjects, and for the more speedy bringing the Offenders to Justice." 9 Geo. I, c. 22 (1723).

82. *Hansard* Commons Sitting, Second Series, vol. 9, May 21, 1823, 426.

83. This distinction as it related to threats to accuse of an infamous crime was made explicit in clauses 7 and 8 of Peel's 1827 legislation. "A Bill (As Amended by the Committee) For consolidating and amending the Laws in England relative to Larceny, and other Offences connected therewith." Ordered by the House of Commons to be Printed, March 13, 1827, 3.

84. "A Bill (As Amended by the Committee) For allowing the benefit of Clergy . . . and to make better provision for the punishment of Persons guilty of sending or delivering threatening Letters." Ordered by the House of Commons to be Printed, June 6, 1823.

85. Charles Upchurch, *Before Wilde: Sex between Men in Britain's Age of Reform* (Berkeley: University of California Press, 2009), 90–92.

86. *Times*, August 4, 1825.

87. *Times*, April 11, 1825.

88. *Times*, November 9, 1825; *Times*, November 16, 1825; PCOM, New Court, February 18, 1825, Middlesex Cases, 417; *Times*, April 16, 1825; *Times*, April 18, 1825; *Times*, March 27, 1825; *Times*, August 4, 1825; For the Barley Mow Public House raid, see *Times*, August 23, 1825; *Times*, August 25, 1825; *Times*, September 2, 1825; *Times*, September 22, 1825.

89. *Times*, August 16, 1825; *Times*, August 26, 1825; *Times*, September 2, 1825.

90. *Times*, September 21, 1825; *Times*, October 18, 1825.

91. *Age*, October 23, 1825. Only the word "when" was removed from the quote.

92. *Times*, August 23, 1825. For other newspaper stories discussing the Muirhead case, see *Morning Chronicle*, August 23, 1825; *Times*, August 25, 1825; *Morning Chronicle*, August 25, 1825; *Age*, August 28, 1825; *Weekly Dispatch*, August 28, 1825; *Bell's Weekly Messenger*, August 28, 1825; *Examiner*, August 28, 1825; *Bristol Mercury*, August 29, 1825; *Weekly Dispatch*, September 4, 1825; *Times*, September 6, 1825; *Times*, September 7, 1825; *Times*, September 24, 1825; *Examiner*, September 25, 1825; *Times*, September 26, 1825; *Morning Chronicle*, October 22, 1825; *Times*, October 22, 1825; *Age*, October 23, 1825; *Bell's Weekly Messenger*, October 23, 1825; *Age*, November 6, 1825; *Times*, November 17, 1825; *Morning Chronicle*, October 21, 1826; *Age*, October 22, 1826; *Morning Chronicle*, April 26, 1827; *Examiner*, April 29, 1827; *Times*, May 17, 1827; *Sun*, April 29, 1830.

93. *Times*, August 23, 1825.

94. *Times*, August 26, 1825.

95. Ibid.

96. Hon. Henry Grey Bennet, (1777–1836), in D. R. Fisher, *The House of Commons, 1820–1832* (Cambridge: Cambridge University Press, 2009); Louis Crompton, "*Don Leon*, Byron, and Homosexual Law Reform," in *Literary Visions of Homosexuality*, ed. Stuart Kellogg (New York: Haworth Press, 1983), 65–66.

97. Peel Papers and Additional Manuscripts, General Correspondence, vol. CC (July 9–August 1825). Add. MS 40380, ff. 227–231, 234–236, 257, 258, 315.

98. Eric Richards, 2004, "Horton, Sir Robert John Wilmot-, third baronet (1784–1841)," *Oxford Dictionary of National Biography*, August 2018.

99. Add. MS 40380, ff. 315. Reginald was only the second bishop of Calcutta, a diocese that included not only all of India but southern Africa and Australia. Michael Laird, 2004, "Heber, Reginald (1783–1826)," *Oxford Dictionary of National Biography*, August 2018.

100. Arthur Sherbo, 2004, "Heber, Richard (1774–1833)," *Oxford Dictionary of National Biography*, August 2018. The Roxburghe Club was the most exclusive group of bibliophiles in Britain, with Sir Walter Scott, the Duke of Devonshire, and the Duke of Marlborough among its thirty-one members in 1825.

101. Emphasis original. See the chapter-opening paragraph for the full quote. Add. MS 40380, ff. 229–230.

102. One word was left out of the quote, due to the ambiguity of the manuscript source.

103. Add. MS 40380, ff. 321. In the original letter, "deeply regret" and "not understand" are underlined twice.

104. Emphasis original. Add. MS 40380, ff. 234.

105. Emphasis original. Add. MS 40380, ff. 236.

106. Hobhouse held this position from 1817 to 1827. G. C. Boase, 2004, "Hobhouse, Henry (1776–1854)," *Oxford Dictionary of National Biography*, August 2018.

107. Emphasis original. Add. MS 40380, ff. 257, 258. Letter of H. H. [Henry Hobhouse], July 27, 1825.

108. Peel Papers and Additional Manuscripts: Add. MS 40381, ff. 169. Add. MS 40381, ff. 166, 169, 220, 284, 310.

109. Add. MS 40381, ff. 169.

110. Add. MS 40381, ff. 310.

111. Add. MS 40381, ff. 284.

CHAPTER 5

1. *Don Leon; A Poem by the Late Lord Byron . . . to Which Is Added Leon to Annabella: An Epistle from Lord Byron to Lady Byron* (London, Printed for the Booksellers, 1866).

2. Most work discussing religion and *Don Leon* to date has emphasized the criticisms of religion in the text. See George Wilson Knight, "Who Wrote *Don Leon*?" *Twentieth Century* 156 (1954): 67–79; Louis Crompton, "*Don Leon*, Byron, and Homosexual Law Reform," *Journal of Homosexuality* 8, nos. 3–4 (Spring/Summer 1983):

53–71; Peter Cochran, *Byron and Hobby-O: Lord Byron's Relationship with John Cam Hobhouse* (Newcastle upon Tyne, UK: Cambridge Scholars, 2010), 275.

3. Iain McCalman, *Radical Underworld: Prophets, Revolutionaries, and Pornographers in London, 1795–1840* (Cambridge: Cambridge University Press, 1988), 204–206.

4. Also noticing this shift in tone in *Don Leon*, but without basing interpretation on it, is Iain McCalman. "The biting anti-clericalism and moral nihilism of the libertinist canon was often reduced to ludicrous burlesque." Ibid., 215.

5. Louis Crompton's *Byron and Greek Love* is the most thorough previous analysis. For a complete historiography on the range of interpretations that have appeared concerning *Don Leon*, see Charles Upchurch, "The Consequences of Dating *Don Leon*," in *Queer Difficulty in Art and Poetry: Rethinking the Sexed Body in Verse and Visual Culture*, ed. Chris Reed and Jongwoo Jeremy Kim (New York: Routledge, 2017), 24–33.

6. In addition to the other authors previously cited, Anne Sebba also supports 1833 as the probable date when *Don Leon* was written. Anne Sebba, *The Exiled Collector: William Bankes and the Making of an English Country House* (London: John Murray, 2004), 152.

7. Page DuBois, *Sappho Is Burning* (Chicago: University of Chicago Press, 1995), 31.

8. John Emil Vincent, *Queer Lyrics: Difficulty and Closure in American Poetry* (New York: Palgrave Macmillan, 2002), 3.

9. *Don Leon*, lines 14, 16.

10. Emphasis added. Ibid., lines 24, 36, 40.

11. Ibid., lines 127–133.

12. Ibid., lines 133–134.

13. Ibid., lines 147–150.

14. Fiona MacCarthy, *Byron: Life and Legend* (New York: Farrar, Straus and Giroux, 2002), 26–27, 34, 78–79, 88, 91.

15. *Don Leon*, lines 152, 154, 169–172.

16. Emphasis added. "Sympathetic ink" is a term for invisible ink. Ibid., lines 175–176, 183–185.

17. One primary source, cited by Crompton, indicates that Rushton was someone whom Byron had "corrupted." Louis Crompton, *Byron and Greek Love: Homophobia in 19th-Century England* (Berkeley: University of California Press, 1985), 67, 131.

18. Ibid., 67. Leslie Alexis Marchand, *Byron: A Portrait* (New York: Knopf, 1970), 20.

19. Crompton, *Byron and Greek Love*, 83, 236.

20. Children cannot consent to sex with an adult. Any sexual act between a child and an adult is an assault. The age of consent has varied in Britain over the modern period, but that principle of an age of consent has remained largely consistent, with the age of fourteen, at which point an individual was considered competent to give evidence in court, acting as a de facto age of consent in this period. Linda Martin Alcoff, "Dangerous Pleasures: Foucault and the Politics of Pedophilia," in *Feminist Interpretations of Michel Foucault*, ed. Susan J. Hekman (University Park: Pennsylvania State University Press, 1996), 99–136; Louise Jackson, *Child Sexual Abuse in Victorian England* (New York: Routledge, 2000), 102–106.

21. Dror Wahrman has argued that the last two decades of the eighteenth century ushered in a new identity regime, where the more relational, changeable, and unfixed

idea of the self that dominated in the early and mid-eighteenth century gave way to self-understandings that emphasized a core inner self, where individuals "went to great lengths to explain how developments from early childhood entrenches personal identity as if it had an essential, natural existence after all." Dror Wahrman, *The Making of the Modern Self: Identity and Culture in Eighteenth-Century England* (New Haven, CT: Yale University Press, 2004), xv, 273.

22. Rather than being someone who refused to control their impulses and who had become degraded through overindulgence in a range of pleasures. See Harry Oosterhuis, *Stepchildren of Nature: Krafft-Ebing, Psychiatry, and the Making of Sexual Identity* (Chicago: University of Chicago Press, 2000), 53–55; Ivan Crozier, "Nineteenth-Century British Psychiatric Writing about Homosexuality before Havelock Ellis: The Missing Story," *Journal of the History of Medicine and Allied Sciences* 63, no. 1 (2007); Thomas Laqueur, *Solitary Sex: A Cultural History of Masturbation* (New York: Zone Books, 2003); Harry Cocks, *Visions of Sodom: Religion, Homoerotic Desire, and the End of the World in England, c. 1550–1850* (Chicago: University of Chicago Press, 2017), 180.

23. Scholars who have examined how Byron and his Cambridge friends used coded language to discuss illicit sexuality, including pederasty and other forms of same-sex desire, include Marchand, *Byron: A Portrait*; Doris Langley Moore, *Lord Byron: Accounts Rendered* (New York: Harper and Row, 1974); MacCarthy, *Byron*, 65–68. Castlereagh, when traveling to Cambridge for the first time with his father, paid a visit to the Ladies of Llangollen, with whom he remained friends for more than thirty-five years. Hyde, *Strange Death*, 142.

24. *Don Leon*, line 198.

25. Ibid., lines 214–218.

26. Ibid., lines 221–222, 228.

27. Ibid., lines 235, 243–244.

28. Ibid., lines 253–254.

29. Ibid., lines 256, 258, 260.

30. Ibid., lines 271–272.

31. Ibid., lines 286, 293.

32. Ibid., line 318. Another echo of Bentham seems evident when the poet builds an analysis point on the premise that "man's pursuit through life is happiness." Ibid., line 326.

33. Ibid., lines 327–328.

34. Ibid., lines 392–393.

35. Ibid., line 415.

36. Ibid., lines 422–423; Moore, *Byron*.

37. *Don Leon*, lines 447, 469–470; Afsaneh Najmabadi, *Women with Mustaches and Men without Beards: Gender and Sexual Anxieties of Iranian Modernity* (Berkeley: University of California Press, 2005).

38. *Don Leon*, lines 452, 467–468.

39. Ibid., lines 493–494, 500.

40. Ibid., lines 505, 519–520.

41. Ibid., lines 521–543; Ian Worthington, ed., *Demosthenes: Statesman and Orator* (New York: Routledge, 2000).

42. *Don Leon*, lines 544–545, 551. The *Don Leon* poet follows Thomas Moore's biography of Byron in identifying this individual, Giraud, as the son of his host. The individual on whom this representation is based, Nicolo Giraud, is his host's brother-in-law. Crompton, *Byron and Greek Love*, 351.

43. *Don Leon*, lines 544–574.

44. Ibid., lines 592–603.

45. The story of the separation between Byron and Annabella, and Stephen Lushington's role in it, is recounted at the start of Chapter 7.

46. See Chapter 1.

47. Chew does not state his reasons for believing this. Chew is more accurate than most in dating *Don Leon*, which he places between 1824 and 1830. Samuel C. Chew, *Byron in England: His Fame and After-Fame* (New York: Russell and Russell, 1965), 174, 177.

48. Margaret Maria Elizabeth Beckford was born in 1784, and Susan Euphemia Beckford was born in 1786. Lewis Melville, *The Life and Letters of William Beckford of Fonthill* (London: William Heinemann, 1970), 172.

49. Crompton, *Byron and Greek Love*, 353n, 378n; Leslie A. Marchand, *Byron: A Biography* (New York: Knopf, 1957), 2:587n; G. Wilson Knight, *Lord Byron's Marriage: The Evidence of Asterisks* (New York: Macmillan, 1957), 74–76, 237–240.

50. "Leon to Annabella," lines 161–163.

51. Ibid., lines 173–174.

52. Ibid., lines 73–74.

53. Ibid., lines 195–196.

54. Ibid., lines 199–200, 204.

55. Ibid., lines 209–210, 187–188.

56. Ibid., lines 232–240.

57. Ibid., lines 267–264.

58. Ibid., lines 317–318.

59. This tension between the sacrament of marriage and the enforcement of the sodomy law is long-standing. See Cocks, *Visions of Sodom*, 35–36.

60. "Leon to Annabella," lines 75–108.

61. McCalman, *Radical Underworld*, 204–206.

62. *Don Leon*, line 1061.

63. Ibid., lines 1065, 1069–1070.

64. Ibid., lines 1075–1180.

65. Ibid., lines 1194–1240.

66. For an overview of the Beckford newspaper-clippings collection, see Rictor Norton, "Oddities, Obituaries and Obsessions: Early Nineteenth-Century Scandal and Social History Glimpsed through William Beckford's Newspaper Cuttings," in *The Beckford Society Annual Lectures 2004–2006*, ed. Richard Allen (Warminster, UK: Beckford Society, 2008), 53–72.

67. *Don Leon*, lines 761–783, 784–785.

68. Ibid., lines 788–849.

69. Ibid., line 881. The Barley-Mow is discussed in Beckford's clippings, in a story about the bail arrangements for the keeper of the house. The story also mentions

"John Grosset Muirhead," who is extensively discussed in the "Notes to *Don Leon*" and discussed in other Beckford newspaper clippings. Papers of William Beckford (1772–1857), Newspaper cuttings (1780–1847), MS BECKFORD, c. 71, f. 34, *Age*, September 1825. MS BECKFORD, c. 75, f. 68, *Morning Chronicle*, October 22, 1825, on the trial of J. G. Muirhead, esq., Westminster Sessions. See also MS BECKFORD, c. 75, f. 69, *Morning Chronicle*, July 27, 1829, for a story on the rearrest in Dover of "The Well-known Mr. Muirhead," where the events of 1825 are recounted. For two of the many reports involving soldiers in the Beckford clippings, see MS BECKFORD, c. 67, f. 152, *Morning Chronicle*, November 24, 1827; *News*, September 23, 1827, MS BECKFORD, c. 83, fol. 139. For one of the stories that Beckford collected about clergymen sexually assaulting those entrusted to their care, see MS BECKFORD, c. 83, f. 81, *News*, April 29, 1822.

70. *Don Leon*, line 929.

71. Ibid., lines 930–943.

72. For the best work on Heber and Hartshorne related to their relationship, see Arnold Hunt, "A Study in Bibliomania: Charles Henry Hartshorne and Richard Heber," *Book Collector* 42 (1993): 25–43, 185–212.

73. *Annual Register*, 1833, 245–247. For other obituaries for Heber, see *Morning Chronicle*, October 10, 1833; *Examiner*, October 6, 1833; *North Wales Chronicle*, October 15, 1833; *Jackson's Oxford Journal*, October 19, 1833.

74. Beckford kept two obituaries for Heber and several earlier stories related to him and Charles Henry Hartshorn. MS BECKFORD, c. 63. *Morning Chronicle*, October 8, 1833; *Morning Chronicle*, October 10, 1833. Both reports are related to Heber's death and mention the scandal that surrounded him. For the material related to the 1827 trial, see MS BECKFORD, c. 83, f. 73, *John Bull*, May 7, 1826. "Mr. Heber, the late Member for Oxford University, will not return to this country for some time—the backwardness of the season renders the Continent more congenial to some constitutions"; MS BECKFORD, c. 83, f. 72, *News*, November 14, 1826 [handwritten title and date]. This story repeated the two reports that implied that Hartshorn and Heber had had a sexual affair. Then, "to enable our readers the better to comprehend the *venom* of these paragraphs, we may state, that *Mr. Heber*, the Member for the University of Oxford, and the brother of the late Bishop of Calcutta, is supposed (for after all it is but supposition) to have left England for much the same reason that my *Lord Courtenay*—the Bishop of Clogher, *cum multis aliis*, have deemed it expedient to emigrate to foreign climes"; emphasis original, MS BECKFORD, c. 73, f. 77, "Further Memoranda Relating to Richard Heber, Esq."

75. Margaret Escott, "Bennet, Hon. Henry Grey (1777–1836)," Member Biographies, *The History of Parliament: The House of Commons, 1820–1832*, ed. D. R. Fisher (Cambridge: Cambridge University Press, 2009).

76. Roland Thorne, 2008, "Bennet, Henry Grey (1777–1836), politician," *Oxford Dictionary of National Biography*, April 2019.

77. *Don Leon*, lines 978–987.

78. "Notes to *Don Leon*," Note 66.

79. *John Bull*, November 27, 1825; *John Bull*, December 11, 1825; *London Evening Standard*, July 30, 1827.

80. "His plight, amatory prowess, and exile to Florence attracted much public attention." Escott, "Bennet, Hon. Henry Grey," *History of Parliament*.

81. *Galignani's Messenger* recorded his death in Florence a few days before June 16, 1836, as did at least a dozen other newspapers. Bennet's wife returned to Britain after his death.

82. MS BECKFORD, c. 76, f. 4, *Age*. The *Age* (1825–1843) was a leading weekly conservative journal. See also *Morning Post*, November 14, 1825; *Age*, November 13, 1825.

83. David R. Fisher and Terry Jenkins, "Stanhope, Hon. James Hamilton (1788–1825)," Member Biographies, *The History of Parliament: The House of Commons 1820–1832*, ed. D. R. Fisher (Cambridge: Cambridge University Press, 2009).

84. *Don Leon*, lines 956–971.

85. James Stanhope was the brother of the present Lord Stanhope. "Notes to *Don Leon*," Note 65. For the *Times* obituary for Stanhope, see *Times*, March 8, 1825.

86. For further support of this point using other examples, see Upchurch, "Consequences of Dating *Don Leon*," 24–33.

87. MS BECKFORD, c. 73, f. 55, *Morning Chronicle*, March 6, 1833. "The eyes of the public are on their proceedings, and will be scrupulously directed to any discrepancy between the evidence on which a Member of Parliament was held to bail, and that which may be adduced on his trial at the Clerkenwell Sessions. Great fortune and connexions must not be suffered to interfere with the impartial administration of justice." MS BECKFORD, c. 81, *Morning Chronicle*, May 10, 1842. In 1841, Bankes, a former MP, was again brought into Bow Street for indecently assaulting a soldier in the enclosed grounds of St. James's Park. He failed to appear at his Old Bailey trial, but the case was removed by certiorari to the Court of Queen's Bench. He paid a new bail but, again, went abroad and did not show up for his trial. The "government have resolved that offenders of this description shall not be allowed to set the law at defiance." The Treasury Solicitor filed a writ to start the process of declaring Bankes an outlaw so that all his property could be seized if he did not return to go on trial.

88. *Don Leon*, lines 1002–1010.

89. The quoted text is the full contents of Note 69, save for two reproduced lines of the poem itself.

90. Anna Clark, *Women's Silence, Men's Violence: Sexual Assault in England 1770–1845* (New York: Pandora, 1987), 60–64.

91. After a 1781 judicial decision, proof of penetration and emission was needed for a sodomy conviction, while after 1828, proof of penetration alone was sufficient for a sodomy conviction. Jeffrey Weeks, *Coming Out: Homosexual Politics in Britain from the Nineteenth Century to the Present* (London: Quartet Books, 1977), 13.

92. Richard Martin was an MP from 1801 to 1812 and again from 1818 to April 11, 1827, for Galway. He earned the nickname "Humanity Dick," the animal's friend. There were only three Martins in Parliament in this period. The other two, John Martin and Sir Thomas Byam Martin, had no involvement with the treatment of animals. *The History of Parliament*, Member Biographies, available at http://www.historyofparliamentonline.org.

93. James Brogden, Whig, served as an MP for Launceston (Dunheved) from 1796 to 1832. Sir James Mackintosh served as an MP for Nairnshire from 1813 to 1818 and for Knaresborough from 1818 to 1832. *The History of Parliament*, Member Biographies, available at http://www.historyofparliamentonline.org.

94. MS BECKFORD, c. 67, f. 64, *Morning Chronicle*, March 17, 1825, report on "Mr. Martin" and his "Cruelty to Animals Act" of 1823 as well as his current efforts in the same area in 1825. MS BECKFORD, c. 76, f. 4, *Age*, contains a long discussion of Mr. Martin's bill. For Beckford's clippings on cruelty to animals not mentioning Martin, see MS BECKFORD, c. 69, f. 168, *Times*, July 11, 1828, letter to the editor on cruelty to animals by HOMO and another story about the cruelties at dog-fighting and bear-baiting pits. MS BECKFORD, c. 71, f. 39, *Morning Chronicle*, March 25, 1826.

95. *Don Leon*, line 1443.

96. "Notes to *Don Leon*," Note 91.

97. Thomas Moore, *Life of Lord Byron: With His Letters and Journals* (Boston: Little, Brown, 1853), 3:249.

98. "Leon to Annabella," title page and lines 249–260.

99. Crompton, *Byron and Greek Love*, 353n, 378n; Marchand, *Byron: A Biography*, 2:587n; Knight, *Lord Byron's Marriage*, 74–76, 82–83.

100. Marchand, *Byron: A Portrait*, 217–225.

101. MS BECKFORD, c. 64, f. 17, *Examiner*, February 14, 1841, containing a story from House of Commons session held on Tuesday, February 9, 1841. The story discussed Fitzroy Kelly and the Punishment of Death Bill; MS BECKFORD, c. 82, f. 145–146, *Morning Post*, March 25, 1843, letter to the editor arguing against the death penalty, titled "The Punishment of Death," but not pertaining specifically to sodomy cases; MS BECKFORD, c. 73, f. 34, *Times*, September 17, 1832, a short clipping about Lushington presenting an antislavery petition to the U.S. Congress.

102. MS BECKFORD, c. 63, *Times*, January 4, 1833; *Morning Chronicle*, January 24, 1833; *Morning Chronicle*, January 25, 1833; *Literary and Dramatic Register and Varieties*, January 27, 1833; *Age*, January 27, 1833.

103. MS BECKFORD, c. 83, f. 131, *Morning Chronicle*, February 14, 1826.

104. MS BECKFORD, c. 83, f. 51, *Morning Chronicle*, November 28, 1822.

105. MS BECKFORD, c. 83, f. 80, taken from *Dublin Morning Register*, [October 1834].

106. Leon Radzinowicz, *A History of English Criminal Law and Its Administration from 1750*, vol. 1, *The Movement for Reform 1750–1833* (New York: Macmillan, 1948), 585.

107. Ibid., 1:574.

108. Ibid., 1:577.

109. Ibid., 1:588.

110. Ibid., 1:589–590.

111. Ibid., 1:569.

112. *Don Leon*, lines 1347–1350.

113. Ibid., lines 1341–1346.

114. Louis Crompton, *Homosexuality and Civilization* (Cambridge, MA: Belknap Press of Harvard University Press, 2003), 524–528.

115. Brian Joseph Martin, *Napoleonic Friendship: Military Fraternity, Intimacy, and Sexuality in Nineteenth-Century France* (Durham: University of New Hampshire Press, 2011), 1–15; Ronald Hyam, *Empire and Sexuality: The British Experience* (Manchester: Manchester University Press, 1990).

116. Letter dated May 20, 1830. HO 44 20. Home Office: Domestic Correspondence from 1773 to 1861.

117. HO 44 20, letter dated May 20, 1830.

118. HO 44 20, letter dated May 20, 1830.

119. Emphasis added. HO 44 20, letter dated May 20, 1830.

120. *Calcutta Monthly Journal and General Register*, 1838, 203.

121. Arthur Burns and Joanna Innes, eds., *Rethinking the Age of Reform: Britain 1780–1850* (Cambridge: Cambridge University Press, 2003), 46–47.

CHAPTER 6

1. HO 17/120/60, Petition for James Pratt and John Smith, sentenced to death for sodomy. Letter of Hensleigh Wedgwood, Magistrate at the Union Hall Police Office, to Lord John Russell, explaining why he has dismissed similar cases in the past rather than commit individuals for trial on sodomy charges, as Russell was considering requests for clemency for James Pratt and John Smith.

2. Fr. Frank Ryan, OMI, "The Execution of James Pratt and John Smith, 27th November, 1835: 'The Law to Take Its Course'" (Unpublished manuscript, 2014).

3. Letter of Thomas Baker, dated May 20, 1830. Home Office: Domestic Correspondence from 1773 to 1861. HO 44 20.

4. Arthur Burns and Joanna Innes, eds., *Rethinking the Age of Reform: Britain 1780–1850* (Cambridge: Cambridge University Press, 2003), 2–4, 71–97.

5. It was during the short-lived "Ministry of All the Talents," which included Charles James Fox, that the abolition of the slave trade was passed. Michael Lobban, "'Old Wine in New Bottles': The Concept and Practice of Law Reform c. 1780–1830," in *Rethinking the Age of Reform*, ed. Burns and Innes, 114–135.

6. Peter Mandler, *Aristocratic Government in the Age of Reform: Whigs and Liberals, 1830–1852* (Oxford: Clarendon Press, 1990); E. W. Woodward (Ernest Llewelyn), *The Age of Reform, 1815–70*, 2nd ed. (Oxford: Clarendon Press, 1962); A. S. Turberville (Arthur Stanley), *The House of Lords in the Age of Reform, 1784–1837; with an Epilogue on Aristocracy and the Advent of Democracy, 1837–67* (London: Faber and Faber, 1858); Michael J. Turner, *British Politics in an Age of Reform* (Manchester: Manchester University Press, 1999).

7. Burns and Innes, *Rethinking the Age of Reform*, 1.

8. Leon Radzinowicz, *A History of English Criminal Law and Its Administration from 1750*, vol. 4, *Grappling for Control* (London: Stevens and Sons, 1968), 303–304.

9. Ibid., 4:307.

10. Brian P. Block and John Hostettler, *Hanging in the Balance: A History of the Abolition of Capital Punishment in Britain* (Winchester, UK: Waterside Press, 1997), 121–151.

11. Radzinowicz, *History of English Criminal Law*, 4:310.

12. House of Commons, *First Report from His Majesty's Commissioners on Criminal Law*, June 24, 1834 (published July 30, 1834). Commissioners for the *First Report*: Charles Henry Bellenden Ker, Thomas Starkie, Sir William Wightman, Andrew Amos, and John Austin.

13. Radzinowicz, *History of English Criminal Law*, 4:309–310.

14. Ibid., 4:311.

15. Ibid.

16. James Gregory, *Victorians against the Gallows: Capital Punishment and the Abolitionist Movement in Nineteenth-Century Britain* (London: I. B. Tauris, 2012), 18–19; Basil Montagu, *An Account of the Origin and Object of the Society for the Diffusion of Knowledge upon the Punishment of Death and the Improvement of Prison Discipline* (London: Printed by Richard Taylor and Co., 1812).

17. Gregory, *Victorians against the Gallows*, 18–19; Randall McGowen, "A Powerful Sympathy: Terror, the Prison, and Humanitarian Reform in Early Nineteenth-Century Britain," *Journal of British Studies* 25, no. 3 (July 1986); Richard R. Follett, *Evangelicalism, Penal Theory and the Politics of Criminal Law Reform in England, 1808–30* (New York: Palgrave, 2001).

18. The full citation, as it appears in *Index Librorum Prohibitorum*, is "A Free Examination into the Penal Statutes xxv Henr VIII cap 6 and v Eliz c 17 addrest to Both Houses of Parliament, by A. Pilgrim, &c. London Sold in Little Queen Street MDCCCXXXIII." Pisanus Fraxi [pseud. of Henry Spencer Ashbee], *Index Librorum Prohibitorum: Being Notes Bio- Biblio- Icono-graphical and Critical, on Curious and Uncommon Books* (Privately Printed, 1877), 461. Louis Crompton suggests that *A Free Examination* was "printed probably in Paris." Louis Crompton, "*Don Leon*, Byron, and Homosexual Law Reform," *Journal of Homosexuality* 8, nos. 3–4 (Spring/Summer 1983): 57.

19. Philip Schofield, Catherine Pease-Watkin, and Michael Quinn, eds., *Of Sexual Irregularities, and Other Writings on Sexual Morality*, Collected Works of Jeremy Bentham Series (Oxford: Clarendon Press, 2014).

20. Fraxi/Ashbee, *Index Librorum Prohibitorum*, 461.

21. Emphasis added. "Notes to *Don Leon*," Note 8, 7–8, quoting *A Free Examination*, 22.

22. Ibid., Note 8, quoting *A Free Examination*, 22.

23. Ibid., Note 24, 14, quoting *A Free Examination*.

24. Fraxi/Ashbee, *Index Librorum Prohibitorum*, 339.

25. "Notes to *Don Leon*," Note 42, 23, quoting *A Free Examination*.

26. Ibid., Note 53, 37–38, quoting *A Free Examination*.

27. Fraxi/Ashbee, *Index Librorum Prohibitorum*, 339–340.

28. "Notes to *Don Leon*," Note 68, 47, quoting *A Free Examination*, 74.

29. Ibid., quoting *A Free Examination*, 74.

30. S. M. Farrell, 2008, "Bankes, Henry (1757–1834), Politician and Parliamentary Diarist," *Oxford Dictionary of National Biography*, January 2019.

31. Fiona MacCarthy, *Byron: Life and Legend* (New York: Farrar, Straus and Giroux, 2002), 58.

32. Dorothy U. Seyler, *The Obelisk and the Englishman: The Pioneering Discoveries of Egyptologist William Bankes* (Amherst, NY: Prometheus Books, 2015), 30–44.

33. MacCarthy, *Byron*, 58–62, 65–67, 140–141.

34. David R. Fisher, ed., "Bankes, William John (1786–1855)," Member Biographies, *The History of Parliament: The House of Commons 1820–1832* (Cambridge: Cambridge University Press, 2009).

35. Seyler, *Obelisk and the Englishman*, 62; Anna Sebba, *The Exiled Collector: William Bankes and the Making of an English Country House* (London: John Murray, 2004), 31–32, 47–48.

36. Seyler, *Obelisk and the Englishman*, 93–107; Sebba, *Exiled Collector*, 85–112.

37. Emphasis original. Seyler, *Obelisk and the Englishman*, 16.

38. Fisher, "Bankes, William John," *History of Parliament*.

39. Elizabeth Baigent, 2004, "Bankes, William John (1786–1855), Traveller and Antiquary," *Oxford Dictionary of National Biography*, January 2019.

40. Fisher, "Bankes, William John," *History of Parliament*.

41. Police, Queen-square, *Times*, June 8, 1833; *Morning Chronicle*, June 8, 1833; *Galignani's Messenger*, June 10, 1833.

42. *Morning Chronicle*, June 8, 1833; *Times*, June 8, 1833.

43. That scene gives a detailed description of a debate in the 1825 parliamentary session, which occurred when William Bankes was an MP.

44. "Notes to *Don Leon*," Note 56, 40–43. *Galignani's Messenger* was available in Europe and Britain. The use of the French-language newspaper, and the calling out of Peel by name, in *A Free Examination* and *Don Leon*, years after Peel was out of office, suggests a further link between the authors of *A Free Examination* and *Don Leon*. *Galignani's* reports are reprinted from English-language British newspapers, from March 1828; May, June, and August 1833; May and June 1836; and November 1842. The "Notes to *Don Leon*" authors also use Galignani's edition of Thomas Moore's *Life of Byron*. Thomas Moore and George Gordon Byron, *Letters and Journals of Lord Byron: with Notices of his Life*, complete in one volume (Paris: A. and W. Galignani, 1831).

45. "Notes to *Don Leon*," Note 27, citing *Theorie des Peines et des Récompenses, Ouvrage Extrait des Manuscrits de M. Jeremie Bentham, Jurisconsulte Anglais*, 3rd ed. (Paris: Bossange Freres, Libraires, Rue de Seine, no. 12, 1825), 1:55.

46. Howard Spencer, "Wall, Charles Baring (1795–1853), of Norman Court," Member Biographies, *The History of Parliament: The House of Commons 1820–1832*, ed. D. R. Fisher (Cambridge: Cambridge University Press, 2009).

47. Keele University Library, Sneyd (Ralph) mss SC17/39, 52; Spencer, "Wall, Charles Baring," *History of Parliament*.

48. Harriet was one of the leaders of the 1815 Western Schism, a sizable group that seceded *en masse* from the Church of England. Grayson Carter, 2004, "Wall [née Baring], Harriet (1768–1838), Religious Controversialist," *Oxford Dictionary of National Biography*, January 2019.

49. Spencer, "Wall, Charles Baring," *History of Parliament*.

50. Ibid.

51. Miss Eden to Miss Villiers, Bigods, Essex, Sunday, July 1827. Violet Dickinson, ed., *Miss Eden's Letters* (London: Macmillan, 1919).

52. *Morning Chronicle*, May 13, 1833; *Times*, March 4, 1833.

53. *Evening Mail*, May 13, 1833; *Newry Telegraph*, May 17, 1833.

54. The *Times* reported the event second-hand, noting that "in the daily police report of Thursday last" from the *Observer*. *Times*, March 4, 1833; *Birmingham Journal*, March 16, 1833; *Bell's New Weekly Messenger*, April 28, 1833; *Taunton Courier and Western Advertiser*, March 27, 1833.

55. "Criminal Trials, Court of King's Bench, Westminster, May 11," *Times*, May 13, 1833; *Morning Chronicle*, May 13, 1833. There were approximately two-and-a-half columns of text on the trial in the *Times* and in the *Morning Chronicle*.

56. *Newry Telegraph*, May 17, 1833; *London Courier and Evening Gazette*, May 11, 1833.

57. *Bell's Life in London and Sporting Chronicle*, May 12, 1833; *Newry Telegraph*, May 17, 1833.

58. One of the men who spoke for Wall was the Liberal MP Henry Labouchere, uncle of the man who would successfully propose the amendment that effectively lessened the term of imprisonment for certain forms of sex between men in 1885.

59. *Windsor and Eton Express*, November 23, 1833; *Morning Post*, February 6, 1834.

60. Norman Gash, *Aristocracy and People: Britain, 1815–1865* (Cambridge, MA: Harvard University Press, 1981); Asa Briggs, *The Age of Improvement, 1783–1867* (Harlow, UK: Longman, 2000).

61. Radzinowicz, *History of English Criminal Law*, 4:309.

62. G. F. R. Barker, 2004, "Law, Charles Ewan (1792–1850), Judge," *Oxford Dictionary of National Biography*, January 2019.

63. "A Bill for Amending the Law Relating to Offences against the Person in Certain Cases," 5 Will. IV. Sess. 1835 (Prepared and Brought in by Mr. Jervis and Mr. Pryme, June 5, 1835).

64. "Offences against the Person Bill. Clauses to be Proposed in Committee," by Mr. Law, June 1835.

65. Bill No. 276, *Journals of the House of Commons*, vol. 90 (5 Will. IV), June 5, 1835, 312.

66. *Journals of the House of Commons*, vol. 90 (5 Will. IV), July 13, 1835, 447. "A Bill (as Amended by the Committee) for Amending the Law Relating to Offences against the Person in Certain Cases," 6 Will. IV. Sess. 1835, printed July 1, 1835. *House of Commons Parliamentary Papers Online*.

67. Emphasis original. MS Beckford, c. 75, ff. 147, August 16, 1835.

68. *Hansard*, Lords Sitting, Third Series, vol. 30, August 28, 1835, 1069.

69. Ibid., 1066–1067.

70. Ibid., 1067.

71. *Journals of the House of Commons*, vol. 90 (5 Will. IV), August 29–30, 1835, 609. The committee comprised Mr. Ewart, Sir George Strickland, Mr. Pryme, Mr. Brotherton, Mr. Aglionby, Mr. Elphinstone, Mr. Potter, and Mr. Chalmers; "And they are to withdraw, immediately, into the Speaker's Chamber."

72. *Second Report from His Majesty's Commissioners on Criminal Law* (dated June 9, 1836, published June 20, 1836), 1–2.

73. Ryan, "The Execution of Pratt and Smith," citing Central Criminal Court, Appendix to Capital Convictions, Eleventh Session, 1835, before Mr. Baron Gurney, The King v. James Pratt, John Smith, and William Bonill. "Ref: Old Bailie f18350921, dated September 21, 1835," 19.

74. Ibid., 39.

75. Ibid., 19.

76. Ibid., 19–21.

77. Boyd Hilton, *The Age of Atonement: The Influence of Evangelicalism on Social and Economic Thought, 1795–1865* (New York: Oxford University Press, 1987), 298–339.

78. Harry Potter, *Hanging in Judgment: Religion and the Death Penalty in England from the Bloody Code to Abolition* (London: SCM Press, 1993); Vic Gatrell, *The Hanging Tree: Execution and the English People, 1770–1868* (Oxford: Oxford University Press, 1994).

79. Gregory, *Victorians against the Gallows*, 16.

80. CRIM 6/1, Central Criminal Court: Court Books Old Court, November 1834—June 1837, 50. Minutes of the Saturday Meeting between the Recorder and Two Aldermen. Ryan, "Execution of Pratt and Smith," 35–36, 50.

81. HO 6/20 Judges and Recorders Returns, 1835. Cited in Ryan, "Execution of Pratt and Smith," 54.

82. HO 13/68 Home Office: Criminal Entry Books, Correspondence and Warrants, 10 October 1835—21 March 1836. Cited in Ryan, "Execution of Pratt and Smith," 51–52.

83. "Richard Johnson and the Imperial Self," in Anna Clark, *Alternative Histories of the Self: A Cultural History of Sexuality and Secrets, 1762–1917* (New York: Bloomsbury Academic, 2017), 77–98; Anna Clark and Aaron Windel, "The Early Roots of Liberal Imperialism: 'The Science of a Legislator' in Eighteenth Century India," *Journal of Colonialism and Colonial History* 14, no. 2 (2013).

84. Leon Radzinowicz, *A History of English Criminal Law and Its Administration from 1750*, vol. 1, *The Movement for Reform 1750–1833* (London: Stevens, 1948), 593–594.

85. Ibid., 1:107.

86. Ibid., 1:116, 1:120.

87. Ibid., 1:128.

88. Ibid., 1:137.

89. HO 17/120/60, Petition for James Pratt and John Smith, Petition of Elizabeth Pratt.

90. HO 17/120/60, Petition for James Pratt and John Smith, Petition of John Wilson.

91. HO 17/120/60, Petition for James Pratt and John Smith. John Berkshire and Jane Berkshire with 56 supporting signatures.

92. HO 17/120/60, Petition for James Pratt and John Smith, Petition of William Scott Preston.

93. Radzinowicz, *History of English Criminal Law*, 1:111, 1:114.

94. Emphasis original. Ibid., 1:243; Matthew McCormack, ed., *Public Men: Masculinity and Politics in Modern Britain* (New York: Palgrave Macmillan, 2007); Marie

Laure Legay, "The Beginnings of Public Management: Administrative Science and Political Choices in the Eighteenth Century in France, Austria, and the Austrian Netherlands," *Journal of Modern History* 81, no. 2 (June 2009).

95. Charles Dickens, "A Visit to Newgate," in *Sketches by "Boz": Illustrative of Every-Day-Life and Every-Day-People* (Philadelphia: T. B. Peterson, 1839), 109–115.

96. Ibid., 114.

97. Ibid.

98. Holly Furneaux, *Queer Dickens: Erotics, Families, Masculinities* (New York: Oxford University Press, 2009).

99. The character was Tommy Traddles in *David Copperfield.* The 1837 volume form of the *Pickwick Papers* is dedicated to Talfourd. Talfourd was friends with Leigh Hunt, radical editor, publisher, and associate of Byron, who authored *Lord Byron and Some of His Contemporaries* in 1828. Edwin Pugh, *The Charles Dickens Originals* (London: Foulis, 1912), 315; J. W. T. (James William Thomas) Ley, *The Dickens Circle: A Narrative of the Novelist's Friendships* (London: Chapman and Hall, 1918), 41.

100. Edith Hall, 2004, "Talfourd, Sir Thomas Noon (1795–1854), writer, judge, and politician," *Oxford Dictionary of National Biography*, January 2019.

101. Cumberland Clark, *Dickens and Talfourd: With an Address and Three Unpublished Letters to Talfourd* (London: Chiswick, 1919); "A Memoir of Mr. Justice Talfourd," *Law Magazine* 51 (1854).

102. Hall, "Talfourd, Sir Thomas Noon," *Oxford Dictionary of National Biography.*

103. Thomas Sadler, ed., *Diary, Reminiscences, and Correspondence of Henry Crabb Robinson* (Boston: Houghton, Mifflin, 1898).

104. Norman MacKenzie and Jeanne MacKenzie, *Dickens, a Life* (New York: Oxford University Press, 1979); *Hansard*, Commons Sitting, vol. 57, March 8, 1841, 47–57; "A Bill, For taking away the Punishment of Death in certain Cases, and substituting other Punishments in lieu thereof . . . (Prepared and brought in by Mr. Kelly, Dr. Lushington, and Mr. Serjeant Talfourd)," February 12, 1840—4 Vict.

105. John Foster, *The Life of Charles Dickens*, vol. 2, *1842–1852* (London: Chapman and Hall, 1873), 42; also quoted in Edwin P. Whipple, "Oliver Twist," *Atlantic Monthly* 38 (October 1876): 478.

106. *Second Report from His Majesty's Commissioners on Criminal Law*, June 9, 1836 (published June 20, 1836). Commissioners for *Second Report*: Charles Henry Bellenden Ker, Thomas Starkie, Sir William Wightman, Andrew Amos, and John Austin.

107. Ibid., 19–21.

108. Ibid., 32.

109. Ibid., 33.

110. Wilfrid E. Rumble, 2008, "Austin, John (1790–1859), Legal Philosopher," *Oxford Dictionary of National Biography*, January 2019.

111. John Austin, *Lectures on Jurisprudence, or, the Philosophy of Positive Law*, posthumously published (London: J. Murray, 1869), 420.

112. John Austin, *The Province of Jurisprudence Determined* (London: J. Murray, 1832).

113. Radzinowicz, *History of English Criminal Law*, 4:317.

114. Ibid.

115. Radzinowicz, *History of English Criminal Law*, 1:607; Block and Hostettler, *Hanging in the Balance*, 45–57; Radzinowicz, *History of English Criminal Law*, 4:317.

116. Radzinowicz, *History of English Criminal Law*, 4:321. See also Chapter 4.

117. Block and Hostettler, *Hanging in the Balance*, 45–57; Radzinowicz, *History of English Criminal Law*, 4:317.

118. *Fourth Report from His Majesty's Commissioners on Criminal Law*, March 8, 1839 (London: Clowes and Sons, for his Majesty's Stationery Office, 1839). Commissioners: Charles Henry Bellenden Ker, Thomas Starkie, Sir William Wightman, Andrew Amos, and David Jardine.

119. Ibid., 45. The *Second Report* was the last one on which Austin worked. He had repeatedly clashed with the other law commissioners, who believed that Austin's ideas were "too abstract and scientific," and he resigned his position in 1836. Rumble, "Austin, John," *Oxford Dictionary of National Biography*; "John Austin," *Law Magazine* 9 (1860): 167.

120. Walter E. Houghton, *The Victorian Frame of Mind, 1830–1870* (New Haven, CT: Yale University Press, 1957).

121. The last known execution for sex between men in Europe was in 1803, in Rotterdam. Louis Crompton, *Homosexuality and Civilization* (Cambridge, MA: Belknap Press of Harvard University Press, 2003), 533.

122. Roger Chadwick, *Bureaucratic Mercy: The Home Office and the Treatment of Capital Cases in Victorian Britain* (New York: Garland Publishing, 1992), 12–13.

CHAPTER 7

1. See argument associated with note 19 on the next page for direct evidence of *Hansard*'s not mentioning sodomy when it was under discussion in debate in the House of Commons.

2. Brian P. Block and John Hostettler, *Hanging in the Balance: A History of the Abolition of Capital Punishment in Britain* (Winchester: Waterside Press, 1997), 57. Works not discussing the 1841 work of Fitzroy Kelly include Elizabeth Orman Tuttle, *The Crusade against Capital Punishment in Great Britain* (London: Stevens, 1961); Vic Gatrell, *The Hanging Tree: Execution and the English People, 1770–1868* (Oxford: Oxford University Press, 1994); Harry Potter, *Hanging in Judgment: Religion and the Death Penalty in England from the Bloody Code to Abolition* (London: SCM Press, 1993); W. A. Munford, *William Ewart, M.P., 1798–1869: Portrait of a Radical* (London: Grafton, 1960); John Laurence, *A History of Capital Punishment, with Special Reference to Capital Punishment in Great Britain* (Port Washington, NY: Kennikat Press, 1971); Roger Chadwick, *Bureaucratic Mercy: The Home Office and the Treatment of Capital Cases in Victorian Britain* (New York: Garland Publishing, 1992); M. J. Wiener, *Men of Blood: Violence, Manliness and Criminal Justice in Victorian England* (Cambridge: Cambridge University Press, 2004); Randall McGowen, "A Powerful Sympathy: Terror, the Prison, and Humanitarian Reform in Early Nineteenth-Century Britain," *Journal of British Studies* 25, no. 3 (July 1986). For passing reference to Kelly's work

in 1840–1841 on this issue, see James Gregory, *Victorians against the Gallows: Capital Punishment and the Abolitionist Movement in Nineteenth-Century Britain* (London: I. B. Tauris, 2012), 44, 142.

3. This is demonstrated by analyzing the final votes in the Commons on the 1841 version of Kelly, Lushington, and Talfourd's bill and the ways in which Lord John Russell reshaped the bill through these votes on May 3, 1841.

4. Simon Devereaux, "Inexperienced Humanitarians? William Wilberforce, William Pitt, and the Execution Crisis of the 1780s," *Law and History Review* 33, no. 4 (November 2015).

5. Joan Scott, "Gender: A Useful Category of Historical Analysis," *American Historical Review* 91, no. 5 (1986).

6. Joan Pierson, 2006, "Noel [née Milbanke], Anne Isabella [Annabella], suo jure Baroness Wentworth, and Lady Byron (1792–1860), philanthropist," *Oxford Dictionary of National Biography*, April 2019; Harriet Beecher Stowe, *Lady Byron Vindicated: A History of the Byron Controversy* (Boston: Fields, Osgood, 1870).

7. Fiona MacCarthy, *Byron: Life and Legend* (New York: Farrar, Straus and Giroux, 2002), 267.

8. Ibid., 268.

9. Ibid., 264.

10. Ibid., 265.

11. *Hansard*, Commons Sitting, vol. 55, July 15, 1840, 736. Kelly had originally intended to introduce his bill on May 14, 1840, announcing this on the day that the Commons debated the merits of transportation as a punishment and the degree to which it resulted in unnatural crime. Kelly agreed to postpone the presentation of his bill due to the recent murder of Lord John Russell's uncle, resulting in Russell's not having had time to study the bill. "House of Commons, Tuesday, May 5," *Times*, May 6, 1840; "House of Commons, Thursday, May 14," *Times*, May 15, 1840.

12. *Hansard*, Commons Sitting, vol. 55, July 15, 1840, 737.

13. Ibid.

14. Ibid. When Kelly had presented his bill several weeks earlier, his argument that the law was supposed to not be a moral judge but prevent crime or keep offenders from repeating their crimes was reported. "House of Commons, Tuesday, June 23," *Times*, June 24, 1840.

15. *Hansard*, Commons Sitting, vol. 55, July 15, 1840, 740. The precedent was set in 1786, although not always subsequently followed, that "any project aiming at a reform of the criminal law should originate with the judges or, if coming from another quarter, should be approved by them before being submitted for the consideration of Parliament." Leon Radzinowicz, *A History of English Criminal Law and Its Administration from 1750*, vol. 1, *The Movement for Reform 1750–1833* (London: Stevens, 1948), 509.

16. *Hansard*, Commons Sitting, vol. 55, July 15, 1840, 742.

17. Ibid., 743–744.

18. Ibid., 744.

19. Compare ibid.; and "A Bill: for taking away the Punishment of Death in certain Cases . . . ," June 23, 1840—4 Vict.

20. Emphasis added. *Hansard*, Commons Sitting, vol. 55, July 15, 1840, 744. This debate was extensively reported in the *Times*, including Russell's attempt to remove the clause that would have ended the death penalty for rape and "certain other crimes against the person." This speech by Hobhouse was summarized in roughly the same way as it appeared in *Hansard*. Hume, Lushington, Ewart, Kelly, and Talfourd were also reported as urging the members of the Commons to keep the clause. "Parliamentary Intelligence," *Times*, July 16, 1840.

21. MacCarthy, *Byron*, 90; Dorothy U. Seyler, *The Obelisk and the Englishman: The Pioneering Discoveries of Egyptologist William Bankes* (Amherst, NY: Prometheus Books, 2015), 33–41; Robert E. Zegger, *John Cam Hobhouse: A Political Life, 1819–1852* (Columbia: University of Missouri Press, 1973); Michael Joyce, *My Friend H: John Cam Hobhouse, Baron Broughton of Broughton De Gyfford* (London: J. Murray, 1948); Eric Reginald Pearce Vincent, *Byron, Hobhouse and Foscolo: New Documents in the History of a Collaboration* (Cambridge: Cambridge University Press, 2013).

22. For the "very thin House" comment, see *Hansard*, Commons Sitting, vol. 56, February 9, 1841, 463. *Hansard*, Commons Sitting, vol. 55, July 15, 1840, 746. A letter to the editor on the state of the majority on the House of Commons mentions that Charles Baring Wall switched to the Whig-Radicals and raised the majority to sixteen. "To the Editor of the *Times*," *Times*, August 21, 1840.

23. *Hansard*, Commons Sitting, vol. 55, July 15, 1840, 748.

24. *Hansard*, Commons Sitting, vol. 55, July 22, 1840, 880.

25. *Hansard*, Commons Sitting, vol. 55, July 15, 1840, 749. In a leading article published shortly after this debate, the *Times* expressed an opinion against Kelly and Lushington's bill. The *Times* argued that Kelly was too quick to want to protect the guilty and instead should have been protecting the innocent, drawing attention in particular to the issues of rape and the burning of the ships. Sodomy was not mentioned, only the "moral thimble-riggery" of Kelly and his supporters. *Times*, July 18, 1840.

26. *Hansard*, Commons Sitting, vol. 55, July 22, 1840, 881.

27. *Hansard*, Commons Sitting, vol. 55, July 29, 1840, 1081. The debate accompanying the third reading of Kelly and Lushington's bill in the House of Commons was covered in an extensive report in the *Times*. Russell's speech was covered in detail, as was Lushington's speech in favor of the bill. "Parliamentary Intelligence," *Times*, July 30, 1840.

28. *Hansard*, Commons Sitting, vol. 55, July 29, 1840, 1079.

29. Emphasis added. Ibid., 1082.

30. *Hansard*, Commons Sitting, vol. 56, February 9, 1841, 466.

31. *UK Parliamentary Papers*, "Hansard Member Profile: Earl of Darlington," Henry Vane (1788–1864); 2nd Duke of Cleveland (Hereditary) 1842. Darlington first became an MP in 1812 and joined the British Army in 1815. He would achieve the rank of major-general by 1851. George E. Cokayne, *The Complete Peerage of England, Scotland, Ireland, Great Britain and the United Kingdom, Extant, Extinct, or Dormant* (London: St. Catherine Press, 1910), 426.

32. *Hansard*, Commons Sitting, vol. 55, July 29, 1840, 1088.

33. Ibid.

34. Ibid., 1089.

35. Ibid., 1090, 1091, 1094.

36. Ibid., 1085.

37. Ibid., 1086.

38. Frederick "was cared for in vacations from Eton by his uncle Lord Castlereagh*, the foreign secretary, at North Cray Farm, Kent." Stephen Farrell, "Stewart, Frederick William Robert, Visct. Castlereagh (1805–1872)," Member Biographies, *The History of Parliament: The House of Commons 1820–1832*, ed. D. R. Fisher (Cambridge: Cambridge University Press, 2009).

39. *Hansard*, Commons Sitting, vol. 56, February 9, 1841, 463.

40. Ibid., 1841, 463, 466.

41. *Hansard*, Commons Sitting, vol. 57, March 8, 1841, 47–57. "A Bill, For taking away the Punishment of Death in certain Cases, and substituting other Punishments in lieu thereof . . . (Prepared and brought in by Mr. Kelly, Dr. Lushington, and Mr. Serjeant Talfourd.)," February 12, 1841—4 Vict. Thomas Talfourd, discussed in Chapter 6, was added as a sponsor for the 1841 version of the bill.

42. See Chapter 1.

43. *Hansard*, Commons Sitting, vol. 57, March 8, 1841, 54. Russell's speech on the clauses of the bill was reported at length in the *Times*. His discussion of whether the death penalty had a deterrent effect for cases of rape was recounted, followed by the observation that "there are other offences," after which he began a discussion of slander and ruining families. Several sentences on slander and the ruin of families followed, which have been omitted from the quoted passage. *Hansard* introduced this with the ambiguous phrase "There was the case of slander—the slander he would suppose, of a young and innocent woman by some disappointed person," while the *Times* report introduced the same material with "In cases of slander, where reputation was destroyed, where the peace of families was annihilated, innocence unjustly assailed, and where the greatest injury might be inflicted from motives the most malicious," without mentioning a woman as the subject of the discussion. "House of Commons, Monday, March 8," *Times*, March 9, 1841.

44. See Chapters 1 and 5. This statement also seems to draw on Montesquieu's argument that "where there is no public act, there can be no criminal matter, the whole passes betwixt man and God, who knows the measure and time of his vengeance." As quoted in Radzinowicz, *History of English Criminal Law*, 1:272.

45. *Hansard*, Commons Sitting, vol. 57, March 8, 1841, 56.

46. "A Bill, to amend an Act of the Ninth Year of the Reign of King George the Fourth, for consolidating and amending the Statutes of England relive to Offences against the Person . . . (Prepared and brought in by Lord John Russell and Mr. Fox Maule.)," March 8, 1841—4 Vict. Fox Maule served as Undersecretary of State in the Home Department under Russell from 1835 to 1841. John Sweetman, 2014, "Maule, Fox [afterwards Fox Maule-Ramsay], second Baron Panmure and eleventh earl of Dalhousie (1801–1874), army officer and politician," *Oxford Dictionary of National Biography*, April 2019.

47. *Hansard*, Commons Sitting, vol. 57, March 22, 1841, 454; For the withdrawal of the bill by the Attorney General, see *Hansard*, Commons Sitting, vol. 58, June 17, 1841, 1563.

48. "Breviates of Pending Bills," *Morning Chronicle*, July 9, 1840.

49. *Times*, July 16, 1840.

50. Ibid. See also *London Evening Standard*, July 16, 1840; *Morning Chronicle*, July 16, 1841; *Globe*, July 16, 1840; *Evening Mail*, July 17, 1840.

51. Emphasis added. *Times*, July 30, 1840. See also *Evening Chronicle*, July 31, 1840; *Globe*, July 30, 1840; *Morning Post*, July 30, 1840; *London Evening Standard*, July 30, 1840.

52. Report on parliamentary events of February 9, 1841. MS BECKFORD c. 64, f. 17.

53. "To the surprise of [John Cam] Hobhouse, the dinner guests in April 1841 included William Bankes*, another Member who had been dubiously acquitted of a homosexual offence and was about to repeat his transgression." Spencer, "Wall, Charles Baring," *History of Parliament*; Benjamin Disraeli, *Benjamin Disraeli Letters: 1835–37*, vol. 2, ed. J. A. W. Gunn, John Matthews, Donald M. Schurman, and M. G. Wiebe (Toronto: University of Toronto Press, 1982), 514; William Bankes had been mentioned in print a few months before as attending a social event. "Rolls' Court, Westminster, Friday, November 20," *Times*, November 21, 1840.

54. Seyler, *Obelisk and the Englishman*, 237; John Brooke and Julia Gandy, eds., *The Prime Ministers' Papers, Wellington, Political Correspondence, I: 1833–Nov. 1834* (London: H. M. Stationery Office, 1975), 378; Anne Sebba, *The Exiled Collector: William Bankes and the Making of an English Country House* (London: John Murray, 2004), 155.

55. It was reported that Kelly had asked Russell whether May 3 would be a good day to bring his bill into committee. Russell had agreed and added that the debate should take place on a day when there was full attendance in the Commons. "House of Commons, Friday, April 30," *Times*, May 1, 1841. On May 3, it was reported that the House of Commons went into committee on the Punishment of Death Bill, but only after a petition supporting the total abolition of the death penalty had been presented by Lord Castlereagh. "House of Commons, Monday, 3 May," *Times*, May 4, 1841.

56. For the 1841 version, Sir Thomas Noon Talfourd (Mr. Sergeant Talfourd) was listed with Kelly and Lushington as having prepared and brought in the bill.

57. *Hansard*, Commons Sitting, vol. 57, May 3, 1841, 1408.

58. Ibid., 1409–1410.

59. Ibid., 1414–1415.

60. Ibid., 1416–1420.

61. Ibid., 1420. Obituary, Capt. Polhill, *Gentleman's Magazine*, 1848, 546.

62. "4. 9 G. 4. c. 31, 15, 16, 17. Sodomy, Rape, &c., . . . it was amongst other things enacted, that every person convicted of the abominable crime of Buggery, committed either with mankind or with any animal, should suffer Death as a Felon, and that every person convicted of the crime of Rape should suffer Death as a Felon, and that if any person should unlawfully and carnally know and abuse any girl under the age of ten years, every such offender should be guilty of Felony, and, being convicted thereof, should suffer Death as a Felon: AND whereas it is expedient that the said several offences hereinbefore last specified should no longer be punishable with Death; BE it therefore further Enacted, That from and after the commencement of this Act,

if any person shall be convicted of any of the said offences hereinbefore last specified, such person shall not be subject to any sentence, judgment or punishment of death . . ." "A Bill, For taking away the Punishment of Death in certain Cases . . ." February 12, 1841—4 Vict., 6.

63. *Hansard*, Commons Sitting, vol. 57, May 3, 1841, 1422–1426.

64. Ibid., 1426–1428.

65. "To Lord John Russell, on His Bill for the Amendment of the Criminal Law," *Times*, May 20, 1841. In the third letter from "A Priori" (the others dated April 8 and 12), it was again argued that punishments must be proportionate to the crime. The author argued strenuously against Russell's position that the law was not an instrument for passing moral judgment. Many of the specifics of the argument related to the crime of rape, but there were also points where references to sodomy may also have been made. The author argued that the whole clause should be taken out of the bill.

66. The remaining two votes taken that night were 73 to 100 and 122 to 110. *Hansard*, Commons Sitting, vol. 57, May 3, 1841, 1428–1431.

67. Comparative data were gathered from the Hansard Member Profiles, Pro-Quest, UK Parliamentary Papers.

68. Linda Colley, *Britons: Forging the Nation, 1707–1837* (New Haven, CT: Yale University Press, 2009).

69. *Hansard*, Lords Sitting, vol. 58, June 17, 1841, 1554–1555. After the committee amendments, the rape and sodomy provisions of the bill were in the third clause. "A Bill [as Amended by the Committee] For taking away the Punishment of Death in certain Cases, and substituting other Punishments in lieu thereof . . . (Prepared and brought in by Mr. Kelly, Dr. Lushington, and Mr. Serjeant Talfourd.)," May 24, 1841—4 Vict.

70. *Times*, June 18, 1841. See also "House of Lords, Friday, June 11," *Times*, June 12, 1841; "House of Lords, Monday, June 14," *Times*, June 15, 1841.

71. *Hansard*, Lords Sitting, vol. 58, June 17, 1841, 1557.

72. Ibid.

73. *Morning Chronicle*, June 19, 1841. The *Times* report was more detailed and just as clear on the issue under discussion. *Times*, June 19, 1841. The *Examiner* had a much shorter report. *Examiner*, June 20, 1841.

74. *Hansard*, Lords Sitting, vol. 58, June 18, 1841, 1568.

75. Ibid., 1568–1569.

76. Richard Davenport-Hines, 2008, "Phipps, Constantine Henry, first marquess of Normanby (1797–1863), politician and diplomatist," *Oxford Dictionary of National Biography*, May 2019; *Arthur Wellesley Wellington, Wellington and His Friends: Letters of the First Duke of Wellington to the Rt. Hon. Charles and Mrs. Arbuthnot, the Earl and Countess of Wilton, Princess Lieven, and Miss Burdett-Coutts* (London: Macmillan, 1965), 122.

77. *Hansard*, Lords Sitting, vol. 58, June 18, 1841, 1568.

78. *Morning Post*, June 19, 1841.

79. G. C. Boase, 2004, "Hatton, George William Finch-, tenth earl of Winchilsea and fifth earl of Nottingham (1791–1858), politician," *Oxford Dictionary of National Biography*, May 2019.

80. *Times*, September 3, 1841; *Times*, September 8, 1841; *Times*, September 9, 1841; *Times*, September 10, 1841. See also Seyler, *Obelisk and the Englishman*, 249.

Conclusion

1. John A. Phillips and Charles Wetherell, "The Great Reform Act of 1832 and the Political Modernization of England," *American Historical Review* 100 (April 1995); Matthew McCormack, ed., *Public Men: Masculinity and Politics in Modern Britain* (New York: Palgrave Macmillan, 2007); John Tosh, *Manliness and Masculinities in Nineteenth-Century Britain: Essays on Gender, Family, and Empire* (London: Routledge, 2016), 83–102.

2. Catherine Hall, Keith McClelland, and Jane Rendall, eds., *Defining the Victorian Nation: Class, Race, Gender and the Reform Act of 1867* (Cambridge: Cambridge University Press, 2000), 186, 200–204; Seymour Drescher, *The Mighty Experiment: Free Labor vs. Slavery in British Emancipation* (New York: Oxford University Press, 2002), 202–230; Thomas R. Metcalf, *Ideologies of the Raj* (New York: Cambridge University Press, 1994), 160–165; Dror Wahrman, *Imagining the Middle Class: The Political Representation of Class in Britain, c. 1780–1840* (Cambridge: Cambridge University Press, 1995).

3. Christopher Leslie Brown, *Moral Capital: Foundations of British Abolitionism* (Chapel Hill: University of North Carolina Press, 2006), 33–102.

4. *Hansard*, Commons Sitting, Third Series, vol. 300, August 6, 1885, 1397.

5. F. B. Smith, "Labouchere's Amendment to the Criminal Law Amendment Bill," *Historical Studies* 17 (1976): 165; Morris B. Kaplan, *Sodom on the Thames: Sex, Love, and Scandal in Wilde Times* (Ithaca, NY: Cornell University Press, 2005), 175; Weeks, *Sex, Politics and Society*, 1st ed., 126, 151.

6. "There were by that time no more than eight offences remaining capital, including the very rare ones of piracy and treason." Leon Radzinowicz, *A History of English Criminal Law and Its Administration from 1750*, vol. 4, *Grappling for Control* (London: Stevens and Sons, 1968), 325, 330.

7. Ibid., 4:330.

8. Ibid., 4:331–333.

9. Ibid., 4:325, 4:329.

10. Ibid., 4:334.

11. John Hostettler, *The Politics of Criminal Law Reform in the Nineteenth Century* (Chichester: Barry Rose Law Publishers, 1992), 192–207; William Cornish, Jenifer Hart, A. H. Manchester, and J. Stevenson, *Crime and Law in Nineteenth Century Britain* (Dublin: Irish University Press, 1978).

12. *Hansard*, Lords Sitting, vol. 156, January 30, 1860, 253.

13. *Hansard*, Commons Sitting, vol. 159, June 11, 1860, 271.

14. *Hansard*, Lords Sitting, vol. 156, January 30, 1860, 253–254.

15. A. H. Manchester, "Simplifying the Sources of the Law: An Essay in Law Reform," *Anglo-American Law Review* 2 (1973).

16. *Hansard*, Commons Sittings, vol. 161, February 14, 1861, 442.

17. For a discussion of the role of the expert in a democratizing process, see Ian Burney, "Making Room at the Public Bar: Coroners' Inquests, Medical Knowledge and the Politics of the Constitution in Early 19th-Century England," in *Re-Reading the Constitution: New Narratives in the Political History of England's Long Nineteenth Century*, ed. James Vernon (New York: Cambridge University Press, 1996), 123–153.

18. Radzinowicz, *History of English Criminal Law*, 4:336.

19. *Hansard*, Lords Sitting, Third Series, vol. 146, June 22, 1857, 115.

20. Ibid., 118.

21. Ibid., 119.

22. *Hansard*, Commons Sitting, vol. 150, May 20, 1858, 925.

23. "A Bill to Consolidate and amend the Statute Law of England and Ireland relating to Offences against the Person," (Prepared and brought in by Mr. Attorney General, Mr. Attorney General for Ireland, and Mr. Secretary Sotheron Estcourt), April 14, 1859—22 Vict.

24. Emphasis added. Ibid., 14.

25. *Hansard*, Commons Sitting, vol. 153, April 14, 1859, 1771.

26. *Hansard*, Commons Sitting, vol. 154, June 30, 1859, 485.

27. Ibid., 500.

28. Ibid., 490.

29. Ibid., 491–492.

30. *Hansard*, Lords Sitting, vol. 156, January 30, 1860, 254–255.

31. "Offences against the Person. A Bill . . . to consolidate and amend the Statute Law of England and Ireland relating to Offences against the Person" (Brought from the Lords 15th May 1860), printed May 21, 1860—23 Vict. Radzinowicz, *History of English Criminal Law*, 4:337.

32. The delays were procedural. *Hansard*, Commons Sitting, vol. 160, August 7, 1860, 894–895.

33. *Reports from the Select Committee on the Offences against the Person &c. Bills, with the Proceedings of the Committee* (Ordered, by the House of Commons, to be Printed, May 7, 1861).

34. Those subject to life sentences were most often considered for a ticket of leave after ten years. "A Bill [As Amended by the Select Committee] to Consolidate and amend the Statute Law of England and Ireland relating to Offences against the Person" (Prepared and brought in by Mr. Solicitor General, Viscount Palmerston, Mr. Attorney General, and Sir George Lewis) Ordered, by the House of Commons, to be Printed, April 25, 1861.

35. Emphasis added. Ibid., 17.

36. *Reports from the Select Committee on the Offences against the Person &c. Bills*, 7.

37. One member suggested that because there were material alterations to some clauses, "he thought it better that they should be deferred to a future session." *Hansard*, Lords Sitting, vol. 164, July 5, 1861, 370.

38. *Hansard*, Lords Sitting, vol. 164, July 30, 1861, 1780.

39. Ibid., 1782.

40. Ibid., 1783.

41. CRIM 10/51. Old Court, First Session, November 28, 1861. "Guilty of the Attempt—Ten Years Penal Servitude." CRIM 9/7 for occupation and education information, see CRIM 9/7. Worship Street Police Court, November 15, 1861.

42. *Old Bailey Proceedings Online*, June 5, 1875, trial of William Smith (33). "GUILTY—Five Years' Penal Servitude." *Digital Panopticon*, William Smith b. 1842, Life Archive ID obpdef1-383-18750605.

43. *Old Bailey Proceedings Online*, June 24, 1878, trial of Pierre Frongier (48) (t18780624–661). "GUILTY **—Five Years' Penal Servitude." *Digital Panopticon*, Pierre Frongier b. 1830, Life Archive ID obpdef1-661-18780624.

44. *Times*, July 6, 1863 (Police, Hammersmith, Morrison, Chas., for Indecent Assault).

45. Ibid.

46. *Times*, August 18, 1863 (Criminal Trials, CCC, Morrison, Chas., for Indecent Assault); *Digital Panopticon*, Charles Morrison b. 1827, Life Archive ID obpdef1-31-18791124; *Old Bailey Proceedings Online*, August 1863, trial of Charles Morrison (36) (t18630817-968); CRIM 9/9, Hammersmith Police Court, July 4, 1836.

47. Central Criminal Court, Eighth Session, New Court, Wednesday, June 8, 1870, George Brown, 141. See CRIM 9/16 for education and occupation information.

48. CRIM 10, Volume LXXIV, Seventh Session, New Court, Wednesday, May 3, 1871, 397. William Mahoney (17), and George Grant (50). See CRIM 9/17 for occupation and education information. Hammersmith Police Court, April 21, 1871. Initial charge was "B___y with each other," reduced to the attempt.

49. Jeff Evans also documents this increase in sentences for attempted sodomy in his work on Lancashire. Jeff Evans, "The Criminal Prosecution of Inter-Male Sex 1850–1970: A Lancashire Case Study," Ph.D. diss., Manchester Metropolitan University, 2016.

50. *Report of the Select Committee on Criminal Laws* (1819); Phil Handler, "Forging the Agenda: The 1819 Select Committee on the Criminal Laws Revisited," *Journal of Legal History* 25, no. 3 (December 2004).

51. Roger Chadwick, *Bureaucratic Mercy: The Home Office and the Treatment of Capital Cases in Victorian Britain* (New York: Garland Publishing, 1992), 21.

52. The final version of the 1860 Bill (the 1861 Act) leaves only murder subject to the death penalty. Radzinowicz, *History of English Criminal Law*, 4:341.

53. In 1853, an individual identified only as "I. W." wrote in *Notes and Queries* that he had seen a copy of *Don Leon* that was printed outside Britain "many years since." Samuel C. Chew, "'*Don Leon*' Poems," *TLS: Times Literary Supplement* (July 9, 1954): 447, citing *Notes and Queries*, First Series (1853), 7:66. The copy of *Don Leon* held by the Morgan Library in New York is similar in almost all respects to the 1866 copy held in the British Library; however, the few pages remaining after page 48 are in a different typeface. The last line on page 48 is "Whose hand had helped to prop thy tottering place" (line 1340 in the original typeface of the poem). The change in typeface occurs in the middle of the section on Bankes, added sometime after 1833. This adds further weight to the argument that the bawdy puns and sexual allusions that end the 1866 version, appearing between lines 1401 and 1465, are a later addition.

54. All these double notes appear side-by-side, except for the second Note 76, which appears after Note 85. This second Note 76 is in addition to Note 86, which follows it. "Notes to *Don Leon*," 55–56.

55. James Gregory, *Victorians against the Gallows: Capital Punishment and the Abolitionist Movement in Nineteenth-Century Britain* (London: I. B. Tauris, 2012), 24.

56. In such works as Alfred H. Dymond, *Law on Its Trial* (London: Alfred W. Bennett, 1865). The SACP also does not seem to have petitioned privately to the Home Office on sodomy cases. Chadwick, *Bureaucratic Mercy*.

57. Walter E. Houghton, *The Victorian Frame of Mind, 1830–1870* (New Haven, CT: Yale University Press, 1957).

58. Criminal Code Bill, 43 Vict., 1880. Part XIII, Crimes against Morality, 44–45. The "indecent acts" provision was also in the Royal Commission Report on which this bill was based. See *Royal Commission to Consider Law Relating to Indictable Offences*. Report, Appendix (Draft Code) Command Papers: Reports of Commissioners Parliament: 1878–1879, 95.

59. Emphasis added. Criminal Code Bill (1880), 44–45.

60. House of Commons, *Memorandum on Principal Changes Proposed in Law by Criminal Code (Indictable Offences) Bill*, as Settled by Criminal Code Commissioners, 140 (April 1879), 3.

61. *Royal Commission to Consider Law Relating to Indictable Offences* (1879), 95.

62. Emphasis added. *Hansard*, Commons Sitting, Third Series, vol. 300, August 6, 1885, 1397.

63. Emphasis added. Ibid.

64. Ibid., 1398. Fourteen had been established in case law as the age of consent for boys since the eighteenth century, while the Consent of Young Persons Act of 1880 established thirteen as the age of consent for boys and girls, raising the previous age of consent by one year for girls and lowering by the same for boys. Louise Jackson, *Child Sexual Abuse in Victorian England* (New York: Routledge, 2000), 100–101.

65. *Hansard*, Commons Sitting, Third Series, vol. 300, August 6, 1885, 1398.

66. MS BECKFORD, c. 75, f. 31, *Courier*, 1827 [letter in paper dated January 31]. Letter to the editor of the *Courier*, "Harrow School."

67. *Inspector of Reformatory Schools of Great Britain, Twenty-Second Report*, Command Papers: Reports of Commissioners (London: 1878–1879), 56; *Inspector of Reformatory Schools, Twenty-Third Report* (London: 1880), 122; *Inspector of Reformatory Schools, Twenty-Fifth Report* (London: 1882), 60; *Inspector of Reformatory Schools, Twenty-Eighth Report* (London: 1884–1885), 133, 269; *Inspector of Reformatory Schools, Thirtieth Report* (London: 1887), 63, 83. Starting in 1886, "gross indecency" begins to appear as a category in criminal returns. See *Commissioner of Police of Metropolis, Report, 1886*, House of Commons: Command Papers, Reports of Commissioners (London: 1887), 22.

68. Emphasis added. Andrew Doyle, W. H. T. Hawley, John Walsham, and Sir Robert Weale, *Reports to Poor Law Board on Education of Pauper Children by Poor Law Inspectors* (House of Commons Papers: Accounts and Papers, 1862), 510C, 83.

69. *Hansard*, Commons Sitting, Third Series, vol. 255, August 12, 1880, 1086.

70. Bill to amend Criminal Law as to Indecent Assaults on Young Persons 304 (1880).

71. Smith, "Labouchere's Amendment," 165.

72. Weeks, *Sex, Politics and Society*, 1st ed., 126, 151.

73. Kaplan, *Sodom on the Thames*, 175.

74. Herbert Sidebotham, 2004, revised by H. C. G. Matthew, 2009, "Labouchere, Henry Du Pré (1831–1912)," *Oxford Dictionary of National Biography*, March 2019.

75. Ibid.; Algar Thorold, *The Life of Henry Labouchere* (New York: G. P. Putnam's Sons, 1913), 8–42.

76. Hesketh Pearson, *Labby: The Life and Character of Henry Labouchere* (New York: Harper and Brothers, 1937).

77. Thorold, *Life of Henry Labouchere*; Pearson, *Labby*; R. J. Hind, *Henry Labouchere and the Empire, 1880–1905* (London: Athlone Press, 1972).

78. Sidebotham, "Labouchere, Henry Du Pré," *Oxford Dictionary of National Biography*.

79. Smith, "Labouchere's Amendment," 166.

80. Ibid., 167.

81. Ibid.

82. Ibid., 166.

83. Kaplan, *Sodom on the Thames*, 178. "Labouchere later claimed that he had drafted section II in response to what he perceived as the growth of homosexual activity in the capital," citing Henry Labouchere, *Truth*, 11 April 1895, 1331. Matt Cook, *London and the Culture of Homosexuality, 1885–1914* (New York: Cambridge University Press, 2003), 45, 67, 69; Harry Cocks argues that "he justified his clause by arguing that before 1885, 'the law was insufficient to deal with it, because the offence had to [be] proved by an accessory, and many other offences very much of the same nature were not regarded as crimes at all,'" citing *Hansard*, Third Series, CCCXLI, February 28, 1890, cols. 1534, 1535, and *Truth*, May 30, 1895. H. G. Cocks, *Nameless Offences: Speaking of Male Homosexual Desire in Nineteenth-Century England* (London: I. B. Tauris, 2003), 17.

84. For an analysis of how liberal reform often couples greater freedoms with greater demands for discipline, see Patrick Joyce, *The Rule of Freedom: Liberalism and the Modern City* (London: Verso, 2003), 105.

85. Randolph Trumbach, "London's Sodomites: Homosexual Behavior and Western Culture in the 18th Century," *Journal of Social History* 11, no. 1 (Fall 1977); Randolph Trumbach, *Sex and the Gender Revolution* (Chicago: University of Chicago Press, 1998); Arthur Gilbert, "Buggery and the British Navy, 1700–1861," *Journal of Social History* 10 (1976).

86. Michel Foucault, *The History of Sexuality*, vol. 1, *An Introduction* (New York: Vintage Books, 1990).

87. David Halperin, *How to Do the History of Homosexuality* (Chicago: University of Chicago Press, 2002); Martha Vicinus, *Intimate Friends: Women Who Loved Women, 1778–1928* (Chicago: University of Chicago Press, 2004), 7–18; Richard Godbeer, *The Overflowing of Friendship: Love between Men and the Creation of the American Republic*

(Baltimore: Johns Hopkins University Press, 2009); Alan Bray, *The Friend* (Chicago: University of Chicago Press, 2003); Brian Joseph Martin, *Napoleonic Friendship: Military Fraternity, Intimacy, and Sexuality in Nineteenth-Century France* (Durham: University of New Hampshire Press, 2011), 1–15.

88. Anna Clark, *Alternative Histories of the Self: A Cultural History of Sexuality and Secrets, 1762–1917* (New York: Bloomsbury Academic, 2017), 12–18.

89. For the importance of social and material contexts for sustaining identities in relation to sexuality, see John D'Emilio, "Capitalism and Gay Identity," in *Powers of Desire: The Politics of Sexuality*, ed. Ann Snitow, Christine Stansell, and Sharan Thompson (New York: Monthly Review Press, 1983), 100–113.

90. For a discussion of sources for queer history and gender history, see Doan, *Disturbing Practices*, 48–50. For an examination of this issue when analyzing gender history and the history of enslaved people, see Marisa J. Fuentes, *Dispossessed Lives: Enslaved Women, Violence, and the Archive* (Philadelphia: University of Pennsylvania Press, 2018), 1–12.

91. Margot Canaday, *The Straight State: Sexuality and Citizenship in Twentieth-Century America* (Princeton, NJ: Princeton University Press, 2011), 1–15.

92. Joyce, *Rule of Freedom*; James Vernon, *Distant Strangers: How Britain Became Modern* (University of California Press, 2014); Tom Crook, *Governing Systems: Modernity and the Making of Public Health in England, 1830–1910* (Oakland: University of California Press, 2016).

93. Fuentes, *Dispossessed Lives*, 68–9, 83–5; Sarah Haley, *No Mercy Here: Gender, Punishment, and the Making of Jim Crow Modernity* (Chapel Hill: The University of North Carolina Press, 2016).

94. For an analysis of the differences between ancestral genealogy, queer genealogy, and critical history, see Chapter 2, "Genealogy Inside and Out," in Doan, *Disturbing Practices*, 58–93.

95. Briggs, *Age of Improvement*; Burns and Innes, *Rethinking the Age of Reform*, 46–7.

96. Laura Doan, *Disturbing Practices: History, Sexuality, and Women's Experience of Modern War* (Chicago: University of Chicago Press, 2013), 83–84; Regina Kunzel, "The Power of Queer History," *American Historical Review* 123, no. 5 (December 2018); Joan Scott, "Gender: A Useful Category of Historical Analysis," *American Historical Review* 91, no. 5 (1986); Joanne Meyerowitz, Heidi Tinsman, Maria Bucur, Dyan Elliott, Gail Hershatter, Wang Zheng, and Joan W. Scott, "AHR Forum: Revisiting 'Gender: A Useful Category of Historical Analysis,'" *American Historical Review* 113, no. 5 (December 2008). For an example of how a focus on ethics can lead to new questions and approaches, see Seth Koven, *The Match Girl and the Heiress* (Princeton, NJ: Princeton University Press, 2014).

97. Craig A. Williams, *Roman Homosexuality* (New York: Oxford University Press, 2010), 139–144.

98. *Don Leon*, line 295.

99. Uday Singh Mehta, *Liberalism and Empire: A Study in Nineteenth-Century British Liberal Thought* (Chicago: University of Chicago Press, 1999).

100. Harry Oosterhuis, *Stepchildren of Nature: Krafft-Ebing, Psychiatry, and the Making of Sexual Identity* (Chicago: University of Chicago Press, 2000), 161–170.

101. Matt Cook, *Queer Domesticities: Homosexuality and Home Life in Twentieth-Century London* (London: Palgrave Macmillan, 2014); H. G. Cocks, "Religion and Spirituality," in *Palgrave Advances in the Modern History of Sexuality*, ed. H. G. Cocks and Matt Houlbrook (New York: Palgrave Macmillan, 2006), 157–179; Sheila Rowbotham, *Edward Carpenter: A Life of Liberty and Love* (New York: Verso, 2009).

Bibliography

Government Documents

"A Bill [As Amended by the Committee] For allowing the benefit of Clergy . . . and to make better provision for the punishment of Persons guilty of sending or delivering threatening Letters." June 6, 1823.

"A Bill [As Amended by the Committee] For Amending the Law Relating to Offenses Against the Person in Certain Cases." July 1, 1835.

"A Bill [As Amended by the Committee] For taking away the Punishment of Death in certain Cases . . . Prepared and brought in by Mr. Kelly, Dr. Lushington, and Mr. Serjeant Talfourd." May 24, 1841—4 Vict.

"A Bill [As Amended by the Select Committee] to Consolidate and amend the Statute Law of England and Ireland relating to Offences against the Person," (Prepared and brought in by Mr. Solicitor General, Viscount Palmerston, Mr. Attorney General, and Sir George Lewis) Ordered, by the House of Commons, to be Printed, 25 April 1861.

"A Bill for Amending the Law Relating to Offences against the Person in Certain Cases," 5 Will. IV. Sess. 1835. (Prepared and Brought in by Mr. Jervis and Mr. Pryme, 5 June 1835.)

"A Bill For enabling the Judges to abstain from pronouncing Sentence of Death, in certain Capital Felonies (Ordered by the House of Commons to be Printed, 27 May 1823)," 4 Geo. IV.—Sess. 1823.

"A Bill, For taking away the Punishment of Death in certain Cases, and substituting other Punishments in lieu thereof . . . (Prepared and brought in by Mr. Kelly, Dr. Lushington, and Mr. Serjeant Talfourd)," February 12, 1841—4 Vict.

"A Bill: for taking away the Punishment of Death in certain Cases . . . Prepared and brought in by Mr. Kelly and Dr. Lushington," June 23, 1840—4 Vict.

"A Bill, to amend an Act of the Ninth Year of the Reign of King George the Fourth, for consolidating and amending the Statutes of England relative to Offences against the Person . . . (Prepared and brought in by Lord John Russell and Mr. Fox Maule)," March 8, 1841—4 Vict.

"A Bill to Amend Criminal Law as to Indecent Assaults on Young Persons," 304 Ordered, by the House of Commons, to be Printed, 6 August 1880.

"A Bill to Consolidate and amend the Statute Law of England and Ireland relating to Offences against the Person" (Prepared and brought in by Mr. Attorney General, Mr. Attorney General for Ireland, and Mr. Secretary Sotheron Estcourt), April 14, 1859—22 Vict.

Commissioner of Police of Metropolis, Report, 1886, House of Commons: Command Papers, Reports of Commissioners (London: 1887).

CRIM 9/7. Worship Street Police Court, November 15, 1861.

CRIM 9/9. Hammersmith Police Court, July 4, 1836.

CRIM 9/16. New Court, Wednesday, June 8, 1870, George Brown.

CRIM 9/17. Hammersmith Police Court, April 21, 1871. Mahoney (17), and Grant (50).

CRIM 10. New Court, Wednesday, May 3, 1871. 397. Mahoney (17), and Grant (50).

CRIM 10/51. Old Court, First Session, November 28, 1861.

Criminal Code Bill, 43 Vict., 1880.

The Digital Panopticon, Charles Morrison b. 1827, Life Archive ID obpdef1-31-18791124.

The Digital Panopticon, Pierre Frongier b. 1830, Life Archive ID obpdef1-661-18780624.

The Digital Panopticon, William Smith b. 1842, Life Archive ID obpdef1-383-18750605.

First Report from His Majesty's Commissioners on Criminal Law, June 24, 1834 (published July 30, 1834).

Fourth Report from His Majesty's Commissioners on Criminal Law, March 8, 1839 (London: Clowes and Sons, for his Majesty's Stationery Office, 1839).

Great Britain. Parliament. House of Commons. *Report of the Select Committee on Criminal Laws*, July 8, 1819.

Hansard, Commons Sitting, Second Series, vol. 9, May 1823.

Hansard, Commons Sitting, Third Series, vol. 55, July 1840.

Hansard, Commons Sitting, Third Series, vol. 56, February 1841.

Hansard, Commons Sitting, Third Series, vol. 57, March 1841.

Hansard, Commons Sitting, Third Series, vol. 57, May 1841.

Hansard, Commons Sitting, Third Series, vol. 58, June 1841.

Hansard, Commons Sitting, Third Series, vol. 150, May 1858.

Hansard, Commons Sitting, Third Series, vol. 153, April 1859.

Hansard, Commons Sitting, Third Series, vol. 154, June 1859.

Hansard, Commons Sitting, Third Series, vol. 155, July 1859.

Hansard, Commons Sitting, Third Series, vol. 159, June 1860.

Hansard, Commons Sitting, Third Series, vol. 160, August 1860.

Hansard, Commons Sitting, Third Series, vol. 161, February 1861.

Hansard, Commons Sitting, Third Series, vol. 164, July 1861.

Hansard, Commons Sitting, Third Series, vol. 255, August 1880.

Hansard, Commons Sitting, Third Series, vol. 300, August 1885.

Hansard, Lords Sitting, Third Series, vol. 30, August 1835.

Hansard, Lords Sitting, Third Series, vol. 58, June 1841.

Hansard, Lords Sitting, Third Series, vol. 146, June 1857.

Hansard, Lords Sitting, Third Series, vol. 156, January 1860.

Hansard, Lords Sitting, Third Series, vol. 156, February 1860.

Hansard, Lords Sitting, Third Series, vol. 158, May 1860.

Hansard, Lords Sitting, Third Series, vol. 164, July 1861.

HO 6/20 Judges and Recorders Returns, 1835.

HO 13/68 Home Office: Criminal Entry Books, Correspondence and Warrants, October 10, 1835–March 21, 1836.

HO 17/120/60. Petition for James Pratt and John Smith.

HO 44 20. Home Office: Domestic Correspondence from 1773 to 1861.

House of Commons, *Memorandum on Principal Changes Proposed in Law by Criminal Code (Indictable Offences) Bill,* as Settled by Criminal Code Commissioners, 140 (April 1879).

Inspector of Reformatory Schools of Great Britain, Twenty-Second Report, Command Papers: Reports of Commissioners (London: 1878–1879).

Inspector of Reformatory Schools, Twenty-Third Report (London: 1880).

Inspector of Reformatory Schools, Twenty-Fifth Report (London: 1882).

Inspector of Reformatory Schools, Twenty-Eighth Report (London: 1884–1885).

Inspector of Reformatory Schools, Thirtieth Report (London: 1887).

Isabella Hedgeland (née Kelly) to the Committee of the Literary Fund, British Library, Western Manuscripts, Loan 96 RLF 1/632/9, 1832.

Journals of the House of Commons, vol. 90 (5 Will. IV), June 1835.

Journals of the House of Commons, vol. 90 (5 Will. IV), July 1835.

Journals of the House of Commons, vol. 90 (5 Will. IV), August 1835.

"Offences against the Person. A Bill . . . to consolidate and amend the Statute Law of England and Ireland relating to Offences against the Person" (Brought from the Lords 15th May 1860), printed May 21, 1860—23 Vict.

"Offences against the Person Bill, Clauses to be Proposed in Committee, by Mr. Law," June 1835, 6 Will. IV.—Sess. 1835.

Old Bailey Proceedings Online, April 20, 1726, trial of George Redear.

Old Bailey Proceedings Online, April 20, 1726, trials of Gabriel Lawrence, William Griffin, and Thomas Wright.

Old Bailey Proceedings Online, December 4, 1776, trial of Thomas Burrows.

Old Bailey Proceedings Online, February 15, 1797, trial of William Winklin.

Old Bailey Proceedings Online, August 17, 1863, trial of Charles Morrison (36).

Old Bailey Proceedings Online, June 5, 1875, trial of William Smith (33).

Old Bailey Proceedings Online, June 24, 1878, trial of Pierre Frongier (48).

Reports from the Select Committee on the Offences against the Person &c. Bills, with the Proceedings of the Committee (Ordered, by the House of Commons, to be Printed, 7 May 1861).

Reports to Poor Law Board on Education of Pauper Children by Poor Law Inspectors, Andrew Doyle, W. H. T. Hawley, John Walsham, Sir Robert Weale (House of Commons Papers: Accounts and Papers, 1862).

Royal Commission to Consider Law Relating to Indictable Offences. Report, Appendix (Draft Code) Command Papers: Reports of Commissioners Parliament: 1878–1879.

Second Report from His Majesty's Commissioners on Criminal Law, June 9, 1836 (published June 20, 1836).

Primary Sources

Arbuthnot, Harriet. *The Journal of Mrs. Arbuthnot, 1820–1832.* Edited by Gerald Wellesley Wellington and Francis Bamford. London: Macmillan, 1950.

Arbuthnot Papers, King's College Library, Aberdeen.

Aspinall, A. *The Correspondence of Charles Arbuthnot.* London: Royal Historical Society, 1941.

Austin, John. *Lectures on Jurisprudence, or, the Philosophy of Positive Law,* posthumously published. London: J. Murray, 1869.

———(Jurist). MSS 1972. "Annotations to Bentham." Inner Temple Library, London.

———. *The Province of Jurisprudence Determined.* London: J. Murray, 1832.

Papers of William Beckford, 1772–1857, Bodleian Library, University of Oxford, newspaper cuttings, 1780–1847.

    MS BECKFORD, c. 63.

    MS BECKFORD, c. 64.

    MS BECKFORD, c. 67.

    MS BECKFORD, c. 69.

    MS BECKFORD, c. 71.

    MS BECKFORD, c. 73.

    MS BECKFORD, c. 75.

    MS BECKFORD, c. 76.

    MS BECKFORD, c. 81.

    MS BECKFORD, c. 82.

    MS BECKFORD, c. 83.

William Beckford Collection, Beinecke Rare Book and Manuscript Library, Yale University, GEN MSS 102.

Benbow, William. *The Crimes of the Clergy; or, the Pillars of the Priest-Craft Shaken.* London: Benbow, 1823.

Bentham, Jeremy. *An Introduction to the Principles of Morals and Legislation,* printed in the year 1780, and now first published. London: T. Payne and Son, 1789.

———. *An Introduction to the Principles of Morals and Legislation.* London: Printed for W. Pickering, 1823.

Bentham Collection, University College London Library.

    BENTHAM, 161a, ff. 1–19, Letter to Beckford and Part II Prospectus.

    BENTHAM, Box 74a.

Blackstone, William. *Commentaries on the Laws of England.* Vol. 4. Oxford: Clarendon Press, 1769.

Brooke, John, and Julia Gandy, eds. *The Prime Ministers' Papers: Wellington, Political Correspondence, I: 1833–November 1834.* London: H. M. Stationery Office, 1975.

Brown, John. *The Historical Gallery of Criminal Portraitures, Foreign and Domestic Containing a Selection of the Most Impressive Cases of Guilt and Misfortune to Be Found in Modern History*. Manchester: J. Gleave, 1823.

Byrne, James. *Sketch of the life, and unparalleled sufferings, of James Byrne, late Coachman to the Honourable John Jocelyn*, brother to the Honourable and Right Rev. "Father in God," the Lord Bishop of Clogher: *together with some observations on the conduct of the Jocelyn family: as well as that of Alderman Archer, then Lord Mayor of Dublin, on his detaining two letters indispensably necessary for the victim's defence*. London: Printed and published (for Francis O'Neill) by T. Dolby, at the Britannia Press, 1822.

Byrne, James, Percy Jocelyn, and William Cobbett. *The Trial of Unfortunate Byrne, (Late Coachman to the Hon. John Jocelyn) . . . Which Is Annexed the Opinion of That Great Political Writer Mr. Cobbett on the Late Abominable and Disgusting Transaction*. Dublin: Published at No. 1 Princes Street, 1811.

Cholmondeley, R. H., and Richard Heber. *The Heber Letters, 1783–1832*. London: Batchworth Press, 1950.

Don Leon; A Poem by the Late Lord Byron . . . to Which Is Added Leon to Annabella: An Epistle from Lord Byron to Lady Byron. London: Printed for the Booksellers, 1866.

Copies of *Don Leon* in the following collections were examined:
    The British Library.
    Hathi Trust.
    The Moran Library.

Dickens, Charles. *Sketches by "Boz": Illustrative of Every-Day-Life and Every-Day-People*. Philadelphia: T. B. Peterson, 1839.

Dickinson, Violet, ed. *Miss Eden's Letters*. London: Macmillan, 1919.

Disraeli, Benjamin. *Benjamin Disraeli Letters: 1835–37*. Vol. 2. Edited by J. A. W. Gunn, John Matthews, Donald M. Schurman, and M. G. Wiebe. Toronto: University of Toronto Press, 1982.

Duke of Wellington: Political Correspondence, British Library.

Duke of Wellington: Public Papers, Southampton University.

Dymond, Alfred H. *Law on Its Trial*. London: Alfred W. Bennett, 1865.

Fairburn, John. *The Bishop!! Particulars of the Charge against the Hon. Percy Jocelyn, Bishop of Clogher, for an Abominable Offence with John Movelley, a Soldier of the First Regiment of Foot Guards: Including the Evidence before the Magistrate at Marlborough-Street*. London: Printed and published by John Fairburn, 1822.

Fraxi, Pisanus [Henry Spencer Ashbee]. *Index Librorum Prohibitorum: Being Notes Bio- Biblio- Icono-graphical and Critical, on Curious and Uncommon Books*. Privately printed, 1877.

Holloway, Robert. *The Phoenix of Sodom, or, the Vere Street Coterie: Being an Exhibition of the Gambols Practised by the Ancient Lechers of Sodom and Gomorrah, Embellished and Improved with the Modern Refinements in Sodomitical Practices, by the Members of the Vere Street Coterie, of Detestable Memory*. London: J. Cook, . . . to be had of all the booksellers, 1813.

Jerdan, William. *Autobiography, with His Literary, Political, and Social Reminiscences and Correspondence during the Last Fifty Years.* Vol. 1. London: A. Hall, Virtue, 1852–1853.

Keele University Library, Sneyd (Ralph) mss SC17/39, 52.

Lewis, Matthew Gregory. *Journal of a West Indian Proprietor: Kept during a Residence in the Island of Jamaica.* London: John Murray, 1834.

Lewis, M. G., and Cornwell Baron-Wilson. *The Life and Correspondence of M. G. Lewis: with Many Pieces in Prose and Verse, Never before Published.* London: H. Colburn, 1839.

Lieven, Dorothea, Peter Quennell, and Dilys Powell. *The Private Letters of Princess Lieven to Prince Metternich, 1820–1826.* New York: E. P. Dutton, 1937.

Montagu, Basil. *An Account of the Origin and Object of the Society for the Diffusion of Knowledge upon the Punishment of Death and the Improvement of Prison Discipline.* London: Printed by Richard Taylor and Co., 1812.

Moore, Thomas. *Life of Lord Byron: With His Letters and Journals.* Vol. 3. Boston: Little, Brown, 1853.

Moore, Thomas, and George Gordon Byron. *Letters and Journals of Lord Byron: With Notices of his Life,* complete in one volume. Paris: A. and W. Galignani, 1831.

Neumann, Philipp, and E. Beresford Chancellor. *The Diary of Philipp Von Neumann.* Vol. 1, *1819 to 1850.* Boston: Houghton Mifflin, 1928.

Peel Papers and Additional Manuscripts: British Library.

 Add. MS—40380, ff. 227–231, 234–236, 257, 258, and 315.

 Add. MS—40381, ff. 166, 169, 220, 284, 310.

 General Correspondence, vol. CC (July 9–August 1825).

Richardson, John. *Recollections, Political, Literary, Dramatic, and Miscellaneous: Of the Last Half-Century.* London: C. Mitchell, 1856.

Romilly, Sir Samuel. *Memoirs of the Life of Sir Samuel Romilly: Written by Himself; With a Selection from his Correspondence.* Edited by his sons. Vol. 2. 2nd ed. London: J. Murray, 1840.

Schofield, Philip, Catherine Pease-Watkin, and Michael Quinn, eds. *Of Sexual Irregularities, and Other Writings on Sexual Morality.* Collected Works of Jeremy Bentham Series. Oxford: Clarendon Press, 2014.

Smith, Gamaliel, esq. [Jeremy Bentham]. *Not Paul, but Jesus.* London: Printed for John Hunt, Old Bond Street, 1823.

Stowe, Harriet Beecher. *Lady Byron Vindicated: A History of the Byron Controversy.* Boston: Fields, Osgood, 1870.

Theorie des Peines et des Récompenses, Ouvrage Extrait des Manuscrits de M. Jeremie Bentham, Jurisconsulte Anglais. Vol. 1. 3rd ed. Paris: Bossange Freres, Libraires, Rue de Seine, no. 12, 1825.

Toynbee, William. *Glimpses of the Twenties.* London: A. Constable, 1909.

Wellington, Arthur Wellesley. *Wellington and His friends: Letters of the First Duke of Wellington to the Rt. Hon. Charles and Mrs. Arbuthnot, the Earl and Countess of Wilton, Princess Lieven, and Miss Burdett-Coutts.* London: Macmillan, 1965.

Primary Sources (Additional)

Bentham, Jeremy, and Louis Crompton. "Jeremy Bentham's Essay on 'Paederasty.'" *Journal of Homosexuality* 4, no. 1 (1978): 91–107.

———. "Offences against One's Self." *Journal of Homosexuality* 3, no. 4 (1978): 389–406.

Broughton, John Cam Hobhouse, Baron. John Cam Hobhouse Manuscript Material, 1818–1864. Pforzheimer Collection, New York Public Library (NYPL) Pforz MS.

Buxton, Charles, ed. *Memoirs of Sir Thomas Fowell Buxton, Baronet. With Selections from His Correspondence.* London: John Murray, 1860.

Byron, George Gordon, and J. W. Lake. *The Complete Works of Lord Byron, Including His Lordship's Suppressed Poems, with Others Never before Published. [With "The Life of Lord Byron" Abridged from the Life by J. W. Lake, a Facsimile of a Letter from Lord Byron to the Editor of "Galignani's Messenger," and a Portrait.]* Paris: A. and W. Galignani, 1831.

Clarkson, Thomas. *Prospectus of the Society for the Diffusion of Information on the Subject of Capital Punishments.* Farmington Hills, MI: Thomson Gale, 2005.

Cobbett, William. *The "Thing," or, a Full Exposition of an Alleged Crime, of a Particular Nature, against the Right Rev. Percy Jocelyn, Lord Bishop of Clogher, with a Private Soldier of the Foot Guards: At the White Lion Public-House, in Alban's-Place, St. James's, London, on Friday the 19th July, 1822: to Which Is Annexed, a Report of the Trial of James Byrne, at Green-Street, October 1811.* Cork: Printed by John Connor, 1822.

Combe, Abram. *An Address to the Conductors of the Periodical Press upon the Causes of Religious and Political Disputes with Remarks on the Local and General Definition of Certain Words and Terms.* Edinburgh: Sold by Bell and Bradfute, 1823.

Dickinson, Violet, ed. *Miss Eden's Letters.* London: Macmillan, 1919.

Joyce, Michael. *My Friend H: John Cam Hobhouse, Baron Broughton of Broughton De Gyfford.* London: J. Murray, 1948.

Macready, William Charles, and William Toynbee. *The Diaries of William Charles Macready, 1833–1851.* Vol. 1. London: Chapman and Hall, 1912.

———. *The Diaries of William Charles Macready, 1833–1851.* Vol. 2. London: Chapman and Hall, 1912.

Marshall. *An Account of the Melancholy Death of Lord Castlereagh, Alias Lord Londonderry; Who Put an End to His Own Existence, by Cutting His Throat, at His Residence at North Cray, in Kent, on Monday Morning Last, the 12th of August, 1822.* Newcastle: Marshall, 1822.

McCormick, Ian. *Sexual Outcasts 1750–1850.* Vol. 1, *Sexual Anatomies.* London: Routledge, 2000.

———. *Sexual Outcasts 1750–1850.* Vol. 2, *Sodomy.* London: Routledge, 2000.

Medwin, Thomas. *Conversations of Lord Byron: Noted during a Residence with His Lordship at Pisa, in the Years 1821 and 1822.* London: Printed for Henry Colburn, New Burlington Street, 1824.

Partington, Wilfred, ed. *The Private Letter-Books of Sir Walter Scott: Selections from the Abbotsford Manuscripts.* New York: Frederick A. Stokes, 1930.

Phillips, Charles, J. W. Parkins, and James Byrne. *The Irishman in London, Byrne versus Parkins, the Celebrated Speech of C. Phillips, Esq. The Whole of the Trials at the Court of King's Bench, in the Case of Byrne v. Parkins, before Lord Chief Justice Abbott, on Monday, February 16th, 1824, and Tuesday, Feb. 17th.* London: G. Hebert, 1824.

Shelley, Percy Bysshe. "A Discourse on the Manners of the Ancient Greeks Relative to the Subject of Love." In *Shelley on Love: An Anthology*, edited by Richard Holmes, 101–112. Berkeley: University of California Press, 1980.

Society for the Diffusion of Information on the Subject of Capital Punishments. *The Punishment of Death: A Series of Short Articles, to Appear Occasionally in Numbers Designed for General Circulation*, nos. 1–5. London: Harvey and Darton for the Society for the Diffusion of Information on the Subject of Capital Punishments, 1831.

Sodomy Trials: Seven Documents. New York: Garland Publishers, 1986.

Toynbee, William. *Lays of Common Life.* London: Remington, 1890.

———. *Phases of the Thirties.* London: H. J. Glaisher, 1927.

———. *Vignettes of the Regency: And Other Studies Political and Social.* London: Ambrose, 1907.

<h2 style="text-align:center">PERIODICALS</h2>

The Age.
Annual Register.
Aris's Birmingham Gazette.
The Atlantic Monthly, a Magazine of Literature, Science, Art, and Politics.
Bath Chronicle and Weekly Gazette.
Bell's Life in London and Sporting Chronicle.
Bell's New Weekly Messenger.
Bell's Weekly Messenger.
Birmingham Journal.
Black Dwarf.
Bristol Mercury.
Bury and Norwich Post.
Calcutta Monthly Journal and General Register.
Caledonian Mercury.
Cambridge Chronicle and Journal.
Carlisle Journal.
Cheltenham Chronicle.
Chester Chronicle.
Cobbett's Weekly Political Register.
The Courier.
Dublin Morning Register.
The Ecclesiastical and University Annual Register.
Edinburgh Review.

Essex Standard.
Evening Mail.
Galignani's Messenger.
Globe.
Hampshire Chronicle.
Harper's New Monthly Magazine.
The Independent Whig.
Inverness Courier.
Jackson's Oxford Journal.
John Bull.
Kentish Gazette.
Kentish Weekly Post or Canterbury Journal.
Lancaster Gazette.
Law Magazine.
Leeds Intelligencer.
The Liberal.
Literary and Dramatic Register and Varieties.
Liverpool Mercury.
London Courier and Evening Gazette.
London Evening Post.
London Evening Standard.
Manchester Mercury.
Morning Advertiser.
Morning Chronicle.
Morning Herald.
Morning Post.
Newry Telegraph.
New Times.
Norfolk Chronicle.
Northampton Mercury.
North Wales Chronicle.
Notes and Queries.
Public Ledger.
Public Ledger and Daily Advertiser.
Salisbury and Winchester Journal.
The Satirist or the Censor of the Times.
Saunders's News-Letter.
Scots Magazine.
Sheffield Independent.
Stamford Mercury.
Star.
Suffolk Chronicle; or Weekly General Advertiser and County Express.
Sun.
Sussex Advertiser.

Taunton Courier and Western Advertiser.
The Times.
Truth.
Waterford Mail.
Windsor and Eton Express.

DATABASES

The British Newspaper Archive.
The Digital Panopticon.
England Births and Baptisms. https://www.findmypast.co.uk.
The History of Parliament: British Political, Social and Local History, edited by R. G. Thorne. History of Parliament Trust, Great Britain, Boydell and Brewer. http:// www.historyofparliamentonline.org/.
House of Commons Parliamentary Papers Online. https://parlipapers-proquest-com .proxy.lib.fsu.edu/parlipapers.
Old Bailey Proceedings Online. Version 8.0.
Ordinary of Newgate's Accounts.
The 17th–18th Century Burney Collection Newspapers Database.
The Times Digital Archive.
Wiltshire Marriages Index, 1538–1933, Parish Marriages, England.

SECONDARY SOURCES (BOOKS)

Andrew, Donna T. *Aristocratic Vice: The Attack on Duelling, Suicide, Adultery, and Gambling in Eighteenth-Century England.* New Haven, CT: Yale University Press, 2013.

Barker, Hannah. *Newspapers, Politics and English Society, 1695–1855.* Harlow, UK: Longman, 2000.

———. *Newspapers, Politics, and Public Opinion in Late Eighteenth-Century England.* Oxford: Clarendon Press, 1998.

Baron-Wilson, Cornwell, Mrs. *The Life and Correspondence of M. G. Lewis: With Many Pieces in Prose and Verse, Never before Published.* London: H. Colburn, 1839.

Bartlett, C. J. *Castlereagh.* New York: Charles Scribner's Sons, 1966.

Behrendt, Stephen C. *Romanticism, Radicalism, and the Press.* Detroit: Wayne State University Press, 1997.

Bew, John. *Castlereagh: A Life.* Oxford: Oxford University Press, 2012.

Blain, Virginia, Patricia Clements, and Isobel Grundy, eds. *The Feminist Companion to Literature in English: Women Writers from the Middle Ages to the Present.* New Haven, CT: Yale University Press, 1990.

Blakey, Dorothy. *The Minerva Press, 1790–1820.* London: Printed for the Bibliographical Society at the University Press, Oxford, 1939.

Block, Brian P., and John Hostettler. *Hanging in the Balance: A History of the Abolition of Capital Punishment in Britain.* Winchester, UK: Waterside Press, 1997.

Brady, Sean. *Masculinity and Male Homosexuality in Britain, 1861–1913.* New York: Palgrave Macmillan, 2005.

Bray, Alan. *The Friend.* Chicago: University of Chicago Press, 2003.

———. *Homosexuality in Renaissance England.* New York: Columbia University Press, 1995.

Briggs, Asa. *The Age of Improvement, 1783–1867.* Harlow, UK: Longman, 2000.

British Library. *The Pleasures of Bibliophily: Fifty Years of The Book Collector: An Anthology.* London: British Library, 2003.

Brockman, Harold Alfred Nelson. *The Caliph of Fonthill.* London: W. Laurie, 1956.

Brown, Christopher Leslie. *Moral Capital: Foundations of British Abolitionism.* Chapel Hill: University of North Carolina Press, 2006.

Burnard, Trevor. *Mastery, Tyranny, and Desire: Thomas Thistlewood and His Slaves in the Anglo-Jamaican World.* Chapel Hill: University of North Carolina Press, 2004.

Burns, Arthur, and Joanna Innes, eds. *Rethinking the Age of Reform: Britain 1780–1850.* Cambridge: Cambridge University Press, 2003.

Butler, Judith. *Undoing Gender.* New York: Routledge, 2004.

Canaday, Margot. *The Straight State: Sexuality and Citizenship in Twentieth-Century America.* Princeton, NJ: Princeton University Press, 2011.

Chadwick, Roger. *Bureaucratic Mercy: The Home Office and the Treatment of Capital Cases in Victorian Britain.* New York: Garland Publishing, 1992.

Charmley, John. *The Princess and the Politicians: Sex, Intrigue and Diplomacy, 1812–40.* London: Viking, 2005.

Châtel, Laurent. *William Beckford: The Elusive Orientalist.* Oxford: Voltaire Foundation, 2016.

Chatterjee, Partha. *The Black Hole of Empire: History of a Global Practice of Power.* Princeton, NJ: Princeton University Press, 2012.

Chew, Samuel C. *Byron in England: His Fame and After-Fame.* New York: Russell and Russell, 1965.

Clark, Anna. *Alternative Histories of the Self: A Cultural History of Sexuality and Secrets, 1762–1917.* New York: Bloomsbury Academic, 2017.

———. *Scandal: The Sexual Politics of the British Constitution.* Princeton, NJ: Princeton University Press, 2004.

———. *The Struggle for the Breeches: Gender and the Making of the British Working Class.* Berkeley: University of California Press, 1995.

———. *Women's Silence, Men's Violence: Sexual Assault in England 1770–1845.* New York: Pandora, 1987.

Clark, Cumberland. *Dickens and Talfourd: With an Address and Three Unpublished Letters to Talfourd.* London: Chiswick, 1919.

Clark, Richard. *Capital Punishment in Britain.* Hersham, UK: Ian Allan, 2009.

Cochran, Peter. *Byron and Hobby-O: Lord Byron's Relationship with John Cam Hobhouse.* Newcastle upon Tyne, UK: Cambridge Scholars, 2010.

Cocks, Harry. *Visions of Sodom: Religion, Homoerotic Desire, and the End of the World in England, c. 1550–1850.* Chicago: University of Chicago Press, 2017.

Cocks, H. G. *Nameless Offences: Speaking of Male Homosexual Desire in Nineteenth-Century England*. London: I. B. Tauris, 2003.

Cohen, Ed. *Talk on the Wilde Side: Towards a Genealogy of a Discourse on Male Sexualities*. New York: Routledge, 1993.

Cokayne, George E. *The Complete Peerage of England, Scotland, Ireland, Great Britain and the United Kingdom, Extant, Extinct, or Dormant*. London: St. Catherine Press, 1910.

Colley, Linda. *Britons: Forging the Nation, 1707–1837*. New Haven, CT: Yale University Press, 1992.

———. *Captives: Britain, Empire and the World, 1600–1850*. New York: Pantheon Books, 2002.

Cook, Matt. *London and the Culture of Homosexuality, 1885–1914*. New York: Cambridge University Press, 2003.

———. *Queer Domesticities: Homosexuality and Home Life in Twentieth-Century London*. London: Palgrave Macmillan, 2014.

Cornish, William, Jenifer Hart, A. H. Manchester, J. Stevenson. *Crime and Law in Nineteenth Century Britain*. Dublin: Irish University Press, 1978.

Crompton, Louis. *Byron and Greek Love: Homophobia in 19th-Century England*. Berkeley: University of California Press, 1985.

———. *Homosexuality and Civilization*. Cambridge, MA: Belknap Press of Harvard University Press, 2003.

Crook, Tom. *Governing Systems: Modernity and the Making of Public Health in England, 1830–1910*. Oakland: University of California Press, 2016.

Dabhoiwala, Faramerz. *The Origins of Sex: A History of the First Sexual Revolution*. New York: Oxford University Press, 2012.

Davis, Michael T., and Paul A. Pickering. *Unrespectable Radicals? Popular Politics in the Age of Reform*. Aldershot, UK: Ashgate, 2008.

Derry, John W. *Castlereagh*. London: A. Lane, 1976.

Deslandes, Paul. *Oxbridge Men: British Masculinity and the Undergraduate Experience, 1850–1920*. Bloomington: Indiana University Press, 2005.

Dickinson, H. T. *British Radicalism and the French Revolution, 1789–1815*. New York: Blackwell, 1985.

Dinwiddy, J. R. *Radicalism and Reform in Britain, 1780–1850*. London: Hambledon Press, 1992.

Doan, Laura. *Disturbing Practices: History, Sexuality, and Women's Experience of Modern War*. Chicago: University of Chicago Press, 2013.

Drescher, Seymour. *Abolition: A History of Slavery and Antislavery*. New York: Cambridge University Press, 2009.

———. *The Mighty Experiment: Free Labor vs. Slavery in British Emancipation*. New York: Oxford University Press, 2002.

DuBois, Page. *Sappho Is Burning*. Chicago: University of Chicago Press, 1995.

Dyck, Ian. *William Cobbett and Rural Popular Culture*. New York: Cambridge University Press, 1992.

Dyer, Gary. *British Satire and the Politics of Style, 1789–1832*. Cambridge: Cambridge University Press, 1997.

Emsley, Clive. *Crime and Society in England, 1750–1900*. New York: Longman, 1996.

Epstein, James. *Scandal of Colonial Rule: Power and Subversion in the British Atlantic during the Age of Revolution*. New York: Cambridge University Press, 2012.

Evans, Eric J. *Sir Robert Peel: Statesmanship, Power, and Party*. London: Routledge, 1991.

Fisher, D. R. *The House of Commons, 1820–1832*. Vols. 1–7. Cambridge: Published for the History of Parliament Trust by Cambridge University Press, 2009.

Follett, Richard. *Evangelicalism, Penal Theory and the Politics of Criminal Law Reform in England, 1808–30*. New York: Palgrave, 2001.

Foster, John. *The Life of Charles Dickens*. Vol. 2, *1842–1852*. London: Chapman and Hall, 1873.

Foucault, Michel. *The Archaeology of Knowledge*. New York: Pantheon Books, 1972.

———. *The History of Sexuality*. Vol. 1, *An Introduction*. New York: Pantheon Books, 1978.

French, Henry, and Mark Rothery. *Man's Estate: Landed Gentry Masculinities 1660–1900*. Oxford: Oxford University Press, 2012.

Fuentes, Marisa J. *Dispossessed Lives: Enslaved Women, Violence, and the Archive*. Philadelphia: University of Pennsylvania Press, 2018.

Furneaux, Holly. *Queer Dickens: Erotics, Families, Masculinities*. New York: Oxford University Press, 2009.

Gash, Norman. *Aristocracy and People: Britain, 1815–1865*. Cambridge, MA: Harvard University Press, 1981.

Gatrell, Vic. *The Hanging Tree: Execution and the English People, 1770–1868*. Oxford: Oxford University Press, 1994.

Genovese, Eugene D. *Fatal Self-Deception: Slaveholding Paternalism in the Old South*. New York: Cambridge University Press, 2011.

Gibson, William, and Joanne Begiato. *Sex and the Church in the Long Eighteenth Century: Religion, Enlightenment and the Sexual Revolution*. New York: I. B. Tauris, 2017.

Gillis, John R. *A World of Their Own Making: Myth, Ritual, and the Quest for Family Values*. New York: Basic Books, 1996.

Gilmartin, Kevin. *Print Politics: The Press and Radical Opposition in Early Nineteenth-Century England*. New York: Cambridge University Press, 1996.

———. *Writing against Revolution: Literary Conservatism in Britain, 1790–1832*. Cambridge: Cambridge University Press, 2007.

Godbeer, Richard. *The Overflowing of Friendship: Love between Men and the Creation of the American Republic*. Baltimore: Johns Hopkins University Press, 2009.

Green, Daniel. *Great Cobbett: The Noblest Agitator*. London: Hodder and Stoughton, 1983.

Gregory, James. *Victorians against the Gallows: Capital Punishment and the Abolitionist Movement in Nineteenth-Century Britain*. London: I. B. Tauris, 2012.

Haggerty, George E. *Queer Gothic*. Urbana: University of Illinois Press, 2006.

Haley, Sarah. *No Mercy Here: Gender, Punishment, and the Making of Jim Crow Modernity*. Chapel Hill: University of North Carolina Press, 2016.

Hall, Catherine. *Civilising Subjects: Metropole and Colony in the English Imagination, 1830–1867*. Chicago: University of Chicago Press, 2002.

Hall, Catherine, Nicholas Draper, Keith McClelland, Katie Donington, and Rachel Lang. *Legacies of British Slave-Ownership: Colonial Slavery and the Formation of Victorian Britain.* Cambridge: Cambridge University Press, 2014.

Hall, Catherine, Keith McClelland, and Jane Rendall. *Defining the Victorian Nation: Class, Race, Gender and the British Reform Act of 1867.* Cambridge: Cambridge University Press, 2000.

Halperin, David. *How to Do the History of Homosexuality.* Chicago: University of Chicago Press, 2002.

Harris, Bob. *A Patriot Press: National Politics and the London Press in the 1740s.* New York: Oxford University Press, 1993.

Hilton, Boyd. *The Age of Atonement: The Influence of Evangelicalism on Social and Economic Thought, 1795–1865.* New York: Oxford University Press, 1987.

———. *A Mad, Bad, and Dangerous People? England, 1783–1846.* Oxford: Oxford University Press, 2006.

Hind, R. J. *Henry Labouchere and the Empire, 1880–1905.* London: Athlone Press, 1972.

Hinde, Wendy. *Castlereagh.* London: Collins, 1981.

The History of the Times. Vol. 1, *"The Thunderer" in the Making, 1781–1841.* New York: Macmillan, 1935.

Hobson, Christopher. *Blake and Homosexuality.* New York: Palgrave, 2001.

Hostettler, John. *The Politics of Criminal Law Reform in the Nineteenth Century.* Chichester: Barry Rose Law Publishers, 1992.

Houghton, Walter. *The Victorian Frame of Mind, 1830–1870.* New Haven, CT: Yale University Press, 1957.

Hunt, Giles. *The Duel: Castlereagh, Canning and Deadly Cabinet Rivalry.* New York: I. B. Tauris, 2008.

Hurd, Douglas. *Robert Peel: A Biography.* London: Weidenfeld and Nicolson, 2007.

Hyam, Ronald. *Empire and Sexuality: The British Experience.* Manchester: Manchester University Press, 1990.

Hyde, H. Montgomery. *The Other Love: A History and Contemporary Survey of Homosexuality in Britain.* London: Heinemann, 1970.

———. *The Strange Death of Lord Castlereagh.* London: Heinemann, 1959.

Jackson, Louise. *Child Sexual Abuse in Victorian England.* New York: Routledge, 2000.

James, C. L. R. *The Black Jacobins: Toussaint L'Ouverture and the San Domingo Revolution.* New York: Vintage Books, 1963.

Janes, Dominic. *Oscar Wilde Prefigured: Queer Fashioning and British Caricature, 1750–1900.* Chicago: University of Chicago Press, 2016.

———. *Picturing the Closet: Male Secrecy and Homosexual Visibility in Britain.* New York: Oxford University Press, 2015.

Jones, Gareth Stedman. *Languages of Class: Studies in English Working Class History, 1832–1982.* Cambridge: Cambridge University Press, 1983.

Joyce, Michael. *My Friend H: John Cam Hobhouse, Baron Broughton of Broughton De Gyfford.* London: J. Murray, 1948.

Joyce, Patrick. *The Rule of Freedom: Liberalism and the Modern City.* London: Verso, 2003.

Kaplan, Morris B. *Sodom on the Thames: Sex, Love, and Scandal in Wilde Times.* Ithaca, NY: Cornell University Press, 2005.

Kissinger, Henry. *A World Restored: Metternich, Castlereagh, and the Problems of Peace, 1812–22.* New York: Grosset and Dunlap, 1964.

Knight, G. Wilson. *Lord Byron's Marriage: The Evidence of Asterisks.* New York: Macmillan, 1957.

Koven, Seth. *The Match Girl and the Heiress.* Princeton, NJ: Princeton University Press, 2014.

Lacey, Brian. *Terrible Queer Creatures: Homosexuality in Irish History.* Dublin: Wordwell Books, 2008.

Laqueur, Thomas. *Solitary Sex: A Cultural History of Masturbation.* New York: Zone Books, 2003.

Laurence, John. *The History of Capital Punishment.* Secaucus, NJ: Citadel Press, 1983.

——. *A History of Capital Punishment, with Special Reference to Capital Punishment in Great Britain.* Port Washington, NY: Kennikat Press, 1971.

Lewis, Brian, ed. *British Queer History: New Approaches and Perspectives.* Manchester: Manchester University Press, 2013.

Ley, J. W. T. (James William Thomas). *The Dickens Circle: A Narrative of the Novelist's Friendships.* London: Chapman and Hall, 1918.

Linebaugh, Peter, and Marcus Rediker. *The Many-Headed Hydra: Sailors, Slaves, Commoners, and the Hidden History of the Revolutionary Atlantic.* Boston: Beacon Press, 2000.

Lonsdale, Roger, ed. *Eighteenth Century Women Poets: An Oxford Anthology.* New York: Oxford University Press, 1989.

Lovell, Ernest, ed. *His Very Self and Voice: Collected Conversations of Lord Byron.* New York: Macmillan, 1954.

MacCarthy, Fiona. *Byron: Life and Legend.* New York: Farrar, Straus and Giroux, 2002.

Macdonald, David Lorne. *Monk Lewis: A Critical Biography.* Toronto: University of Toronto Press, 2000.

MacKenzie, Norman, and Jeanne MacKenzie. *Dickens, a Life.* New York: Oxford University Press, 1979.

Mandler, Peter. *Aristocratic Government in the Age of Reform: Whigs and Liberals, 1830–1852.* Oxford: Clarendon Press, 1990.

Marchand, Leslie Alexis. *Byron: A Biography.* 3 vols. New York: Knopf, 1957.

——. *Byron: A Portrait.* 1st ed. New York: Knopf, 1970.

Martin, Brian Joseph. *Napoleonic Friendship: Military Fraternity, Intimacy and Sexuality in Nineteenth-Century France.* Durham: University of New Hampshire Press, 2011.

Matthews, Gelien. *Caribbean Slave Revolts and the British Abolitionist Movement.* Baton Rouge: Louisiana State University Press, 2006.

Maxwell, Sir Herbert. *The Life of Wellington: The Restoration of the Martial Power of Great Britain.* 2 vols. London: S. Low, Marston, 1899.

McCalman, Iain. *Radical Underworld: Prophets, Revolutionaries, and Pornographers in London, 1795–1840.* Cambridge: Cambridge University Press, 1988.

McCormack, Matthew, ed. *Public Men: Masculinity and Politics in Modern Britain.* New York: Palgrave Macmillan, 2007.

McLaren, Angus. *Sexual Blackmail: A Modern History*. Cambridge, MA: Harvard University Press, 2002.

Mehta, Uday Singh. *Liberalism and Empire: A Study in Nineteenth-Century British Liberal Thought*. Chicago: University of Chicago Press, 1999.

Melville, Lewis. *The Life and Letters of William Beckford of Fonthill*. London: William Heinemann, 1970.

Metcalf, Thomas R. *Ideologies of the Raj*. New York: Cambridge University Press, 1994.

Moore, Doris Langley. *Lord Byron: Accounts Rendered*. New York: Harper and Row, 1974.

Mosse, George. *The Image of Man: The Creation of Modern Masculinity*. New York: Oxford University Press, 1996.

———. *Nationalism and Sexuality: Respectability and Abnormal Sexuality in Modern Europe*. New York: H. Fertig, 1985.

Munford, W. A. *William Ewart, M.P., 1798–1869: Portrait of a Radical*. London: Grafton, 1960.

Najmabadi, Afsaneh. *Women with Mustaches and Men without Beards: Gender and Sexual Anxieties of Iranian Modernity*. Berkeley: University of California Press, 2005.

Nattrass, Leonora. *William Cobbett: The Politics of Style*. New York: Cambridge University Press, 1995.

Norton, Rictor, ed. *Homosexuality in Nineteenth-Century England: A Sourcebook*. http://rictornorton.co.uk.

———. *Mother Clap's Molly House: The Gay Subculture in England, 1700–1830*. 1st ed. London: GMP, 1992.

———. *Mother Clap's Molly House: The Gay Subculture in England, 1700–1830*. Rev. 2nd ed. Stroud, Gloucestershire: Chalfont Press, 2006.

Oosterhuis, Harry. *Stepchildren of Nature: Krafft-Ebing, Psychiatry, and the Making of Sexual Identity*. Chicago: University of Chicago Press, 2000.

Parekh, Bhikhu. *Jeremy Bentham: Critical Assessments*. Vol. 3, *Law and Politics*. London: Routledge, 1993.

Parris, Matthew, and Nick Angel. *The Great Unfrocked: Two Thousand Years of Church Scandal*. London: Robson Books, 1998.

Pearl, Morris Leonard. *William Cobbett, a Bibliographical Account of His Life and Time*. London: Oxford University Press, 1953.

Pearson, Hesketh. *Labby: The Life and Character of Henry Labouchere*. New York: Harper and Brothers, 1937.

Peck, Louis F. *A Life of Matthew G. Lewis*. Cambridge, MA: Harvard University Press, 1961.

Potter, Harry. *Hanging in Judgment: Religion and the Death Penalty in England from the Bloody Code to Abolition*. London: SCM Press, 1993.

Pugh, Edwin. *The Charles Dickens Originals*. London: Foulis, 1912.

Radzinowicz, Leon. *A History of English Criminal Law and Its Administration from 1750*. Vol. 1, *The Movement for Reform 1750–1833*. London: Macmillan, 1948.

———. *A History of English Criminal Law and Its Administration from 1750*. Vol. 4, *Grappling for Control*. London: Stevens and Sons, 1968.

Rediker, Marcus. *Villains of all Nations: Atlantic Pirates in the Golden Age.* Boston: Beacon Press, 2004.

Reynolds, Elaine A. *The First English Detectives: The Bow Street Runners and the Policing of London, 1750–1840.* New York: Oxford University Press, 2012.

Robb, Graham. *Strangers: Homosexual Love in the Nineteenth Century.* New York: W. W. Norton, 2004.

Rosenthal, Caitlin. *Accounting for Slavery: Masters and Management.* Cambridge, MA: Harvard University Press, 2018.

Rothschild, Emma. *The Inner Life of Empires: An Eighteenth-Century History.* Princeton, NJ: Princeton University Press, 2011.

Rowbotham, Sheila. *Edward Carpenter: A Life of Liberty and Love.* New York: Verso, 2009.

Rumble, Wilfrid E., and John Austin. *Doing Austin Justice: The Reception of John Austin's Philosophy of Law in Nineteenth-Century England.* London: Continuum, 2004.

Sadler, Thomas, ed. *Diary, Reminiscences, and Correspondence of Henry Crabb Robinson.* Boston: Houghton, Mifflin, 1898.

Sambrook, James. *William Cobbett.* London: Routledge and Kegan Paul, 1973.

Samuelian, Kristin Flieger. *Royal Romances: Sex, Scandal, and Monarchy in Print, 1780–1821.* New York: Palgrave Macmillan, 2010.

Scherer, Paul. *Lord John Russell: A Biography.* Selinsgrove, PA: Susquehanna University Press, 1999.

Scott, Joan. *The Fantasy of Feminist History.* Durham: Duke University Press, 2012.

Sebba, Anne. *The Exiled Collector: William Bankes and the Making of an English Country House.* London: John Murray, 2004.

Seyler, Dorothy U. *The Obelisk and the Englishman: The Pioneering Discoveries of Egyptologist William Bankes.* Amherst, NY: Prometheus Books, 2015.

Shattock, Joanne. *The Oxford Guide to British Women Writers.* Oxford: Oxford University Press, 1993.

Shore, Heather. *London's Criminal Underworlds, c. 1720–c.1930: A Social and Cultural History.* New York: Palgrave Macmillan, 2015.

Smith, E. A. *Wellington and the Arbuthonts, a Triangular Friendship.* Dover, NH: Alan Sutton Publishing, 1994.

Snorton, C. Riley. *Black on Both Sides, a Racial History of Trans Identity.* Minneapolis: University of Minnesota Press, 2017.

Summers, Montague. *The Gothic Quest: A History of the Gothic Novel.* New York: Russell and Russell, 1964.

Temple, Kathryn. *Loving Justice: Legal Emotions in William Blackstone's England.* New York: New York University Press, 2019.

Thompson, E. P. *Customs in Common.* New York: New Press, W. W. Norton, 1991.

———. *Whigs and Hunters: The Origin of the Black Act.* New York: Pantheon Books, 1975.

Thorne, R. G., ed. *The House of Commons, 1790–1820.* 5 vols. London: Published for the History of Parliament Trust by Secker and Warburg, 1986.

Thorold, Algar. *The Life of Henry Labouchere.* New York: G. P. Putnam's Sons, 1913.

Tilby, A. Wyatt. *Lord John Russell, a Study in Civil and Religious Liberty.* New York: Richard R. Smith, 1931.

Todd, Janet, ed. *A Dictionary of British and American Women Writers, 1660–1800.* Totowa, NJ: Rowman and Allanheld, 1985.

Tosh, John. *Manliness and Masculinities in Nineteenth-Century Britain: Essays on Gender, Family, and Empire.* London: Routledge, 2016.

Trumbach, Randolph. *Sex and the Gender Revolution.* Chicago: University of Chicago Press, 1998.

Turberville, A. S. (Arthur Stanley). *The House of Lords in the Age of Reform, 1784–1837; with an Epilogue on Aristocracy and the Advent of Democracy, 1837–67.* London: Faber and Faber, 1858.

Ward, Richard. *Print Culture, Crime and Justice in 18th-Century London.* London: Bloomsbury Academic, 2014.

Wardroper, John. *Wicked Ernest: The Truth about the Man Who Was Almost Britain's King: An Extraordinary Royal Life Revealed.* London: Shelfmark Books, 2002.

Weeks, Jeffrey. *Coming Out: Homosexual Politics in Britain from the Nineteenth Century to the Present.* London: Quartet Books, 1977.

———. *Sex, Politics, and Society: The Regulation of Sexuality since 1800.* London: Longman, 1981.

———. *Sex, Politics and Society: The Regulation of Sexuality since 1800.* 3rd ed. New York: Pearson, 2012.

White, Deborah Gray. *Ar'n't I a Woman? Female Slaves in the Plantation South.* New York: W. W. Norton, 1999.

Wiener, M. J. *Men of Blood: Violence, Manliness and Criminal Justice in Victorian England.* Cambridge: Cambridge University Press, 2004.

Williams, Craig A. *Roman Homosexuality.* New York: Oxford University Press, 2010.

Wilson, Kathleen. *The Sense of the People: Politics, Culture, and Imperialism in England, 1715–1785.* Cambridge: Cambridge University Press, 1995.

Woodham-Smith, Cecil. *Queen Victoria: Her Life and Times.* Vol. 1, *1819–1861.* London: Cardinal, 1975.

Woodward, E. L. (Ernest Llewelyn). *The Age of Reform, 1815–70.* 2nd ed. Oxford: Clarendon Press, 1962.

Zamoyska, Priscilla Stucley. *Arch Intriguer: A Biography of Dorothea De Lieven.* London: Heinemann, 1957.

Zegger, Robert E. *John Cam Hobhouse: A Political Life, 1819–1852.* Columbia: University of Missouri Press, 1973.

Secondary Sources (Journal Articles and Chapters)

Alcoff, Linda Martin. "Dangerous Pleasures: Foucault and the Politics of Pedophilia." In *Feminist Interpretations of Michel Foucault,* edited by Susan J. Hekman, 99–136. University Park: Pennsylvania State University Press, 1996.

Allen, C. J. W. 2004. "Kelly, Sir Fitzroy Edward (1796–1880), Judge." *Oxford Dictionary of National Biography,* April 2019.

Baigent, Elizabeth. 2004. "Bankes, William John (1786–1855), Traveller and Antiquary." *Oxford Dictionary of National Biography*, January 2019.

Barber, Giles. "Galignani's and the Publication of English Books in France from 1800 to 1852." *The Library* s5-XVI, no. 4 (December 1961): 267–286.

———. "J. J. Tourneisen of Basle and the Publication of English Books on the Continent c. 1800." *The Library* s5-XV, no. 3 (September 1960): 193–200.

Barker, G. F. R. 2004. "Law, Charles Ewan (1792–1850), Judge." *Oxford Dictionary of National Biography*, January 2019.

Barrow, Robin J. "Rape on the Railway: Women, Safety, and Moral Panic in Victorian Newspapers." *Journal of Victorian Culture* 20, no. 3 (September 2015): 341–356.

Beckett, John. "Politician or Poet? The 6th Lord Byron in the House of Lords, 1809–13." *Parliamentary History* 34, no. 2 (June 2015): 201–217.

Begiato, Joanne. "Tears and the Manly Sailor in England, c. 1760–1860." *Journal for Maritime Research* 17, no. 2 (2015): 117–133.

Boase, G. C. 2004. "Hatton, George William Finch-, Tenth Earl of Winchilsea and Fifth Earl of Nottingham (1791–1858), Politician." *Oxford Dictionary of National Biography*, May 2019.

———. 2004. "Hobhouse, Henry (1776–1854)." *Oxford Dictionary of National Biography*, August 2018.

———. 2009. "Stoddart, Sir John (1773–1856), Writer and Lawyer." *Oxford Dictionary of National Biography*, April 2019.

Broad, John. "Whigs and Deer-Stealers in Other Guises: A Return to the Origins of the Black Act." *Past and Present* 119 (May 1988): 56–72.

Brooke, John. "Meredith, Sir William, 3rd Bt. (1725–90)." Member Biographies, *The History of Parliament: The House of Commons 1754–1790*. Edited by L. Namier and J. Brooke. Cambridge: Cambridge University Press, 1964.

Brunstrom, Conrad, and Tanya Cassidy. "'Scorn Eunuch Sports': Class, Gender and the Context of Early Cricket." *Journal for Eighteenth-Century Studies* 35, no. 2 (2012): 223–237.

Burney, Ian. "Making Room at the Public Bar: Coroners' Inquests, Medical Knowledge and the Politics of the Constitution in Early 19th-Century England." In *Re-Reading the Constitution: New Narratives in the Political History of England's Long Nineteenth Century*, edited by James Vernon, 123–153. New York: Cambridge University Press, 1996.

Capdeville, Valérie. "Gender at Stake: The Role of Eighteenth-Century London Clubs in Shaping a New Model of English Masculinity." *Culture, Society and Masculinities* 4, no. 1 (2012): 13–32.

Carter, Grayson. 2004. "Wall [née Baring], Harriet (1768–1838), Religious Controversialist." *Oxford Dictionary of National Biography*, January 2019.

Carter, Philip. "Men about Town: Representations of Foppery and Masculinity in Early Eighteenth-Century Urban Society." In *Gender in Eighteenth-Century England: Roles, Representations and Responsibilities*, edited by Hannah Barker and Elaine Chalus, 31–57. New York: Longman, 1997.

Chase, Malcolm. 2015. "Benbow, William (1787–1864), Radical and Publisher." *Oxford Dictionary of National Biography*, April 2019.

Clark, Anna. "The Chevalier d'Eon and Wilkes: Masculinity and Politics in the Eighteenth Century." *Eighteenth-Century Studies* 32, no. 1 (1998): 19–48.

Clark, Anna, and Aaron Windel. "The Early Roots of Liberal Imperialism: 'The Science of a Legislator' in Eighteenth-Century India." *Journal of Colonialism and Colonial History* 14, no. 2 (2013). https://muse.jhu.edu/.

Cocks, Harry. "Religion and Spirituality." In *Palgrave Advances in the Modern History of Sexuality*, edited by H. G. Cocks and Matt Houlbrook, 157–179. New York: Palgrave Macmillan, 2006.

———. "Safeguarding Civility: Sodomy, Class and Moral Reform in Early Nineteenth-Century England." *Past and Present* 190, no. 1 (2006): 121–146.

Crompton, Louis. "*Don Leon*, Byron, and Homosexual Law Reform." In *Literary Visions of Homosexuality*, edited by Stuart Kellogg, 53–72. New York: Haworth Press, 1983.

———. "Jeremy Bentham's Essay on 'Paederasty.'" *Journal of Homosexuality* 3, no. 4 (1978): 383–388.

Cross, Paul. "The Private Case: A History." In *The Library of the British Museum: Retrospective Essays on the Department of Printed Books*, edited by P. R. Harris, 201–240. London: British Library, 1991.

Crozier, Ivan. "Nineteenth-Century British Psychiatric Writing about Homosexuality before Havelock Ellis: The Missing Story." *Journal of the History of Medicine and Allied Sciences* 63, no. 1 (January 2008): 65–102.

Cruickshanks, Eveline, and Howard Erskine-Hill. "The Waltham Black Act and Jacobitism." *Journal of British Studies* 24, no. 3 (July 1985): 358–365.

Dabhoiwala, Faramerz. "Lust and Liberty." *Past and Present* 207, no. 1 (May 2010): 89–179.

Davenport-Hines, Richard. 2008. "Phipps, Constantine Henry, First Marquess of Normanby (1797–1863), Politician and Diplomatist." *Oxford Dictionary of National Biography*, May 2019.

Davis, David Brion. "Capitalism, Abolitionism, and Hegemony." In *British Capitalism and Caribbean Slavery: The Legacy of Eric Williams*, edited by Barbara Solow and Stanley Engerman, 209–277. Studies in Interdisciplinary History. New York: Cambridge University Press, 1987.

D'Emilio, John. "Capitalism and Gay Identity." In *Powers of Desire: The Politics of Sexuality*, edited by Ann Snitow, Christine Stansell, and Sharan Thompson, 100–113. New York: Monthly Review Press, 1983.

Devereaux, Simon. "Inexperienced Humanitarians? William Wilberforce, William Pitt, and the Execution Crisis of the 1780s." *Law and History Review* 33, no. 4 (November 2015): 839–885.

Drescher, Seymour. "Cart Whip and Billy Roller: Antislavery and Reform Symbolism in Industrializing Britain." *Journal of Social History* 15, no. 11 (September 1981): 3–24.

Escott, Margaret. "Bennet, Hon. Henry Grey (1777–1836)." Member Biographies, *The History of Parliament: The House of Commons, 1820–1832*. Edited by D. R. Fisher. Cambridge: Cambridge University Press, 2009.

Farrell, S. M. 2008. "Bankes, Henry (1757–1834), Politician and Parliamentary Diarist." *Oxford Dictionary of National Biography*, January 2019.

Farrell, Stephen. "Stewart, Frederick William Robert, Visct. Castlereagh (1805–1872)." Member Biographies, *The History of Parliament: The House of Commons 1820–1832*. Edited by D. R. Fisher. Cambridge: Cambridge University Press, 2009.

Fisher, David R. "Bankes, William John (1786–1855)." Member Biographies, *The History of Parliament: The House of Commons 1820–1832*. Edited by D. R. Fisher. Cambridge: Cambridge University Press, 2009.

Fisher, David R., and Terry Jenkins. "Stanhope, Hon. James Hamilton (1788–1825)." Member Biographies, *The History of Parliament: The House of Commons 1820–1832*. Edited by D. R. Fisher. Cambridge: Cambridge University Press, 2009.

Foster, Thomas A. "The Sexual Abuse of Black Men under American Slavery." *Journal of the History of Sexuality* 20, no. 3 (September 2011): 445–464.

Gilbert, Arthur. "Buggery and the British Navy, 1700–1861." *Journal of Social History* 10 (1976): 72–98.

———. "The Regimental Courts Martial in the Eighteenth Century British Army." *Albion* 8, no. 1 (1976): 50–66.

———. "Sodomy and the Law in Eighteenth- and Early Nineteenth-Century Britain." *Societas* 8, no. 3 (1978): 225–241.

Gladfelter, Hal. "The Indictment of John Purser, Containing Thomas Cannon's *Ancient and Modern Pederasty Investigated and Exemplify'd*." *Eighteenth-Century Life* 31, no. 1 (Winter 2007): 39–61.

———. "In Search of Lost Texts: Thomas Cannon's *Ancient and Modern Pederasty Investigated and Exemplify'd*." *Eighteenth-Century Life* 31, no. 1 (Winter 2007): 22–38.

Greene, Richard. 2016. "Kelly [née Fordyce; other married name Hedgeland], Isabella (bap. 1759, d. 1857), Poet and Novelist." *Oxford Dictionary of National Biography*, April 2019.

Haggerty, George. "Literature and Homosexuality in the Late Eighteenth Century: Walpole, Beckford, and Lewis." *Studies in the Novel* 18, no. 4 (Winter 1986): 341–352.

Hall, Edith. 2004. "Talfourd, Sir Thomas Noon (1795–1854), Writer, Judge, and Politician." *Oxford Dictionary of National Biography*, January 2019.

Handler, Phil. "Forging the Agenda: The 1819 Select Committee on the Criminal Laws Revisited." *Journal of Legal History* 25, no. 3 (December 2004): 249–268.

Harkin, Maureen. "Matthew Lewis's Journal of a West India Proprietor: Surveillance and Space on the Plantation." *Nineteenth-Century Contexts* 24, no. 2 (June 2002): 139–150.

Huddleston, David. 2008. "Jocelyn, Percy (1764–1843), Bishop of Clogher." *Oxford Dictionary of National Biography*, April 2019.

Hunt, Arnold. "A Study in Bibliomania: Charles Henry Hartshorne and Richard Heber." *Book Collector* 42 (1993): 25–43, 185–212.

Hunt, Lynn. "The Long and the Short of the History of Human Rights." *Past and Present* 233 (2016): 323–331.

Jenkins, Terry. "Lushington, Stephen (1782–1873)." Member Biographies, *The History of Parliament: The House of Commons 1820–1832*. Edited by D. R. Fisher. Cambridge: Cambridge University Press, 2009.

Knight, George Wilson. "Who Wrote *Don Leon?" Twentieth Century* 156 (1954): 67–79.

Kunzel, Regina. "The Power of Queer History." *American Historical Review* 123, no. 5 (December 2018): 1560–1582.

Laird, Michael. 2004. "Heber, Reginald (1783–1826)." *Oxford Dictionary of National Biography*, August 2018.

Leask, Nigel. 2015. "Lewis, Matthew Gregory [called Monk Lewis] (1775–1818), Novelist and Playwright." *Oxford Dictionary of National Biography*, April 2019.

Legay, Marie Laure. "The Beginnings of Public Management: Administrative Science and Political Choices in the Eighteenth Century in France, Austria, and the Austrian Netherlands." *Journal of Modern History* 81, no. 2 (June 2009): 253–293.

LeJacq, Seth Stein. "Buggery's Travels: Royal Navy Sodomy on Ship and Shore in the Long Eighteenth Century." *Journal for Maritime Research* 17, no. 2 (2015): 103–116.

MacDonald, Simon. "English-Language Newspapers in Revolutionary France." *Journal for Eighteenth-Century Studies* 36, no. 1 (2013): 17–33.

Malenas, Ellen. "Reform Ideology and Generic Structure in Matthew Lewis's 'Journal of a West India Proprietor.'" *Studies in Eighteenth Century Culture* 35 (January 2006): 27–51.

Manchester, A. H. "Simplifying the Sources of the Law: An Essay in Law Reform." *Anglo-American Law Review* 2 (1973): 395–413.

McConnell, Anita. 2009. "Beckford, William Thomas (1760–1844), Writer and Art Collector." *Oxford Dictionary of National Biography*, April 2019.

McDowell, R. B. 2004. "Hyde, Harford Montgomery (1907–1989)." *Oxford Dictionary of National Biography*, July 2018.

McGowen, Randall. "A Powerful Sympathy: Terror, the Prison, and Humanitarian Reform in Early Nineteenth-Century Britain." *Journal of British Studies* 25, no. 3 (July 1986): 312–334.

Melikan, R. 2008. "Romilly, Sir Samuel (1757–1818), Lawyer and Politician." *Oxford Dictionary of National Biography*, June 2018.

Merrick, Jeffrey. "Commissioner Foucault, Inspector Noël, and the 'Pederasts' of Paris, 1780–3." *Journal of Social History* 32, no. 2 (Winter 1998): 287–307.

Meyerowitz, Joanne, Heidi Tinsman, Maria Bucur, Dyan Elliott, Gail Hershatter, Wang Zheng, and Joan W. Scott. "AHR Forum: Revisiting 'Gender: A Useful Category of Historical Analysis.'" *American Historical Review* 113, no. 5 (December 2008): 1344–1429.

Norton, Rictor. "Oddities, Obituaries and Obsessions: Early Nineteenth-Century Scandal and Social History Glimpsed through William Beckford's Newspaper Cuttings." In *The Beckford Society Annual Lectures 2004–2006*, edited by Richard Allen, 53–72. Warminster, UK: Beckford Society, 2008.

Palmer, Alan. 2009. "Ernest Augustus (1771–1851), King of Hanover." *Oxford Dictionary of National Biography*, April 2019.

Paton, Diana. "Witchcraft, Poison, Law, and Atlantic Slavery." *William and Mary Quarterly* 69, no. 2 (April 2012): 235–264.

Phillips, John A., and Charles Wetherell. "The Great Reform Act of 1832 and the Political Modernization of England." *American Historical Review* 100 (April 1995): 411–436.

Pierson, Joan. 2006. "Noel [née Milbanke], Anne Isabella [Annabella], Suo Jure Baroness Wentworth, and Lady Byron (1792–1860), Philanthropist." *Oxford Dictionary of National Biography*, April 2019.

Prothero, Iorwerth. "Benbow, William." *Dictionary of Labour Biography*, edited by Joyce M. Bellamy and John Saville. Vol. 6. London: Macmillan, 1972–2010.

———. "William Benbow and the Concept of the 'General Strike.'" *Past and Present* 63 (1974): 132–171.

Radzinowicz, L. "The Waltham Black Act: A Study of the Legislative Attitude Towards Crime in the Eighteenth Century." *Cambridge Law Journal* 9, no. 56 (1945): 465–486.

Ragan, Bryant T., Jr., and Jeffrey Merrick. "Eighteenth-Century Homosexuality in Global Perspective." *Historical Reflections/Réflexions Historiques* 33, no. 1 (Spring 2007): 1–5.

Richards, Eric. 2004. "Horton, Sir Robert John Wilmot-, Third Baronet (1784–1841)." *Oxford Dictionary of National Biography*, August 2018.

Robertson, Lisa Ann. "'Sensible' Slavery." *Prose Studies* 29, no. 2 (August 2007): 220–237.

Rosen, F. 2014. "Bentham, Jeremy (1748–1832), Philosopher, Jurist, and Reformer." *Oxford Dictionary of National Biography*, May 2014.

Rumble, Wilfrid E. 2008. "Austin, John (1790–1859), Legal Philosopher." *Oxford Dictionary of National Biography*, January 2019.

Rustigan, Michael A. "A Reinterpretation of Criminal Law Reform in Nineteenth Century England." *Journal of Criminal Justice* 8, no. 4 (1980): 205–219.

Scott, Joan. "Gender: A Useful Category of Historical Analysis." *American Historical Review* 91, no. 5 (1986): 1053–1075.

Sherbo, Arthur. 2004. "Heber, Richard (1774–1833)." *Oxford Dictionary of National Biography*, August 2018.

Shoemaker, Robert B. "The Old Bailey Proceedings and the Representation of Crime and Criminal Justice in Eighteenth-Century London." *Journal of British Studies* 47, no. 3 (July 2008): 559–580.

Sidebotham, Herbert. 2004. Revised by H. C. G. Matthew. 2009. "Labouchere, Henry Du Pré (1831–1912)." *Oxford Dictionary of National Biography*, March 2019.

Smith, F. B. "Labouchere's Amendment to the Criminal Law Amendment Bill." *Historical Studies* 17 (1976): 165–173.

Sokol, Mary. "Jeremy Bentham on Love and Marriage: A Utilitarian Proposal for Short-Term Marriage." *Journal of Legal History* 30, no. 1 (2009): 1–21.

Spencer, Howard. "Wall, Charles Baring (1795–1853), of Norman Court." Member Biographies, *The History of Parliament: The House of Commons 1820–1832*. Edited by D. R. Fisher. Cambridge: Cambridge University Press, 2009.

Sweetman, John. 2014. "Maule, Fox [afterwards Fox Maule-Ramsay], Second Baron Panmure and Eleventh Earl of Dalhousie (1801–1874), Army Officer and Politician." *Oxford Dictionary of National Biography*, April 2019.

Taylor, Howard. "Rationing Crime: The Political Economy of Criminal Statistics since the 1850s." *Economic History Review* 51, no. 3 (August 1998): 569–590.

Thorne, Roland. 2008. "Bennet, Henry Grey (1777–1836), Politician." *Oxford Dictionary of National Biography*, April 2019.

————. 2004. "Stewart, Robert, Viscount Castlereagh and Second Marquess of Londonderry (1769–1822)." *Oxford Dictionary of National Biography*, July 2018.

Trumbach, Randolph. "The Birth of the Queen: Sodomy and the Emergence of Gender Equality in Modern Culture, 1660–1750." In *Hidden from History: Reclaiming the Gay and Lesbian Past*, edited by Martin Duberman, Martha Vicinus, and George Chauncey, 129–140. New York: Penguin, 1990.

————. "London's Sodomites: Homosexual Behavior and Western Culture in the 18th Century." *Journal of Social History* 11, no. 1 (Fall 1977): 1–33.

Upchurch, Charles. "The Consequences of Dating *Don Leon*." In *Queer Difficulty in Art and Poetry: Rethinking the Sexed Body in Verse and Visual Culture*, edited by Chris Reed and Jongwoo Jeremy Kim, 24–33. New York: Routledge, 2017.

————. "Full-Text Databases and Historical Research: Cautionary Results from a Ten-Year Study." *Journal of Social History* 45 (Fall 2012): 89–105.

————. "Politics and the Reporting of Sex between Men in the 1820s." In *British Queer History: New Approaches and Perspectives*, edited by Brian Lewis, 17–38. New York: University of Manchester Press, 2013.

————. "Undoing Difference: Academic History and the *Downton Abbey* Audience." *Journal of British Cinema and Television* 16, no. 1 (January 2019): 28–41.

van der Meer, Theo. "Sodomy and Its Discontents: Discourse, Desire, and the Rise of a Same-Sex Proto-Something in the Early Modern Dutch Republic." *Historical Reflections* 33, no. 1 (Winter 2007): 41–67.

Waddams, S. M. 2004. "Lushington, Stephen (1782–1873), Judge." *Oxford Dictionary of National Biography*, April 2019.

Williams, Glanville. "The Reform of the Criminal Law and of Its Administration." *Journal of the Society of Public Teachers of Law* 4 (1958): 217–230.

Woodland, Patrick. 2004. "Meredith, Sir William, Third Baronet (bap. 1724, d. 1790), Politician." *Oxford Dictionary of National Biography*, April 2019.

Worrall, David. "The Mob and 'Mrs Q': William Blake, William Benbow, and the Context of Regency Radicalism." In *Blake, Politics, and History*, edited by Jackie DiSalvo, G. A. Rosso, and Christopher Z. Hobson, 169–184. New York: Garland Publishing, 1998.

DISSERTATIONS

Evans, Jeff. "The Criminal Prosecution of Inter-Male Sex 1850–1970: A Lancashire Case Study." Ph.D. diss., Manchester Metropolitan University, 2016.

Shipe, Jonathan. "The Cost of a Moral Army: Masculinity and the Construction of a Respectable British Army, 1850–1885." Ph.D. diss., Florida State University, 2016.

UNPUBLISHED MANUSCRIPT

Ryan, Fr. Frank, OMI. "The Execution of James Pratt and John Smith, 27th November, 1835: 'The Law to Take Its Course.'" Unpublished manuscript, 2014.

Index

Page numbers in italics indicate an illustration.

Society for the Diffusion of Information
on the Subject of Capital Punishment
(SDISCP), 143
Society for the Diffusion of Knowledge
Respecting the Punishment of Death and
the Improvement of Prison Discipline
(SDKPDIPD), 143
Society for the Suppression of Vice, 61, 73,
81, 110
Socrates, 120, 203
sodomy: exaggerated denunciations of,
6, 18–19, 25, 68–71, 105–106, 166,
174–175, 183–184; ostracism or banishment as punishment for, 16, 37, 84, 114,
136, 211n27; physical act of, between
men, 105–106, 123, 155, 167–168, 204;
physical act of, between men and women,
7, 124–128, 132–133, 144, 167, 193;
public shame as sufficient punishment
for, 23, 25, 28, 148; radical understanding of, 7, 76–80, 82–85, 117
sodomy law: Christian arguments against,
126–127, 138; class privilege and, 7, 23,
63, 74, 78, 85, 87, 108, 129, 204; and
disruption of companionate relationships, 117, 124–128, 135, 158; majorities for reform of, 5, 12–13, 138, 156,
162–163, 175, 180–183, 204; other arguments against, 24, 25–26, 138, 143–145,
156–157, 175, 177; religious hypocrisy
and, 7, 74–75, 78, 81–83
Spa Fields conspiracy, 62, 80
Stanhope, James, 28, 132–133, 134
Statute Law Commission, 188–190
Stewart, Amelia Anne. *See* Londonderry,
Lady (Amelia Anne "Emily" Stewart,
Lady Castlereagh)
Stewart, Frederick William Robert (Vis-
count Castlereagh, nephew of Robert
Stewart), 176
Stewart, Robert. *See* Castlereagh, Viscount
(Robert Stewart, second marquess of
Londonderry)
St. James's Palace, 10, 63–66
Stoddart, John, 72–73
The Strange Death of Lord Castlereagh
(Hyde), 11, 89–91, 96–97, 99

summer of 1825 prosecutions, 11, 108–111
Summers, Montague, 46
Swan, Robert, 156, 159

Talfourd, Thomas, 159–160, 167, 176–177,
179, 183–184, 245n99
taste and sexuality, 6–7, *25*, 27, 28, 32, 33,
35–36, 46, 129, 136, 144, 153, 154, 202
Toynbee, William, 99–100
Trinidad, 45
Trinity College, Dublin, 74
Trumbach, Randolph, 199

"unnatural" not an argument, 19, 26, 35

Vane, Henry (Earl of Darlington), 174–175,
178
Venice, 147
Vere Street molly-house raid, 10, 62, 67–71,
76–77, 85, 109, 129, 225n40
Vicinus, Martha, 199
vir, 202
Virgil, 120, 128, 203

Wahrman, Dror, 234n21
Wall, Charles Baring, 144–145, 148–150,
153, 154, 163, 172, 178, 181
Walpole, Horace, 135
Walpole, Sir Robert, 107
Wedgwood, Hensleigh, 140, 157
Weeks, Jeffrey, 4, 197
Wellington, Duke of (Arthur Wellesley),
11, 66, *70*, 88, 94, 97, 146–147, 150, 179,
184
Wells, Rev. David Bowker, 104–105
Whiteside, James, 189–190
Wilberforce, William, 48, 58, 137, 145
William IV, 150
Wilmont-Horton, Sir Robert John,
111–113, 139
Wilson, Mrs. Cornwell Baron (Margaret
Wilson), 43, 46
Winchilsea, Earl of, 6, 182–184
Wolfenden Committee, 89

Yelverton, Henry Edward (Lord Grey de
Ruthyn), 119

CHARLES UPCHURCH is an Associate Professor of British History at Florida State University and the author of *Before Wilde: Sex between Men in Britain's Age of Reform*.

Made in United States
Orlando, FL
02 May 2022

17431974R10166